C0-DVT-617

Globalization, Employment and Mobility

Other titles from IDE-JETRO:

Mariko Watanabe (*editor*)
RECOVERING FINANCIAL SYSTEMS
China and Asian Transition Economies

Daisuke Hiratsuka (*editor*)
EAST ASIA'S DE FACTO ECONOMIC INTEGRATION

Hisayuki Mitsuo (*editor*)
NEW DEVELOPMENTS OF THE EXCHANGE RATE REGIMES IN DEVELOPING COUNTRIES

Tadayoshi Terao and Kenji Otsuka (*editors*)
DEVELOPMENT OF ENVIRONMENTAL POLICY IN JAPAN AND ASIAN COUNTRIES

Masahisa Fujita (*editor*)
REGIONAL INTEGRATION IN EAST ASIA
From the Viewpoint of Spatial Economics

Akifumi Kuchiki and Masatsugu Tsuji (*editors*)
INDUSTRIAL CLUSTERS IN ASIA
Analyses of Their Competition and Cooperation

Mayumi Murayama (*editor*)
GENDER AND DEVELOPMENT
The Japanese Experience in Comparative Perspective

Nobuhiro Okamoto and Takeo Ihara (*editors*)
SPATIAL STRUCTURE AND REGIONAL DEVELOPMENT IN CHINA
An Interregional Input–Output Approach

Akifumi Kuchiki and Masatsugu Tsuji (*editors*)
THE FLOWCHART APPROACH TO INDUSTRIAL CLUSTER POLICY

Masahisa Fujita (*editor*)
ECONOMIC INTEGRATION IN ASIA AND INDIA

Globalization, Employment and Mobility

The South Asian Experience

Edited by

Hiroshi Sato
and
Mayumi Murayama

IDE-JETRO

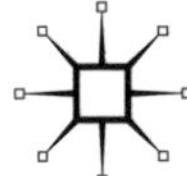

First published 2008 by
PALGRAVE MACMILLAN
Houndmills, Basingstoke, Hampshire RG21 6XS and
175 Fifth Avenue, New York, N.Y. 10010
Companies and representatives throughout the world

PALGRAVE MACMILLAN is the global academic imprint of the Palgrave Macmillan division of St. Martin's Press, LLC and of Palgrave Macmillan Ltd. Macmillan®is a registered trademark in the United States, United Kingdom and other countries. Palgrave is a registered trademark in the European Union and other countries.

ISBN-13: 978–0–230–53803–0 hardback
ISBN-10: 0–230–53803–7 hardback

This book is printed on paper suitable for recycling and made from fully managed and sustained forest sources. Logging, pulping and manufacturing processes are expected to conform to the environmental regulations of the country of origin.

A catalogue record for this book is available from the British Library.

Library of Congress Cataloging-in-Publication Data

Globalisation, employment and mobility : the South Asian experience / [edited by] Hiroshi Sato and Mayumi Murayama.
p. cm.
Includes index.
ISBN 0–230–53803–7 (alk. paper)
1. Labor market—South Asia. 2. Labor supply—South Asia. I. Sato, Hiroshi, 1943– II. Murayama, Mayumi, 1961– III. Ajia Keizai Kenkyujo (Japan)
HD5812.57.A6G66 2008
331.10954—dc22 2008015149

10 9 8 7 6 5 4 3 2 1
17 16 15 14 13 12 11 10 09 08

Printed and bound in Great Britain by
CPI Antony Rowe, Chippenham and Eastbourne

Contents

List of Tables

List of Figures

Acknowledgements

This book is the result of a research project entitled 'Globalization in South Asia: Its Impact on Employment and Labour Issues'. The project was conducted through the Institute of Developing Economies (IDE-JETRO) between 2005/6 and 2006/7. During the course of these two years, researchers benefited from the unlimited help of numerous people and organizations, both in Japan and in South Asia. Though every individual cannot be cited, we are very grateful to all who provided their assistance.

The overall two-year project included four overseas joint research projects in India, Pakistan and Sri Lanka. Smooth coordination of these efforts would have been impossible without the efficient and considerate administrative support provided by Kumiko Sakumoto and Kyoko Miura at IDE-JETRO.

As our research project neared completion, it was the timely support and arrangements made by Masahiro Okada at IDE-JETRO and Alec Dubber at Palgrave Macmillan that led to publication of the results of this research in its current form. Mami Ishigaki and Noriko Wakabayashi at IDE-JETRO took much trouble to arrange the editing of English in the manuscripts. We would like to thank them and also the English editors who spent substantial time and effort not only in correcting sentences but also clarifying our ideas.

We certainly appreciate the invaluable comments given by anonymous referees both inside and outside IDE-JETRO. Although their suggestions have been incorporated where possible, contributing authors are, of course, responsible for remaining errors and any shortcomings. Comments on this book will be most welcome, and we hope that both the book and subsequent discussion will lead to further research with an even wider group of people in the future.

HIROSHI SATO
MAYUMI MURAYAMA

Notes on the Contributors

Etsuyo Arai is a Research Fellow at IDE-JETRO. She has done postgraduate work at Peradeniya University, and her current research interests include economic and social transformation in Sri Lanka. She is the author of 'Sri Lanka: Community Consultants in an Underdeveloped Welfare State' (in Shinichi Shigetomi (ed.), *The State and NGOs: Perspective from Asia*, Institute of Southeast Asian Studies, 2002).

Junko Kiso is currently Professor in the Faculty of Global and Inter-Cultural Studies at Ferris University in Japan. She has been a visiting scholar at Jawaharlal Nehru University in India, and her main areas of interest are in development and labour studies in South Asia. She has contributed to scholarship in these areas with extensive publications and is author of *Labour in Indian Development: Structure and Changes in Urban Labour Market* (2003, in Japanese).

Momoe Makino is a Research Fellow at IDE-JETRO. Her current research interest concerns how the creation of employment has been used to alleviate poverty in South Asia. She is the author of 'Pakistan Labor-Intensive Industry Struggling against Chinese Products: a Case of Footwear Industry' (in *Ajia Keizai*, Vol. 47, No. 6, in Japanese).

Arup Mitra is Professor of Economics at the Institute of Economic Growth, Delhi. His research interests are in issues relating to urban development, labour and welfare, industrial growth and productivity, and gender differentials. His earlier works include *Occupational Choices, Networks and Transfers: an Exegesis Based on Micro Data from Delhi Slums* (2003) and *Urban Development and Urban Ills* (with Edwin S. Mills, 1997). Professor Mitra was the winner of the prestigious Mahalanobis Memorial Medal in 2004.

Mayumi Murayama is a Senior Research Fellow at IDE-JETRO. Her main areas of interest include gender and development issues in South Asia and Japan, and regional relationships in South Asia. Recent publications include *Gender and Development: Japanese Experience in Comparative Perspective* (editor, 2005) and 'Borders, Migration and Sub-Regional Cooperation in Eastern South Asia' (in *Economic and Political Weekly*, Vol. 41, No. 14, 2006).

Hisaya Oda is a Senior Research Fellow at IDE-JETRO and visiting Professor in the Graduate School of Tokyo University of Foreign Studies. He also serves on the editorial boards of *Developing Economies*, *Ajia Keizai* and the *Journal of Humanities and Social Sciences*. His research interests include the economic growth of Pakistan and migration issues in South Asia. He is the author of a number of research papers, and his recent article 'Dynamics of Internal and International Migration in Rural Pakistan: Evidence of Development and Underdevelopment' appears in *Asian Population Studies* (August, 2007).

Hitoshi Ota is a Research Fellow at IDE-JETRO. He specializes in labour economics, industrial relations and human resource management. His published work includes the article 'Flexible Work Organisation, Human Resource Practices and Worker Perception in India: a Case Study of Bangalore City' (in *Indian Journal of Labour Economics,* Vol. 48, No. 1, 2005).

Hiroshi Sato is former Director of the Area Studies Department at IDE. His research interest is in the current politics and political history of South Asia. Earlier works include *Uneasy Federation. The Political Economy of Central Budgetary Transfers in South Asia* (1994) and 'Social Security and Well-Being in a Low-Income Economy: an Appraisal of the Kerala Experience' (in *The Developing Economies*, Vol. 42, No. 2, 2004).

Takahiro Sato is an Associate Professor in the Research Institute for Economics and Business Administration at Kobe University. He was a visiting scholar at the University of California, Berkeley, and his main area of interest relates to economic development issues in India. He is the author of *Development Economics: India's Economic Reforms in the era of Globalization* (2002, in Japanese).

Yoshie Shimane is a Research Fellow at IDE-JETRO. She is currently a scholar affiliated with the Institute of Economic Growth in India, and her research interest lies in industrial development in India, especially in the accumulation of technology and its spillover into indigenous firms. Her earlier works include 'How Inter-Firm Linkage Enhanced the Growth of the Automobile Industry in India' (in *Ajia Keizai*, Vol. 40, No. 8, in Japanese) and 'India's Motorcycle Industry: Indigenous Two-Wheeler Manufacturers and the Development of Capability among Indian Components Suppliers' (in Yuri Sato and Moriki Ohara (eds), *Asia's Motorcycle Industry: the Rise of Local Companies and the Dynamism of Industrial Development*, 2006, in Japanese).

Yuko Tsujita is a Research Fellow at IDE-JETRO. Her major research interests include the social sector, labour, and urban development in India. She is currently completing her Ph.D. at the University of Sussex, and her dissertation is entitled 'The Impact of Education on the Poverty of Urban Slum Dwellers in Delhi, India'.

Introduction: Globalization and Employment in South Asia

Hiroshi Sato and Mayumi Murayama

> People see the world through the optics of their workplace. Success or failure in the labour market determines whether family needs and aspirations can be met, whether girls and boys get a decent education, whether youths are able to build a career or end up on the street. Youth employment is a critical area for action. Loss of work affects dignity and self-esteem, generates stress and other health problems, and undermines social integration. (*A Fair Globalization: Creating Opportunity for All*, World Commission on the Social Dimension of Globalization, February 2004, p. 86)

Background and issues

What is meant by 'globalization'?

Is 'globalization' a new word representing a new phenomenon? Or is it merely a newly coined word to designate an age-old phenomenon? Scholars like Amartya Sen who view 'globalization' in terms of human history over several millennia would argue that globalization, in its basic form, is not particularly new, and that around the year 1000, the globalization of science, technology and mathematics was changing the nature of the old world (Sen 2005: 345). Sen, however, emphasizes here the importance of the migration of peoples and the transmission of ideas, goods and technology. Coming much nearer, we may cite 'world system' theorists like Wallerstein who hold that Western capitalism has woven a globalized network by engendering integrated but basically asymmetric economic relations between metropolitan centres and peripheries. There is certainly merit to extending our intellectual horizons far and wide, but here we have to concentrate our focus on the particular situation which made the word 'globalization' so central to our understanding of the current global political economy.

In this sense of the word, globalization represents a new feature highly visible in the last quarter of the twentieth century, when the volume of transactions in commodities, financial capital and labour, as well as the volume of information mediated by new technology, reached an unprecedented scale. This period broadly coincides with what Standing termed 'the era of market regulation', as contrasted with the 'era of statutory regulation' which had by that time dominated three decades of post-Second World War economy (Standing 1999: xiii). We can go further to be more specific. Commodity trade and capital flow in the form of FDI-cum-portfolio investment, especially the latter, surged in the 1990s (Ghose 2000: 284–5; Gunter and van der Hoeven 2004: 14–15), and their vigorous movement involved reorganization of the workforce across national borders, both horizontally and vertically (Feenstra 1998). Innovation in information technology tremendously facilitated this reorganization (Ito n.d.). Against this backdrop, the labour market and employment underwent significant transformation.

No less important than the direct effect caused by basic economic interaction is the concomitant effect induced by 'homogenization' of policies and institutions related to the labour market (Gunter and van der Hoeven 2004: 7–8). Globalization in the 1990s thus has the twin faces of economic internationalization and institutional homogenization. This broad conceptualization will suffice and be analytically useful for our current volume, which is concerned with several aspects of labour and employment in South Asia since the 1990s.

As our brief quotation above from the World Commission Report amply shows, the issue of labour and employment is crucial in evaluating the human consequences of globalization (Lee 1996, 1997). While employment flexibility and relaxation of labour regulations are being promoted by public and private agencies under globalization, there have emerged grave concerns over this trend on the grounds that these policies essentially overlook the human aspect of labour and work, such that even their economic rationale cannot remain beyond question (Stiglitz 2002).

This introductory chapter will first focus on the several prominent issues related to the labour market in the age of globalization in order to properly locate our research concerns. The other chapters of this book share, in one way or another, a common focus with the issues to be reviewed herein, but with a caveat that the authors of each chapter are neither bound by, nor responsible for, the observations here. This is followed by a compact survey on the current situation of labour and employment in South Asia, with a particular focus on India. Then, a brief summary of the findings and contributions of each chapter is presented.

Globalization and employment

Job loss and a 'race to the bottom'?

As trade and investment constituted major factors involved in the process of globalization, initial concern and early efforts at analysis were addressed to the effects of international trade and investment on domestic employment. Given that, in the world as a whole, the bulk of trade and investment expansion took place among the *developed* countries, their effect on employment in developed countries was the first to be examined as a response to the widely shared concern in the developed world over employment loss and rapid fluctuation due to the relocation, or 'offshoring', of industries. The main concern was whether the relative merit afforded by lower labour standards was necessary for maintenance of export competitiveness and an advantageous investment environment because, if so, a pessimistic outlook for labour conditions was inevitable, as any enterprise would seek to relocate their establishments according to relative advantage. Serious loss of jobs and a 'race to the bottom' would be inevitable. This pessimist view is now largely dispelled by various studies, as competitiveness demands much more than mere cheap labour, but rather it also depends upon higher productivity and better organized industrial structure. However, such adaptation is often ruled out in the case of the less skilled workers with lower-paid jobs who have borne the brunt of the adjustment due to internationalization of trade and investment (Rodrik 1997; Feenstra 1998).

In the further deepening of globalization around the turn of the century, when information technology (IT) was more widely harnessed and as the developing countries, particularly China, became more intensely involved within the trade network, we witnessed radical changes in the situation of world employment and the labour market (Auer 2006: 123–6). Outsourcing and subcontracting of office and factory employment proliferated. It transformed, if not totally obliterated, the Fordist or Taylorist manufacturing process. However, it was not a simple one-way process of 'job loss', but a restructuring process which also involved 'job creation' in different forms. Even a secular decline of employment can be accompanied by a different momentum of job loss and creation, and only the net result may end up decreasing the total number of the employed. In the mid-1990s, the OECD estimated the turnover ratio of employment (i.e. rate of loss + rate of creation per total employment) at nearly 20 per cent per year (OECD 1996: 7).[1]

Developing countries were not exempted from this 'job loss' and 'job creation' dynamism (Rama 2003: 12–16). While foreign direct investment (FDI), Export Processing Zones (EPZs) and Special Economic Zones (SEZs) as well as outsourced services, including in the IT segment, created substantially new varieties of employment, simultaneous employment downsizing and restructuring had taken place in the public as well as the private sectors. This complex process divided public opinion into two opposite camps: one welcoming globalization as job-creating, another accusing it of being job-destructive. Rama (2003) summarizes disparate case studies in developing economies and insists that economic reform had a long-run positive effect on economic growth, while in the short run, it destabilized employment and increased unemployment. However, in spite of Rama's attempt, the total picture is far from clear due to the absence of comprehensive data on job loss–creation dynamics in developing countries including India.[2]

Flexibility and homogenization of the labour market

It is generally observed that the loss and creation of jobs is not a simple replacement of the same types of jobs but involves a significant transformation in the nature of the jobs created. The bulk of the jobs created under globalization tend to be more 'flexible' in many ways. As Standing (1999: 83–127) defined the word 'flexibility', it is applied to multiple dimensions, beginning with the 'organizational', 'wage system', 'labour cost', 'employment (numerical)' and 'work process' dimensions and extending to the 'job structure' dimension. The most common attribute of flexibility may be 'employment flexibility', which is also called 'numerical flexibility' and which comprises various types of employment: casual and temporary workers, consultants, subcontractors, agency workers, homeworkers, teleworkers, part-time workers and concealed workers (Standing 1999: 102, Figure 4.4).[3] Due to 'contractualisation of employment', and 'contracting-out of firms' employment function' (ibid.: 125), flexible employment spread fast among the service sectors, and now it has become pervasive in many of the manufacturing processes, both in developed and developing countries. Permanent workers are often demoted to these kinds of flexible jobs whenever they have to undergo restructuring in their firms (see Ahmedabad case study by Kiso 2003: 256–64).[4] Roy called this flexibilization 'casualisation and informalisation' (Roy 2003: 150).

In fact, it is now widely observed that whatever jobs are currently created tend to be due more to the growth of flexible jobs, or 'casual' or 'irregular' jobs, as they are generally called, than to permanent ones. A Japanese employers' representative in an international forum confessed that 'their foremost concern was to create jobs', apparently desiring to say that they had no concern with the standard of labour conditions (*International Labour Review*, 141(1–2), 2002, p. 163).[5] This wide acceptance of the flexibility norm by employers testifies to another notable trait of globalization, and that is homogenization. Policy homogenization that aims at 'deregulation of labour laws' to make employment more flexible is being sought on a presumed demerit of labour law regulation which discourages employers from hiring more and induces them to adopt more labour-saving technology. This is a widely explored theme of labour economics, where it is examined whether labour law regulation is conducive to stagnation of employment either through discouraging more investment and hiring or through encouraging the adoption of labour-saving technology.[6] However, we may in the first instance have to ask, as Standing (1999: 126) did, if flexibility has already proceeded despite lack of legal reforms, and if it has contributed to the increase in employment at all. Given the empirical fact that labour flexibility preceded legal deregulation, the minimum agreement would be that de facto flexibility does not need *de jure* flexibility as its precondition. As quoted by Standing (1999: 125), an executive of one European temporary staffing company remarked that 'the market is changing faster than the laws are'.

Informal economy and the 'working poor'

The spread of flexible employment has far-reaching significance for understanding the nature of the labour market. One of the outcomes is the redefinition of the concept of the 'informal sector'. Informality ceases to be a phenomenon limited to a particular segment of the industrial sectors. It becomes rather ubiquitous, crossing sector borders. Beattie (2000) points out that 'the informal economy is not really a "sector" as such. It is in fact a phenomenon to be found in almost all sectors. And it includes workers of all categories: employees, the self-employed, home workers, unpaid family workers, etc.' The scale of establishments or the number of employees is no longer an effective indicator of 'informality'; employment status has become the key determinant. Carr and Chen (2004: 132–3) define informal employment as 'employment without secure contracts, work benefits, or social protection'. It is also a job with low average earnings.

For the developing economies, the dominance of the informal economy, rather than unemployment, has been a major characteristic of the labour market, as many people cannot afford to be unemployed. Carr and Chen (2004: 129) emphasize that 'in developing countries, where the majority of the workforce has never had secure long-term employment, the concept of unemployment is somewhat problematic'. We have to ask 'what type of job?' or 'on what terms?' (ibid.)

The growing importance of labour flexibility has brought about a kind of convergence of academic as well as practical concerns into such concepts as 'working poor' and 'decent work'.[7]

The problem of the working poor is not that they are unemployed but that they are working and at the same time poor. Majid (2001: 282) examined worldwide data on employment and poverty and concluded that, in 1997, 534 million people were working poor; their figure was as large as 25% of the total employed labour force, that is, one out of four workers was part of the working poor. The working poor increased in low-income countries, but decreased in middle-income countries. Of the working poor, 95 per cent were in low-income countries. However, among the low-income countries, trends differed from country to country, which suggested polarization in the low-income countries.

Another issue related to the informal economy and the working poor is the problem of gender, although the gender issue has much wider implications of its own.[8] However, the observed rise in the female labour participation rate is often linked to the growth of the informal economy with low-wage jobs (Gunter and van der Hoeven 2004: 25–6), and being excluded from participation in regular employment, female labour tends to concentrate in the informal economy (Carr and Chen 2004). According to Beattie's observation (2000: 132), female labour occupies two-thirds of the jobs in the urban informal economy.

Labour migration

Labour migration, especially migration across national borders, is another field of study in which globalization aroused a new interest. As Sassen (1996: 59) notes:

> Economic globalization denationalizes national economies; in contrast, immigration is renationalizing politics. There is a growing consensus in the community of states to lift border controls for the flow of capital, information, and services, and more broadly, to further globalization. But when it comes to immigrants and refugees, [omitted] the national state claims all its old splendour in asserting its sovereign right to control its borders.

Sassen's observation raises a pertinent question as to whether globalization lowers and makes irrelevant the barriers of national borders across the board. In the age of globalization, states go readily to remove barriers against free movement of capital, information and technology, but go slowly so far as labour migration is concerned.

This asymmetric attitude of the states arises from their inclination to evade the costs of cultural conflicts and political instability rather than respond to economic necessity (as developed nations generally suffer from labour shortage). Even in receiving the flow of migration, states are more or less selective, such that they only accept certain specified service labour within a regulated framework. Movement of unskilled labour becomes increasingly difficult in this selective and exclusivist framework (Gunter and van der Hoeven 2004: 27). Migrants are thus placed in the marginal position of contesting the dynamics of inclusion and exclusion. However, it needs no mention that the economic impact of their earnings and remittances reaches far and wide in the economy of the sending states, with varying impact on micro (household) and macro (national) economies in the emigrants' states.[9]

Workers' well-being and security

Flexibility of labour and deregulation of labour law have radically eroded the basis of the post-war welfare state, particularly in the developed countries. However, even in developing countries where full employment and universal social welfare have never been a reality, the shift from statutory to market regulation (Standing 1999) tends to dismantle the presumably 'protective' labour law regime. Yet ironically enough, the progress of labour market transformation and reforms stirred up awareness of the heightened insecurity of labour conditions. Moreover, there is found an emerging concern both for maintaining 'core labour standards'[10] and for extending the social security network among those layers of people (including informal and household workers) who have so far been left outside the formal social security framework.

Core labour standards have been a major concern of international organizations such as the ILO (Lee 1997), but an increasingly large number of NGOs in the developed world are also becoming actively involved in maintaining core labour standards in developing countries. There is of course a subtle point in distinguishing these endeavours from what is called 'disguised protectionism' (Banks 2006: 95) which is sometimes so vocal in public opinion of the developed economies. However, as we steer between 'globalization enthusiasts' and 'labour rights proponents' (Elliott and Freeman 2003: 2), we will have to attain a broad consensus, both at the level of national politics and international policy forums, as regards maintenance of a decent or minimum level of labour security and welfare. As a matter of fact, the real cost required for minimum security, including light, ventilation, safety measures against accidental fires and so on, could not be so high as to kill the competitiveness of firms even in the developing countries (Lee 1997: 197; Banks 2006: 96). Elliott and Freeman (2003: 2) are perhaps right to argue that discourse on 'globalization vs. labour standards' 'poses the problem incorrectly'. After all, as Kucera (2002) maintains, even FDI decisions do not solely depend upon labour-cost or labour productivity factors. Better standards of socio-economic attainment and human capital can coexist with higher levels of labour standards.

Similarly, social security reform has two contradictory faces. On one hand, reform is oriented towards market-friendly adjustment of the existing institutions. The most typical example is pension reform which releases accumulated funds for investment in the volatile private financial market. Labour flexibility also erodes the basis of the established social security network. However, this erosion itself calls for reformulation of the social safety network. One emerging concern is provision of protective cover to the casual and informal labourers so far unprotected by a social security framework. This is a new challenge for the established social security system, which has catered only to the interests of employees and workers in the formal economy. The concept of social security itself has to be redefined, and institutional adaptation more inclusive for informal labour has to be explored (van Ginneken 2003: 290).[11]

South Asian scene

This section is meant to serve as a bridging piece to link the previous observations with the constituent chapters which deal with various issues of labour and employment in South Asian countries. We begin with a brief review of policies related to employment and labour in South Asia, and then give India a special focus as the majority of the chapters are concerned with the current issues of employment and labour in India.

Policy review across South Asia

For the purpose of policy review, we can begin with the 1980s because that particular decade, in almost all the South Asian countries, was the watershed of policy orientation in economic management. We recognize a clear shift from the post-war, or rather post-independence left-of-centre nationalist policy, outlook to a more market-oriented and externally open economic policy. Incumbent administrations which initiated such a shift were the Janata Party government (1977–80) and Indira Gandhi's (1980–84) in India, Ziaul Haq's (1977–88) in Pakistan, Ziaur Rahman's (1975–81) in Bangladesh and Jayawardene's (1977–84) in Sri Lanka. From the early to late 1980s, South Asian states invariably adopted the 'structural adjustment' policy initiated and backed by the international agencies, then took to the task of macroeconomic reform, including budgetary contraction, and external opening-up and deregulation in varying degrees. However, so far as structural adjustment was sought on the level of the macroeconomy, reforms in individual factor markets, particularly in the labour market, were still far off the reform agenda. Still, public sector employment, hitherto the largest source for educated job-seekers, stagnated. Some governments, Bangladesh for example, totally suspended recruitment of government employees in the 1980s. But the boon in the employment situation in that decade was the rapidly growing labour market for South Asian workers in Middle Eastern oil-producing countries. Countries like Bangladesh, Pakistan and Sri Lanka, along with some of the western and southern parts of India, benefited from the large inflow of remittances from emigrant workers. This inflow, which continued in the following decades, has substantially changed the social and economic landscape in those areas with a high propensity for emigration (see Chapter 10).

However, the picture changed drastically in the 1990s. A wide range of reform measures, including privatization of public enterprises, external opening-up of trade, and investment, were taken up. Public sector employment actually decreased remarkably in Sri Lanka and in India (particularly in the central government)[12] due to downsizing and voluntary retirement schemes. Among the reforms in factor markets, financial and banking sector reform was implemented rather quickly, but labour market reform, especially deregulation of the labour law regime, lagged behind to varying degrees in the South Asian countries. In India, which has the largest workforce in the formal, organized economy, deregulation of labour law became an important item in the major reform agenda for furthering economic liberalization in the 1990s. In other countries including Pakistan, Sri Lanka and Bangladesh, vital sectors of industries which had grown in the late 1980s and 1990s were sorts of 'greenfield' industries such as garments and export-oriented goods, most typically located in economic enclaves (EPZs), and were generally free from trade union pressures and labour law regulation.[13] The political environment surrounding the labour market also differs significantly in these two groups. India has a quite influential group of leftist parties across the country, and trade unions, which are more or less affiliated with the political parties, still exert substantial influence on public policymaking. Sri Lanka may follow India in this respect and has ventured into similar labour law reform in the form of an amendment to the Termination of Employment of Workmen Act (see Chapter 5), but since the mid-1970s, the number of registered trade unions in Sri Lanka has constantly and conspicuously decreased, such that they have lost one-third of their strength.[14] However, a turbulent situation is expected in the case of the garment industries, as the post-MFA situation invites a more volatile market for South Asian countries (including India), especially since the safeguard measures against China are scheduled to be lifted after 2008. The garment workers' agitation in Bangladesh in the summer of 2006 may be a herald of this turbulent stage (see Chapter 2).

A focus on India

We observed, in the 1990s, the most remarkable policy shift in India. Economic liberalization in India, initiated under the Narasimha Rao government of the Indian National Congress (INC), first dismantled the regulatory framework characterized as a 'licence raj' and opened up many closely guarded fields to private enterprises, both domestic and foreign. At the same time, the government downsized public sector enterprises, and private enterprises pursued with renewed vigour the 'hire and fire' policy to restructure employment (see Chapter 1). This first stage of economic liberalization produced the spectacular result of high growth in the manufacturing and services industries, with the GDP growth rate from 1991 to 1996 at an average of 5–6 per cent per year.

The second stage of reform, the so-called 'second-generation reform', was taken up by the 'rightist' Bharatiya Janata Party (BJP) government, which took command in 1998 by forming a coalition government with several regional and minor parties. It appointed the Second National Commission of Labour (SNCL) and initiated an agenda of labour market reform (see Chapter 4). The government's call for flexibility and labour law reform clearly reveals that the wave of homogenization has taken firm root in India. However, one disturbing factor was that, by the turn of the century, Indian reform was found to contribute little to increasing employment opportunities. A Planning Commission task force on employment describes a dismal picture:

> The rate of growth of employment declined sharply from 2.04% per year in the period 1983 to 1993–94 to only 0.98% per year in the period 1993–94 to 1999–2000. This sharp deceleration in the growth of employment has naturally been the focus of much attention and comment, raising concerns that economic growth in the 1990s has been of 'jobless' variety. (Government of India 2001: 18 and Table 2.3)[15]

The remedy for this 'jobless' growth ultimately depends on the diagnosis of the factors inhibiting the growth of employment in spite of the higher level of economic growth in the 1980s and the 1990s. Is the labour law regime counted as one of the inhibiting factors? Three of our chapters examining Indian cases essentially address this issue (see Chapters 4, 7 and 8).

However as we have already mentioned, aggregate growth or decline in employment over the years is the net result of job creation and destruction during the period (see our observation on p. 3). 'Jobless' growth by no means signifies a stagnant labour market. Chapter 1 as well as Chapter 9 will help us to understand the more dynamic and complex nature of the urban labour market involving a large substratum of informal and casual jobs.

There are several other important issues related to the current employment situation in India which we could not discuss in this volume. A nationwide scheme of rural employment creation (under the new National Rural Employment Guarantee Act) was started in February 2006, overseen by the present United Progressive Alliance (UPA) government led by the INC. The government also intends to introduce a national scheme of social security extension among unorganized sector workers. Public policy on labour and employment appears to have dual objectives, one to further the flexibility and deregulation of the labour market, and another to extend the security network for workers in the informal economy. India, as elsewhere, is faced with the task of tactful renovation of policy and institutional mixing of market-friendly with welfare-oriented reforms in the age of globalization.

Post-MFA garment industry in South Asia

While the forces of globalization have left no sections of the economy unaffected, this book has placed special focus on the ready-made garment industry, as four chapters deal with this sector from different perspectives.[16] The reason for this is twofold; one is its significant position in the four South Asian economies covered in this book, and the other is the timing of this research project, which was conducted during 2005 and 2006.

Since the 1970s, the export-oriented ready-made garment industry has shifted its production centres from the developed to developing countries. The trend, conceptualized in terms such as a 'new international division of labour' (Fröbel et al. 1980) and 'commodity chains' (Gereffi and Korzeniewicz 1994), was precipitated by several factors which also characterize globalization, i.e. global trade regime, development of infrastructure and information technology, and homogenization of economic policies towards export orientation in the less developed countries. At the same time, the outcomes of industrial relocation, which are, for instance, the creation of a new labour force, predominance of female workers in developing countries, types and nature of jobs, competition among the newcomer countries, and job loss in the garment industry of the developed countries, have constructed the very features of globalization.

Looking at South Asia, the garment industry has become one of the most prominent sectors of growth since the late 1970s. In the relatively smaller economies, namely Bangladesh and Sri Lanka, the share of the garment industry in total export earnings is as high as 65 and 45 per cent, respectively, in 2005/6. In India and Pakistan, where the industrial bases are more diversified and include upstream textile industries, the share of garment exports alone is comparatively low, at 8 and 18.6 per cent, respectively, in the same year. Nevertheless, coupled with the textile sector, this sector contributes about 15 and 60 per cent, respectively, to exports.[17]

The significance of this sector is also corroborated in terms of employment creation. The exact number of units and the size of employment are not known because the sector covers a large number of small-scale units along with large and modern factories. As far as the statistical data indicate, however, the share of the garment industry in total manufacturing employment in the four countries, i.e. India, Pakistan, Bangladesh and Sri Lanka, is 3.6, 7.4, 41 and 37 per cent, respectively.[18] A rough estimate suggests that the total size of the workforce employed in the garment industry in these four South Asian countries amounts to around 6.8 million people.[19]

Due to the substantial contribution of the garment industry not only in the economy but also in workers' livelihoods, the possible impact that would be exerted by the withdrawal of the Multi-Fibre Arrangement (MFA) at the end of 2004 was an issue of great concern. In the past, the MFA, which came into force in 1974, had mixed implications for each of the South Asian countries. By imposing quotas on existing export countries, it opened the scope for fresh entry by resource-poor countries with abundant labour, such as Bangladesh and Sri Lanka, while it precluded the larger and more resourceful economies of India and Pakistan from exploiting their full potential. Therefore, once the textile and clothing trade was liberalized, it was expected that the latter group would gain substantially whereas the former would face adverse effects, both in exports of their products as well as in imports of raw materials. In their actual performances in the post-MFA era, the four South Asian countries have recorded an increase of market shares in their major export markets, although the degree of growth varies.[20] The varied outcome reflects the different responses of each country in the changed trade regime, and at the same time, poses different tasks to be solved.

Within the garment industry in South Asia, there is a discernible difference in terms of gender composition of the labour in the region stretching from Pakistan to the northern part of India versus the rest of the region including southern India, Bangladesh and Sri Lanka. In the former region, male workers have been principally used, and in the latter region, the industry is predominantly female. This difference is also related to the size of production as well as to mode of labour management. Therefore, the changes in trade regimes have had different implications in each country, or more precisely, in each garment cluster. Chapters 2 and 3 discuss the issue on the basis of field surveys in Bangalore, India, and in Bangladesh and Pakistan. Along with two articles on the garment industry in Sri Lanka published separately (Tilakaratne 2006; Arai 2006), we expect to present a broader picture of the garment industry across these four South Asian countries in the post-MFA era.

Structure of the volume and major findings

We have divided our volume into four parts, each composed of a set of chapters written with a distinctive focus of interest. We start in Part I by analysing, through 'the optics of the workplaces', the micro-dynamics of the composition and the change in the workforce and in jobs. The scope is enlarged in Part II to focus on the macro and national trends of reforms in labour regulations and policy. These micro and macroscopic findings are expected to offer a complementary view of the major changes in the South Asian labour market where the job profiles are fast changing and institutional reforms are under way. Statutory labour regulations are then put to a test in Part III as to whether they work as restraints against the growth in labour demand and productivity. It needs no mentioning that the analysis here has much to do with the practical relevance of the policy reforms for deregulation of labour laws. Part IV deals with the increasing mobility of labour in the globalized economy and with its effect on well-being by way of domestic as well as international migration. Taken as a whole, this collection of 10 chapters aims to present a comprehensive picture of the current employment scene in South Asia, providing both empirical and theoretical insights into the dynamic process of transformations in the job market and labour regulations.

We shall now briefly introduce the major findings and contributions in each of our chapters. Part I throws light on the current employment status of workers in different workplaces across the three countries of Bangladesh, India and Pakistan. All three of these chapters base their findings on recent first-hand field surveys at workplaces in order to give, among other things, a microanalytic view of the changes and mobility in employment status, structure of wages (incomes) and productivity, and gender composition of the workforce (especially in the garment industries). Each chapter is based on meticulous fieldwork and presents a convincing picture of the changing job organization at a crucial juncture of economic reform and trade liberalization.

Chapter 1 by Junko Kiso, based on field surveys meticulously conducted at three points in time, in 1991, 1998 and 2006, clearly delineates the trajectories of job changes of a substantial number of ex-factory workers in Ahmedabad city in the Indian state of Gujarat. Although the impact of 'job loss' differs across different socio-economic backgrounds as defined by social status, education and work experience, what can be emphasized from two follow-up surveys in 1998 and 2006 is that an experience of 'job loss' from the organized sector was not necessarily accompanied by the chance of reintegration into the organized sector ('one-way flexibility' or 'informalization' as the author terms it). Greater dependence on the earnings of other family members and investment in education to enhance prospective employment chances of younger family members are some of the strategic options to cope with the heightened job insecurity of the workers.

In Chapter 2, Mayumi Murayama conducted surveys of female garment workers in Bangalore, India, and in Bangladesh. Both in Bangalore and Bangladesh, the garment industry workforce is female-dominated, in contrast to northern India and Pakistan where it is largely male-dominated. This difference in the gender composition of workers is linked with the mode of production and the nature of the skills. Female workers in factory production of a larger scale are assigned to work on line assemblies, and their skills are confined to that particular part of garment manufacturing. This precludes women from acquiring higher skills. It is also observed that, with the rapid expansion of production, management has inadequate time to give sufficient training to the workers, despite its intentions to do so. In spite of several important differences in the social and economic backgrounds of the female workers in the two samples, upgrading skills and labour productivity remain central issues for the garment industry in the two countries.

Chapter 3 by Momoe Makino offers a contrasting picture to the preceding chapter by illustrating a specific feature of the Pakistani garment industry, namely that most sewing operators are male workers hired at piece rates. Dominance of a male workforce in the garment industry, particularly in sewing operations, is induced by traditional social divisions and a segregated labour market. It is one of the factors explaining the higher wage level as well as the lack of labour quality in the Pakistani garment industry. The author predicts in the conclusion that, in order for the Pakistani garment industry to survive in intensifying international competition, a shift in the employment system from piece rates to fixed rates will be required.

In Part II, the current attempts by South Asian governments to pursue labour law and policy reforms are examined. Each chapter closely follows the trajectory of labour policy reforms and places it in an appropriate context of economic management and reformation. In Chapter 4, Hitoshi Ota presents a comprehensive picture of labour law reforms undertaken in India in its course of economic liberalization. Although labour legislation is frequently claimed as the cause of rigidity in the labour market and indirectly made the culprit of economic stagnation, India's labour market is quite flexible despite so-called restrictive labour laws. Nonetheless, there may be certain truths in the statement by the proponents of labour law reform that labour legislation in India is archaic and does not conform to the current economic environment characterized by globalization. Ota also suggests some possible directions for labour law reform in India.

Chapter 5 by Etsuyo Arai discusses a similar case of labour law reform in Sri Lanka, particularly with regard to the revision of the Termination of Employment of Workmen Act (TEWA) enacted in 1971. The revision of TEWA took place under the influence of the business community, and in it was stipulated a formula to make it easier to fire workers. However, the labour market in Sri Lanka was distorted due to the behaviour of job seekers and employers; the greatest number of newly created jobs have been in businesses under the authority of the Board of Investment and business in the informal sector, which is not affected by labour regulations. It is quite doubtful whether the TEWA revision itself has contributed much to creation of new employment. Arai concludes that it may be a necessary but certainly not a sufficient condition for growth of employment.

In Chapter 6, Hiroshi Sato discusses the recent debate on extending the employment reservation system to the private sector in India. He contends that the debate is no doubt a product of the globalized Indian economy. Although problems remain if reservation is the optimal policy to redress the marginalization of the less privileged classes in Indian society, the private sector could take some steps to make recruitment more inclusive and to empower the underprivileged so as to make them actors in the globalized economy. In the absence of such initiatives, the author contends, market-oriented reforms will alienate the less privileged classes by enlarging economic as well as social disparities among the people.

Part III contains two chapters which aim at analysing the causal effect of labour regulation on employment and production. Two studies take up the case of the textile and garment industries in India and use the same statistical source material, i.e. the *Annual Survey of Industries*. Their major contribution lies in the critical methodology for identifying new variables to establish a functional relationship between labour regulations and labour demand and productivity. Earlier literature on the subject, including most notably Besley and Burgess (2004), is also critically scrutinized.

Chapter 7 by Takahiro Sato provides an estimate of the labour demand function in the textile and garment industries and claims, among other things, that job security regulation in the organized sector depresses labour demand in that sector, while increasing employment in the informal sector. However, this empirical evidence does not imply that the government should deregulate labour laws in order to absorb the huge surplus of labour in the informal sector, but rather that the government has to prepare social safety nets and support the employment-enhancing textile and garment firms.

In Chapter 8, Yoshie Shimane investigates whether the minimum wage regulations in Indian states have affected the pattern of employment from fiscal years 1993 to 1996. The conclusion is that there is no evidence to show that minimum wage regulation decreases the efficiency of production of ready-made garment manufacturers in India. It is also suggested that, under the political and social climate in India, deregulating the minimum wage might entail large political as well as social costs.

Finally in Part IV, two chapters attempt to assess the economic effects of internal and international migration on the well-being of the households in terms of income, education and other entitlements. Both studies are based on extensive data collected from sample households in urban slums in Delhi and rural villages in Punjab, Pakistan. The studies also share the basic concern of identifying the circumstantial factors which lead from increased mobility to a concomitant improvement in the well-being of migrant households.

Chapter 9 by Arup Mitra and Yuko Tsujita, based on a primary survey of households (2004–5) in the slum clusters of Delhi, examines whether migrants are likely to experience upward mobility in their place of destination, or alternatively, if they merely transfer their poverty from rural areas to large cities. Empirical findings suggest that migrant households which have been in the city for a very long time have a higher well-being index on average than those who migrated in the last 10 years. Implementation of 'employment-cum-shelter' support schemes in the urban areas may contribute to their well-being. The somewhat conventional view of internal migration as an extension of rural poverty is not tenable according to this analysis.

In Chapter 10, Hisaya Oda analyses the impact of workers' remittances from a household perspective, based on a field survey carried out in the Chakwal district of Punjab province in Pakistan. The study reveals the poor economic condition of non-migrant households and the widespread poverty among them. Most households classified as poor are found in this category. The survey also shows a non-negligible incidence of poverty among internal migrant households. This indicates that internal migration does not necessarily improve the economic condition of migrant households. External migration seems to be the best option for upgrading the living standard of the households in these villages. Although globalization has made the movement of human beings easier, unfortunately this option is available only to a handful as it involves high initial costs such as travel expenses, commissions to brokers, and costs associated with information.

Appendix

Statistical information presented here is based on the latest available official data from four South Asian countries. Appendix Tables A.1 and A.2 illustrate the country profile.

1. Labour statistics in South Asia

Bangladesh

The Bangladesh Bureau of Statistics generally publishes a *Report on Labour Force Survey* (hereafter abbreviated as LFS) in intervals of two to three years. Four surveys between 1989 and 2000 (LFS 1989, LFS 1990/1991, LFS 1995/1996 and LFS 1999/2000) used two definitions of economic activities: (1) usual and (2) extended. The extended definition includes any person engaged in household economic activities such as care of poultry and livestock, threshing, cleaning, boiling, drying, processing, and preservation of food, with or without pay or profit, during the reference period. However, the 2002/2003 survey dropped the extended definition and changed the cut-off age of the labour force from '10 and above' to '15 and above'.

Table A.1 Basic socio-economic indicators I

	Population, 2005 (millions)	*Gross national income (GNI), 2005 ($ billions)*	*Per capita GNI, 2005 ($)*	*GDP, 2005 ($ million)*	*Average annual growth, 2000–5 (%)*	*Composition of GDP, 2005 (%)*		
						Agriculture	*Industry*	*Service*
Bangladesh	142	66.2	470	59 958	5.3	21.0	28.0	52.0
India	1 095	793	720	785 468	6.9	19.0	28.0	54.0
Pakistan	156	107.3	690	110 732	4.8	22.0	25.0	53.0
Sri Lanka	20	22.8	1 160	23 479	4.2	17.0	26.0	57.0

Source: World Bank, *World Development Report 2007*.

Table A.2 Basic socio-economic indicators II

	Urban population (%)	*Sex ratio (females per 1000 males)*	*Literacy rates (%)*				*Survey year*
			Both sexes	*Male*	*Female*	*Age criteria*	
Bangladesh	23.1	938	45.3	49.6	40.8	Age 7 years and above	2001
India	27.8	933	65.4	75.9	54.2	Age 7 years and above	2001
Pakistan	32.5	925	45.0	56.5	32.6	Age 10 years and above	1998
Sri Lanka	16.3	1 021	91.1	92.6	89.7	Age 10 years and above	2001

Sources: Bangladesh Bureau of Statistics, *Population Census 2001: National Report (Provisional)*.
Registrar General and Census Commissioner of India, *Census of India 2001: Provisional Population Totals*.
Population Census Organization, *Population and Housing Census of Pakistan 1998*; Federal Bureau of Statistics, *Pakistan Statistical Yearbook 2003*.
Department of Census and Statistics, *Statistical Abstract – 2004 Sri Lanka*.

India

There are several labour-related statistics in India. Besides the decennial census of population, the most updated and comprehensive labour-related data are the National Sample Survey (hereafter NSS) collected by the National Sample Survey Organization (NSSO) of the Ministry of Statistics and Programme Implementation. The NSSO has been conducting surveys on employment and unemployment since its ninth round of operation (May–November 1955). Recent issues are available online (http://mospi.gov.in/mospi_nsso_rept_pubn.htm).

Pakistan

The Federal Bureau of Statistics has regularly published a *Labour Force Survey* (hereafter LFS) since 1963. Recent reports are available on its website (http://www.statpak.gov.pk/depts/ index.html). The *Labour Force Survey 2005–2006* was undertaken on a quarterly basis for the first time.

Sri Lanka

The Department of Census and Statistics (DCS) has published a *Labour Force Survey* (hereafter LFS) on a quarterly basis since the first quarter of 1990. It also publishes an annual report. These are available through the DCS website (http://www.statistics.gov.lk/index.asp). Due to ethnic conflicts, northern and eastern provinces are not covered in the survey.

Sources:

Bangladesh Bureau of Statistics, *Report on Labour Force Survey 2002–2003*, December 2004.

National Sample Survey Organization, *Employment and Unemployment Situation in India 2004–05*, Parts I and II, September 2006.

Government of Pakistan, Statistics Division, Federal Bureau of Statistics, *Labour Force Survey 2005–2006*, October 2006.

Department of Census and Statistics, Ministry of Finance and Planning, *Sri Lanka Labour Force Survey: Final Report – 2006*, June 2007.

Appendix Table A.3 shows the size of the labour force in these four countries.

2. Labour participation rate (Appendix Table A.4)

The definition of 'labour force' (economically active population) is similar for all four countries. It includes both employed and unemployed populations based on their activity status during the reference period. India uses three different reference periods, but for comparison, the current weekly status is presented in the tables.

Pakistan and Sri Lanka set the cut-off age for the labour force at 10 years and above; Bangladesh sets it at 15 years and over. India does not mention an age criterion in its definition of the labour force, but many figures include data for ages 15 years and above.

Table A.3 Size of labour force in four countries (thousands)

	Labour force			*Employed*			*Unemployed*		
	Total	*Male*	*Female*	*Total*	*Male*	*Female*	*Total*	*Male*	*Female*
Bangladesh	46 324	35 978	10 346	44 322	34 478	9 844	2 002	1 500	502
India	395 881	274 203	121 679	378 359	262 728	115 631	17 522	11 475	6 048
Pakistan	50 050	39 970	10 080	46 940	37 810	9 130	3 110	2 160	950
Sri Lanka	7 599	4 837	2 761	7 105	4 611	2 495	493	227	267

Sources: Bangladesh LFS 2002–3, Table 3.4a; India NSS 2004–5, Table (34); Pakistan LFS 2005–6, Tables 8 and 9; Sri Lanka LFS 2006, Tables 2, 15 and 19.

Table A.4 Labour force participation rate (%)

	Both sexes	*Male*	*Female*	*Year*	*Age*
Bangladesh	57.3	87.4	26.1	2002–3	Age 15 and above
Rural	57.5	88.1	25.6		
Urban	56.8	85.1	27.4		
India	n.a.	n.a.	n.a.	2004–5	Age 15 and above
Rural	63.6	84.5	42.6		
Urban	52.0	78.7	23.0		
Pakistan	46.0	72.0	18.9	2005–6	Age 10 and above
Rural	48.9	73.8	23.4		
Urban	40.7	68.7	10.6		
Sri Lanka	51.2	68.1	35.7	2006	Age 10 and above
Rural	52.1	68.4	37.1		
Urban	45.3	66.7	26.2		

Sources: Bangladesh LFS 2002–3, Table 3.8; India NSS 2004–5; Statement 4.1.2; Pakistan LFS 2005–6, Table 6; Sri Lanka LFS 2006, Table 5.

Detailed definitions of the labour force and employment status of each country are as follows.

Bangladesh

An economically active population or labour force is defined as persons aged 15 years and above who are either employed or unemployed during the reference period of the survey (before the week of the day that the survey is made). It excludes disabled and retired persons, income recipients, full-time housewives and students, and beggars or other persons who did not work for pay or profit at least one hour during the reference week.

India

The labour force is comprised of persons who have been either employed (working) or unemployed (but seeking or available for work). A person is considered to be employed if he or she has been engaged in any economic activity or who (despite his or her attachment to economic activity) has not been working for reason of illness, injury or other physical disability, bad weather, festivals, social or religious functions, or other contingencies necessitating temporary absence from work. Unpaid helpers who have been assisting in the operation of an economic activity in the household farm or in non-farm activities are also considered as workers.

In order to determine whether or not a person is employed, unemployed, or not in the labour force, the NSS takes multiple approaches to determine activity status. There are three reference periods for the survey: (1) one year, (2) one week, and (3) each day of the reference week. Based on these periods, three different measures of activity status are decided: (1) usual, (2) current weekly, and (3) current daily.

Usual activity status of a person is measured with respect to principal activity (usual principal activity status) and subsidiary economic activity (usual subsidiary economic activity status). The activity in which a person spent a relatively longer time (major time criterion) during the 365 days preceding the date of survey is considered to be the usual principal activity status of the person. The usual principal activity status of the person is: (1) employed, (2) unemployed, and (3) not in the labour force (neither working nor available for work). Whether a person is employed (working) or unemployed (not working but seeking or available for work) is determined by the major time criterion, a relatively longer time spent in accordance with either of the two statuses.

A person whose usual principal status has been determined on the basis of the major time criterion may have pursed some economic activity for a shorter time throughout the reference year of 365 days preceding the date of survey, and this is not less than 30 days. The status in which such economic activity has been pursued would be the subsidiary economic activity status of the person.

Usual status, determined on the basis of the usual principal activity and usual subsidiary economic activity of a person taken together, is considered to be the usual activity status of the person.

The current weekly activity status of a person is his or her activity status during a reference period of seven days preceding the date of survey. A person is considered to be working (or employed) if he or she has been working for at least one hour on at least one day during the seven days. A person is considered unemployed, or seeking or available for work, if no economic activity was pursued during the reference period.

Current daily activity status is based on a person's activity status on each day of the reference week. For assigning activity status, each day of the reference week is viewed as either two 'half days' or a 'full day'. If a person has been working for four hours or more during the day, then he or she is considered to be employed. If a person has been working for one hour or more but less than four hours, then he or she is considered to have been employed for a half day and either unemployed (seeking or available for work) or not in the labour force (neither seeking nor available for work) for the other half of the day. If a person has not been engaged in any work, even for one hour on a day, but has been seeking or has been available for work for four or more hours, then he or she is considered to have been unemployed for the entire day. However, if he or she has been seeking or has been available for work for only a period that is more than one hour and less than four hours, then he or she is considered to have been unemployed for one half day and not in the labour force for the other half day.

Pakistan

The labour force or currently active population is comprised of all persons of 10 years of age and above who fulfil the requirement for being included among the employed or unemployed during the reference period (one week preceding the date of interview). A person is employed if he or she has worked at least one hour during the reference period and has been either a paid employee or has been self-employed. Persons employed on a permanent or regular basis, who have not worked for any reason during the reference period, are also treated as employed, regardless of the duration of their absence and whether or not they have continued to receive a salary during that time.

Sri Lanka

The labour force is composed of the economically active population 10 years of age and over. Persons who have been employed or unemployed during the reference period of one week preceding the survey are included in the labour force. Those who were working as paid employees, as employers, as their own account workers (self-employed), or as unpaid family workers during the reference period, are considered to have been employed. This includes persons with a job but who were not at work during the reference period.

3. Unemployment (Appendix Table A.5)

Bangladesh

Persons age 15 years and over are considered to be unemployed if they did not work at all during the preceding week of the survey (even for an hour in the reference

Table A.5 Unemployment rate (%)

	Both sexes	*Male*	*Female*
Bangladesh	4.3	4.2	4.9
Rural	4.1	4.0	4.4
Urban	5.0	4.6	6.2
India	n.a.	n.a.	n.a.
Rural	3.9	3.8	4.2
Urban	6.0	5.2	9.0
Pakistan	6.2	5.4	9.3
Rural	5.4	4.6	7.7
Urban	8.0	6.9	15.8
Sri Lanka	6.5	4.7	9.7
Rural	6.6	4.7	9.9
Urban	5.5	4.6	7.7

Sources: Bangladesh LFS 2002–3, Table 5.1; India NSS 2004–5, Statement 6.1; Pakistan LFS 2005–6, Table 18; Sri Lanka LFS 2006, Table 19.

week) and were actively looking for work or were available for work but did not work due to temporary illness or because there was no work available.

India

As with the other three countries, unemployment status is described as current weekly activity status. A person is considered unemployed if, during the reference week, no economic activity was pursued, but he or she made efforts to get work or was available for work any time during that week though not actively seeking work in the belief that no work was available.

Pakistan

All persons 10 years of age and above are considered to be unemployed if, during the reference period, they were: (1) without work (were not in paid-employment or were self-employed and (2) were currently available for work (were available for paid employment or self-employment), or (3) were not currently available due to illness, willing to take a job within a month, temporary layoff, or an apprentice and not willing to work).

Sri Lanka

Persons who are seeking and available for work, but who had no employment during the reference period (week), are considered to be unemployed.

4. Underemployment (Appendix Table A.6)

Bangladesh, Pakistan and Sri Lanka use similar definitions to estimate the size of underemployment (less than 35 work hours in the reference week). For the underemployment rate, however, Pakistan uses the total labour force including the unemployed as the denominator. Bangladesh and Sri Lanka use the ratio of those

Table A.6 Underemployment rate (%)

	Both sexes	*Male*	*Female*
Bangladesh	34.2	23.1	72.3
Rural	36.4	25.3	75.9
Urban	26.7	16.0	71.8
Pakistan	1.9	1.7	2.5
Rural	2.2	2.2	2.2
Urban	1.1	0.7	3.7
Sri Lanka	5.3	4.8	6.3
India			
Measure 1			
Rural		4.3	16.7
Urban		2.3	8.6
Measure 2			
Rural		10.7	34.3
Urban		5.6	20.2
Measure 3			
Rural		6.9	20.7
Urban		3.3	12.9
Measure 4			
Rural		11	13.9
Urban		6.2	8.9
Measure 5			
Rural		10.7	7.4
Urban		6.2	6.5
Measure 6			
Rural		9.2	5.9
Urban		5.5	5.2

Sources: Bangladesh LFS 2002–3, Table 5.5; India NSS 2004–5, Statement 7.1–7.6; Pakistan LFS 2005–6, Table 21; Sri Lanka LFS 2006, Table 30.

who worked shorter hours to those who were employed. India adopts different measures, and these are presented in Appendix Table 6.

Bangladesh

The underemployment rate is the percentage of those who worked less than 35 hours per week to the total number of employed persons.

Pakistan

'Time-related underemployed' comprises all employed persons who, during the reference period, satisfied the following two criteria simultaneously: (1) worked less than 35 hours per week, and (2) sought or were available for alternative or additional work. The underemployment (time-related) rate is the time-related underemployed population expressed as a percentage of the currently active population.

Sri Lanka

Employed persons are visibly underemployed if they have worked less than the normal duration in their main activity. In Sri Lanka, 35 hours per week is the cut-off point applicable to all workers except government teachers. The underemployment rate is defined as the percentage of underemployed persons among the employed.

India

Two types of underemployment are calculated in India: (1) visible and (2) invisible. Visible underemployment is the state in which a person categorized as usually employed is not working relative to a shorter reference period. It is measured by cross-classifying persons by: (1) their usual and current weekly status (Measure 1), (2) their usual and current daily status (Measure 2), and (3) their current weekly and current daily statuses (Measure 3).

Invisible underemployment is the state in which an employed person may appear to work throughout the year but wants additional or alternative work for various reasons. The NSS calculates the invisible underemployment using a set of probing questions. One measure is the number of 'usually employed' who answer that they did not work regularly throughout the year (Measure 4). Another is the proportion of those who indicate their availability for additional (Measure 5) or alternative (Measure 6) work to the 'usually employed'.

5. Employment status (Appendix Table A.7)

Pakistan and Sri Lanka use similar categories of employment status, but Bangladesh and India are different.

Bangladesh

An 'employer' is defined as a person who may employ one or more persons in a commercial or industrial enterprise. A person employing non-productive servants such as domestic servants is not considered as an employer.

'Self-employed' is defined as a person who works for his or her own household farm or non-farm enterprise(s) for profit or family gain. Such persons do not receive any wages or salary for work performed.

An 'unpaid family worker' is defined as a person who works at least one hour in the reference period (other than household work) without pay or profit in a family-operated farm or in a business owned and/or operated by the household head or other members of the household to whom he or she is related by kinship, marriage, adoption or dependency. Unpaid family workers who work at least one or more hours during the reference period are considered as a part of the labour force.

An 'employee' is one who has regular employment and receives wages or a salary from the enterprise, establishment or organization to which they are attached for performing the assigned work.

A 'day-labourer' is a wage earner whose services are solicited only for periodic time intervals during the reference period.

Table A.7 Distribution of employed persons by employment status (%)

	Sri Lanka			*Pakistan*		
	Both sexes	*Male*	*Female*	*Both sexes*	*Male*	*Female*
Employer/self-employed/unpaid family worker						
'Employer'	3.1	4.4	0.8	0.9	1.1	0.1
'Own account worker'	30.8	35.2	22.7	34.9	39.8	15.0
'Unpaid family worker'	10.5	4.4	21.7	26.9	19.1	59.2
Subtotal	44.4	44.0	45.2	62.7	60.0	74.3
Employee						
Employee	55.6	56.0	54.8	37.3	40.0	25.7
Subtotal	55.6	56.0	54.8	37.3	40.0	25.7
Total	100.0	100.0	100.0	100.0	100.0	100.0

	India			
	Rural		*Urban*	
	Male	*Female*	*Male*	*Female*
Employer/self-employed/unpaid family worker				
'Self-employed'	58.1	63.7	44.8	47.7
Subtotal	58.1	63.7	44.8	47.7
Employee				
'Regular employee'	9.0	3.7	40.6	35.6
'Casual labour'	32.9	32.6	14.6	16.7
Subtotal	41.9	36.3	55.2	52.3
Total	100.0	100.0	100.0	100.0

	Bangladesh		
	Both sexes	*Male*	*Female*
Employer/self-employed/unpaid family worker			
Employer	0.4	0.4	0.2
'Self-employed'	44.8	50.6	24.5
'Unpaid family worker'	18.4	9.9	48.0
Subtotal	63.6	60.9	72.7
Employee			
'Employee'	13.7	13.8	13.4
'Day labourers'	20.0	22.9	9.6
'Domestic worker'	0.6	0.1	2.5
'Apprentice'	0.9	1.0	0.6
'Others'	1.2	1.2	1.2
Subtotal	36.4	39.0	27.3
Total	100.0	100.0	100.0

Sources: Bangladesh LFS 2002–3, Table 4.8b; India NSS 2004–5, Statement 5.7; Pakistan LFS 2005–6, Table 12; Sri Lanka LFS 2006, Table 15.

In addition to those categories mentioned above, the categories of 'domestic worker' and 'apprentice' are identified with no further explanation regarding each of them.

India

'Self-employed' includes the following:

1. 'Own-account workers' who are those self-employed persons operating enterprises on their own account or with one or a few partners and who, during the reference period, generally run their enterprise without hiring any labour. They could, however, have had unpaid helpers to assist them in the activity of the enterprise.
2. 'Employers' who are those self-employed persons working on their own account or with one or a few partners and, who generally run their enterprise by hiring labour.
3. 'Helpers in the household enterprise' who are those self-employed persons (mostly family members) who are engaged in household enterprises, working full or part-time, and who do not receive any regular salary or wages in return for the work performed. They do not run the household enterprise on their own but assist the related person living in the same household in running that enterprise.

'Regular salaried/wage employees' are those who work in others' farms or non-farm enterprises (both household and non-household) and in return receive salary or wages on a regular basis (not on the basis of daily or periodic renewal of work contracts). This category includes not only persons getting time wages but also those receiving piece wages or salary and paid apprentices (both full and part-time).

'Casual wage labour' includes persons who are casually engaged in others' farm or non-farm enterprises (both household and non-household) and in return receive wages according to the terms of a daily or periodic work contract.

Pakistan

An 'employer' is a person working during the reference period on their own account or with one or a few partners at a 'self-employment job' with one or more employees engaged on a continuous basis.

An 'own account worker' is a person working during the reference period on their own account or with one or more partners at a 'self-employment job', without any employee engaged on a continuous basis, but possibly with one or more contributing family workers or employees engaged on an occasional basis. It includes owner cultivators, sharecroppers and contract cultivators.

An 'unpaid family worker' is a person who works without pay in cash or in kind on an enterprise operated by a member of his or her household or other related persons.

Table A.8 Distribution of employed population by main industry (%)

	Agriculture	Industry	Service
Bangladesh	51.7	13.7	34.6
Male	49.8	12.3	37.9
Female	58.6	17.4	23.0
India			
Rural male	66.5	15.5	18.0
Urban male	6.1	34.4	59.5
Rural female	83.3	10.2	6.5
Urban female	18.1	32.4	49.5
Pakistan	43.4	19.9	36.7
Male	37.2	21.2	41.6
Female	68.8	15.0	16.2
Sri Lanka	32.2	26.6	41.2

Sources: Bangladesh LFS 2002–3, Table 4.1; India NSS 2004–5, Statement 5.9; Pakistan LFS 2005–6, Table 10; Sri Lanka LFS 2006, Table 10.

An 'employee' is a person who works for a public or private employer and receives remuneration in wages, salary, commission, tips, piece rates, or pay in kind. Employees are divided into regular paid employees with fixed wages, casual paid employees, paid workers by piece rate or work performed, and paid non-family apprentices.

Sri Lanka

Status categories of Sri Lanka are the same as those applied in Pakistan and include: (1) 'employers', (2) 'own account workers', (3) 'unpaid family workers' and (4) 'employees'.

6. Distribution of employed population by main industry

Three broad industries are classified as follows (see Appendix Table A.8):

1. 'Agriculture' which includes agriculture, forestry, fishing and related works.
2. 'Industry' which includes manufacturing, mining and quarrying, electricity, gas and water, and construction (Bangladesh, India and Sri Lanka); manufacturing and construction (Pakistan).
3. 'Service' which includes all remaining sectors.

Notes

1. Genda (2004: 13) puts the turnover rates (rate of loss plus rate of creation per total employment) in OECD countries at: Japan (1989–2000) 8.2 per cent, USA (1973–88) 19.4 per cent, UK (1980, 1984, 1990) 9.5 per cent, Germany (1983–90) 12.1 per cent,

France (1984–92) 13.0 per cent. Figures are for all industries, except in the USA where the figure is only for manufacturing industries.

2. For India, Roy (2003) made an exploratory attempt to measure job loss in India based on *Annual Survey of Industries* data.
3. For further discussion on 'flexibility', see Chapter 4 on Indian labour law reforms.
4. Cases of reabsorption of workers who lost jobs into the informal economy are discussed in detail in Chapter 1.
5. In Japan, the share of 'irregular employment' in total employment increased from 20.9 per cent in 1995 to 32.3 per cent in 2005. In the manufacturing sector, it increased from 18.2 per cent in 2000 to 21.9 per cent in 2005. The number of 'regular' employees among the permanent employees decreased during the period from 2003 to 2005, while the number of part-time, contract and staffing company workers among them sharply increased (Ito n.d.: 6, 10, 11).
6. Theoretical issues related to labour law regulation and growth of employment and productivity are reviewed in more detail in Chapters 7 and 8.
7. For the concept of 'decent work' and the search for appropriate indicators of 'decent work', which is something similar to the Human Development Index, see Reich (2002), Ghai (2003), Anker et al. (2003), Bescond et al. (2003) and Bonnet et al. (2003).
8. While arguing on the role of female labour in garment industries, Chapter 2 discusses much wider aspects of female labour participation in South Asia.
9. Chapter 10 studies the case of Pakistani migrants and the economic effects of overseas remittances on households.
10. Core labour standards, in ILO terminology, include elimination of child labour, abolition of forced labour, encouragement of non-discrimination in employment, and freedom of association and collective negotiation. They are more or less well reflected in statutory provisions (either in the constitutions or basic labour laws) of contemporary nations. For the Indian case see Chapter 4.
11. In India, a few state governments and a number of NGOs have taken initiatives to institutionalize a social security network among the employees and workers in the informal economy. The key element in successful institution is the presence of associational initiatives by the beneficiaries themselves. Sato (2004) discussed this theme by examining the case of Kerala state in southern India.
12. Total stagnation or decrease in public sector employment led to a renewed demand for employment reservation for Scheduled Castes and Scheduled Tribes in the *private* sector enterprises in India. This issue is discussed in Chapter 6.
13. Among these three countries, only Sri Lanka witnessed a major debate on labour law reforms, especially with regard to the revision of the Termination of Employment of Workmen Act (TEWA). For this see Chapter 5 on Sri Lankan labour law reforms.
14. Information supplied by Etsuyo Arai, the author of Chapter 5.
15. The National Sample Survey result for the sixty-first round 2004–5 (large sample) showed notable recovery of the employment growth rate, which registered 2.89 per cent per annum between 1999–2000 (the year of the previous 'large sample' survey) and 2004–5. However, the most prominent factor of growth during the period is found in self-employment and female work participation in the lower echelons of the income hierarchy. There are also some other disturbing trends in the growth, like a fall in real daily wage earnings, especially among male workers (Unni and Raveendran 2007).
16. A part of our research outcome is published as Murayama (2006), which contains two articles on the garment industry in Sri Lanka not presented in this book.
17. The sources of export data are the Bangladesh Bank, the Central Bank of Sri Lanka, the Department of Commerce, India, and the State Bank of Pakistan.
18. The sources of data are the Annual Survey of Industries 1999/2000 (India), the Census of Manufacturing Industries 2000/1 (Pakistan), the Census of Manufacturing Industries 1999/2000 (Bangladesh) and the Census of Industries 2003/4 (Sri Lanka).
19. Calculated from Table 1.1 in Joshi (2002).

20. India performed best, registering a market share increase of 34 and 32 per cent in the US and EU in 2005 over the previous year, according to data derived from the World Trade Atlas. The remaining three countries marked an increase in the US but a decrease in the EU market during the same period. However, mainly due to implementation of safeguard measures by the EU against Chinese garments, the performance of those countries turned positive in the year 2006.

References

Anker, Richard, Igor Chernyshev, Philippe Egger, Farhad Mehran and Joseph A. Ritter (2003) 'Measuring Decent Work with Statistical Indicators'. *International Labour Review* 142(2): 147–75.

Arai, Etsuyo (2006) 'Readymade Garment Workers in Sri Lanka: Strategy to Survive in Competition'. In Mayumi Murayama (ed.) *Employment in Readymade Garment Industries in Post-MFA Era: the Cases of India, Bangladesh and Sri Lanka*, Joint Research Programme Series no. 140. Tokyo: Institute of Developing Economies.

Auer, Peter (2006) 'Perspectives, the Internationalization of Employment: a Challenge to Fair Globalization?' *International Labour Review* 145(1–2): 119–34.

Banks, Kevin (2006) 'The Impact of Globalization on Labour Standards'. In John Craig and S. Michael Lynk (eds) *Globalization and the Future of Labour Law*. Cambridge: Cambridge University Press.

Beattie, Roge (2000) 'Social Protection for All: But How?' *International Labour Review* 139(2): 129–48.

Bescond, David, Anne Chataignier and Farhad Mehran (2003) 'Seven Indicators to Measure Decent Work: an International Comparison'. *International Labour Review* 142(2): 179–211.

Besley, Timothy and Robin Burgess (2004) 'Can Labour Regulation Hinder Economic Performance? Evidence from India'. *Quarterly Journal of Economics* February: 91–134.

Bonnet, Florence, Jose B. Figueiredo and Guy Standing (2003) 'A Family of Decent Work Indexes'. *International Labour Review* 142(2): 213–38.

Carr, Marilyn and Martha Chen (2004) 'Globalization, Social Exclusion and Gender'. *International Labour Review* 143(1–2): 129–59.

Elliott, Kimberly Ann and Richard B. Freeman (2003) *Can Labor Standards Improve under Globalization*? Washington, DC: Institute of International Economics.

Feenstra, Robert C. (1998) 'Integration of Trade and Disintegration of Production in the Global Economy'. *Journal of Economic Perspectives* 12(4): 31–50.

Fröbel, Folker, Jürgen Heinrichs and Otto Kreye (1980) *The New International Division of Labour: Structural Unemployment in Industrialised Countries and Industrialisation in Developing Countries*. Cambridge and New York: Cambridge University Press.

Genda, Yuji (2004) *Job Creation in Japan* (in Japanese). Tokyo: Nihon Kezai Shinbunsha.

Gereffi, Gary and Miguel Korzeniewicz (eds) (1994) *Commodity Chains and Global Capitalism*. Westport, Conn. and London: Greenwood Press.

Ghai, Dharam (2003) 'Decent Work: Concept and Indicators'. *International Labour Review* 142(2): 113–45.

Ghose, Ajit K. (2000) 'Trade Liberalization, Employment and Global Inequality'. *International Labour Review* 139(3): 281–305.

Government of India (2001) *Report of the Task Force on Employment Opportunities*. New Delhi: Planning Commission, July.

Gunter, Bernhard G. and Rolph van der Hoeven (2004) 'The Social Dimension of Globalization: a Review of the Literature'. *International Labour Review* 143(1–2): 6–43.

Ito, Minoru (n.d.) 'Gurobaruka, IT gijutukakusin no koyoukozo heno eikyou' (Influences by Globalization and IT: Technological Innovation on Employment Structure). Japan Institute of Labour website, accessed on 10 December 2006.

Joshi, Gopal (2002) 'Overview of Competitiveness, Productivity, and Job Quality in South Asian Garment Industry'. In Gopal Joshi (ed.) *Garment Industry in South Asia: Rags or Riches?* New Delhi: South Asia Multidisciplinary Advisory Team, International Labour Organization.

Kiso, Junko (2003) *Indo Kaihatsu no naka no roudousha, Toshiroudousijou no kouzou to henyou* (Workers in Developing India: Structure and Change in Urban Labour Market) (in Japanese). Tokyo: Nihonhyouronsha.

Kucera, David (2002) 'Core Labour Standards and Foreign Direct Investment'. *International Labour Review* 141(1–2): 31–69.

Lee, Eddy (1996) 'Globalization and Employment: Is Anxiety Justified?' *International Labour Review* 135(5): 485–97.

—— (1997) 'Globalization and Labour Standards: a Review of Issues'. *International Labour Review* 136(2) (summer): 173–89.

Majid, Nomaan (2001) 'The Working Poor in Developing Countries'. *International Labour Review* 140(3): 271–91.

Murayama, Mayumi (ed.) (2006) *Employment in Readymade Garment Industries in Post-MFA Era: the Cases of India, Bangladesh and Sri Lanka*. Joint Research Programme Series no. 140. Tokyo: Institute of Developing Economies.

OECD (1996) *Job Creation and Loss, Analysis, Policy and Data Development*. Paris: OECD.

Rama, Martin (2003) 'Globalization and Workers in Developing Countries'. World Bank Policy Research Working Paper 2958. Washington, DC: World Bank.

Reich, Robert B. (2002) 'The Challenge of Decent Work'. *International Labour Review* 141(1–2): 115–22.

Rodrik, Dani (1997) *Has Globalization Gone too Far?* Washington, DC: Institute of International Economics.

Roy, Tirthankar (2003) 'Social Costs of Reforms: a Study of Job Loss with Special Reference to Declining Industries'. In Shuji Uchikawa (ed.) *Labour Market and Institution in India, 1990s and Beyond*. New Delhi: Manohar, pp. 121–54.

Sassen, Saskia (1996) *Losing Control? Sovereignty in an Age of Globalization*. New York: Columbia University Press.

Sato, Hiroshi (2004) 'Social Security and Well-Being in a Low-Income Economy, an Appraisal of the Kerala Experience'. *The Developing Economies* 42(2) (June): 288–304.

Sen, Amartya (2005) *The Argumentative Indian, Writings on Indian History, Culture and Identity*. London: Penguin Books.

Standing, Guy (1999) *Global Labour Flexibility, Seeking Distributive Justice*. London: Macmillan Press.

Stiglitz, Joseph E. (2002) 'Employment, Social Justice and Societal Well-Being'. *International Labour Review* 141(1–2): 9–29.

Tilakaratne, W.M. (2006) 'Phasing Out of MFA and the Emerging Trends in the Readymade Garment Industry in Sri Lanka'. In Mayumi Murayama (ed.) *Employment in Readymade Garment Industries in Post-MFA Era: the Cases of India, Bangladesh and Sri Lanka*. Joint Research Programme Series no. 140. Tokyo: Institute of Developing Economies.

Unni, Jeemol and G. Raveendran (2007) 'Growth of Employment (1993–94 to 2004–05): Illusion of Inclusiveness?' *Economic and Political Weekly* 20 January: 196–9.

van Ginneken, W. (2003) 'Extending Social Security: Policies for Developing Countries'. *International Labour Review* 142(3): 277–94.

Part I

Dissecting the Changes in the Workplace

1

Job Loss and Job Opportunities of Factory Workers in Ahmedabad: Flexible Labour Rethink

Junko Kiso

1.1 Introduction

In the globally expanding market economy, many developing as well as advanced countries have exerted a keen effort to implement labour reforms as one of their measures to adapt to the global economy and to succeed in the highly competitive environment. One among those countries is India. Since the inception of economic reforms in India in the 1990s, there has been much discussion in particular concerning the amendment of the labour laws, such as the Industrial Dispute Act which restricts the free layoff, dismissal and closure of firms employing 100 or more workers, the Contract Labour (Regulation and Abolition) Act which prohibits employment of contract labour in any specific process or operation, and the Factory Act which prohibits women from working at night, and so forth. It has been argued that labour market flexibility should be produced by deregulation of the protective regulations, among other means, based on the premise that the rigidity in the labour market due to these labour-protective laws has not only hindered the efficient allocation of labour resources but has also led to increased labour costs and consequent employment constraints on management, and as a result, has hindered further employment generation. Thus, labour flexibility has become one of the focuses of the labour reforms.

As has been extensively recognized recently, however, there is more flexibility in practice than is commonly believed (Planning Commission 2006; Sharma 2006). Needless to say, dismissal, retrenchment of employees, and the closure of establishments have been carried out legally or illegally even by the firms covered by those restrictive laws. Furthermore, what is not to be forgotten is that the unorganized sector, including the urban informal sector, which has absorbed a large number of workers, is characterized by an extremely fluctuating labour market which is virtually free from employment protection regulations. On the other hand, the organized sector workers, who are covered by the major provisions of labour laws and social security and have been at the centre of organized labour movements, still account for only about 7 per cent of the total workforce, as will be described later.

In fact, the reform of labour institutions has not proceeded far enough and the debate has been protracted. This is attributable to the fact that labour market flexibility is a matter of life or death for management and labour alike, and it has therefore been difficult for the government to adjust mutual interests. It may also be said that this is why the discussion has proved to be a decisive test of the direction of labour policy.

In view of this situation, the objective of this chapter is to explore the implications of actual flexibility in the labour market for the workers, viz. the realities of job loss and job change, because this, as a prerequisite for considering the labour reforms in India, is thought to be as critically important as the studies on the possible effects of flexibility due to legal revisions on employment increases as well as the debate on the past negative impact of job security provisions on employment generation.[1] The objective was also chosen because of the lack of sufficient micro-level studies of this sort, despite their importance, barring some valuable empirical studies (e.g. Patel 1988; Guha 1996; Noronha and Sharma 1999; Breman 2004).

Specifically, the following three points are the main analytical ones. First, an attempt will be made to analyse the influence of job loss on workers' job histories, i.e. what changes job loss brings about in the workers' job areas, employment security, earnings and lives. Second, as determinants of those changes, the influence of previous work experience, caste and level of education will be discussed, Third, considering the probability of their family environment also influencing their living conditions, the possibility of family playing a role as a safety net in their difficulties and alleviating the risks of falling into further impoverishment due to job loss will be discussed. The data sources of the case studies are two follow-up surveys conducted in 1998 and 2006 on the factory workers who were originally surveyed by the author in Ahmedabad, Gujarat, in 1991.

The composition of this chapter is as follows. In Section 1.2, I outline in brief the salient changes which have occurred in the Indian urban labour market during the past decades based on secondary data. Section 1.3 discusses the changes in the labour market of the survey area, viz. urban Gujarat and especially Ahmedabad, and its salient features so as to provide the background of the field survey which constitutes the core of this chapter. Section 1.4 states the changes that occurred in the employment environment of the sample workers during the 15 years between 1991 and 2006 and the field survey methods. Then, Section 1.5 analyses what happened to the sample workers between the 1991 survey and the 1998 survey, mainly based on the differences between those with and those without the experience of job loss. In Section 1.6, using the data of the 2006 survey, the influence of job loss is analysed further, but based on the subjects' work experiences and personal characteristics including educational achievement or caste affiliation. Noteworthy here is that most of the sample workers had experienced job loss up to this point since 1991. Furthermore, in Section 1.7 I briefly consider the role of family in coping with the difficulties, and the summary and conclusion are presented at the end.

Before going on to the main issues, I will briefly explain some basic terms. The organized sector workers generally include those of all establishments in the public sector irrespective of size of employment and non-agricultural establishments in the private sector employing 10 or more persons, and the unorganized sector workers are those of the units whose employment size is less than 10 including the own account units. However, since the analysis is focused on the urban area in this chapter, the term 'informal sector workers' is used mostly instead of 'non-agricultural unorganized sector workers'. Regular and non-regular employments are terms that refer to the status or security of employment. Employees out of regular employment, such as casual, temporary and contract workers, are included among non-regular employees.

1.2 The changing Indian labour market

1.2.1 Stagnant employment growth in the organized sector

Economic growth rates in India averaged 6.8 per cent per annum during the Eighth Five-Year Plan (1992–97) and trended at the slightly lower level of 5.5 per cent during the Ninth Five-Year Plan (1997–2002). Furthermore, the estimated growth rate of GDP over the previous year is over 9 per cent for the year 2006/7, and so these figures emphasize the fact that there has been fairly steady economic growth in recent years in India (Government of India 2007). Meanwhile, employment in the organized sector, which has provided relatively stable employment and relatively 'privileged' working conditions for the workers, has not increased at the same pace. Table 1.1 shows the net changes in the employment figures in the organized sector for every five years, from 1980 to 2004. The employment figures in the organized sector, which had constantly increased before 1980 (not included in the table), subsequently continued to increase in all categories until 1995, although the pace of increase had slowed in all. The figures, however, posted a net decrease in public and male categories from 1995 to 2000, while a net increase continued in other categories, such as private, female, etc. Then, during the four years from 2000 to 2004, the employment figures in the organized sector decreased overall as well as in all categories except female, in which they marginally increased. The average growth rate of employment in the organized sector declined to 1.7 per cent in the 1980s, then decreased further to 0.6 per cent in the 1990s, and slumped to −1.38 per cent during 2000–4. The only organized industries where employment has increased in the same period are wholesale and retail trade (1.92 per cent), finance, insurance and real estate (3.06 per cent), and mining and quarrying (2.17 per cent). In this context, the discussion on jobless growth has picked up momentum.

The low employment growth rate in the manufacturing sector is particularly serious. Nagaraj (2004) revealed a period of jobless growth in the 1980s, a boom for four years during 1992–96, and a subsequent period of retrenchment and highlighted that about 15 per cent of workers had lost their jobs between 1995/96 and 2001/2. It seems to be clear from Table 1.1 that this employment decrease in the manufacturing sector became a cause of the net decrease in employment in the organized sector during 2000–4. According to the result of the Annual Survey of Industries (ASI) 2003/4 (factory sector), the annual growth rate of employment was −0.35 per cent, while the real growth rate of net value added[2] in the organized manufacturing sector was 4.71 per cent between 1990/91 and 2003/4. This is also

Table 1.1 Net changes in employment figures in the organized sector (thousands)

	1980–85	*1985–90*	*1990–95*	*1995–2000*	*2000–4*
Total	227	178	117	44	−152
Public sector	219	150	69	−15	−112
Private sector	8	27	48	59	−40
Male	181	130	59	−26	−153
Female	46	48	58	70	1
Manufacturing	32	15	14	15	−94
Other industries	195	163	104	28	−58

Source: Government of India, *Economic Survey*, various issues.

reflected in its labour distribution rate, which declined from 40 per cent in 1990/91 to 28.7 per cent in 2003/4 (Ministry of Statistics and Programme Implementation, website). In addition, what is to be noted is an increasing share of female workers in the organized sector. Their share in the data from reporting registered factories increased from 9.7 per cent in 1991 to 25.8 per cent in 1998 (Labour Bureau 2004: 17).

Thus, employment in the organized sector has either stagnated or decreased, but the total workforce has been increasing at the same time. According to the population censuses, the total number of workers, including main workers who had worked for the major part of the reference year (i.e. six months or more) and marginal workers who had not worked for the major part of the reference year (i.e. less than six months), increased by an average of 2.5 per cent per annum between 1991 and 2001. This figure increased at the faster rate of 3.6 per cent in urban areas as compared to the corresponding rate of 2.2 per cent in rural areas. In short, if one considers the employment situation in the organized sector, it will be obvious that the increase of the total workforce has been due to an expansion of employment in the unorganized sector. In fact, looking at only the main workers, agricultural employment decreased at the rate of −1.0 per cent annually and employment in the non-agricultural unorganized sector, which includes rural non-farm sectors as well as the urban informal sector, increased by 4.8 per cent during the same period.[3] As a result, in 1991 the total workforce of 402.23 million including marginal workers had the following composition: 58 per cent employed in agriculture, 7 per cent employed in the organized sector and 35 per cent engaged in the non-agricultural unorganized sector.

1.2.2 Changes in quality of employment

The increase in employment in the informal sector is considered to coincide with an increase in self-employed and casual labour to a large extent, though not fully. According to Table 1.2 which is based on National Sample Survey (NSS) data, the share of regular employees in male employment constantly declined from 1987/88 to 2004/5 in urban areas, on which we focus our analysis here, and there was a commensurate increase in casual labour until 1999/2000. However, through 2004/5, the share of self-employment showed a drastic expansion, which was compensated by a decline in the share of casual labour. In addition, although reliable macro data do not exist, an increasing use of contract workers is also said to be a recent conspicuous phenomenon. Noteworthy here is the possibility that contract workers might be included in the category of regular employees to some extent in NSS data because the persons working and getting salaries/wages on a regular basis are treated as regular employees in NSS and some of the contract workers practically work regularly. A more accurate grasp of the number of contract workers would make the share of non-regular employment higher.

For example, Deshpande et al. (2004) attempted to explore the extent of flexibility enjoyed by employers in adjusting employment in the organized manufacturing sector and identified the expanding trend of non-regular employment between 1991 and 1998 based on a large-scale field survey of 1294 factories across 9 industry groups in 10 states. Whereas the number of employees increased by 2.84 per cent yearly, the share of non-permanent employees, which is composed of casual and temporary employees, expanded from 32 to 36 per cent between the two periods. Adding contract workers, the share of non-regular workers reached 42 per cent in 1998.

Furthermore, as revealed by Table 1.2, the expanding share of regular employees among female workers is also noteworthy. This possibly reflects the increasing share of female employment in the data of the reporting registered factories and the increase of female workers in the organized sector. There seem to be reasons from the demand side, such as a lower wage and an easier employment adjustment in the case of female workers compared to their male counterparts, resulting in an increasing demand for female workers.

Behind these phenomena, in the case of manufacturing industry in particular, there seems to be the reality that flexibilization of the labour market has proceeded virtually steadily while institutional reform for producing flexibility has come to be a focus of the debate on labour reform, as we have mentioned above. In other words, reduction of regular and/or organized sector employment seems to have been realized in various ways. One of them is the voluntary retirement scheme (VRS), which started from the public sector around the end of the 1980s and extended widely to the private sector. In addition various legal or illegal measures[4] have also been adopted, such as dismissal for the purpose of reorganization of firms, i.e. a reduction in regular male employees and sometimes their substitution with non-regular contract or casual workers and with female workers, closure of units under various causes or pretexts, and subsequent reopening of the units with a more capital-intensive nature of technology or a new line-up of employees, such as fewer regular and more non-regular employees, etc. Thus, growth has stagnated in the regular and/or organized sector employment, and in contrast, growth has increased in non-regular and/or informal sector employment, or the very flexible labour, which generally has an acute lack of employment security and income security.

Table 1.2 Employment status of those usually employed in urban areas and main cities from 1987/88 to 2004/5 (%)

		Male				*Female*			
		1987/88	*1993/94*	*1999/2000*	*2004/5*	*1987/88*	*1993/94*	*1999/2000*	*2004/5*
India	Self-employed	41.7	41.7	41.5	44.8	47.1	45.8	45.3	47.7
(urban)	Regular employees	43.7	42.0	41.7	40.6	27.5	28.4	33.3	35.6
	Casual labour	14.6	16.3	16.8	14.6	25.4	25.8	21.4	16.7
Gujarat state	Self-employed	38.6	37.3	40.8	41.4	40.2	42.6	41.9	42.9
(urban)	Regular employees	44.8	44.9	35.9	48.2	28.6	24.1	26.4	30.3
	Casual labour	16.6	17.8	23.3	10.4	31.2	33.3	31.7	26.8
Ahmedabad	Self-employed	34.6	35.6	36.9	36.9	36.6	43.9	62.7	38.8
	Regular employees	45.4	51.3	34.0	52.5	30.3	27.0	22.5	29.9
	Casual labour	20.0	13.1	29.1	10.7	33.1	29.1	14.7	31.3
Mumbai	Self-employed	32.4	35.2	29.2	40.3	30.5	27.6	25.9	29.2
	Regular employees	62.8	65.4	67.9	51.7	63.1	69.2	69.0	68.9
	Casual labour	4.8	2.1	3.1	8.0	6.4	3.2	5.2	1.9
Kolkata	Self-employed	36.7	33.9	44.4	36.8	30.7	28.4	29.9	51.6
	Regular employees	54.3	54.4	40.6	43.5	64.5	62.3	54.5	44.2
	Casual labour	9.0	11.7	15.0	19.7	4.8	9.3	15.0	4.2
Delhi	Self-employed	38.2	44.1	43.5	37.1	29.2	24.2	31.3	15.9
	Regular employees	58.1	45.2	54.0	59.0	67.7	57.6	64.6	79.6
	Casual labour	3.7	10.7	2.6	3.9	3.1	18.2	4.1	4.4
Bangalore	Self-employed	28.9	31.8	27.2	35.2	33.1	29.6	25.0	23.9
	Regular employees	52.7	53.5	58.2	46.2	32.0	62.3	58.6	67.2
	Casual labour	18.4	14.7	14.6	18.6	34.9	8.1	16.8	9.0

Note: Usually employed persons include principal status workers and subsidiary status workers who are 15 years of age and above.
Sources: NSSO (2001) *Employment and Unemployment in India 1999–2000*, NSS 55th Round (July 1999–June 2000), Part 1; NSSO website, *National Sample Survey*, other various issues, available at http:mospi.nic.in/mospi_nsso_rept._pubn.htm; NSSO (1990) 'Results of the Fourth Quinquennial Survey on Employment and Unemployment (All India)', NSS 43rd Round (July 1987–June 1988) *Sarvekshana*, special number.

1.3 Survey area: the changing Ahmedabad labour market

1.3.1 Growth and employment in the state of Gujarat

The state of Gujarat, in which the survey area of Ahmedabad city is located, has been counted as one of the advanced states in India. The state government has given priority to industrial development since Gujarat was formed by splitting the state of Bombay in 1960 and has taken a more aggressive approach to industrialization since the economic reforms started (see e.g. Dholakia 2000; Hirway 2000). Gujarat's economic growth rate is relatively high and its per capita income is also very high as compared to the Indian average. The annual compound growth rate of the net state domestic product (NSDP) at constant prices and per capita NSDP grew by 7.3 and 5.2 per cent, respectively, between 1993/94 and 2003/4 (provisional). The manufacturing sector also achieved a high growth rate of 7.1 per cent (Government of Gujarat 2006a: s-43). However, sluggish growth of employment in the organized sector is obvious in the state as well. The average growth rate of employment, which was 2.14 per cent per annum in the 1980s, declined to 0.47 per cent in the 1990s and dipped to –0.49 per cent between 2000 and 2004 (Government of Gujarat 2006a: s-107). Furthermore, Gujarat is also no exception to the paradoxical growth of production and employment in the organized manufacturing sector. Bagchi et al. (2005: 3043–4), using ASI data (factory sector), show that from 1979/80 to 1999/2000 annual compound growth rates of net value added and capital used in the organized manufacturing sector were 7.8 and 11.8 per cent, respectively, while that of employment has been only 0.9 per cent, and have noted that industrial growth in Gujarat has been highly capital-intensive and labour-displacing. But nonetheless the number of workers of working registered factories in Gujarat, which had gradually increased until 2000, continued to go up after a temporary reduction in 2001, and then has been increasing with record high numbers (provisional) since 2003 (Govt. of Gujarat 2006b: 216).

The changes in quality of employment can be reconfirmed in Table 1.2. Compared to urban India, the noticeable point about urban Gujarat is that the share of regular employees, which had dropped drastically from 1993/94 to 1999/2000, subsequently increased considerably through 2004/5, contrary to the trend observed for urban India. Considering the sluggish growth of employment in the organized sector, this phenomenon can be fairly attributed to an increase of 'regular' employees outside the organized sector. Moreover, a possible increase of contract workers might explain this trend to some extent because they often seem to be included among regular employees as stated above, although a contract worker is not typically reckoned in the number of employees of an organized sector unit, no matter how long and continuously he/she has been working there.

1.3.2 The changing economic base in Ahmedabad city

Ahmedabad is the largest city in Gujarat and seventh biggest metropolitan city in India; it has also been known as a city of traditional cotton textile industry in India. The population of the city increased by average rate of 2.25 per cent per annum during the decade of 1991–2001, and reached an estimated total of 3.69 million people at the time of the 2001 census. The city began to develop as one of the

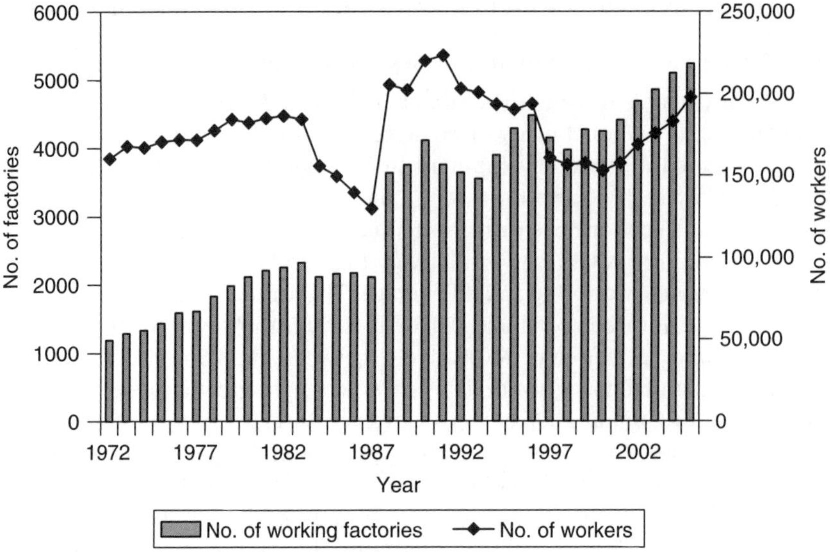

Figure 1.1 Working registered factories and workers employed daily, Ahmedabad, 1972–2005
Notes: Number of workers means the average number of workers employed daily in working factories, including the estimated average number of workers. Figures for 2003–5 are provisional.
Sources: Ahmedabad Municipal Corporation, website, *Statistical Outline of Ahmedabad City for 2003/2004*, available at http://www.egovamc.com/amc_budget/report.asp; Government of Gujarat State, Industrial Safety and Health and Chief Inspector of Inspection (Construction), unpublished data.

industrial centres based on its cotton textile industry under colonial rule and has acquired a position as the most important industrial centre in the state. However, with the decline of the large-scale cotton textile industry in India, retrenchment of workers and closure of mills started here, too, in the late 1970s and continued in big surging waves from the middle of the 1980s through the 1990s, with the result that a large number of mill workers were forced to leave the mills. Consequently, the number of cotton mill workers, which had been close to 160,000 in the late 1970s including temporary workers and contract workers, was estimated to have sharply declined to 25,000 in 1996 (Breman 2004: 143, 145).

As a matter of fact, closure of factories and employment restructuring have been extensively implemented, not only in the textile industry but also in various other industries in Ahmedabad. It is obvious that the number of factories has decreased given the steep decline in the number of factory workers during the 1980s in Ahmedabad (Figure 1.1). The number of working registered factories and the number of their workers, which had reached 2,320 and 184,246, respectively, in 1983, decreased by 9 and 30 per cent, respectively, during the four years up to 1987. Then in the 1990s, the number of factories began increasing but the number of workers remained stagnant or decreased. In addition, the rapid increase of both factories and their employment figures in 1988 seems to have been caused by the expansion of the city area in 1986 and the consequent disclosure of statistical figures covering the new city area starting from 1988. Although the number of workers also finally started displaying an uptrend in the 2000s, it has not returned to the peak of 1991.

Such a radically changing employment environment in the industrial city of Ahmedabad has affected the quality of employment, i.e. the composition of workers by employment status in the city. Table 1.2 clearly shows that in Ahmedabad the share of regular employees declined conspicuously from 1993/94 to 1999/2000, after displaying an uptrend between 1987/88 and 1993/94.[5] So in 1999/2000, only one out of three workers was working as a regular employee, while two out of three were working as casual employees or were self-employed. This share of regular employees was extraordinarily low among major metropolitan cities. But in 2004/5, the share of regular employees again strikingly and quickly increased in Ahmedabad as well. Although it cannot be discussed here because of lack of data, an extreme fluctuation during a short period will require further in-depth examination and analysis, considering the possible causes mentioned for the similar change that occurred in urban Gujarat, transformation of industrial structure and the resulting changes in industrial employment structure, in addition to an increase in the number of factory workers since the 1990s in Ahmedabad, etc., including the data source limitations, if any.

Furthermore, the strikingly large share of self-employed and casual labour combined among the female workforce, compared to the other major cities, is also noteworthy. This seems to be partly attributed to the success of SEWA (Self-Employed Women's Association) which was founded in Ahmedabad in 1972 and has been working for female workers in the informal sector, such as self-employed and home-based workers in the region, by organizing them. This means that the existence of supporting organizations such as SEWA seems to have encouraged women to engage in various jobs in the informal sector and to have turned them from invisible to visible labour statistically. Even though economic activities by female workers are still undoubtedly statistically underestimated[6] in general, the 1993/94 NSS shows that, in urban Gujarat, the workforce participation rate among females aged 15 years and above was 9.7 per cent, whereas in Ahmedabad city it was relatively high, at 19.6 per cent (Mahadevia 2002: 62). According to the population censuses, the number of total workers (main workers plus marginal workers) in Ahmedabad city increased by 2.82 per cent for male workers between 1991 and 2001, whereas for female workers, it increased at the higher rate of 5.72 per cent.[7]

On the basis of our discussion above, we may say that the Ahmedabad labour market, the changes in which have determined the situation of the labour market in urban Gujarat, is also an incomparably peculiar case in the sense that precisely because of the traditional old industrial city, it has been exposed to an extraordinary radical structural change that has led to unpredicted fluctuation. In what follows, the realities of the labour market flexibility will be discussed from the labour side, based on the case studies that were conducted in this city.

1.4 Survey methods and changes in the employment environment in the field

Three field surveys were carried out during a period of 15 years between 1991 and 2006. The first survey (hereinafter 'the 1991 survey') was conducted in August 1991, and all 233 respondents surveyed were factory employees at that time. The number of factories selected was six, and they were all private factories which belonged to one of three industries: textiles, engineering or chemicals. Each industry included one each of a medium/large registered factory (employing 100 or more workers directly) and a small registered factory (employing less than 100 workers directly). The 233 employee samples were male and were randomly selected but were based on the four 'worker categories' of managerial and clerical staff (MCS), technical staff (TS), production workers (PW) and contract workers (CW) according to type of job and employment relation. The first three categories are composed of directly employed employees and the last one is composed of indirectly employed employees. For convenience, we will refer to these four types of employees as '1991 worker categories' in this chapter.

The second survey (hereinafter 'the 1998 survey') was conducted on the same 233 workers in April and June 1998, and we found that their work and employment environment had already changed by that time. First, employment restructuring, such as enforcement of the VRS and replacement of directly employed workers by contract workers, had been carried out in the sample factories for seven years. Second, as a more noteworthy change, two medium/large-scale factories out of six sample factories were closed down in 1994 and 1996, respectively. According to information from the workers, trade unions and the management, the major causes for the closure were said to be, for example, the stoppage of electric power transmission, business problems due to internal trouble in the management of one factory, and for another, supply disruption of a basic ingredient which was declared harmful and banned from importation.

The third survey (hereinafter 'the 2006 survey') was conducted in August 2006. At one medium/large-scale factory, the owner and name of the factory had been changed and all employees had been put under VRS. One of the small factories was closed down due to business trouble, while another small factory had carried out retrenchment on a large scale. As a result, almost all the sample workers of five factories, except for those at one small factory, had experienced job loss at least once during the 15 years from 1991 to 2006. Thus, closure and employment restructuring had been carried out in the factories surveyed as well during those 15 years. These were very common phenomena in Ahmedabad and were just a few examples of cases which frequently occurred in India, as mentioned above. This means that labour flexibility has in fact been secured for the employers of the organized sector in the survey area as well.

As a result, such closure of factories and employment restructuring led to changes in many respondents' residential addresses. In fact, many workers had changed their residences, and therefore their addresses, between 1991 and 1998 and/or between 1998 and 2006. It was our practice in all three field surveys to visit each worker at his residence and interview him there with the help of a schedule prepared in the Gujarati language,[8] so for the last two surveys, we decided to trace their new addresses up to the third migration. Table 1.3 shows the details of the respondents for each survey.

Table 1.3 Number of respondents by the 1991 worker categories and 1991 factory sizes

	Total	*1991 Worker categories*				*1991 Factory sizes*	
		MCS	*TS*	*PW*	*CW*	*Medium/large*	*Small*
1991 survey	233	18	27	158	30	156	77
1998 survey	168	14	20	112	22	115	53
2006 survey	130	11	19	82	18	86	44

Source: The author's surveys.

1.5 Closure of factories and job loss: from the 1998 survey

In the 1998 survey, subtracting the missing persons and migrants to distant places, etc., there were 168 valid responses, which is equivalent to about three-quarters of the valid responses in the 1991 survey. The analysis presented below is based on the data obtained from these 168 respondents. They are divided into two groups: workers from the closed factories (C Group) and workers in the factories still operating (O Group). It follows that the former consists of the workers who were working in the two medium/large but closed factories and the latter consists of the workers who were working in the one medium/large and three small factories which were still working, as mentioned above. Response rates of both groups are almost equal. In the following paragraphs, an attempt is made to analyse what the closures and consequent job losses have meant for the work and living conditions of the workers of the two groups.

1.5.1 Jobs and earnings

Three-quarters of the respondents were distributed in the age groups of thirties and forties, and their average age was 42.4 years. Almost all were married. Table 1.4 reveals that while the number of employed persons is 151 (90%), the rest were unemployed, retired or out of labour force and not seeking a job. The ratios of the employed were 95 per cent in the O Group and 84 per cent in the C Group. While more than half of the employed persons remained working at the same factories as in 1991, the rest had changed jobs during the seven years. As the same table shows, most of the employed were still employees in the O Group, while the number in the C Group declined by around 70 per cent, and instead, the ratio of self-employed had increased. Furthermore, the ratio of permanent employees, which was 81 per cent in 1991, declined to 59 per cent in 1998, and the ratio of non-regular employees such as contract, casual and temporary workers had increased. This indicates that a process of destabilization of employment had been under way. This trend is conspicuous particularly in the C Group, in which contract workers accounted for almost half the group, and when casual and temporary workers are included, the majority were in unstable employment situations. Furthermore, while in the O Group most of the workers (about 90 per cent) were still employed in the manufacturing and repairing sector, in the C Group the same fell below

Table 1.4 Activities, employment status and employment security in 1998

	Total	*O Group*	*C Group*
Activities			
Total	168 (100.0)	93 (100.0)	75 (100.0)
Employed	151 (89.9)	88 (94.6)	63 (84.0)
Unemployed	4 (2.4)	–	4 (5.3)
Retired	10 (6.0)	3 (3.2)	7 (9.3)
Out of labour force	3 (1.8)	2 (2.2)	1 (1.3)
Employment status of employed			
Total	151 (100.0)	88 (100.0)	63 (100.0)
Employee	122 (80.8)	79 (89.8)	43 (68.3)
Employer	4 (2.6)	2 (2.3)	2 (3.2)
Self-employed	25 (16.6)	7 (8.0)	18 (28.6)
Unpaid family worker	–	–	–
Employment security of employees			
Total	122 (100.0)	79 (100.0)	43 (100.0)
Permanent	72 (59.0)	63 (79.7)	9 (20.9)
Temporary	9 (7.4)	3 (3.8)	6 (14.0)
Casual	12 (9.8)	3 (3.8)	9 (20.9)
Contract	28 (23.0)	10 (12.7)	18 (41.9)
Unknown	1 (0.8)	–	1 (2.3)

Notes:
1. Figures in parentheses show percentages.
2. 'Retired' persons are included in 'Out of labour force'.
Source: The author's survey.

half, and there was an increase in other industrial sectors such as construction, wholesale and retail trade, restaurant/hotel, agriculture and social and personal services, with the result of industrial diversification in their employment.

Next, the changes in net earnings: the basic wage plus fringe benefits minus deductions (contribution to social security, tax, payment for debts, etc.) for employees and gross earnings minus costs for self-employed persons and employers are shown in Table 1.5. This clearly shows that the distribution of the 168 respondents by net earnings became distinctly biased towards the higher-earning classes in 1998 as compared to 1991. Moreover, the average monthly net earnings of the 165 respondents including the unemployed (excluding three whose net earnings were unknown) more than doubled from Rs.866 in 1991 to Rs.1754 in 1998. It increased a bit in real terms as well, since the index number of consumer prices for industrial workers in Ahmedabad rose by 83 per cent during the same period (Government of Gujarat 1996a, 2006).

However, the significant variations between the changes in the earning levels of the O and C Groups should not be overlooked. Average monthly net earnings for C Group workers who were employed by the medium/large factories were Rs.1046 in 1991, which was higher than Rs.719 for O Group workers, many of whom were employed by the small factories at that time. However, the situation was reversed in

Table 1.5 Percentage distribution of respondents by net earnings level in 1991 and 1998 (%)

	Number of employees	*Monthly net earnings (Rs.)*						
		Less than 500	*500–1299*	*1300–2099*	*2100–2899*	*2900–4999*	*5000 and above*	*Unknown*
1991								
Total	168	30.4	47.6	20.2	1.8	–	–	–
O Group	93	41.9	46.2	10.8	1.1	–	–	–
C Group	75	16.0	49.3	32.0	2.7	–	–	–
1998								
Total	168	13.1	38.7	23.8	4.8	13.1	4.8	1.8
O Group	93	7.5	30.1	29.0	7.5	18.3	5.4	2.2
C Group	75	20.0	49.3	17.3	1.3	6.7	4.0	1.3

Source: The author's surveys.

1998, with C Group workers having relatively lower average monthly earnings, at Rs.1340, than the corresponding earnings of O Group workers, at Rs.2091. Whereas the earnings of the latter increased by 190 per cent, surpassing the price hike during the same time, those of the former increased by only 29 per cent. In this sense, loss of jobs led to an unexpected fall in the earnings for the workers of the C Group. Furthermore in the C Group, the distribution of earnings is heavily biased towards the lower levels.

1.5.2 Job changes and their impact

Of the respondents, 57 per cent experienced job changes during the seven years up to 1998. About 80 per cent of the job changers changed jobs only once, while the rest changed more than twice. The job-changing ratio in the C Group (81 per cent)[9] naturally greatly surpassed that in the O Group (37 per cent). About 40 per cent of the respondents had never undergone a job change before 1991, but 70 per cent of them were forced to experience it by 1998. We observed that the turnover rate of workers was distinctly low in the medium/large factories compared to small factories in the 1991 survey, which indicates that the job changes for this period were unexpected for the C Group workers in particular.

The gross number of job changes was 122. However, these figures require some attention because, in case of casual jobs in particular, job changing is possibly underestimated because of the high possibility that workers do not perceive it as a change in job when there was no change in the type of occupation, irrespective of changes in employers or places of work.[10] The major reason for job changes was the closure of factory/company as was expected. Whether the closure was legal or illegal was left to the respondent to judge. 'Illegal closure' and 'legal closure' combined accounted for about half of the 136 responses (in multiple answers), and the former reason was reported in higher proportion (36 per cent) than the latter (12 per cent). For the first job change in particular, 81 per cent of the job changers cited legal or illegal closure of factories, 'dismissal', or 'retrenchment', which underlines the fact that the majority of them had left the factory jobs involuntarily. However, no one cited any involuntary reasons for the second and third job changes; this indicates that they had come to change jobs of their own volition. The types of changes that occurred are as follows.

Categorizing all jobs experienced into three sectors: informal sector, formal sector (which is used in contrast with the informal sector instead of the organized sector here), and agriculture, based on employment scale, industry and employment status in the author's field surveys,[11] we find that the informal sector accounted for more than half, as presented in Table 1.6. While the percentage of the formal sector was higher in the O Group, the percentage of the informal sector was higher in the C Group. All the respondents (including indirectly employed contract workers) were working for formal sector factories in 1991, which indicates the severity of the situation and the difficulty in obtaining a relatively secure job in the formal sector in those days, and the situation was more serious for the C Group. Furthermore, the same table also presents other details of the changes. The shift within the formal sector accounted for about 40 per cent in the O Group,

Table 1.6 Breakdown of job changes between 1991 and 1998

	Total	*O Group*	*C Group*
Sector			
Formal sector	36 (29.5)	20 (43.5)	16 (21.1)
Informal sector	66 (54.1)	21 (45.7)	45 (59.2)
Agriculture	12 (9.8)	3 (6.5)	9 (11.8)
Unknown	8 (6.6)	2 (4.3)	6 (7.9)
Sector change			
Informal → Informal	11 (9.0)	3 (6.5)	8 (10.5)
Formal → Formal	33 (27.0)	18 (39.1)	15 (19.7)
Informal → Formal	2 (1.6)	1 (2.2)	1 (1.3)
Formal → Informal	55 (45.1)	18 (39.1)	37 (48.7)
Formal → Agriculture	12 (9.8)	3 (6.5)	9 (11.8)
Unknown	9 (7.4)	3 (6.5)	6 (7.9)
Wage/salary change			
Up	42 (34.4)	26 (56.5)	16 (21.1)
Down	75 (61.5)	18 (39.1)	57 (75.0)
No change	3 (2.5)	1 (2.2)	2 (2.6)
Unknown	2 (1.6)	1 (2.2)	1 (1.3)
Total	122 (100.0)	46 (100.0)	76 (100.0)
Employment status			
Permanent	26 (29.2)	16 (47.1)	10 (18.2)
Temporary	17 (19.1)	7 (20.6)	10 (18.2)
Casual	19 (21.3)	3 (8.8)	16 (29.0)
Contract	26 (29.2)	8 (23.5)	18 (32.7)
Unknown	1 (1.1)	0 (0.0)	1 (1.8)
Total	89 (100.0)	34 (100.0)	55 (100.0)

Notes: Figures in parentheses show percentages.
Source: The author's survey.

but only 20 per cent in the C Group. Particularly in the C Group, the ratio of the downward shift from the formal to the informal sector was high; in contrast, only one case revealed an upward shift. Thus, it is clear that it was becoming difficult to return to the formal sector once a person fell into the informal sector. Additionally in this connection, the 212 gross job changes that had occurred up to 1991 were mostly shifts from the informal sector or agriculture to the formal sector, or a shift within the formal sector.[12]

Furthermore, it can also be observed that job changing tends to destabilize employment situations. In the C Group, the self-employed accounted for 24 per cent of the new jobs. The remaining jobs were mostly employees, but of these, as shown in Table 1.6, the majority were non-regular unstable employment such as temporary, casual or contract. Turning our eyes to the earnings level, we see it increased in only one-third of all job changes and ordinarily declined; three-quarters of the cases in the C Group experienced decline. Recalling that only a

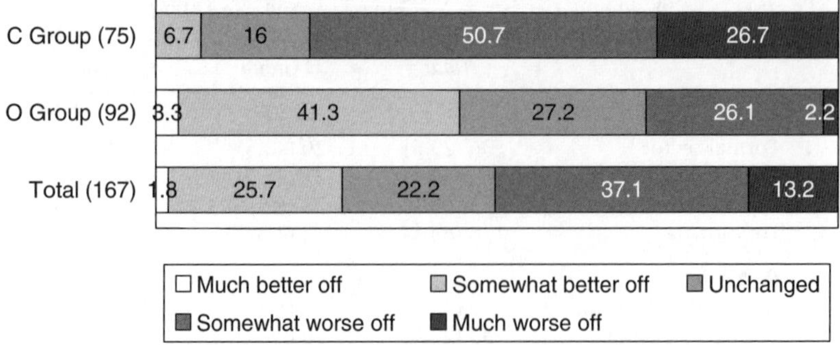

Figure 1.2 Perceptions of changes in living standard as of 1998 (%)
Source: The author's survey.

quarter of the 212 job changes had brought a decrease in earnings in the 1991 survey, we see that the negative economic effects of job changes have become more serious in this respect as well.

However, a point worth noting is that there were persons who avoided a downward shift even in the C Group. For example, those who were MCS or TS in 1991, in more than half of their job changes (14 cases), had shifted within the formal sector. At the same time, most persons with higher education, i.e. college and above, in the C Group did not shift downward but shifted within the formal sector.

Furthermore, I would like to emphasize that as job changing went on, each one brought improvement. When the job changes were repeated, there was a tendency towards increase in the ratio of manufacturing/repairing as the industry, the ratio of employees as the employment status, the ratio of permanent as the employment security, and the ratio of increase in the wage level. This might indicate that persons who could expect to obtain a better job have repeatedly changed jobs, although the number of cases is small. As a matter of fact, around 30 per cent of the persons with two or more job changes were those who were categorized as TS in 1991. Although we cannot make any firm conclusions here for lack of adequate data, we can infer that there is a greater possibility for those who were MCS or TS to avoid a serious decline due to job loss as well as to climb up again. This will be discussed further in the next section.

In addition, 45 persons (27 per cent of respondents) experienced unemployment during the seven years. The average unemployment period for those persons was about 14 months, and 28 persons experienced unemployment for more than one year. The ratio of persons who experienced unemployment was higher in the C Group and was also different depending on their 1991 worker categories. While the ratio was 0 per cent in MCS and a quarter in both TS and PW, it reached 41 per cent in CW, which indicates that re-employment was more difficult for CW.

Thus, it can be concluded that job changes due to job loss have negatively affected the employment situation in most cases. Upward mobility is negligible, indicating an increasing severity in the labour market situation for most of the job losers. Furthermore, such severity was also observed from the changes in respondents' standard of living based on their own perceptions. Asking the question by dividing their evaluations into five broad categories: 'much better off', 'somewhat better off', 'unchanged', 'somewhat worse off', and 'much worse off', 167 responses were obtained. As Figure 1.2 shows, the evaluations were conspicuously different for the O and C Groups.

1.6 Further decline among the workers: from the 2006 survey

In this section, based on the results of the 2006 survey, an attempt is made to explain in what way the process of flexibilization in the labour market has further progressed, what consequently has happened to the workers' jobs and lives, and who were most affected by this process and who were not. As mentioned earlier, job loss and consequent job changes had been experienced by most of the sample workers during the 15 years since 1991 due to closure of factories and employment restructuring. Therefore, taking this circumstance into consideration, and at the same time reflecting on the fact that all the sample workers had once worked for formal sector factories but in different worker categories at some point in their long job histories, the analysis carried out here is again based on the four 1991 worker categories: MCS, TS, PW and CW. There is correlation among the category of work, caste and educational level of the sample workers as revealed in the 1991 survey, and we will return to this issue at the end of the section.

1.6.1 Jobs and earnings

The 2006 survey was to be conducted on the 168 sample workers who had been interviewed in the 1998 survey. The number of respondents decreased to 130, but the valid response rate of 77.4 per cent was higher than expected. These 130 workers will be referred to as the respondents in this section. Others whom we could not interview included migrants (10.1 per cent), deceased (7.1 per cent), missing persons (2.4 per cent) and others including 'no answer' (3 per cent). The respondents have also aged during this period, and those in their fifties are most numerous (38.5 per cent), followed by those in their forties (35.4 per cent). The average age of the respondents was 50.4 years.

Employed persons, numbering 109, accounted for 83.8 per cent of the respondents. According to Table 1.7(A) which shows the changes in the employment status of 108 workers who were also employed in 1998, the share of employees decreased and instead the share of employers or self-employed increased. Almost the same distribution can be observed for all 109 employed in 2006, which also shows that the share of self-employed is relatively high in MCS and TS (Table 1.7(B)).

Furthermore, Table 1.8(A) shows the changes in the employment security of 78 workers who were employees both in 1998 and 2006. Both in absolute and relative terms, there was a sharp decline in permanent workers during this period, and they were mostly replaced by temporary or casual workers. The distribution of 85 employees by employment security in 2006 is also similar (Table 1.8(B)). In addition, it was also confirmed that out of these 78 workers, 17 persons shifted

Table 1.7 Employment status of employed persons in 2006

Employment status	*A (n = 108)*		*B 2006*				
	1998	*2006*	*Total (n = 109)*	*MCS (10)*	*TS (15)*	*PW (66)*	*CW (18)*
Employee	84.3	77.8	78.0	70.0	73.3	78.8	83.3
Employer	3.7	2.8	2.8	0.0	0.0	3.0	5.6
Self-employed	12.0	19.4	19.3	30.0	26.7	18.2	11.1

Notes:
A: 'Employed' both in 1998 and 2006.
B: 'Employed' in 2006 irrespective of employment status in 1998.
Source: The author's surveys.

Table 1.8 Employment security of employees in 2006

Employment security	*A (n = 78)*		*B 2006*				
	1998	*2006*	*Total (n = 85)*	*MCS (7)*	*TS (11)*	*PW (52)*	*CW (15)*
Permanent	56.4	38.5	37.6	85.7	81.8	26.9	20.0
Temporary	3.8	14.1	15.3	0.0	0.0	23.1	6.7
Casual	9.0	21.8	22.4	14.3	18.2	21.2	33.3
Contract	30.8	25.6	24.7	0.0	0.0	28.8	40.0

Notes:
A: 'Employees' both in 1998 and 2006.
B: 'Employees' in 2006 irrespective of employment security in 1998.
Source: The author's surveys.

from permanent employment to non-regular employment while only three workers shifted in the reverse direction. The rest were a shift within permanent or non-regular employment. So, it is obvious that more respondents moved downward than upward in terms of employment security during the eight years. Another important point is, as Table 1.8(B) shows, the difference in the extent of employment destabilization by 1991 worker categories. Destabilization has progressed or deepened conspicuously in PW and CW but not so in MCS and TS. Actually, 85 per cent of casual workers and all contract workers in 2006 were those who had been PW or CW in 1991.

As predicted, monthly net earnings are distinctly different depending on 1991 worker categories. As Figure 1.3 presents, whereas the share of workers with higher earning levels, say Rs.5000 and more, was 70 and 46.7 per cent for MCS and TS, respectively, it was 0 per cent for CW and a mere 4.5 per cent even for PW. In contrast, the workers with lower earnings of less than Rs.2900 reached a high ratio of 94 per cent for CW and 61 per cent for PW, but for TS and MCS, they were few or non-existent. This naturally resulted in a big difference in average net earnings in each worker category: Rs.7063 in MCS, Rs.6860 in TS, and a much lower Rs.2898 in PW and Rs.2071 in CW. In the field, we often found cases of workers who were working on a daily basis and getting only Rs.75 or so as a daily wage. Unstable

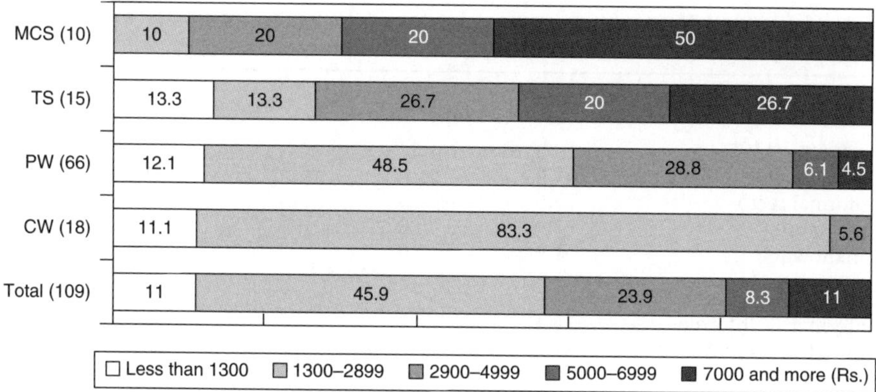

Figure 1.3 Monthly net earnings by the 1991 worker categories in 2006 (%)
Source: The author's survey.

Table 1.9 Number of job changes between 1998 and 2006 by the 1991 worker categories and operating/closed factories

Number of job changes	*Total*	*1991 Worker categories*				*Situation of the sample factories in 1998*	
		MCS	*TS*	*PW*	*CW*	*Operating*	*Closed*
0	47 (39.8)	6 (60.0)	8 (44.4)	27 (37.5)	6 (33.3)	32 (42.1)	15 (35.7)
1	43 (36.4)	2 (20.0)	6 (33.3)	30 (41.7)	5 (27.8)	28 (36.8)	15 (35.7)
2	20 (16.9)	0 (0.0)	3 (16.7)	11 (15.3)	6 (33.3)	12 (15.8)	8 (19.0)
3	5 (4.2)	2 (20.0)	1 (5.6)	1 (1.4)	1 (5.6)	2 (2.6)	3 (7.1)
4	3 (2.5)	0 (0.0)	0 (0.0)	3 (4.2)	0 (0.0)	2 (2.6)	1 (2.4)
Total	118 (100.0)	10 (100.0)	18 (100.0)	72 (100.0)	18 (100.0)	76 (100.0)	42 (100.0)

Source: The author's survey.

and insufficient working days add to the miseries of this extremely low wage rate. Furthermore, the 1991 survey highlighted the great differences in earning levels among the 1991 worker categories, which suggests that a similar earning gap has remarkably held even after their experience of job loss and job changes.

1.6.2 Job changes and their impact

During the eight years since the 1998 survey, of the 118 respondents who answered the questions on job changes, 60 per cent had experienced job changes (Table 1.9). About 40 per cent of the job changers had changed jobs more than twice. The gross number of job changes was 110, although some attention is still necessary regarding this figure as mentioned in the previous section. CW changed jobs most, followed by PW. Approximately two-thirds of the 51 respondents who had no experience of job changes by 1998 had experienced it by 2006, with the result

Table 1.10 Breakdown of job changes by the 1991 worker categories between 1998 and 2006

	Total	*MCS*	*TS*	*PW*	*CW*
Sector ($n = 110$)					
Formal sector	41.8	62.5	53.3	35.8	45.0
Informal sector	53.6	37.5	46.7	58.2	50.0
Agriculture	2.7	0.0	0.0	3.0	5.0
Unknown	1.8	0.0	0.0	3.0	0.0
Sector change ($n = 110$)					
Informal → Informal	26.4	37.5	13.3	26.9	30.0
Formal → Formal	22.7	62.5	40.0	17.9	10.0
Informal → Formal	18.2	0.0	13.3	16.4	35.0
Formal → Informal	23.6	0.0	20.0	29.9	15.0
Others	4.5	0.0	0.0	4.5	10.0
Unknown	4.5	0.0	13.3	4.5	0.0
Wage/salary change ($n = 110$)					
Up	43.6	50.0	46.7	40.3	50.0
Down	40.9	25.0	26.7	47.8	35.0
No change	11.8	12.5	20.0	9.0	15.0
Unknown	3.6	12.5	6.7	3.0	0.0
Employment security ($n = 86$)					
Permanent	20.9	50.0	50.0	13.5	16.7
Temporary	18.6	0.0	10.0	25.0	11.1
Casual	32.6	50.0	40.0	23.1	50.0
Contract	27.9	0.0	0.0	38.5	22.2

Note: 'Others' in sector change includes the shifts between agriculture and formal sector or informal sector.
Source: The author's survey.

that 85 per cent of the 118 respondents had experienced job loss at least once after the 1991 survey. Furthermore, out of 67 respondents who had experienced job changes by 1998, 57 per cent had repeated job changes afterward as well. As multiple responses were possible, the reasons given for the 105 job changes numbered 115 in total. Circumstances on the management side, such as closure of factory/company, voluntary retirement scheme, retrenchment and other type of dismissal, accounted for 39 per cent of the responses. In addition, low wage (16 per cent), lack of employment guarantee (9 per cent), strenuous work and dissatisfaction with management (each 6 per cent) were also cited.

Details of the 110 job changes are shown in Table 1.10. Compared to Table 1.6 which revealed the job changes up to 1998, the total number of formal sector units increased. However, a significant difference was still observed across the 1991 worker categories: the share of the formal sector is highest in MCS, whereas it is lowest in PW. Furthermore, the shift within the formal sector and the upward shift from the informal to the formal sector accounted for 22.7 and 18.2 per cent, respectively, of the total job changes, whereas the ratios of the shift within the informal sector and the downward shift from the formal to the informal sector were 26.4 and 23.6 per cent, respectively. This indicates a decreasing trend in the downward shift in the 2006 survey compared to the 1998 survey, which seems to be mainly due to the fact that many respondents had already worked in the informal sector at the time of the 1998 survey, after dropping once from formal sector factories to the informal sector. As observed in the previous section, shifts within the formal sector were more common for MCS in this survey as well. However, one thing to note here is that any type of self-employment was automatically included in the informal sector in the author's surveys, which seems to have led to the overestimation of the share of the informal sector in cases of MCS or TS in particular, considering that their occupations were mostly professional and technical work although they were self-employed. At the same time, it should also be noticed that the share of the formal sector is possibly overestimated in the case of contract workers because they frequently mentioned the employment size of the companies to which they were supplied as a size of the unit although they were indirectly and often temporarily employed by those units.

Let us now turn to the changes in earnings before and after job changes. The number of job changes accompanied by a rise in earnings was higher than in the 1998 survey, and the share of job changes accompanied by a decline in earnings became lower. Such a trend may be attributed to the fact that while many of the job changes up to 1998 were accompanied by a decrease in earnings owing to job loss from formal sector factories, a considerable number of job changes after 1998 were those that occurred after once experiencing a downward shift to the informal sector.

As for the changes in employment security, 86 new jobs (76 per cent) were employee jobs, and only one-fifth of those were permanent employee jobs. The rest were casual, temporary or contract jobs, indicating that they have just drifted among the unstable non-regular employment. Even so, it is difficult even to get jobs of this sort without any personal connection. When job changers after 1998 were asked about the process of seeking the latest jobs and employment, 68 respondents replied to this question. Sources of information on jobs were mostly friends or neighbourhoods. None used institutional employment exchanges. Use of advertisements was reported by only three workers. Furthermore, 30 out of 68 respondents mentioned the necessity of recommendation by an acquaintance in order to be hired.

1.6.3 Changes in living conditions

Now we will examine how the respondents evaluated the changes which occurred in their lives after suffering radical changes in their employment and working environment during the eight years. This analysis is based on the same five categories as the 1998 survey. 'Much better off' and 'somewhat better off' accounted for 4.6 and 29.2 per cent, respectively, while 'much worse off' and 'somewhat worse off' accounted for 23.1 and 26.2 per cent, respectively. The remaining 16.9 per cent responded with 'unchanged'. While there were no 'much worse off' in MCS, there were no 'much better off' in CW. Furthermore, by clubbing these five levels of evaluation into the three broader categories of 'better off', 'unchanged' and 'worse

Table 1.11 Changes in respondents' perception of their living standard between 1998 and 2006 by the 1991 worker categories

	Total *n* = *130*		*MCS* *n* = *11*		*TS* *n* = *19*		*PW* *n* = *82*		*CW* *n* = *18*	
	1998	*2006*	*1998*	*2006*	*1998*	*2006*	*1998*	*2006*	*1998*	*2006*
Better off	32.3	33.8	72.7	63.7	52.6	57.9	24.4	28.0	22.2	16.7
Unchanged	22.3	16.9	18.2	18.1	21.1	10.5	20.8	17.2	32.4	22.2
Worse off	45.3	49.3	9.1	18.2	26.3	31.6	54.8	54.8	45.4	61.1

Source: The author's surveys.

off', Table 1.11 reveals the results in comparison with that of the 1998 survey. The ratio of the respondents 'worse off' increased in 2006 compared to 1998, and did so for MCS, TS and CW. Needless to say, those who replied 'worse off' in 2006 were not necessarily the same persons as those who replied thus in 1998. If they were the same, however, this means that they evaluate their living standards as continuing to decline after the 1991 survey. Particularly in CW, those 'worse off' reached 61.1 per cent and accounted for more than half in PW, but in contrast, 'better off' accounted for more than half in MCS and TS. Of course, these results cannot only be attributed to the changes in the employment and working environment that each worker experienced. Changes in their personal family life and changes in their awareness associated with the progressively changing social environment are also considered to have affected them. However, considering that out of those who replied 'better off', 45 per cent cited a wage raise and 14 per cent cited obtaining a better job; out of those who replied 'worse off', 73 and 25 per cent cited a decrease in earnings and unemployment, respectively, as the reasons for their evaluations (in multiple answers), there is a significant possibility that changes in the employment and working environment strongly determined their evaluations. The other reasons were a rise in household income due to employment of other family members (48 per cent), smaller family size (36 per cent) or increase of social status (11 per cent), etc., among those who reported their situation to be 'better off'. Other important reasons cited by those who selected 'worse off' were price hikes (42 per cent), increase of expenditure (28 per cent), increase of expenses for children (28 per cent), sickness of self and/or family members (27 per cent) and bigger family size (22 per cent).

There are large variations in the penetration rates of major durable consumer goods among the 1991 worker categories. Of such goods, colour TVs showed a relatively high penetration rate across all worker categories. During the field survey, we sometimes visited respondents' houses which were poor and extremely small but had a colour TV as about the only durable good. Ownership rates of colour TVs were 100 per cent for MCS and TS, 66 per cent for PW, and reached 50 per cent even for CW. On the other hand, ownership rates of black and white TVs were 21 per cent for PW and 17 per cent for CW. Furthermore, scooters/motorcycles were owned by

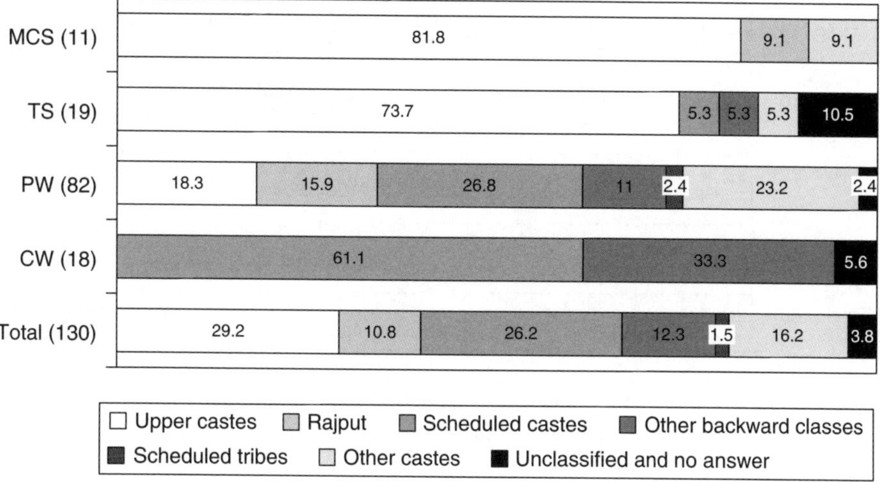

Figure 1.4 Caste composition of respondents by the 1991 worker categories (%)
Source: The author's survey.

91 per cent of MCS, 74 per cent of TS and 34 per cent of PW, but not at all by CW. Cars were owned by 16 per cent of TS and 5 per cent of PW. Ownership of a mobile phone was reported by 55 per cent for MCS, 63 per cent for TS, 32 per cent for PW and the small proportion of 6 per cent for CW. For refrigerators as well, ownership rates were high for MCS (82 per cent) and TS (79 per cent), whereas they were low for PW (28 per cent) and CW (11 per cent). Furthermore, there were toilets in all houses of MCS and TS, but not in 29 and 50 per cent of the houses of PW and CW, respectively. Also, all houses of MCS and TS had their own water taps, but 17 and 28 per cent of the houses of PW and CW, respectively, did not.

1.6.4 Who has experienced decline?

Thus, the labour market, which is flexible in practice, has seriously affected the work and lives of the sampled (ex-) factory workers, and the extent of that effect was distinctly different among the 1991 worker categories. So, more noteworthy at this stage is how visibly different the personal characteristics of the workers in each category are. They are shown in Figures 1.4 and 1.5.

First, as we can see from Figure 1.4, caste distribution is distinctly different among the 1991 worker categories. Upper castes are strongly represented in MCS and TS, accounting for more than 80 and 70 per cent, respectively, whereas the share for upper castes was 0 per cent in CW and was less than 20 per cent in PW. In contrast, the share of scheduled castes was above 60 per cent for CW, 0 per cent for MCS and 5.3 per cent for TS. In addition, the remaining CWs were mostly from other backward classes. Furthermore, in the case of PW, each caste group is distributed evenly.

Next, Figure 1.5 reveals a definite relationship between educational level and the 1991 worker categories. While more than 80 per cent of MCS and around half of TS had an education of college level or above, the corresponding shares were a mere

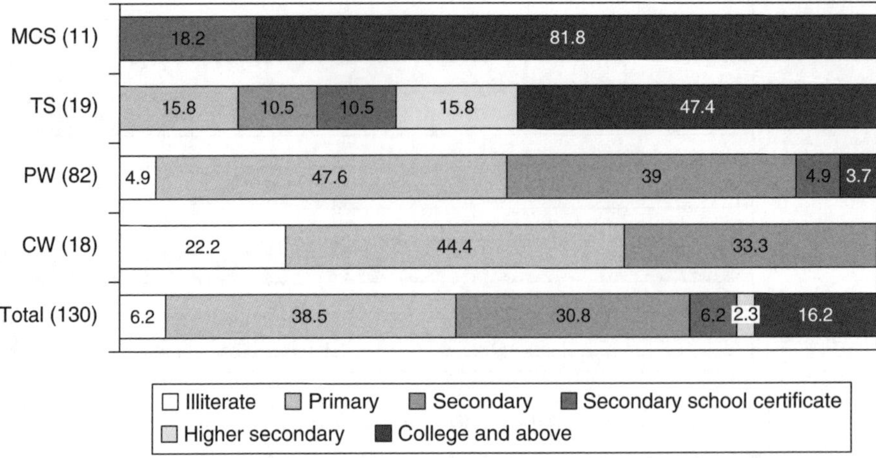

Figure 1.5 Educational level by the 1991 worker categories in 2006 (%)
Source: The author's survey.

3.7 per cent for PW and 0 for CW. In fact, the level of education of CW was generally conspicuously low, with most of them having received no education or having only primary level of education, which combined accounted for two-thirds of them.

It was made clear in the 1991 survey that caste composition and educational level were distinctly different among the worker categories in factories, and similar correlations were again presented in the 2006 survey after 15 years had passed and the number of the sample workers had decreased to less than 60 per cent. Based on the 1991 survey, the author had concluded that personal characteristics such as religion, caste and native place, and educational disparities which presumably occurred through caste differential, reflecting the different formal or informal recruitment and selection methods of different worker categories in factories, had determined the job access and the position of each worker in the factory. As the 2006 survey reveals, their life course as workers still seems to be considerably dependent on this mechanism. However, perhaps it would be more accurate to say that this mechanism, coupled with the drastically fluctuating labour market, has particularly deprived workers of the lower class of a chance to turn their lives around and has condemned them to continue to work at the bottom of the labour market.

1.7 Avoidance of risk of impoverishment or decline

The influence of job loss was analysed as described above when we attempted to consider it at the individual worker level. However, the workers who, as the result of job loss, had lost the legislative safety nets such as the Employees' State Insurance Act and the Employers' Provident Funds Act[13] as well as the stable income source which had been guaranteed by the enterprise, have coped with the risks of impoverishment at the family level as their last resort. Their concrete measures were (1) diversification of income source, (2) raising of the household income through employment of other family members, (3) living in an extended family, (4) usage of savings and access to loans, and so on.

For example, attempts to diversify income sources were often observed in the sample workers' families. In the 1998 survey, around 70 per cent of the respondents reported that they had a source of income other than their own earnings from their main jobs. This mainly included earnings by other family members, and the share of respondents having this sort of earning had increased as compared to the same in 1991. Furthermore, in the 2006 survey, out of 130 respondents, the number of workers who had other income sources was 111 (85.4 per cent), and three out of four had earnings from other family members. Other sources of earnings were their own pension (7.7 per cent), their own earnings from secondary jobs including agriculture (10 per cent), and income by leasing out a house and/or land (5 per cent), etc.

It has been discussed that crisis in the household economy may become one of the reasons for women to participate in the labour market in order to support household income (for example, see Mahadevia 2002). In the 1998 survey, the workforce participation rate for spouses (wives) in the C Group was 45 per cent, compared to 27 per cent in the O Group, which appears to be an expression of that. Furthermore, in the 2006 survey, the number of wives was 117, and their workforce participation rate was 36 per cent. Particularly in CW, more than half of the spouses were involved in economic activities, and this share was considerably higher than that in Ahmedabad (see Section 1.3). However, it should be added that 71 per cent of the working wives were working in the informal sector, especially as home-based workers whose rewards were extremely low. The average monthly earnings of these working wives were Rs.847. By earning level, 45 per cent of the working wives were receiving only Rs.500 or less, and those earning Rs.1000 or less accounted for 71 per cent.

A marked increase in extended families was also one of the major findings in the 2006 survey. This seems to have become one useful measure to sustain livelihoods. We found in the 1991 survey more families belonging to nuclear families than we expected, and the percentage of extended families was only 27 per cent. In contrast, in the 2006 survey the latter increased to about 50 per cent. In our survey, there were many households where respondents' children continued to live with their parents, brothers and sisters, and their siblings' families, after forming their own families, contrary to the belief that nuclear families had recently increased in urban areas, especially in the middle class. Such a phenomenon is partly explained by their preference for living in an extended family in order to pluralize income sources and to save on fixed household costs such as dwelling expenses. Actually in the field, households which seemed unable to split into separate nuclear families and which seemed to be barely surviving by living as an extended family were often observed. However, it should be added that there is still the possibility that the household situation observed in the 1991 survey was a rather exceptional phenomenon due to migration,[14] etc., and that the present household situation is proving precisely that the extended family had persisted as a traditional type of household. Furthermore, recalling that 'bigger family size' was cited as one of the significant reasons for being 'worse off', living in an extended family is, on the contrary, likely to have depressed their living conditions, particularly in cases of families with many non-earning dependants.

Furthermore, savings and access to loans are also considered to be very effective insurance against a crisis, but there were changes in the percentage of the respondents with those. Although the share of respondents with savings decreased from half in the 1991 survey to around a third in the 1998 survey, it increased again to about 42 per cent in the 2006 survey. The savings amount of half of the depositors was more than Rs.50,000 in 2006. On the other hand, the percentage of respondents with loans, or a debtor ratio, had declined from 60 per cent in 1991 to 41 per cent in 1998 and then to below 30 per cent in 2006. Such a low ratio, particularly in 2006, may be partly attributed to the difficulty of obtaining accurate information on loans as well as savings from respondents. In addition, some of the respondents must have liquidated debt with the money they received as compensation or retirement allowance, etc., upon the closure of factories or dismissal or through voluntary retirement schemes, etc. On the contrary, formal loans from the employees' cooperative societies and loans from their factories or employers, which are institutionalized in a sense as an advance on salary, became almost impossible to obtain after they lost their secure employment relationship, and this may also have contributed to the reduction of debt. In fact, 60 per cent of the 233 sample workers in the first survey had debts, and in more than 90 per cent of the loan cases, the loan was obtained from their cooperative societies, factories or employers. In this sense it may be said that the risk of impoverishment became higher.

While some of the respondents alleviated the risk of further impoverishment in these ways, other people who did not have such means seem to have dropped down more easily. In other words, the lack of chance of a secondary job, absence of family members having a source of income, lack of savings, and unavailability of formal or quasi-institutionalized loans, etc., have depressed their lives more seriously, and such cases were not rare in the author's survey. For example, in one of the surveyed areas, there was no chance of even home-based work. This indicates that the extremely low wages in home-based work are basically due to an excess supply of labour, which inevitably leads to some people being left out of the selection process even in the informal sector. Furthermore, with the loss of access to relatively reliable lenders as well as the loss of the legislative safety net including the Employees' State Insurance Act, the lives of workers who suffered from their own or their family members' sickness or accidents have been severely affected. These workers have often fallen into serious poverty. For example, 17 respondents reported sickness as a reason for their living standard being 'worse off' in the 2006 survey and seven of them reported that it was 'much worse off'.

In light of the above discussion, let us examine the household income level of the respondents in 2006. The average amounts of household income were still distinctly different among the 1991 worker categories. The amounts were Rs.11090 for MCS and Rs.10585 for TS, whereas they were much lower for PW, at Rs.5498, and for CW, at Rs.3284. They are 57, 54, 90 and 59 per cent higher, respectively, than the average own net earnings of each worker category. Ultimately, it is concluded that even various efforts at the family level are not enough to bridge the economic gap among the 1991 worker categories. However, it seems to be certain that those measures have decreased the risk of further impoverishment, particularly for the workers of the poorer classes.

To add another word or two, membership of trade unions and other sorts of social organizations is also considered useful as a measure for avoiding the risk of impoverishment, but very few respondents had such memberships. Organization, as a measure of risk avoidance, no longer exists for them.

1.8 Conclusion

Allow me to summarize the main points. First, as shown in Section 1.2, jobless growth (in the organized sector), and therefore an increase in non-regular and/or informal sector employment, have become recent conspicuous trends in the urban labour market, while the argument for and against labour market flexibility has been extensively conducted. As shown in Section 1.3, Gujarat, which is seen as one of the advanced industrialized states in India, was also not an exception in this respect. In addition, the biggest industrial centre in the state, Ahmedabad, developed with a heavy reliance on the cotton textile industry, and the decline of this industry has had a most serious impact on the city's economy. Many factories, including textile mills, have been closed or otherwise have carried out employment restructuring. With the changing industrial structure, the employment environment has also undergone many changes here as well. Then, in Section 1.4, it was mentioned that many sample workers had also experienced closure of factories, dismissal and voluntary retirement, etc. Based on this fact, in Section 1.5, the changes which have occurred in the work and lives of (ex-) factory workers were analysed, based on the differences between those with and without the experience of job loss. What was observed is that a considerable gap has developed, in terms of their jobs, earnings and lives, between those who experienced job loss and those who did not. More precisely, the impact of job loss was strong enough to reverse the situation between the workers of the O Group, whose factories were mostly small but still operating in 1998, and the workers of the C Group, whose factories were medium or large size but had been closed by 1998. Thus, the risk of job loss, which should have been reduced at least institutionally for the FS workers, easily became a reality, and the consequent job loss has brought about an unanticipated change in the lives of people. Furthermore in Section 1.6, based on the fact that most of the sample workers had experienced job loss by 2006, the impact of job loss was again analysed. Even though their experience is also described with the words 'job loss', the impact was not same. Therefore, the analysis focused on the extent of the differences and the factors leading to the differences. The gap observed in work and life remained very great among the 1991 worker categories even after 15 years. Caste, related educational level, and work experience as influenced by caste and education have surfaced as some of the possible factors causing the gap. In addition, what can be emphasized from the two follow-up surveys is that the experience of job loss from the organized sector (= decline) was not necessarily accompanied by a chance of reintegration into the organized sector. This means that flexibilization of employment has been realized as one-way flexibility, with an exit but without an entrance. Thus, many of the workers have floated among jobs without employment security. Finally in Section 1.7, it was indicated that while many sample workers were working in unstable and severe employment and work environments, diversification of income sources, living in extended families, and savings and access to loans, etc., possibly played a role at the family level to prevent them from falling into further impoverishment.

Obviously, plenty of new middle-class people have been created by the steady growth of the economy since the inception of economic reforms in India. The social and economic transformation which has occurred in Ahmedabad is also astonishing. On the other hand, it is also true that behind those attention-grabbing social changes, employment flexibility has actually increased, resulting in a large number of workers missing out on the wave of growth and ending up living in huddled masses of poverty. In fact, the field surveys reported in this chapter also showed that some people had a better chance to move upwardly, while many others have faced a serious decline in their jobs and lives during these 15 years. Needless to say, behind such phenomena there were also changes in the labour demand associated with changing industrial structure and technological improvements as well as a sluggish growth in organized and regular employment opportunities in Ahmedabad. So, we can also argue that the workers whose labour quality was mismatched with present demands could not escape a downward shift. Furthermore, undoubtedly employment and working conditions in the informal sector have remained without any drastic improvement, which made it impossible for people who had once dropped down to the informal sector to turn things around. Besides, other aspects may come into focus when an analysis on intergenerational social mobility is added, based on the result of the field surveys on the children of the respondents which was carried out at the same time as the 2006 survey. The author and investigators observed in the process of the field survey that more than a few children of the respondents had realized upward mobility in some ways in their generation; however, details of the results of the children's survey will be discussed elsewhere.

Lastly, a suggestion derived through these small case studies is that separate measures should be considered for existing old-fashioned workers and for potential or new entrants into the labour market. For the existing workers, including many of our respondents, who have suffered adverse effects and who are characterized by obsolete skills, low educational level, and older age, it is very difficult to re-enter the organized sector because of their mismatch with labour demand in the present labour market, even if more employment opportunities were to be generated in the organized sector. What is required for them is provision of retraining and job placement services. Also required is support to improve productivity in the informal sector and to distribute the benefits to the workers in an attempt to seriously improve employment and working conditions.

On the other hand, for potential and new entrants, a higher priority should be given to preventing the persistence, across generations, of poverty which is reflected in the gap among social status stratifications like caste. To that end, it seems indispensable that more emphasis is placed on increasing the job opportunities in the organized sector and regular employment than in the informal sector and non-regular employment. In addition, restructuring the labour market system will also be necessary. This means that an attempt is required to ensure fairer opportunities for education and skill development which is matched with the newly emerging economic scene and the consequent changing labour demand, as well as to ensure more practical job placement services for the new generations. These attempts are not only expected to help in changing lives in the generation of potential and new entrants by bridging the social and economic gaps among people in the different strata; they are also expected to lead to support of the older generation at the family level, as long as the social security system is neither widely realized nor sufficiently effective (although the government has tried to extend its coverage)[15] and as long as the family continues to fulfil an insurance function against risks.

In India, where recent economic growth is very impressive, further flexibility in the labour market should be pursued with a blueprint for job growth not only in the informal sector but also in the organized sector.

Acknowledgement

A portion of the field surveys on which this chapter is based, i.e. the 2006 survey, was conducted as part of the author's research project supported financially by the Japan Society for the Promotion of Science (JSPS).

Notes

1. Sundar (2005) reviews the debate.
2. The wholesale price index of manufactured products was used as a deflator.
3. This figure is the growth rate of the following unorganized sector workers: main workers – (agriculture-related main workers + workers in the organized sector) (Government of India 1993, 2004, 2007). Looking at examples of other estimates, Sakthivel and Joddar (2006) indicated based on NSS and other data that the workforce in the unorganized sector increased from 275.6 million in 1983 to 371.2 million in 1999/2000, and Rani and Unni (2004) estimated that in the unorganized sector, manufacturing employment grew negatively during 1984–90 and the early 1990s but in the late 1990s grew positively by 2.16 per cent per annum.
4. For illegal measures, see Datt (1993) and Chowdhury (1996).
5. Mahadevia (2002) explains that this increase between 1987/88 and 1993/94 is due to the fact that, after once losing regular employment, males might have found another regular employment, quoting the case studies of the retrenched textile workers who were absorbed into other jobs (p. 64). Further investigation will be required as to whether the expansion of the city area in 1986 influenced the data of 1987/88, and if so, to what extent.
6. For example, Kantor (2003), based on a field survey in Ahmedabad, revealed a serious undercount of home-based producers in the national data sources in India.
7. For calculation, data from the Ahmedabad Municipal Corporation (website) was used. Figures for 2001 are provisional. For further reference, the percentage of the working population out of the total population rose from 49.9 to 52.7 per cent for males, whereas for females, it rose from 6.07 to 8.48 per cent during the period.

8. Interviews were conducted by the author and local investigating staff for all three surveys. A few of the local staff participated in all three surveys. One in particular participated in all field surveys as an assistant cum interpreter for the author, who does not understand Gujarati. The author wishes to express her sincere gratitude for his deep understanding and generous support of these surveys. Thanks are also due to the investigators as well. Moreover, the author extends her deepest appreciation to the interviewees who cooperated with the field surveys.
9. The respondents in the C Group with no experience of job change were retired, unemployed, out of work, or persons who remained at factories as security guards, etc.
10. In questions concerning job history, we requested that the respondents answer with information on all jobs, including when started, when terminated, and the length of employment in order to prevent the omission of any job. However, there is a possibility that they omitted some jobs.
11. For units other than agriculture, 20 as the number of employees was used as a tentative criterion of formal or informal in the analysis of the field surveys. The reason why we used 20 employees as a criterion is as follows. In the first 1991 survey, all the respondents were factory workers and many of their previous jobs were also related to manufacture and repair. In general, in the manufacturing and repair industry, the criterion of formal or informal is defined by the Factories Act, which is basically applicable to any premises using power where 10 or more workers are employed, or 20 or more workers where power is not used. Therefore, to avoid overestimation of the formal sector by including cases with 10 or more employees where power is not used (although there is a possible overestimation of the informal sector on the other hand), the size of 20 employees was tentatively used as a criterion. Thus, units with 20 or more employees were regarded as the formal sector, and the rest as the informal sector. Furthermore, the units were included in the informal sector if the employment status was self-employed or unpaid family worker or if the occupation was that of labourer, such as construction worker, loader or unloader, etc. We also used the same criterion in the succeeding field surveys for purposes of comparison.
12. Hereinafter the results of the 1991 survey are based on Kiso (2002).
13. The ESI Act aims at providing workers with medical relief, etc. and the EPF Act attempts to guarantee economic security for the future life of the employee after his retirement, both of which primarily apply to every factory covered by the Factories Act and some other industries' establishments where 20 or more persons are employed. Therefore, many of our respondents who are now (ex-) factory workers were covered by those Acts and the high extent of application of the provisions under those two Acts had been confirmed by deductions shown in each payslip in the 1991 survey.
14. In 1991 51 per cent of the respondents were from outside the Ahmedabad district.
15. Social security schemes have so far mainly covered the organized sector workers in India. However, expansion of social security to unorganized workers has been controversial during the past years in particular, and at present, the passage of the related bill is one of the matters of concern for the United Progressive Alliance regime.

References

Bagchi, Amiya Kumar, Das Pancharnan and Sadhan Kumar Chattopadhyay (2005) 'Growth and Structural Change in the Economy of Gujarat, 1970–2000'. *Economic and Political Weekly* 40(28): 3039–47.

Breman, Jan (2004) *The Making and Unmaking of an Industrial Working Class: Sliding Down the Labour Hierarchy in Ahmedabad, India*. Amsterdam: Amsterdam University Press.

Chowdhury, S.R. (1996) 'Industrial Restructuring, Unions and the State: Textile Mill Workers in Ahmedabad'. *Economic and Political Weekly* 31(81): L7–L13.

Datt, R. (1993) 'Lockout, Closure and the Role of the State'. In T. S. Papola, P. P. Ghosh and A. N. Sharma (eds) *Labour, Employment and Industrial Relations in India*. Patna: Indian Society of Labour Economics.

Deshpande, Lalit K., Alakh N. Sharma, Anup K. Karan and Sandip Sarkar (2004) *Liberalisation and Labour: Labour Flexibility in Indian Manufacturing*. New Delhi: Institute for Human Development.

Dholakia, Ravindra H. (2000) 'Liberalisation in Gujarat: Review of Recent Experience'. *Economic and Political Weekly* 35(35 and 36): 3121–4.

Guha, B.P. (1996) *Voluntary Retirement: Problems and Prospects of Rehabilitation*. New Delhi: Shri Ram Centre for Industrial Relations and Human Resources.

Hirway, Indira (2000) 'Dynamics of Development in Gujarat: Some Issues'. *Economic and Political Weekly* 35(35 and 36) 3106–20.

Kantor, Paula (2003) 'Improving Estimates of the Number and Economic Contribution of Home-Based Producers in Urban India'. *The Indian Journal of Labour Economics* 46(2): 235–46.

Kiso, Junko (2002) 'Factory Workers and Their Mobility in Ahmedabad City'. In T. Shinoda (ed.) *The Other Gujarat: Social Transformations among Weaker Sections*. Mumbai: Popular Prakashan.

Mahadevia, Darshini (2002) 'Changing Economic Scenario: Informalisation and Increased Vulnerability'. In Amithbh Kundu and Darshini Mahadevia (eds) *Poverty and Vulnerability in a Globalising Metropolis Ahmedabad*. New Delhi: Manak Publications Pvt. Ltd.

Nagaraj, R. (2004) 'Fall in Organised Manufacturing Employment: a Brief Note'. *Economic and Political Weekly* 39(30): 3387–90.

Noronha, E. and R. N. Sharma (1999) 'Displaced Workers and Withering of the Welfare State'. *Economic and Political Weekly* 34(23): 1454–60.

Patel, B. B. (1988) *Workers of Closed Textile Mills: Patterns and Problems of Their Absorption in a Metropolitan Labour Market*. New Delhi: Oxford and IBH Publishing.

Rani, Uma and Jeemol Unni (2004) 'Unorganised and Organised Manufacturing in India: Potential for Employment Generating Growth'. *Economic and Political Weekly* 39(41): 4568–80.

Sakthivel, S. and Pinaki Joddar (2006) 'Unorganised Sector Workforce in India: Trends, Patterns and Social Security Coverage'. *Economic and Political Weekly* 41(21): 2107–14.

Sharma, A. N. (2006) 'Flexibility, Employment and Labour Market Reforms in India'. *Economic and Political Weekly* 41(21): 2078–85.

Sundar, K. R. S. (2005) 'Labour Flexibility Debate in India – a Comprehensive Review and Some Suggestions'. *Economic and Political Weekly* 40(22 and 23): 2274–85.

Government publications

Ahmedabad Municipal Corporation, website, *Statistical Outline for 2003–4*. Available at http://www.egovamc.com/amc_budget/report.asp.

Government of Gujarat (1996) *Socio-Economic Review: Gujarat State 1995–96*. Gandhinagar.

Government of Gujarat (2006a) *Socio-Economic Review: Gujarat State 2005–6*. Gandhinagar.

Government of Gujarat (2006b) *Statistical Abstract of Gujarat State 2006*. Gandhinagar.

Government of India (1993) *Census of India 1991: Final Population Totals – Brief Analysis of Primary Census Abstract, Series-1*.

Government of India (2004) *Census of India 2001: Primary Census Abstract – Total Population: Table A-5, Series-1*. Delhi.

Government of India, Ministry of Statistics and Programme Implementation, available at http:mospi.nic.in/mospi_asi.htm

Government of India, Ministry of Finance (2004) *Economic Survey 2003–4*. Delhi.

Government of India, Ministry of Finance (2007) *Economic Survey 2006–7*. Delhi.

Government of India, Ministry of Labour, Labour Bureau (2004) *Statistical Profile on Women Labour 2004*.

Government of India, Planning Commission (2006) *Towards Faster and More Inclusive Growth: an Approach to the 11th Five Year Plan*, available at http://www.planningcommission.nic.in

2
Female Garment Workers in India and Bangladesh in the Post-MFA Era

Mayumi Murayama

2.1 Introduction

The manner in which globalization has affected employment and people's lives from a gender perspective has been an issue of potent concern not only in the developing countries but also in the developed ones. What is clear thus far is that the impacts are multifarious and preclude any hasty evaluation as to whether they are positive or negative. This is because, first, globalization, despite its core connotation of universalism, actually takes many forms. Globalization proceeds simultaneously in multiple dimensions, not only in economic but also in social and cultural dimensions. Second, people who are engaged in globalization have different combinations of social and economic attributes, such as gender, class, ethnicity and age, which differentiate the material and interpretative impacts of globalization at the level of individuals or any given social group. In other words, the effects of globalization are mediated by the local or contextual factors in which individuals are embedded.

Although it is impossible to make an across-the-board analysis of globalization, this does not lessen the significance of investigating what changes globalization has brought about in the lives of people. This chapter will investigate the state of female employment in the export-oriented ready-made garment industries in two places, Bangalore, India, and Bangladesh.

The reason for the selection of this particular industry is that the garment industry offers a typical case where globalization and gender coalesce into production of economic and social relations. Since the 1970s, there has been a growing body of literature on female factory workers.[1] The ready-made garment industry has been the one most often discussed in those studies because, in many countries, this is the industry which pioneered the extensive mobilization of women into wage labour. Women have been preferred as workers in the garment industry mainly because they constitute a cheap, flexible and docile workforce, which is an essential factor for the success of this particular labour-intensive industry.

While it is observed across many countries that young and single women of rural origin predominantly constitute the workforce in the garment industry, the experience of being a garment worker differs depending on the objective as well as the subjective conditions of each individual woman. In other words, the social embeddedness of production has been of great importance in understanding the gendered implications of globalization. Some studies have compared the impact of factory work on women in different countries. For instance, comparing the status of female factory workers of Singapore and South Korea, Phongpaichit (1988) finds a marked difference between these two successful cases of industrialization. In her analysis, besides the existence of a relatively abundant pool of potential labour in Korea, another and very important factor that undermines the economic value of women's work there is the strong social bias against women that prevails not only in the labour market but also in general. Wolf's study on central Java shows that daughters working in factories there are subject to fewer controls by their parents than are their Taiwanese counterparts. Wolf notes that local kinship systems as well as gender and family ideologies have a strong bearing on the effects of industrialization on women's lives (Wolf 1992). Based on ethnographical research in the two factories, one located in Hong Kong and the other in Shenzhen, Lee (1998) describes how different modes of control mechanisms and distinct work cultures are produced even though they are under the control of the same managerial staff and the same set-up of assembly lines. In her analysis, the differences in the two factories are brought about primarily by embedded differences in gender and labour markets.

Added to the differences in local contexts, the garment industry has been subject to changes in the global context. The industry currently stands at a critical juncture of trade liberalization as the result of the withdrawal of the Multi-Fibre Arrangement (MFA) regime at the end of 2004.[2] The MFA, which governed global trade of textiles and clothing for 30 years by way of imposing quantitative restrictions on textile and clothing exports, had varied effects, thus its withdrawal is having different implications on individual countries engaged in the garment trade.

Both India and Bangladesh are the major world garment exporters. However, as will be discussed later in the following section, the garment industries in India and Bangladesh have tread different paths of development and have been structured differently on the basis of their respective economic, social and political endowments. In the years immediately before the complete withdrawal of the MFA, the general opinion was that India, with the advantage of having textile industries with better infrastructure, would be a winner along with China, while Bangladesh, whose good performance heretofore was largely due to export ceilings in the form of quotas that the MFA imposed on other more competitive countries, would lose its share in the liberalized global market. More than two years have passed since then, and both countries are surviving well in their major markets. Nevertheless, this does not mean that the situation surrounding the workers is the same as before. Simultaneously, the conditions of the workers in India and Bangladesh may also be different.

The major concern of this chapter is to investigate the situation of female garment workers who are embedded in the different socio-economic settings and who are affected by the forces of global competition in different ways. It is not, however, a comparative study in the pure sense of the term, due to limitations in the data and the author's depth of understanding of the local context. It is, therefore, first meant to be a preparatory study to gather and present fundamental information regarding the workers' profiles and their positions in the workplace and in the households. Second, keeping this limitation in mind, this chapter intends to delineate the effects of the changing trade and industrial environment on the workers and explore the implications of these effects in the broader context of globalization and female employment.

For the sake of shedding light upon the local context, I have chosen as my research fields Bangladesh and Bangalore, one of the garment clusters in India. Unlike the more or less homogeneous structure of the garment industry within Bangladesh, the Indian garment industry is composed of many garment production centres dispersed over various parts of the country. Due to the wide variations in socio-economic settings within the country, each garment hub has distinct characteristics in terms of products, size of individual units and type of workforce. The most prominent distinction related to gender is observed between the hubs in the northern and the southern parts of India. While the garment industry in North India is comprised of many smaller units with predominantly male labour, the gender composition of workers is generally reversed in South India, while the average size of units varies from hub to hub.

Garment production in Bangalore is structured with relatively large factories and predominantly female labour. This feature of Bangalore distinguishes it from other Indian garment hubs but at the same time presents similarities with the garment industry in Bangladesh, which shares these common characteristics with the majority of countries including those in East and South East Asia. Is this specific nature of the Bangalore garment industry associated with sociocultural factors related to gender? As for women's position in society, South India is considered to be less patriarchal than North India. However, Bangladesh, in contrast, is known for persistent gender disparities, although recently the gap has been narrowing in terms of educational and health-related indicators. Thus, I would assume that feminization of labour has taken place not solely by the gender-related factors but in conjunction with other factors such as economic imperatives. This question will be examined first by tracing the development process of the garment industry in both countries, and second, through surveys of the workers' profiles and conditions in the two places to extract similarities and dissimilarities. Further, to check the relevance of the findings, some references will be made to other garment centres, particularly Tiruppur in Tamil Nadu, one of the southern states. Tiruppur is the largest knitwear cluster, contributing 56 per cent of India's total knitwear exports.[3] It is also characterized by increasing feminization of its labour force. The remarkable growth of Tiruppur has attracted the interest of a number of researchers (Cawthorne 1995; Swaminathan and Jeyaranjan 1999; Neetha 2002; Awasthi 2003). By way of re-examining my own findings from the surveys in Bangalore and Bangladesh in the light of information available from the studies on Tiruppur, I intend to draw more general conclusions regarding the situation of garment workers under intensified global competition.

Following this introduction, Section 2.2 overviews the process of development of the garment industry as well as the process of feminization of labour in that particular industry in Bangalore, India, and Bangladesh. Based on the field surveys, the socio-economic profile of female workers is presented in Section 2.3. Section 2.4 discusses some changes taking place in their work and issues of concern after the MFA withdrawal. In the Conclusion, after summarizing the main findings from the surveys, I will also locate some of the findings in the wider context of South Asia.

This study reveals the relatively more independent agency of Bangladeshi female workers with respect to migration and employment, compared not only with the Bangalorean sample but also with the general view about Bangladeshi women. The labour process, as well as the implications for garment work, differs between Bangalorean and Bangladeshi workers. However, there are many commonalities, which seem to be true also for garment industries other than those in Bangalore and Bangladesh. This indicates an ongoing trend of feminization of garment workers in the wider context of South Asia, which is linked with the changing mode of production and payment that is working unfavourably against the workers.

2.2 Garment industries in India and Bangladesh

The export-oriented ready-made garment industries in India and Bangladesh have traversed different paths of development. In a nutshell, while India had a garment industry catering to its domestic market prior to the development of an export-oriented garment industry backed by an upstream textile industry, such indigenous factors were almost non-existent in Bangladesh, where the garment industry began as a new industry, implanted based on the East and South East Asian model, with an important role played by foreign capital and with little linkage with other domestic industries, at least in the initial stage.

2.2.1 Garment industry in India

The origin of garment making for the domestic market in India, or the subcontinent, is said to date back to the Mughal period when Muslim rulers wore sewn clothing. This was followed by the colonial period during which demand for Western clothes, particularly uniforms, increased greatly (Banerjee 1991: 252). The mode of production during those periods was artisanal. This traditional garment sector still exists today, and it is not unrelated to the export-oriented garment sector.

Garments for export emerged in the 1960s. According to Chatterji and Mohan (1993: M-95), there were two phases of development. During 1970/71–1975/76, the first export boom in Indian garments was witnessed. It was driven by the high demand for Indian handloom garments and other indigenous fabrics in the US and Europe. The second phase began from the mid-1980s, which was marked by a relatively steadier growth and a rise of knitwear garments. Handloom garments were gradually replaced by mill-made garments. Between the mid-1980s and 2000, knitwear exports increased at a higher rate than woven (handloom and mill-made) garments. In 2005/6, garment exports reached about $8.6 billion ($3.2 billion of knitwear and $5.4 billion of woven garments), accounting for 8 per cent of India's total export earnings.[4]

Due to the existence of a strong traditional garment sector, the initial policy stance of the Indian government towards this sector placed emphasis on the protection of small-scale establishments from competition with large-scale, modern factories. Until 2001, the ready-made garments industry was reserved for the small-scale sector with an investment ceiling imposed, although companies with a certain proportion of exports were exempted from this. The export obligation was considered to be an unduly stiff imposition by large-scale undertakings (Chatterji and Mohan 1993: M-111). It resulted in a sector that consisted of a large number of small firms and a decentralized and networked production structure, which made India's minimum efficient scale of operation much lower than that of China or Bangladesh (Vijayabaskar 2002: 56). Nevertheless, owing to deregulation of the industry from 1985 onward,[5] capacity increases and investments in technical modernization began in the late 1980s and 1990s (Tewari 2005: 22).

2.2.2 Garment industry in Bangalore

As a consequence of the specific development path of the industry as stated above, India has several garment hubs across the country, each with its own distinctive characteristics. The major industrial clusters are Delhi, Mumbai, Kolkata, Chennai, Bangalore, Jaipur, Tiruppur, Ludhiana, Cochin and Hyderabad. Each region is independent in terms of sourcing raw materials and labour and has developed unique product specialities, with Delhi, for instance, being the multi-product hub, Chennai being the leader in shirts, Tiruppur in knitwear and Jaipur as a growing hub of ladies fashion. In such typology, Bangalore is characterized as 'the techno-savvy structured garment manufacturing centre'.

> The factories in this hub are, by and large, huge setups with the latest technology and IT systems for high productivity in basic garments like trousers and jackets. Many trouser factories have come up in this region in the last few years, and the same is true for jackets. Even factories from the north have invested in Bangalore for production of trousers and jackets to take advantage of the skilled labour and technical know-how that this region has acquired over time.... The focus in this region is on production efficiency and training to match international standards in manufacturing.[6]

There have been studies on different garment industrial clusters, such as Delhi (Mazumdar 2003; Rao and Husain 1991), Kolkata (Banerjee 1991), Chennai (Kalpagam 1994), Hyderabad (Chakravarty 2004, 2005), Ahmedabad (Unni et al. 1999), Kerala (Varghese 1999), Thane and Pune (Pore 1991) and Tiruppur (Cawthorne 1995; Swaminathan and Jeyaranjan 1999; Neetha 2002; Awasthi 2003). However, regarding Bangalore, despite its growing prominence, only a few studies have been published (RoyChowdhury 2005; New Trade Union Initiative 2005).

Overshadowed by the booming IT industry with which the name of Bangalore has become almost synonymous, the ready-made garment industry, nevertheless, is no less important in the state of Karnataka. In 2004/5, Karnataka, of which Bangalore is the capital, exported ready-made garments worth Rs.45 billion (approximately $US1 billion), which is approximately 15 per cent of all Indian ready-made garment exports. In terms of state exports, garments ranked fourth, accounting for 7.3 per cent in 2004/5, following electronics, computer software and biotechnology (Rs.315 billion, 51 per cent of state exports), petroleum and petroleum products (Rs.62 billion, 10 per cent), and gems and jewellery (Rs.46 billion, 7.5 per cent).[7]

One significance of this particular sector also lies in its employment creation for women. It is the second largest provider of female employment, next to the *beedi* (small hand-rolled cigarette) industry (RoyChowdhury 2005: 2251). The exact amount of employment is not certain, however. Labour Department statistics say that there are 797 garment units and that 140,000 workers are employed in these units. However, some workers' union estimates say that there are more than 1000 units in Bangalore and that close to 400,000 people work in these units.[8] Another official estimate says that there are about 15,000 garment manufacturing units of differing capacities and that the sector provides employment to over 300,000 people, of which about 90 per cent are women (Government of Karnataka 2006: 230).

The estimate of 15,000 garment units seems to include numerous tailor shops along with very small-scale factories.[9] Despite the presence of those small-scale units, what is better known as a salient feature of the garment industry in Bangalore, besides the dominance of female workers, is that it is relatively well organized in factory-based production, unlike other garment hubs. Why has Bangalore become a garment cluster with such distinct characteristics?

Karnataka had a long tradition of industrial development even before independence. Bangalore was a flourishing centre of textile production. By the early twentieth century, there were three large textile mills and a large number of smaller cotton, silk and woollen textile units (Nair 2005: 38–40, 81; also Nair 1998). From the 1940s to the 1970s, Bangalore attracted the establishment of many public sector units, including the Hindusthan Aircraft Factory (later Hindusthan Aeronautics Limited), Bharat Electronics Limited and Bharat Heavy Electricals Limited. In addition, several large private sector units such as Motor Industries Company Limited, International Instruments and Kirloskar Electric invested in the city.[10]

The inception of the garment industry in Bangalore occurred in the mid-1970s. The two large factories were Gokaldas Exports and Samrat Ashoka Exports, of which the former has turned out to be India's current top garment exporter, while the latter was closed down in 1997 partly due to labour unrest.[11] Until the mid-1980s, the number of garment units remained at less than 100, and they were mostly concentrated in the Lalbagh area, a crowded commercial–industrial neighbourhood. It should be noted that before the 1980s, the workers were predominantly male

(RoyChowdhury 2005: 2251). It was after the mid-1980s that the industry extended outward and the factories dispersed to many parts of the city. The Textile Policy of 1985, as mentioned already, could have been a reason for the spurt.

Throughout the 1980s and 1990s, Bangalore saw the proliferation of new garment units, with some relocated from other apparel hubs such as Delhi and Mumbai or added as new units, while a lesser number of other units closed down. Gokaldas Exports, India's largest garment manufacturer, owns more than 40 units located in Bangalore and employs around 44,000 workers, of which 75 per cent are women.[12]

There are several reasons why Bangalore has become the choice as a base for garment production. Besides the good climate throughout the year, the reason most often mentioned by management is the relatively peaceful industrial relations and availability of docile labour.[13] What should be emphasized here is that the industrialists, especially those who have the experience of running garment units in other garment clusters, point out the availability of female workers who are docile – meaning that they are free from labour movement activities and are easily trained – as a strong advantage of Bangalore. Along with the favourable policy shift as mentioned above, lower need for concern about labour problems could be considered as the major reason why a relatively large investment in garment factories was possible in Bangalore.

2.2.3 Garment industry in Bangladesh

The beginning of the export-oriented garment industry in Bangladesh was slightly delayed compared to that of Bangalore. In 1977, the first consignment was exported to then West Germany by Jewel Garments. The industry's achievement is noteworthy, particularly for a country plagued with poor resource endowments and adverse conditions for industrialization. Exports increased from approximately $32 million in 1983/84 to $1.4 billion in 1992/93. In 1987/88, the garment export share surpassed that of raw jute and allied products, the country's long-standing primary export items. The figure rose further to $6 billion in 2005/6, accounting for about 65 per cent of the country's total export earnings in that year.[14]

The number of units, which remained a meagre 46 until the end of 1983, underwent a phenomenal increase over the last two decades, reaching more than 4000. Factories are concentrated mostly in the capital, Dhaka, the surrounding region, and Chittagong, the port city. The garment units of Bangladesh are comprised of relatively large-scale factories. Around 80 per cent of the units employ more than 100 workers, with the highest concentration of 200–499 workers seen at 55 per cent of the total units (Bangladesh Bureau of Statistics 2004). However, there is a discernible difference between woven-garment and knit-garment factories. First, the woven-garment units are much larger than the knit-garment units in terms of both employment and fixed assets. For example, more than 90 per cent of the woven-garment establishments employ more than 100 employees, whereas only 1 per cent of the knit-garment units belong to this category. Second, knit garments are more capital-intensive than woven garments. Third, there is a difference in the gender composition of the workforce. The employment generated by the sector is estimated to be around 2 million jobs, of which around 70 per cent are filled by women. However, the share of jobs filled by male workers is higher in case of knitwear factories, at around 43 per cent (Bangladesh Bureau of Statistics 2004).

Several factors account for the outstanding growth of the industry in Bangladesh. The country's industrialization after independence in 1971 followed the same path, from state-led to privatization, as that of a majority of developing countries. The state sector, which controlled 92 per cent of the modern industrial fixed assets in 1972 as a result of the nationalization policy, had suffered chronic losses due to various internal and external constraints (Sobhan and Ahmad 1980). Successive governments from the mid-1970s gradually shifted their policy stance, with more emphasis on private initiatives. The policies implemented thereafter included measures such as opening up sectors which were previously reserved for the state sector, divestiture of state enterprises, establishment of export processing zones, and ensuring access for private enterprises to credit and foreign exchange facilities. Export promotion was one of the top priorities of these policy initiatives. Alongside liberal policies for foreign direct investment, including allowing 100 per cent equity share ownership, export-oriented units have been offered lucrative incentives such as tax holidays, bonded warehouse facilities and a duty drawback system. Thus by the early 1980s, the policy environment became quite favourable for export industries, whether of domestic or foreign origin.

Nevertheless, the congenial policy environment would have remained unexploited without external actors ready to make use of it. As in many other countries and industries – with the exception of India's garment industry – foreign multinational companies played a catalyst role in promoting the garment industry in Bangladesh. They brought the initial technology and other know-how for the modern production of garments that meet international requirements. Simultaneously, through controlling product development and marketing operations, they have successfully linked Bangladesh as a competitive production base to the international market. The foreign multinationals further contributed to diffusing technology and know-how to local firms by generating spin-offs.[15] Currently, it is local rather than foreign capital that constitutes the majority of the garment firms.

For foreign capital, the advantages of Bangladesh as a site of garment production were mainly the availability of cheap labour and the initially quota-free status of the country under the MFA regime. Initiated by the US with the objective of protecting domestic textile industry, the MFA restricted the volume of textile and garment products, mainly in the form of bilateral quotas negotiated within the MFA framework.

There have been two contrasting views regarding the effect of the MFA on developing countries. One view has criticized the increasing protectionism in major OECD markets as neo-protectionism, whereas the other view has taken note of the positive impacts of the MFA in promoting the textile and garment industry in developing countries. In reality, the actual effects of the MFA differed from country to country because of the varying economic conditions and experiences in global trade. The implications of the MFA differed particularly between long-standing exporting countries and new exporters of textile and clothing. For new entrants such as Bangladesh, the MFA, even after taking into account its negative effect, proved to be a blessing. It initially induced industrial relocation from more advanced economies to Bangladesh, and subsequently it provided Bangladesh with a guaranteed market secured from the more competitive producer countries.

The sudden surge of Bangladeshi garments in the OECD markets led in 1985 to a fresh imposition of quotas by some countries like the UK, France, the US and Canada. Later, the UK and France lifted restrictions, and subsequently only the US and Canada were implementing quotas for Bangladeshi garment exports. The US restrictions affected Bangladesh's garment sector significantly because the export growth at that time was mainly due to the US market. Implementation of quotas caused a decline in absolute terms for most items in the first months of 1986. However after a transition period, the level of growth increased again in 1987, mainly due to diversification into non-quota items (Wiig 1990: 154–9). One of the successful areas of product diversification was knitwear, which was outside the purview of the MFA. In the initial period, it was the woven-garment sector that dominated the structure of garment exports, while in recent years it has been the knit garment sector which has demonstrated more robust growth. The growth of knit garments was spurred by a growing demand in the EU market and was also stimulated by domestic incentives in the form of cash compensation and duty drawbacks (Bhattacharya and Rahman 2001: 4).

As already mentioned, the gender composition of garment workers is predominantly female. Although the garment industry is considered in general to be a female-intensive industry in many parts of the world because it requires the 'nimble fingers' of women which are suitable for sewing (Elson and Pearson 1981), the formula did not work automatically. The strong gender norms which separate the worlds of male and female, along with class differences, have resulted in the creation of a labour market segregated along the lines of gender and class. Until the advent of the garment industry, the employment opportunities for women, especially those from poor households, were extremely limited to such informal work as domestic maids and construction workers. Not only factory employment but also small-scale tailoring work has had male attributes. It was by the mediation of foreign capital, which also provided the seed money, that space was created for females in the industry in Bangladesh. Desh Garments (described in note 15) was instrumental in gaining acceptance for employment of female workers by sending 14 women among a total of 130 workers to the Daewoo Pusan Plant in 1979.[16] Seeing that factory's successful operation, other new factories followed suit, and the gender-specific concerns regarding women turned out to be an advantage for garment employers, who came to recognize that female workers were docile, dexterous and cheaper than male workers (Ahmad 1990: 20). Once the new employment opportunity was opened, women, whose economic needs were becoming increasingly pressing in both urban and rural areas, immediately took advantage of it.[17]

2.3 Garment workers in Bangalore and Bangladesh

2.3.1 Source of data and limitations

As already noted, the export-oriented garment industries in Bangalore and Bangladesh have common features, i.e. predominance of female workers and relatively large-scale factory production. In this section, based on small sample surveys of female garment workers, we will examine the similarities and dissimilarities in their socio-economic profiles.

The two surveys were carried out with slightly different objectives and at different times. The survey in Bangladesh was conducted in December 2005. Exploring the impact of the MFA withdrawal on workers was the primary objective, hence data on workers in employment and retrenched workers were collected (see Murayama 2006 for details). On the other hand, the survey in Bangalore, which was conducted in December 2006, was more focused on garnering basic information about the profiles of workers and working conditions. This was because, first, there is less literature available than in the case of Bangladeshi garment workers, and second, the author's exposure to Bangalore in general is much more limited than that to Bangladesh. Both surveys were conducted on the basis of pre-designed interview schedules with the help of NGOs engaged in activities for the welfare of garment workers.[18]

Besides the differences in the time and objectives, sample size is a major problem. Due to time constraints, data on 100 female workers for each category were ready for analysis at the time of this writing. Therefore, the whole analysis remains exploratory, although secondary materials were consulted whenever possible to augment the analysis. Nevertheless, under a broad comparative framework regarding who the garment workers are, what their working conditions are, what garment employment means for their livelihood, and what impact global competition has made on their work, I hope that a somewhat more concrete picture will emerge to assist in identifying the existing gap in knowledge.

2.3.2 Socio-economic profile of garment workers

For the sake of comparison, the data on workers in employment in the Bangladeshi survey are presented along with data on Bangalorean workers. The Bangladeshi sample is taken from the country's three industrial clusters, Dhaka, Savar and Chittagong, and it covers both those workers working in units located in the Export Processing Zones (EPZs) and those outside of the zones.[19] On the other hand, the sample from Bangalore was collected from the three main concentrations of garment units within the city. The employment size of the factories where sample workers are employed is presented in Table 2.1.

2.3.2.1 Age

The average age of Bangalorean and Bangladeshi workers is 29.9 and 24.1 years old, respectively. The age-wise distribution of Bangalorean workers is skewed to higher ages than Bangladeshi workers (Table 2.2). Whereas there are a substantial number

Table 2.1 Employment size of factories (persons)

	Bangalore	*Bangladesh*
Less than 100	4	0
100–499	18	2
500–999	56	21
1000–1999	8	42
2000–4999	10	23
5000–9999	3	8
10,000 and above	1	4
Total	100	100

Note: Employment size is based on information provided by the respondents.
Source: Author's survey.

of workers who are in their thirties in Bangalore, the prominent concentration among the Bangladeshi workers is in the age cohort of 20–24 years.

The age of Bangalorean workers is high compared with the findings of other studies. Nearly half of the female workers of Tiruppur belonged to the 15–20 age group (Neetha 2002). Many of them entered the industry as child or adolescent workers. In the case of the Bangalorean sample, the lowest age of the sample workers was 17 (only one worker). The higher minimum age of workers may reflect the degree of legal compliance by the factories in Bangalore.[20]

2.3.2.2 Religion, caste and language

Since questions related to religion, caste and language were not included in the survey in Bangladesh, only information on Bangalorean workers is presented here.[21] With respect to religion, 87 per cent of the workers are Hindu, while of the remaining 13 per cent, 9 per cent are Muslim and 4 per cent are Christian. According to the 1991 census, the percentages of the three religious communities in Karnataka are 85.4, 11.64 and 1.91 per cent, respectively. Within the considerable limitations of the number and nature of the sample, we could say that garment work has drawn women from different religious communities, with a slightly higher representation of Hindus and Christians.

In terms of the caste distribution of Hindu workers, the highest number of workers belong to the Vokkaliga caste (35 per cent) followed by Lingayaths (6 per cent) and Kurubas (6 per cent). Excluding Scheduled Castes (SCs), Scheduled Tribes (STs) and Muslims, those three are the dominant castes in the state of Karnataka in terms of population. Among them, the concentration of Vokkaligas in our data exceeds their share in the state population, which was about 11 per cent in 1988[22] (Government of Karnataka 1990). The proportion of SCs and STs in our sample is 5 and 3 per cent, while that in Karnataka state according to the 2001 census is 16.2 and 6.6 per cent, respectively (Directorate of Census Operations 2001a). Thus, compared with the state average, the representation of the SCs and STs is low in our sample. This contrasts with the garment workers in Tiruppur investigated by

Table 2.2 Age distribution (persons)

Age range	*Bangalore*	*Bangladesh*
Less than 15 years	0	0
15–19 years	12	14
20–24 years	14	47
25–29 years	28	28
30–39 years	35	10
40–49 years	8	1
50 and above	3	0
Total	100	100

Source: Author's survey.

Table 2.3 Distribution of main language (%)

	Sample	*1991 Census*
Kannada	72	66.22
Urdu	9	9.96
Telugu	11	7.39
Tamil	5	3.84
Marathi	3	3.65
Others	0	8.94
Total	100	100

Source: Author's survey.

Neetha (2002). There, the share of the SCs and backward castes was 30.1 and 66.9 per cent, respectively, among the workers, thus much higher than our sample. In case of Tiruppur, women of the weaving community (*gounders*, who belong to the backward castes) were the initial entrants as workers. Later, with the coming of migrants, women of SCs, who were traditionally agricultural labourers, joined the industry (Neetha 2002). Due to the limited size of our sample, it is difficult to draw a definite conclusion. However, as far as our data are concerned, garment workers in Bangalore do not necessarily belong to the lowest echelon of society, as shown by the fact that the industry has drawn women of higher and dominant castes in Karnataka.[23] A relation between garment employment and weaver castes in Karnataka could not be substantiated.

Seventy-two workers mentioned Kannada, the main language spoken in the state, as their mother tongue. This percentage is higher than the state average shown in Table 2.3. However, considering that more non-Kannada speakers have begun to adopt Kannada as their main language,[24] it could be said that the linguistic profile of the workers is more or less similar to the ethno-linguistic composition of the state. In other words, garment employment spread among the various communities residing in the state of Karnataka.

Table 2.4 Marital status (persons)

	Bangalore	*Bangladesh*
Married	57	49
Unmarried	26	44
Divorced	3	0
Separated	8	6
Widowed	6	1
Total	100	100

Source: Author's survey.

Table 2.5 Education level (persons)

	Bangalore	*Bangladesh*
No schooling	5	0
No schooling but able to sign name	6	3
Grades 1–5	12	20
Grades 6–7 (India)	19	–
Grades 6–8 (Bangladesh)	–	37
Grades 8–10 (India)	52	–
Grades 9–10 (Bangladesh)	–	37
Grades 11–12	6	3
Total	100	100

Source: Author's survey.

2.3.2.3 Marital status

The proportion of those who have been married, including those divorced, separated or widowed, is higher among the Bangalorean workers (Table 2.4). This may be due to the age composition of the samples, in which the Bangladeshi sample is younger than its Bangalorean counterpart. The mean age of marriage in the Bangalorean and Bangladeshi samples is 17.5 and 18.7 years, respectively, which is younger than Karnataka's average of 20.14 (2001 census)[25] and Bangladesh's average of 19.0 (2001 census). Within the small samples, there are a substantial number of women who were divorced, separated or widowed. In our samples, the number is greater among the Bangalorean workers.

2.3.2.4 Educational status

The educational status of the workers is presented in Table 2.5. The mean years of schooling are almost same, i.e. 7.57 years (Bangalore) and 7.65 years (Bangladesh). There are more workers without any formal education in the Bangalorean sample, while in that sample there is also a higher proportion with a high school education (grades 8–10) and a pre-university (PU) education (grades 11–12), which is more or less equivalent to Bangladesh's secondary education (grades 9–10) and higher secondary education (grades 11–12). Thus, there is a wider variation in the Indian sample.

The educational level of our Bangladeshi sample seems to be higher than that in other surveys with a larger data sample. For instance, a survey of 589 female workers in 1997 found the mean level of schooling was 6.8 years (Paul-Majumder and Begum 2006: 17). Comparable data regarding garment workers in Karnataka are not available for reference. As for Bangladesh, the level of the education of garment workers in Bangladesh has been on the increase (Paul-Majumder and Begum 2006: 21). Previously, a large number of garment workers had no formal education. However, with the rise of the general educational level of girls in the country along with increasing demands for educated workers, illiterate workers are becoming a minority. The literacy rate (7 years and above) of garment workers is also much higher than that of the general female population, where it is 40.83 per cent (Bangladesh Bureau of Statistics 2003). The same holds true for garment workers in Karnataka. The female literacy rate in Karnataka is 57.45 per cent, while that in the Bangalore district is 78.98 per cent (Directorate of Census Operations 2001b), both of which are lower than the rate in our sample.

2.3.2.5 Migratory status

In the Bangladeshi sample, all but two workers were migrants at the location where the factories were located. This share seems relatively higher than earlier studies, which found the proportion of migrants to be around 70 per cent of garment workers (Paul-Majumder and Begum 2006: 19). The share of migrants among Bangalorean workers is similar to that figure, i.e. 66 per cent, including six persons who migrated from other states.[26] The migration rate among the urban females of Karnataka state is about 40 per cent (NSSO 2001: Table 2.3). Therefore, the rates of migration are much higher among garment workers.

As for Bangladesh, there are no comparable gender-segregated data. One estimate suggests that more than three-quarters of urban population is composed of migrants (Afsar 2000: 8). Female rural–urban migration was very limited in the pre-independence period, as suggested by the high sex ratio (number of males per 100 females) of 142.3 among the urban population in 1961. The ratio has been on the decline since then, reaching 117.2 in 2001. In fact, female migration became a visible phenomenon only with the advent of the garment industry during the last two decades (Paul-Majumder and Begum 2006: 123).

As far as our data show, there are several differences between Bangalorean and Bangladeshi workers. First, the migrant workers in Bangalore tend to be long-time migrants compared with the Bangladeshi workers (Table 2.6). Second, a majority of Bangalorean workers migrated to the city with family, whereas among Bangladeshi workers, accompaniment of relatives rather than immediate kin is the dominant mode of migration (Table 2.7). Accompaniment of relatives, friends or neighbours is a common mode of movement used by women to avoid the possible risks of moving alone, and thereby it is a means rather than an end of movement. The significance of family-related factors in aspects of decision making regarding migration is also corroborated in Table 2.8. Although job searching is the main reason for

Table 2.6 Duration of stay in city (persons)

	Bangalore	*Bangladesh*
Less than 6 months	0	1
6 months to 1 year	3	5
1–3 years	8	17
3–5 years	9	31
5–10 years	19	33
More than 10 years	27	11
Total*	66	98

* Only migrants are included in total.
Source: Author's survey.

Table 2.7 Mode of migration (persons)

	Bangalore	*Bangladesh*
Migrated alone	6	13
Migrated with family	53	21
Migrated with friends/neighbours	3	7
Migrated with relatives	2	56
Others	2	1
Total	66	98

Source: Author's survey.

Table 2.8 Reason for migration (persons)

	Bangalore	*Bangladesh*
Job search	33	78
Economic hardship	7	–
Accompanying family	19	10
Familial conflict	4	3
To study	1	4
Other	2	3
Total	66	98

Source: Author's survey.

both Bangalorean and Bangladeshi workers, accompanying family is mentioned by a larger number of Bangalorean workers.

From the features enumerated so far, we could summarize that Bangalorean workers are older and more likely to be married than Bangladeshi workers. Probably because of these dispositions, the familial factor seems to weigh more among the Bangalorean workers. On the other hand, the Bangladeshi workers in our sample are younger and better educated, especially in light of Bangladesh's standards. The latter are more specific about their purpose of migration, i.e. job seeking.

Table 2.9 First year of factory employment (persons)

	Bangalore	*Bangladesh*
Before 1980	3	0
1980–84	4	1
1985–89	6	1
1990–94	15	2
1995–99	25	30
2000–5	43	66
2000	(7)	(18)
2001	(2)	(26)
2002	(2)	(8)
2003	(11)	(6)
2004	(11)	(6)
2005	(10)	(2)
2006	4	–
Total	100	100

Note: Since the Bangladesh survey was conducted in 2005, 2006 data are not available for Bangladesh.
Source: Author's survey.

2.3.3 Becoming a garment worker

2.3.3.1 Work experience

The Indian workers in our sample have longer experience in garment factories than the Bangladeshi workers (Table 2.9). This is probably related to the history of the garment industry in both countries, as discussed in Section 2.2. In response to the question concerning when the workers began working in the industry, the earliest year mentioned in the Indian sample is 1977 while that in the Bangladeshi sample is 1984. From the same table, it is noted that in both countries, a large proportion of workers began factory employment in 2000 or thereafter. A distinction, however, is that the peak of employment was observed during the early part of the 2000s in Bangladesh, while that of the Bangalorean workers is more recent. This could be an indication of the different impact of the MFA withdrawal in the two countries, such that Bangalore has become an increasingly popular site for investment for expanding production of export garments.

In contrast to the Bangladeshi sample, in which only four workers had wage work experience other than that in the garment industry (as housemaids), 57 per cent of the Indian workers had worked in various occupations, of which housemaid was the most common, mentioned by 29 per cent of the workers. The remaining 28 per cent mentioned varied work such as tailoring at home, *agarbathi* (incense sticks) making, construction work, work in factories and so on. This suggests different paths of labour participation by Bangalorean and Bangladeshi women, a different position for garment employment in the labour market, and consequently, different implications for individual lives as well as for society. In other words, while the garment industry is the first and still the only employment opportunity for the large majority of female job seekers in Bangladesh, women in Bangalore have had more exposure to wage work, especially in small-scale industries and home-based manufacturing operations.

Workers in both samples mentioned the better income prospects in garment employment as the main reason for leaving their previous occupations, followed by other reasons such as proximity of the workplace and a better physical environment. The four Bangladeshi workers who had previously worked as housemaids felt garment employment was better because of the regularity and the higher amount of income. On the other hand, Indian workers who had varied work experiences show a mixed picture. Out of 57 Indian workers who had wage work experience before joining garment factories, setting aside 13 no-responses, 35 workers found garment employment better than their previous job primarily because of the regularity in income (21 responses) followed by proximity to residence (6 responses). Conversely, 9 workers who view garment employment negatively cited the requirement of hard work (4 responses) and sexual harassment at the workplace (2 responses) as their reasons.

For some of the Indian workers, garment employment was not their first choice. At least 14 workers out of 100 sought job opportunities other than garment work, such as office jobs or sales clerk jobs, but failed due to lack of education or experience. For a majority of the sample, however, garment employment has been perceived as a fine choice, though it might not be the optimum one, promising good income and future prospects for their lives. Most of them found their jobs through informal sources such as friends, relatives and workers in the factories. Information regarding garment employment was well dispersed even in rural areas through family members, relatives and neighbours who found employment in garment factories before them. Out of 100 Indian workers, 32 of them had family or close relatives who were garment workers before them. The situation is similar in Bangladesh.

2.3.3.2 Employment status

In India as in many other countries including both developed and developing countries, contract workers are one of the most notable features of employment flexibilization or casualization. In Karnataka, contract work has been on the rise, drawing workers mainly from rural areas when failure in weather-sensitive agriculture forced them to migrate to cities (Rajeev 2006). The extensive use of contract workers in the ready-made garment industry has been mentioned (Mazumdar 2003; Vijayabaskar 2002; Neetha 2002; Aswathi 2003). In the case of Bangalore's garment industry, however, it has been stated by management that instead of contract work, own-payroll workers have been the norm, which contrasts with garment industries in northern India.[27] Notwithstanding, our sample shows almost three-quarters are contract workers employed directly by the factory, and only 26 per cent are permanent workers.

The term 'contract worker' has been used rather vaguely in recent years, which might reflect the diversification of employment arrangements, or the intensifying

Table 2.10 Present position of workers (persons)

	Bangalore	*Bangladesh*
Tailor/operator	58	65
Helper	20	5
Quality controller	14	25
Ironman	3	0
Folding/finishing	3	2
Others	2	3
Total	100	100

Source: Author's survey.

flexibility of employment. In our sample, there were no contract workers hired through labour contractors. The system where contract workers are hired directly by employers is also prevalent in Tiruppur (Awasthi 2003: 30). Aswathi (2003) has used the term to refer to all non-regular workers, which include many in forms of employment such as seasonal, part-time, casual, temporary and piece rate. Here, as far as our sample is concerned, there are differences between permanent and contract workers regarding the mode of payment, wage level and availability of other benefits, as discussed below. The difference, however, is not very distinct. The distinction becomes critical at the time of dismissal. Whereas permanent workers cannot be easily dismissed and at least legally have access to a set of norms, a structure of permanency such as a trade union, and entitlement to claim compensation or approach the Labour Commissioners' Office and Labour Courts, those recourses are not readily available to contract workers.[28]

In contrast, in our sample, 92 per cent of Bangladeshi workers are permanent and the remaining 8 per cent are on probation, thus no contract workers were included. In Bangladesh, the practice of contract work is more prevalent in the knitwear industry, where the share of male workers is higher. In reality, the permanent status of a worker, however, does not ensure job security, as discussed below.

The current position of workers is presented in Table 2.10. Our Indian sample has a larger number of helpers than does the Bangladeshi sample. Promotion from helper to tailor/operator, checker/quality controller or any other position is rather limited in the Indian case. Compared with the Bangladeshi sample, in which 35 per cent of workers experienced promotion in their current factory, only 16 per cent of Indian workers experienced promotion in their current factory, despite the fact that the average duration of service in the factories concerned is longer in the Indian sample (4.3 years) than in the Bangladeshi sample (2.6 years). In total, only 29 per cent of Indian workers ever experienced a promotion in their work history in various garment factories. Furthermore, Indian workers are less optimistic than their Bangladeshi counterparts about future prospects, as only 38 of the Indians, in contrast to 73 Bangladeshis, are hopeful of future promotion. Lack of education and training is often cited as the grounds for their low level of anticipation, while

Table 2.11 System of payment (persons)

	Bangalore			*Bangladesh*
	Permanent workers	*Contract workers*	*Total*	
Fixed salary plus overtime	25	43	68	70
Fixed salary without overtime	1	31	32	23
Piece rate				7
Total	26	74	100	100

Source: Author's survey.

Table 2.12 Wage levels (US dollars)

	Bangalore			*Bangladesh*
	Permanent workers	*Contract workers*	*Total*	
Tailor/operator	68	59	61	33
Helper	60	51	52	15
Total workers	64	56	58	31

Notes: Exchange rates taken from the Reserve Bank of India for 15 December 2006 and from the Bangladesh Bank for December 2005. $US1 = 44.66 rupees, 66.07 taka.
Source: Author's survey.

several workers mention that they do not want promotion because of work pressure or other reasons.

2.3.3.3 Wages and other benefits

The payment system in both samples is summarized in Table 2.11. In both sets of data, the dominant payment method is fixed salary plus overtime. However, the practice of fixed salary without overtime is also observed among a non-negligible number of workers. In this regard, there is a discernible difference between permanent and contract workers in India: while almost all the permanent workers receive overtime along with a fixed salary, a considerable number of contract workers are employed without overtime payment. In both countries, the exploitative nature of the payment system is evident, since around 70 per cent of those whose payment is fixed without overtime reported that they do overtime work to varied extents.[29]

Total monthly wages in terms of US dollars are shown in Table 2.12. Several points should be noted. First, the wage difference is considerably high; Bangalorean workers earn almost twice that of Bangladeshi workers. Second, among Indian workers, contract workers earn less than permanent workers. Third, the wage gap between the tailor/operator and helper categories is much wider in Bangladesh.

Although the condition of contract workers is inferior in terms of wage levels, all contract workers except six enjoy other benefits, such as bonuses, ESI (Employees' State Insurance) and EPF (Employees' Provident Fund).[30] Moreover, all 100 workers have weekly holidays and other types of paid holidays, such as festival holiday, earned leave, sick leave and maternity leave, although the latter holidays are not granted equally among all the workers. The condition of Bangladeshi workers is much less favourable. Weekly holidays and other types of holidays are granted only to 81 workers. The biggest difference in responses was with regard to availability of maternity leave; while 46 Indian workers mentioned the availability of maternity leave in their factories, only one Bangladeshi worker responded to the question.

None of our Indian sample has ever worked in a different employment status. Further study is required as to whether or not the path between permanent and contract employment is very limited. Out of 74 contract workers, only 15 expressed a desire to become a permanent worker for the sake of higher wages, while three declined and the rest did not give clear reactions. With respect to working environment, three-quarters of the Indian workers mentioned that they are satisfied. Such facilities as first aid, doctor clinic, safe drinking water, a sufficient number of clean toilets, crèche and canteen are available, not for all but for a substantial number of workers in our data.

Despite the more or less favourable views about their working conditions, 78 Indian workers (18 permanent and 60 contract workers), or more than three-quarters, feel their job is not secure. This view is expressed irrespective of their employment status, whether permanent or contract. The most often mentioned reason is insecurity of their employment status both by permanent workers (17 responses) and contract workers (50 responses). It should be noted that among all the sample workers only 31 of them (8 permanent and 23 contract workers) received formal letters of appointment from management. Among the Bangladeshi workers, it was almost same; only 32 of them had a letter of appointment. However, the concern regarding employment status was less pronounced (53 per cent) among the Bangladeshi workers. Nevertheless, one should not overlook the fact that a majority of workers both in Bangalore and Bangladesh expressed strong concern about their job security.

2.3.3.4 *Garment workers' contribution to households*

Most of Bangalore's workers live with their family members. Their households consist of 4.5 persons on average, including the workers themselves. Each household averages 2.4 earning members. Thus, there are more earners than economically dependent family members. In terms of contribution to household income, 42 per cent of workers mentioned that they were the main earners in their households, followed by husband (29 per cent), brother (12 per cent), father (9 per cent) and so forth. This shows their participation in this occupation is essential for the survival of the family.[31] The occupations of family members include service sector occupations such as driver and electrician, private industry occupations (mainly garment industry), construction work and so on. The importance of garment employment for the economic welfare of households is also corroborated by the fact that 34 per cent of workers have at least one garment worker besides themselves among their family members.[32]

As already mentioned, there are a larger number of independent migrant workers in our Bangladesh sample. Therefore, only 31 of them live with their family members while the rest live with friends/colleagues (22 per cent), in hostels (43 per cent), with relatives (3 per cent) or alone (1 per cent).[33] The average size of a household (the economic unit to which the workers contribute financially, therefore not necessarily the unit of cohabitation) and the number of earners are 3.5 and 2.2 persons, respectively, including the workers themselves. The smallness of the household size indicates that it includes couples without children and also female-headed households. The occupations of other family members are farmers (28 households), garment workers (16 households), small business (8 households), drivers (7 households), construction workers (5 households) and so forth. Among the workers who contribute to household income regularly, more than half of them are the main earners of the households.

Garment employment has enabled the workers to save some of their earnings. In both Bangalore and Bangladesh, more than 60 per cent of the workers save out of their income. The allocation for savings is much higher among Bangladeshi workers (27.6 per cent of wages) than their Bangalorean counterparts (6.4 per cent). It is mainly because the latter allocate a larger portion of their income for family expenditures. The uses of savings are similar: purchase of consumer durables and immovable properties such as land and houses, children's education, investment in family business and so on.

Both Bangalorean and Bangladeshi workers send remittances to their families who are living separately. The number of remittance senders as well as allocation out of total wages is higher among Bangladeshi workers (57 per cent of workers and 40 per cent of wages) than Bangalorean workers (22 per cent of workers and 30 per cent of wages). The difference may be due to the fact that a larger number of Bangalorean workers live together with family, thus obviating the need for remittance. On the other hand, although many Bangladeshi workers are physically separate from their families, they maintain close ties with them through their economic contributions.

2.3.3.5 Social status of garment workers

When garment workers in Bangladesh appeared on the social scene during the early 1980s, it was questioned whether they would bring about a social revolution. In a society where a gender-based division of labour and space was maintained more or less strictly, women, mostly young and unmarried, transgressing the boundaries in large numbers, were definitely a challenge to established gender norms and relations. Gender norms such as *purdah* (female seclusion) have largely lost their material significance at both ends of the social strata. Education and changing perceptions about lifestyles of the upper and upper-middle class, and economic imperatives for the poorer section of the society, have led to expansion of female mobility. Nevertheless, the symbolic meaning of purdah, which confers high value on such dispositions as domesticity and modesty, has not totally disappeared. Rather, it is sometimes tactically strengthened by opponents of change by labelling female factory workers as 'fallen women'. With the expansion of industry, the sources of garment workers are not confined to poor households, and women from educated families are also joining the industry (Paul-Majumder and Begum 2006: 23). Our data also corroborate this trend. Nevertheless, our observations suggest that garment workers, as a socially constructed category, are not yet free from a persistent social stigma in Bangladesh today.

On the other hand, such social stigma is not so pervasive among Bangalorean workers. Twenty-six workers responded that that the social status of garment work is low. They cite reasons such as no respect, inferior work, exploitation, problems with marriage, and harassment at the workplace. Notwithstanding, three-quarters of workers denied that the social status of garment work is low and stated totally opposite reasons, such as that it is a respectable job in society. At a focus group discussion with around 10 workers, all of the participants gave a negative answer to the question of whether, back in their villages, people speak ill of garment workers because they work side by side with men, which is an often uttered statement by Bangladeshi garment workers.

The above difference may be attributable to two factors in Karnataka. First, there is higher social acceptance of women's mobility,[34] and second, there is the fact that the position of the garment industry differs in that, unlike in Bangladesh, it is not the first and only source of employment opportunities for women. Conversely, the conspicuousness of garment workers as a new category for women in Bangladesh has resulted in the severe scrutiny of the workers by society. In that respect, a comparable new social category of workers in Bangalore could be business process outsourcing (BPO) workers (Upadhya and Vasavi 2006). BPO workers have a socially negative reputation as being carefree and not very sober, and marriage prospects even of male workers are grim.[35] The new style of work, especially the night shifts and the relatively high disposable income, has conferred a negative social assessment on BPO workers who are mostly young people of urban middle-class background.

Of course, the fact that a higher social status is accorded to garment workers in Bangalore than in Bangladesh does not imply that they are not subject to gender discrimination at home, in the workplace and in society. An important question remains as to in what way and to what extent garment work has affected the lives of women as gendered beings.

2.4 Changing environment and workers

2.4.1 Change in workload

Since the withdrawal of the MFA, garment exports of both India and Bangladesh have performed well in their major markets, the US and EU (Table 2.13). Behind the good performance of the industry, what changes are occurring in the workplace?

Table 2.13 Major garment exporters in the US and the EU markets ($million)

	US market				*EU market*		
	2005	*% Share 2005*	*% Change 05/04*		*2005*	*% Share 2005*	*% Change 05/04*
China	16,810	23.7	56.8	China	20,361	29.1	48.5
Mexico	6,230	8.8	−9.0	Turkey	9,776	14.0	4.6
Hong Kong	3,524	5.0	−9.1	Bangladesh	4,356	6.2	−4.9
India	3,059	4.3	34.3	Romania	4,287	6.1	−6.2
Indonesia	2,882	4.1	20.0	India	3,992	5.7	32.2
Honduras	2,685	3.8	−2.1	Tunisia	3,059	4.4	−4.9
Vietnam	2,665	3.8	6.4	Morocco	2,814	4.0	−6.3
Bangladesh	2,268	3.2	21.2	Hong Kong	2,056	2.9	−14.2
Thailand	1,833	2.6	0.6	Indonesia	1,468	2.1	−10.3
Dominican Republic	1,831	2.6	−10.1	Bulgaria	1,331	1.9	2.4
World	70,811	100.0	5.9	World	69,863	100.0	6.6

Source: Compiled from *World Trade Atlas*.

Bangalorean workers mention that workload has been on the increase. Regarding the changes in workload since January 2005, 47 per cent of workers answered that it had increased heavily. Coupled with the 35 answers of 'slight increase', more than 80 per cent of the workers are experiencing increased workload. The maintenance of productivity is ensured by a system of 'targets' (New Trade Union Initiative 2005). Out of 100 workers, 98 said they are given targets. According to an NGO activist, these 'targets' have been raised very high recently, and consequently, workers are under heavy pressure, although wages have also been on the increase to some extent.[36] Out of the 98 workers bound by 'targets', 52 expressed their inability to achieve the targets within stipulated working hours. Reported reasons for non-fulfilment include excessive targets, problems with machines and pieces, and requirements for good quality products. In order to fulfil targets, most of the workers do overtime. As already mentioned, many workers work on a fixed salary without overtime. Therefore, this lack of compensation for extra work may lead to the exploitation of labour at least in the short run.

I do not possess information about the current working situation of Bangladeshi workers. Regarding workload at the time of our survey (December 2005), 55 per cent of workers reported a large decrease, while 11 per cent reported a slight increase, and 30 per cent said there was no change. More than one year has passed since then, and so their situation is likely to be different. Notwithstanding, it is certain that for those paid only a fixed salary without overtime, the mechanism of labour exploitation functions the same as in the case of Bangalore if their workload has been increased, especially in the labour market where alternative employment options are severely limited.

2.4.2 Welfare issues and workers

While the quota stipulated by the MFA no longer exists, what has become an issue of concern for many garment exporters instead is the issue of social compliance. In a so-called 'buyer driven commodity chain' like the ready-made garment industry (Gereffi and Korzeniewicz 1994), it is always the buyers in the developed market that have decisive power over the producers in various countries. Motivated by human and labour rights concerns of consumers in developed countries, large buyers are increasingly emphasizing social compliance, i.e. corporate responsibility for labour conditions, as a necessary criterion for placing orders. The issue of social compliance has actually opened institutional space for civil society organizations to be associated with the workers' welfare as some of the stakeholders.

The two NGOs which assisted with our field surveys in Bangalore and Bangladesh have been deeply involved in the welfare of workers. Both NGOs have been supporting the livelihoods of workers outside the workplace. Civil Initiatives for Development (CIVIDEP), established in 2000 by a former left-wing activist and former garment workers, has been engaged in forming social organizations to do community work and run the micro-finance programme (for saving and borrowing) among garment workers in Bangalore (see RoyChowdhury 2005 for details). On the other hand, Nari Uddug Kendra (NUK) of Bangladesh was established in 1991 to promote women's causes. As an important part of its activities, NUK has been running hostels for garment workers since the early 1990s. Through those activities, both CIVIDEP and NUK have also been raising awareness of labour and women's rights.

Both NGOs associate themselves with social compliance initiatives by taking part in social auditing and organizing workshops on management of factories. In addition, they carry out extensive lobbying of government to press for improved welfare of garment workers. However, what has remained beyond the scope of their activities is direct negotiation with management on behalf of workers, especially wage bargaining, because they are not trade unions.

The activities of trade unions in the garment industry have been circumscribed by adverse factors. In Bangalore, ever since 1996 when the Centre of Indian Trade Unions (CITU), the front organization of the Communist Party of India (Marxist), organized a strike at Samrat Ashoka Exports which ended in miserable failure, no large trade unions have been engaged with garment workers (RoyChowdhury 2005). Outside Bangalore, some unionism was observed mainly among male workers in northern India, and this was mentioned by management as the major reason for their shift to Bangalore. However, the predominance of female workers makes organizing difficult since the workers are burdened both at the factories and at home and thus have no time to spare for a labour movement. Moreover, management tries to nip labour activism in the bud, which is possible because of the abundant fresh supply of female labour. The situation was the same in Bangladesh. While older industries, particularly public sector establishments, are plagued with politicized trade union activities, management – with the tacit support of government – has tried to keep the garment industry isolated from unionization. Although there are several federations purportedly involved with garment workers, most of them were initiated by males who were not involved with garment workers (Khan 2002). In more recent years, a union was organized by female workers (Dannecker 2002). Nevertheless, internal rivalries and interventions by foreign donors led to the split of the organization. Until now, those efforts have not succeeded in organizing labour activism among garment workers.

Global concern about labour conditions, which has led to social compliance, has surely contributed to improvement of working conditions, although coverage is basically limited to large factories.[37] In addition, many civil society organizations have been engaged in welfare programmes for garment workers, including various kinds of skill training, legal assistance, health services, dispatching of trained *ayas* for factory crèches and so on. Nevertheless, there still remains the issue of lack of collective bargaining power, and there are discords particularly over wages.[38] Recently, CIVIDEP has taken a step forward to support the formation of a trade union among workers. CIVIDEP's view is that NGOs are agents of change, not bodies that represent workers, and that only worker representation can solve in-factory problems. At the same time, they are cautious about depending solely on trade unions because the system of global commodity chains has severely reduced the scope and range of problems that can only be solved through negotiation with management.[39]

In Bangladesh, there occurred a sudden eruption of labour unrest in 2006. It was the first and largest labour unrest in the history of garment industry there. The precise causes are unknown, but a solution was sought through negotiation of a minimum wage rise. Ultimately, it seems that the core problems of workers will remain unsolved unless labour activism finds its own voice.

2.5 Concluding remarks

Our sample survey shows that there are similarities and dissimilarities in the socio-economic characteristics of workers in Bangalore and Bangladesh. The common disposition of workers of both places may be summarized as follows: they are mostly young, relatively educated migrants from rural areas. Moreover, as the level of education and caste attributes indicate, garment workers do not necessarily belong to the most disadvantaged group in society. Furthermore, their earnings contribute a significant portion of household income, thereby indicating the indispensability of garment employment in their livelihoods.

A notable difference between the two groups of workers, inasmuch as our sample reveals, is that Bangladeshi workers are younger, more likely to be single and more independent in their decisions and actions regarding migration for job search. This does not correspond to the general perception of patriarchal severity and social constraints over female mobility in Bangladesh. Although the scope of sample bias cannot be overlooked, we could minimally state that young women in Bangladesh as embodied in garment workers are no less mobile and independent than women in Karnataka. This study indicates a more dynamic exercise of Bangladeshi workers' agency in favour of migration and employment than is generally conceived. Nevertheless, social valuation of garment workers, in contrast to their economic valuation in terms of their financial contribution to the households and the country, remains low in Bangladesh compared to Bangalore.

While Bangalorean workers enjoy a higher social acceptance and better working facilities and environment than their Bangladeshi counterparts, this does not mean that they are better off. In this regard, further in-depth, qualitative studies beyond the workplace are needed to elucidate the comprehensive implications of garment work on the lives of female workers, whose life worlds spread over households, communities and workplaces.

In the examination of the long-term effects of their employment, a noteworthy concern is the strong sense of insecurity about their employment expressed by both Bangalorean and Bangladeshi workers despite the good performance of the garment industries in both countries. More than three-quarters of Bangalorean workers and more than half of Bangladeshi workers feel their employment is not secure. It should be noted that this concern is shared by a larger number of Bangalorean workers, who appear to be provided with better working facilities and environment including provision of leave, than by Bangladeshi garment workers. The lack of employment security undermines the bargaining position of workers against management in the short term and the bargaining position of women in households and communities since their earnings constitute the fundamental basis of their power.

Finally, allow me to locate some of the findings in the wider context of the changes taking place around garment workers.

As mentioned repeatedly, the garment industries in both Bangalore and Bangladesh are female-dominated. If we take a wider view of the garment industry in South Asia, we find similar female domination in Sri Lanka (Tilakaratne 2006; Arai 2006). In contrast, the garment industry in Pakistan is sustained by male labour as discussed in Chapter 3. The same pattern is observed in northern India. The garment industry in Nepal, which was largely promoted by Indian capital, previously had a higher male ratio among workers and many were Indians. However, these ratios have gradually changed in favour of both females and local labour (Pant and Pradhan 2002).

This difference in the gender composition of workers is linked to the mode of production and the nature of the skills. Male-dominated factories are relatively small in scale and each tailor has the skill to make a complete garment. Conversely, female workers employed in factory production of a larger scale are assigned to work on line assemblies, and their skills are confined to that particular part of garment manufacturing.[40] This precludes women from acquiring higher skills (Mazumdar 2003). It is also observed that, with the rapid expansion of production, management finds less time to impart sufficient training to workers, even if they intend to.

We can see that a similar process of deskilling of tailoring took place in Tiruppur. Its geographical advantage, i.e. being centrally located for the sale and processing of raw cotton, has facilitated the development of the industry (Cawthorne 1995: 44). A prominent feature of the knitwear industry in Tiruppur is the dominance of small units of production with inter-unit transactional relationships. This mode of production has impacted on labour in many ways. While small-scale production has been geared towards stricter control of the labour force with resultant low wages and exploitative working conditions, at the same time it has provided some scope for workers to acquire a wider range of skills (Cawthorne 1995: 53; Swaminathan and Jeyaranjan 1999: 111–12). It has even enabled highly skilled workers to become entrepreneurs (Swaminathan and Jeyaranjan 1999: 112). Subsequently, the dramatic growth of Tiruppur as India's largest knitwear export hub was spurred by the feminization of the workforce.[41] The process was advanced through both replacement of male by female labour and the creation of jobs specifically for women. The jobs occupied predominantly by female workers tend to be categorized as 'feminine' and 'unskilled'. Neetha (2002) argues that the definition of skill is not only technical-based but also gender-based. It should be emphasized that integration of Tiruppur with the export market has precipitated this process.

Another change taking place simultaneously at different locations of garment production is the shift from a piece-rate to a time-rate mode of payment. In contrast to the piece-rate payment prevalent among male workers in northern India and Pakistan (Chapter 3), female workers are mostly paid time-rate wages.

Again, Tiruppur presents a typical example of this phenomenon. In Tiruppur, there have been shifts between time-rate and piece-rate wages. In the early 1960s when the industry was catering to the needs of the domestic market, production was organized as composite units, with workers employed on a permanent basis and paid on a time-rate system. With the outward expansion of the market as well as the rise of numerous interconnected small-scale units, piece-rate payment with few other fringe benefits became the dominant mode of payment (Swaminathan and Jeyaranjan 1999: 99). According to the study by Neetha (2002), 92 per cent of workers were employed under a piece-rate wage contract. Notwithstanding, the study also finds there has been recourse to the time-rate system recently, especially in core operations like cutting and stitching, in which women's participation is quite substantial.

One of the benefits of the time-rate system is that it functions better than the piece-rate system for maintaining the quality standard of products. However, as we have already discussed, if it is linked with a system of production targets, workers are left in limbo. Their predicament grows increasingly dire when overtime wages are not paid.

Notes

1. See Murayama (2005) for issues addressed by preceding studies on female factory labour.
2. The MFA officially expired and was succeeded by the Agreement on Textile and Clothing (ATC) in December 1994. The ATC called for a gradual phasing out of all MFA restrictions by the year 2005.
3. 'Knitwear Industry in Tirupur' (http://www.aepcindia.com/portal/tirupur.asp).
4. Department of Commerce data.
5. According to Tewari (2005) the Textile Policy of 1985 was a turning point in spurring garment exports. Under that policy, the government deregulated the hitherto heavily controlled textile industry by raising the investment ceiling, allowing firms to diversify

their fabric and fibre base, promoting exports through a variety of programmes and supporting technical modernization through the disbursement of credits and so forth (Tewari 2005: 16, 21). The policy, however, brought some negative consequences particularly with respect to employment, such as retrenchment from non-viable textile mills, loss of jobs in the handloom sector, and harsher working conditions in the powerloom sector, which as a whole precipitated the casualization of employment (Uchikawa 1998: 152–64).

6. 'India on the Move: Hubs of Manufacturing Excellence Propel Indian Garment Industry to Greater Growth'. *Apparel Online*. 16–31 Jan. 2006.
7. Figures taken from http://www.vitcblr.org/state_export.htm.
8. An article published in *The Hindu*, 16 Oct. 2006.
9. The study by Narayana (2004) shows textiles including garments accounted for about 17 per cent, the highest share, of all small-scale industries of Karnataka in 2002/3.
10. See Inoue (1992) for the industrial development policy of Karnataka up to the early 1990s.
11. Gokaldas Exports was founded by the father, a silk merchant, of the present directors (three brothers) in 1970. Samrat Ashoka exported to Germany, where the wife of the owner hailed from. Information was provided by K.R. Jayaram, a former garment worker and one of the founding members of CIVIDEP (see note 18).
12. Interview with one of the executive directors of Gokaldas Exports.
13. Interview with several owners and managers of garment factories located in Bangalore. K.R. Jayaram (note 11) also listed the same reasons.
14. Bangladesh Bank data.
15. See the case of Desh Garments, a pioneer garment firm promoted with the technical collaboration of Daewoo, a leading Korean business group (Rhee 1990).
16. According to Rhee (1990) the Bangladeshi founder of Desh Garments was so impressed by the efficiency and sheer numbers of women at Daewoo and other garment factories in Korea that he persuaded the Bangladeshi government to support female trainees and obtained permission from the parents and guardians of 14 women.
17. See Murayama (2006) for the details about the structure of, and changes in, the female labour market in Bangladesh.
18. The Bangladeshi survey was conducted with the help of a local NGO, Nari Uddug Kendra (Centre for Women's Initiatives), while the Bangalore survey was a part of research collaboration with the Institute for Social and Economic Change (Bangalore). The actual interviews were carried out in collaboration with a local NGO, CIVIDEP (Civil Initiatives for Development). The author expresses her deepest gratitude to the organizations as well as to all the people who extended generous assistance.
19. The working conditions and environment of EPZ factories are generally better than non-EPZ factories. Out of 100 workers in the sample, 44 workers are working in EPZ factories.
20. According to India's Factories Act, 1948, a child below 14 years of age is not allowed to work in any factory. An adolescent between 15 and 18 years can be employed in a factory only if s/he obtains a certificate of fitness from an authorized medical doctor. A child between 14 and 18 years of age cannot be employed for more than four and a half hours/day. Although there is the practice among workers of overstating their ages, management seems to avoid employing child labour for the sake of social compliance (interview by the author).
21. According to the 2001 census, 89.7 per cent of the population of Bangladesh is Muslim, followed by Hindu (9.2) and other religious communities. The issue of religion and caste, though it may not be insignificant, has also received little attention in other studies, mainly because of the overwhelming share of the Muslim population and the low amount of attention given to communal issues in the country.
22. The estimated share of Lingayaths and Kurubas was 15 and 6 per cent, respectively.
23. Our sample included two Brahmans.

24. For instance, some Telugu speakers among the Vokkaliga caste adopted Kannada as their main language through marriages with Kannada-speaking Vokkaligas. Also, there is a shift from Tulu to Kannada (interview with K. Rajakumar, an active member of Kannada Sahitya Parishad. See also Nair 1996).
25. http://www.kar.nic.in/dwcd/womenstatistics.htm.
26. Four workers are from Tamil Nadu and two are from Andhra Pradesh.
27. Author's interviews with several owners and managers of garment factories.
28. Views shared by Supriya RoyChowdhury of ISEC.
29. Eighty-five per cent of Bangladeshi workers and 77 per cent of Indian workers do overtime to varied extents. Of them, 17 per cent of Bangladeshi workers and 21 per cent of Indian workers are not paid for overtime.
30. All permanent workers in our sample receive all those benefits. Thus, the disadvantageous condition of contract workers cannot be denied. However, the situation of Bangalorean workers is far better than that in Tiruppur as surveyed by Neetha (2002). There, among 296 workers, only eight reported getting any ESI or EPF benefits.
31. Women's contribution is higher in the case of Tiruppur studied by Neetha (2002). Among the sample of 296 workers, about 54.7 per cent of the workers contribute more than half of the family income.
32. This is true also in the case of Tiruppur. Many female workers have family members working in the same industry (Neetha 2002).
33. Since the collaborating NGO is running hostels for garment workers, there were a large number of hostel residents in our sample. However, including the arrangement of living with friends/colleagues, which is common among migrant unmarried workers so as to share rent and ensure security, it is clear that the lives of these workers are more independent than those of workers in the Bangalorean sample.
34. According to A.R. Vasavi of the National Institute of Advanced Studies in Bangalore, patriarchy is much more muted in Karnataka than in the states in the north (interview by the author).
35. Views shared by Carol Upadhya, National Institute of Advanced Studies, who recently conducted detailed research on IT workers, jointly with A.R. Vasavi.
36. Information provided by Prativha, also a former garment worker and one of the founding members of CIVIDEP.
37. In recent years, the miserable conditions of subcontracting work and home-based production have become known to consumers through various media. As a result, buyers started considering the extension of compliance coverage to those types of production (information provided by an executive of a large buying house).
38. Among the various compliance issues, payment of overtime, which is double the rate of the basic hourly wage, is the issue that factory management resists most (information source same as note 37).
39. Interview with Gopinath, founder-director of CIVIDEP.
40. Interview with a Japanese proprietor of a buying house. According to him, orders from Japanese buyers are more concentrated in garment factories in the north since each lot is not very large and workers in the north have flexible skills to adjust designs according to the varied and complicated orders.
41. Between 1994–96 and 2000–1, female employment grew much faster relative to male employment (Awasthi 2003: 35).

References

Afsar, Rita (2000) *Rural–Urban Migration in Bangladesh: Causes, Consequences and Challenges.* Dhaka: University Press.

Ahmad, Q.K. (1990) 'Study on Female Garment Workers in Bangladesh' (Draft Report). Dhaka: Bangladesh Unnayan Parishad.

Arai, Etsuyo (2006) 'Readymade Garment Workers in Sri Lanka: Strategy to Survive in Competition'. In Mayumi Murayama (ed.) *Employment in Readymade Garment Industry in Post-MFA Era: the Cases of India, Bangladesh and Sri Lanka*. JRP Series no. 140. Chiba: Institute of Developing Economies.

Awasthi, I.C. (2003) 'Globalisation and Knitwear Industry: a Case of Tirupur'. *Manpower Journal* 38(4): 18–40.

Banerjee, Nirmala (1991) 'The More it Changes, the More it is the Same: Women Workers in Export Oriented Industries'. In Nirmala Banerjee (ed.) *Indian Women in a Changing Industrial Scenario*. New Delhi: Sage Publications.

Bangladesh Bureau of Statistics (2003) *Population Census 2001: National Report (Provisional)*.

—— (2004) *Report on Bangladesh Census of Manufacturing Industries 1999–2000*.

Bhattacharya, Debapriya and Mustafizur Rahman (2001) 'Bangladesh's Apparel Sector: Growth Trend and the Post-MFA Challenges'. In Pratima Paul-Majmder and Binayak Sen (eds) *Growth of Garment Industry in Bangladesh: Economic and Social Dimensions*. Dhaka: Bangladesh Institute of Development Studies.

Cawthorne, Pamela M. (1995) 'Of Networks and Markets: the Rise and Rise of a South Indian Town, the Example of Tiruppur's Cotton Knitwear Industry'. *World Development* 23(1): 43–56.

Chakravarty, Deepita (2004) 'Expansion of Markets and Women Workers: Case Study of Garment Manufacturing in India'. *Economic and Political Weekly* 39(45): 4910–16.

—— (2005) 'Women Workers, Entrepreneurs and Behavioral Rationality: a Case of Indian Garment Manufacturing'. *Indian Journal of Labour Economics* 48(1): 101–13.

Chatterji, S. and R. Mohan (1993) 'India's Garment Exports'. *Economic and Political Weekly* 28(35): M95–M119.

Dannecker, Petra (2002) *Between Conformity and Resistance: Women Garment Workers in Bangladesh*. Dhaka: University Press.

Directorate of Census Operations (2001a) *Census of India 2001: Primary Census Abstract, Karnataka*.

—— (2001b) *Census of India 2001: Provisional Population Totals, Karnataka*.

Elson, Diane and Ruth Pearson (1981) ' "Nimble Fingers Make Cheap Workers": an Analysis of Women's Employment in Third World Export Manufacturing'. *Feminist Review* no. 7 (Spring): 87–107.

Gereffi, Gary and Miguel Korzeniewicz (eds) (1994) *Commodity Chains and Global Capitalism*. Westport, Conn. and London: Greenwood Press.

Government of Karnataka (1990) *Report of the Karnataka Third Backward Classes Commission*.

—— (2006) *Economic Survey 2005–6*. Planning and Statistics Department.

Inoue, Kyoko (1992) *Industrial Development Policy of India*. Tokyo: Institute of Developing Economies.

Kalpagam, U. (1994) *Labour and Gender: Survival in Urban India*. New Delhi: Sage Publications.

Khan, Shamsul I. (2002) 'Trade Unions, Gender Issues and the Ready-Made Garment Industry of Bangladesh'. In Carol Miller and Jessica Vivian (eds) *Women's Employment in the Textile Manufacturing Sectors of Bangladesh and Morocco*. Geneva: UNRISD and UNDP.

Lee, Ching Kwan (1998) *Gender and the South China Miracle: Two Worlds of Factory Women*. Berkeley and Los Angeles: University of California Press.

Mazumdar, Indrani (2003) 'Impact of Globalization on Women Workers in Garment Exports: the Indian Experience'. In Veena Jha (ed.) *Trade, Globalisation and Gender: Evidence from South Asia*. Delhi: UNIFEM and the United Nations.

Murayama, Mayumi (2005) 'Factory Women under Globalization: Incorporating Japanese Women into the Global Factory Debate'. In Mayumi Murayama (ed.) *Gender and Development: the Japanese Experience in Comparative Perspective*. Basingstoke and New York: Palgrave Macmillan.

—— (2006) 'Globalization and Female Employment in Bangladesh: Readymade Garment Workers in Post-MFA Era'. In Mayumi Murayama (ed.) *Employment in Readymade Garment*

Industry in Post-MFA Era: the Cases of India, Bangladesh and Sri Lanka. JRP Series no. 140. Chiba: Institute of Developing Economies.

Nair, Janaki (1996) 'Memories of Underdevelopment: Language and Its Identities in Contemporary Karnataka'. *Economic and Political Weekly* 31(41–42) (12–19 Oct.): 2809–16.

—— (1998) *Miners and Millhands: Work, Culture and Politics in Princely Mysore*. New Delhi: Sage Publications.

—— (2005) *The Promise of the Metropolis: Bangalore's Twentieth Century*. New Delhi: Oxford University Press.

Narayana, M.R. (2004) 'Small Scale Industries in Karnataka: Impact of Growth, Sickness and Closure on Production and Employment'. *The Indian Journal of Labour Economics* 47(4): 967–83.

Neetha, N. (2002) 'Flexible Production, Feminisation and Disorganisation – Evidence from Tiruppur Knitwear Industry'. *Economic and Political Weekly* 37(21): 2045–52.

New Trade Union Initiative, South India Coalition for the Rights of Garment Workers: Bangalore (2005) 'Status of Garment Industry in Bangalore'. Paper presented at the First Asia-Level Consultation on International Garment Campaign, held in Bangalore, 2–4 Dec. 2005.

NSSO (National Sample Survey Organization) (2001) *Migration in India 1999–2000: NSS 55th Round*. New Delhi: Government of India.

Pant, Dinesh and Devendra Pradhan (2002) 'Garment Industry in Nepal'. In Gopal Joshi (ed.) *Garment Industry in South Asia: Rags or Riches*? New Delhi: South Asia Multidisciplinary Advisory Team, International Labour Organization.

Paul-Majumder, Pratima and Anwara Begum (2006) *Engendering Garment Industry: the Bangladesh Context*. Dhaka: University Press.

Phongpaichit, Pasuk (1988) 'Two Roads to the Factory: Industrialisation Strategies and Women's Employment in Southeast Asia'. In Bina Agarwal (ed.) *Structure of Patriarchy: State, Community and Household in Modernising Asia*. London and New Delhi: Zed Books and Kali for Women.

Pore, Kumud (1991) 'Women at Work – a Secondary Line of Operation: a Study of the Socio-Economic Conditions of Women Workers in the Garment Industry and the Electronics Industry in Thane and Pune, Maharashtra'. In Nirmala Banerjee (ed.) *Indian Women in a Changing Industrial Scenario*. New Delhi: Sage Publications.

Rajeev, Meenakshi (2006) 'Contract Labour in Karnataka: Emerging Issues and Options'. *Economic and Political Weekly* 41(21): 2086–88.

Rao, V. Rukumini and Sahba Husain (1991) 'Invisible Hands: the Women behind India's Export Earnings'. In Nirmala Banerjee (ed.) *Indian Women in a Changing Industrial Scenario*. New Delhi: Sage Publications.

Rhee, Yung Whee (1990) 'The Catalyst Model of Development: Lessons from Bangladesh's Success with Garment Exports'. *World Development* 18(2): 333–46.

RoyChowdhury, Supriya (2005) 'Labour Activism and Women in the Unorganised Sector: Garment Export Industry in Bangalore'. *Economic and Political Weekly* 40(22/23): 2250–5.

Sobhan, Rehman and Muzaffer Ahmad (1980) *Public Enterprise in an Intermediate Regime: a Study in the Political Economy of Bangladesh*. Dhaka: Bangladesh Institute of Development Studies.

Swaminathan, Padmini and J. Jeyaranjan (1999) 'The Knitwear Cluster in Tiruppur: an Indian Industrial District in the Making?' In Amiya Kumar Bagchi (ed.) *Economy and Organization: Indian Institutions under Neoliberal Regime*. New Delhi: Sage Publications.

Tewari, Meenu (2005) 'Post-MFA Adjustments in India's Textile and Apparel Industry: Emerging Issues and Trends'. Working Paper no. 167, Indian Council for Research on International Economic Relations.

Tilakaratne, W.M. (2006) 'Phasing Out of MFA and the Emerging Trends in the Readymade Garment Industry in Sri Lanka'. In Mayumi Murayama (ed.) *Employment in Readymade Garment Industry in Post-MFA Era: the Cases of India, Bangladesh and Sri Lanka*. JRP Series no. 140. Chiba: Institute of Developing Economies.

Uchikawa, Shuji (1998) *Indian Textile Industry: State Policy, Liberalization and Growth*. New Delhi: Manohar.

Unni, Jeemol, Namrata Bali and Jignasa Vyas (1999) *Subcontracted Women Workers in the Global Economy: Case of Garment Industry in India*. Ahmedabad: Gujarat Institute of Development Research and Self Employed Women's Association.

Upadhya, Carol and A.R. Vasavi (2006) *Work, Culture, and Sociality in the Indian IT Industry: a Sociological Study*. Bangalore: School of Social Sciences, National Institute of Advanced Studies.

Varghese, Sheela (1999) 'Employment of Women in the Garment Industry'. Discussion Paper no. 9. Thiruvananthapuram: Centre for Development Studies.

Vijayabaskar, M. (2002) 'Garment Industry in India'. In Gopal Joshi (ed.) *Garment Industry in South Asia: Rags or Riches*? New Delhi: South Asia Multidisciplinary Advisory Team, International Labour Organization.

Wiig, Arne (1990) 'Non-Tariff Barriers to Trade and Development: the Case of the Garments Industry in Bangladesh'. In Ole David Koht Norbye (ed.) *Bangladesh Faces the Future*. Dhaka: University Press.

Wolf, Diane L. (1992) *Factory Daughters: Gender, Household Dynamics, and Rural Industrialization in Java*. Berkeley: University of California Press.

3 Competitiveness of the Garment Industry in Pakistan with Particular Focus on Piece Rate Workers*

Momoe Makino

3.1 Introduction

When the Multi-fibre Arrangement (MFA) was phased out on 1 January 2005, textile and garment[1] exporters in World Trade Organization (WTO) member countries in principle became subject to tough competition in the non-quota market (WTO 1996; Raffaelli 1998; Nordås 2004). Before 2005, there was concern about the possible negative impact of the MFA phase-out in countries such as Bangladesh that believed they were protected by the quota regime (Bhattacharya and Rahman 2001: 9–12). Since January 2005, however, Bangladesh has continued to perform well. There are several explanations for this performance such as: (1) that the effect of MFA phase-out was and still is limited because China agreed to export restrictions on textile and garment products to the US and EU in 2005 (Yamagata 2006),[2] (2) that international textile and garment buyers would not import exclusively from China in order to diversify risks (Saxena and Wiebe 2005), or (3) that more time is needed to truly assess the effects of phasing out the MFA.

About 60 per cent of Pakistan's exports are in textile and garment goods. Thus, the impact of phasing out the MFA was of great concern. These concerns were somewhat similar to those of Bangladesh, but Pakistan was more optimistic about the post-MFA situation. Unlike Bangladesh, Pakistan has excelled in relatively capital-intensive products such as yarn, fabrics and home textile products. Import ceilings in US and EU markets had suppressed exports of these products under the MFA regime (Zaidi 1999: 186–7). As would be expected, Pakistani textile exports have been growing steadily since the MFA was phased out. However, exports of downstream garment products, especially knitwear (which accounts for the largest share value-wise in total garment exports), have been stagnant.

One reason for sluggish knitwear performance could be related to phasing out the MFA.[3] This chapter does not include a detailed examination of the impact of the MFA phase-out but rather includes a search for the indigenous factors behind the weak performance of the knitwear industry in Pakistan, given that the garment industry has to face intensifying competition in the post-MFA international market. This chapter focuses on production workers since the garment industry is one of the most labour-intensive industries, and worker competitiveness is relatively important in such an industry. The significance of this study lies in its inclusion of a detailed survey of production workers in the garment industry. First, there are only a few substantial studies on production workers in the manufacturing industries of Pakistan. Second, the garment industry expects intensified competition in the post-MFA era, and its performance is crucial for the economy of Pakistan because it is an important source of employment as well as foreign currency.

The objective of this chapter is to examine factors, specifically characteristics of sewing operators, which may make the Pakistani garment industry uncompetitive in the post-MFA international market. In order to achieve this objective, survey interviews with managers and production workers were conducted in the garment industry in Lahore in November 2005 and in August 2006. This chapter proceeds as follows. Through use of official data, Section 3.2 presents an overview of the Pakistani garment industry and a possible scenario that the garment industry may face in the post-MFA era. Section 3.3 includes an examination of issues related to whether or not the Pakistani garment industry can contend with its competitors in the post-MFA era. Particular focus is placed on wage levels. China, India and Bangladesh are viewed as main competitors of Pakistan. China is seen as a threat for all countries that export garments, while the Pakistani garment industry must compete directly with India and Bangladesh.[4] Section 3.4 includes interviews with managers in the Pakistani garment industry. They were asked about wage levels and their perceptions of possible bottlenecks related to competing in export markets. Interviews with production workers in the garment industry are included in Section 3.5. In addition to verifying wage levels, these interviews also sought to determine whether or not managerial perceptions of possible bottlenecks (for example, lack of quality labour due to the piece rate payment system), were reasonable from a worker perspective.

3.2 The garment industry in Pakistan and the MFA phase-out

3.2.1 Significance of the Pakistani garment industry

Cotton is a major agricultural crop in Pakistan; the textile and garment industries make use of that cotton as a raw material. Together, they share a major role in Pakistan's manufacturing base. The total amount of Pakistan's exports in 2005/6[5] was $US16.45 billion; textile and garment exports comprised 60 per cent of this total (Table 3.1). Cotton fabrics comprised the largest share of total exports at 12.8 per cent. This was followed by bedwear[6] at 12.4 per cent and knitwear at 10.6 per cent. The export of ready-made garments, excluding leather garments and knitwear, comprised 8.0 per cent. Thus, total garment exports made up 18.6 per cent of total exports.

There is no recent Census of Manufacturing Industries (CMI).[7] Despite the lack of data, Makino (2006b) estimated current shares of the garment industry. These calculations yield 11.1 and 20.1 per cent as shares of the garment industry in manufacturing value-added and in manufacturing employment respectively (Makino 2006b: 58–9). Makino suggests that these percentages may be underestimates of the actual share of the garment industry. Although it is difficult to obtain

Table 3.1 Value-wise share of textile and garment products in total Pakistan exports (US$ million)

	2004/5[1] *value*	*2005/6 value*	*2005/6 % share*	*04/05–05/06 % change*
Total exports	14,391	16,451	100.0	14.3
Textile and garment	8,445	9,835	59.8	16.5
Cotton yarn	1,057	1,383	8.4	30.9
Cotton fabrics	1,863	2,108	12.8	13.2
Knitwear	1,635	1,751	10.6	7.1
Bedwear	1,450	2,038	12.4	40.6
Ready-made garments (excluding leather garments and knitwear)	1,088	1,310	8.0	20.4
Towels	520	588	3.6	12.9
Artificial silk and synthetic textiles	300	200	1.2	–33.3

Note: 1. Year description such as '2004/5' refers to the fiscal year in Pakistan which in this case would be from July 2004 to June 2005.
Source: Compiled from State Bank of Pakistan, *Statistical Bulletin 2006*, Table 4.15.

correct figures, the importance of the garment industry in creating employment in Pakistan cannot be denied. Evidently, the garment industry is very important for Pakistan. It has a 19 per cent share in total Pakistani exports and makes a substantial contribution to total manufacturing value-added and employment.

In 2005, China ranked first internationally in exports of both knitwear and woven wear (Table 3.2). In total garment exports of $US237.63 billion, the value of exports from China was $US65.90 billion, a 27.7 per cent share. In comparison, Pakistan's share in the garment export market was marginal.

3.2.2 Prospects of the post-MFA era

The garment industry, particularly the knitwear industry in Pakistan, is of course concerned about increasing competition in the post-MFA international market. Though it is too early to assess the full impact of the MFA phase-out, a possible scenario that the Pakistani garment industry may face in the post-MFA era can be constructed using both domestic and international data.

Viewing domestic data in Table 3.1, it can be seen that exports of textiles and garments increased dramatically in 2005/6. While exports of knitwear also increased 7.1 per cent, the increase was relatively slow compared with other textile and garment subcategories.

International data found in Table 3.2 show that Pakistan recorded a 0.6 per cent decrease in knitwear exports in 2005, while woven exports increased dramatically by 42.5 per cent. Both knitwear and woven wear exports from China and India increased immensely. Bangladeshi data for 2005 are missing in the UN database (as of June 2007), but they are available in the US import statistics compiled by the Office of Textile and Apparel (OTEXA), US Department of Commerce. These US import data are useful because in Pakistani items sold abroad, 62.4 per cent of knitwear and 39.8 per cent of woven wear exports go to the US market. Table 3.3

Table 3.2 Overview of international garment exports[1] (US$ million)

Rank	Country	(HS2002 Code 61) Knitwear				Rank	Country	(HS2002 Code 62) Woven wear			
		Value 2004	*Value 2005*	*% share (2005)*	*% change (2004–5)*			*Value 2004*	*Value 2005*	*% share (2005)*	*% change (2004–5)*
1	China	25,803	30,871	28.4	19.6	1	China	28,981	35,031	27.2	20.9
2	Hong Kong	12,202	13,317	12.3	9.1	2	Hong Kong	11,236	12,252	9.5	9.0
3	Italy	6,830	6,706	6.2	−1.8	3	Italy	10,517	10,774	8.4	2.4
4	Turkey	6,259	6,590	6.1	5.3	4	Germany	6,767	6,708	5.2	−0.9
5	Germany	4,443	4,440	4.1	−0.1	5	India	3,676	5,456	4.2	48.4
6	India	2,474	3,203	2.9	29.5	6	Turkey	4,537	4,862	3.8	7.2
7	France	3,027	3,188	2.9	5.3	7	France	4,346	4,639	3.6	6.8
8	Belgium	2,386	2,685	2.5	12.5	8	Mexico	4,546	4,575	3.5	0.6
9	Mexico	2,789	2,589	2.4	−7.2	9	Belgium	3,356	3,654	2.8	8.9
10	US	2,699	2,579	2.4	−4.4	10	Romania	3,465	3,417	2.7	−1.4
	Bangladesh	2,388	–	–	–		Bangladesh	2,020	–	–	–
	Pakistan	1,665	1,655	1.5	−0.6		Pakistan	933	1,330	1.0	42.5
	Total	107,096	108,709	100.0	1.5		Total	121,685	128,917	100.0	5.9

Note: 1. Data for Vietnam, which is considered to be among top 10, are missing.
Source: United Nations, *COMTRADE Database*.

Table 3.3 Major exporters of cotton garment products to the US (US$ million)

Rank	*Country*	*(MFA category 338) Men's knit shirts*			*Rank*	*Country*	*(MFA category 347) Men's trousers*		
		Value 2004	*Value 2005*	*% change*			*Value 2004*	*Value 2005*	*% change*
	World	5,182.4	5,556.6	7.2		World	5,023.4	5,291.5	5.3
1	Honduras	710.6	717.7	1.0	1	Mexico	1,469.9	1,430.2	−2.7
2	Pakistan	452.4	505.9	11.8	2	China	110.3	383.0	247.2
3	Mexico	555.5	428.9	−22.8	3	Dominican Republic	449.7	365.8	−18.7
4	India	291.3	412.1	41.5	4	Bangladesh	177.0	308.6	74.3
5	El Salvador	373.6	360.2	−3.6	5	Hong Kong	247.5	225.6	−8.8
6	Peru	251.9	305.4	21.2	6	Nicaragua	147.0	175.6	19.4
7	China	110.3	235.5	113.5	7	Colombia	124.2	163.3	31.5
8	Vietnam	251.7	209.1	−16.9	8	Honduras	132.0	148.1	12.2
9	Guatemala	216.9	184.5	−15.0	9	Vietnam	147.4	142.9	−3.0
10	Haiti	135.9	174.2	28.2	10	India	93.2	139.3	49.5
15	Sri Lanka	96.4	117.9	22.3	12	Pakistan	105.1	134.4	27.9
19	Bangladesh	55.3	105.0	90.0	19	Sri Lanka	75.3	88.2	17.2

Source: OTEXA (Office of Textile and Apparel).

shows the import value of men's knit shirts and trousers in 2004 and 2005 from major exporting countries to the US. These are the two main Pakistani garment export items[8] to the US market. In both categories, imports to the US from China and Bangladesh increased greatly, and this may have been an effect of phasing out the MFA. Compared with the Central American countries such as Mexico and Honduras, Pakistan shows relatively good performance, but the increase seems relatively slow when compared with that of China and its direct competitors India and Bangladesh.

Several concerns related to garment exports remain for Pakistan. One of the reasons why significant effects of the MFA phase-out have not yet been seen may be related to safeguard measures[9] implemented by the US on garment imports from China and restrictions of Chinese exports to the US market.[10] Figure 3.1 shows the monthly import value of men's cotton shirts going from China to the US. It clearly shows the huge increase at the beginning of 2005 and the subsequent large decrease after safeguard measures were implemented. Other main export items from Pakistan to the US, such as men's cotton trousers, were subject to the same safeguard measures and show the same tendency seen in Figure 3.1. It seems probable that the safeguard measures and the subsequent export restrictions benefited Pakistan. This implies a negative prospect for Pakistani garment exports after the end of 2008, because restrictions on exports from China to the US will expire. Further, as shown in Table 3.3, the performance of Pakistani garment exports is inferior to that

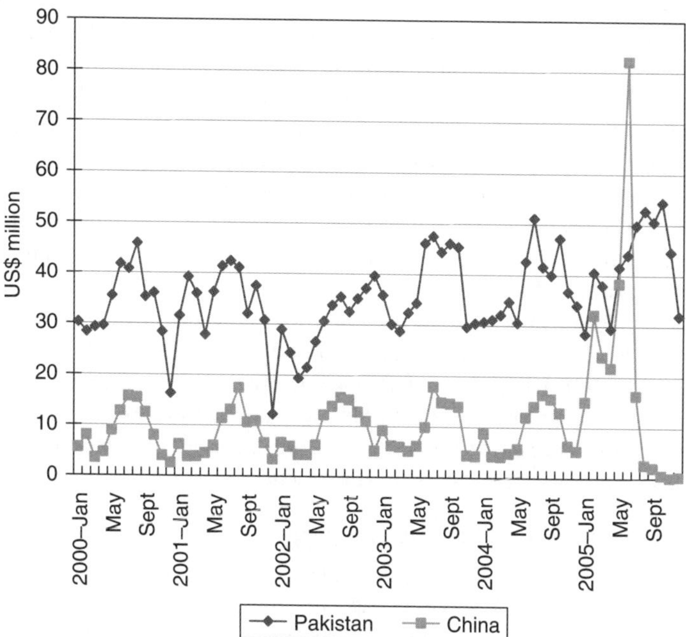

Figure 3.1 Value of monthly imports of men's knit shirts (MFA category 338)
Source: OTEXA

of its direct competitors India and Bangladesh. Thus, the Pakistani knitwear industry, which showed weak performance following the MFA phase-out, has expressed serious concern that Pakistan's knitwear exports could be swept away by India and Bangladesh.

3.3 Competitiveness of the Pakistani garment industry

3.3.1 Labour endowment and productivity in Pakistan

The effects of phasing out the MFA cannot yet be measured precisely, but an increase in Chinese exports in the post-MFA era can be expected. Intensified competition with India and Bangladesh can also be predicted. The garment industry is labour-intensive, and the labour-to-capital endowment ratio is higher in Pakistan than in China or India.[11] Therefore, according to the Heckscher–Ohlin trade theory, Pakistan should have a comparative advantage over China and India in the garment industry. However, as Krugman and Obstfeld (2000) point out, competitiveness is not in reality necessarily determined by factor endowment. For example, Fukunishi (2005) compared the garment industry in Kenya with that in Bangladesh and indicated that Kenyan manufacturers 'can only create less products and employment than expected from the pattern of its factor endowment due to wage rigidity' (Fukunishi 2005: 251). The garment industry in Pakistan seems to have the same problem. Thus, the competitiveness of the Pakistani garment industry, focusing on wage levels, is further examined in this chapter.

High labour productivity reduces labour cost, so in principle, a comparison of labour costs should include not only wage levels but also labour productivity. Labour productivity in Pakistan may be assumed to be lower than in China and India. A study conducted by World Bank and SMEDA (Small and Medium Enterprise Development Authority) (2003) shows that Pakistan's labour productivity is lower than that of China and India, despite its higher capital intensity per labour. With this assumption, it would be sufficient to show that Pakistan has a higher wage level than China or India in order to show that Pakistan's labour cost is higher than these two countries. On the other hand, it is necessary to examine the difference in labour productivity between Pakistan and Bangladesh in order to show that Pakistan's labour costs are higher than those of Bangladesh. The same study shows that Pakistan's labour productivity is higher than that of Bangladesh, but the difference in productivity between the two countries can be explained primarily by Pakistan's higher capital intensity per labour. Thus, Pakistan's labour quality can be assumed to be no higher than that of China, India or Bangladesh, and focusing on wage levels does not detract from the objectives of this study.

3.3.2 Level of per capita income and wages

Following the method used by Hirano (2005: 135), Table 3.4(a) shows a comparison of both nominal and real wages of the garment sector[12] and the ratio of the wage in the garment sector to GNP per capita and to the average wage of manufacturing sectors in major knitwear-exporting countries (except high-income countries). Latest data available for Pakistan are those from 1996, so the 1996 current price data for

Table 3.4(a) Wages in the garment sector (1996): comparison with GNP per capita (US$)

Major knitwear-exporting countries (except high-income countries)	*Wage[1] in garment sector (nominal)*	*Wage in garment sector (real)[2]*	*Ratio of wage in garment sector to average wage in manufacturing sectors*	*Ratio of wage in garment sector to GNP per capita*
Pakistan	1,883	1,883	0.92	3.92
India	730	911	0.57	1.92
Bangladesh	519	605	0.91	2.00
Cambodia	532	–	0.78	1.77
Thailand	3,049	2,070	0.79	1.03
Vietnam	772	1,254	0.82	2.66
Turkey	2,842	1,826	0.48	1.00
Mexico	2,389	1,496	0.48	0.65
Indonesia	1,120	1,030	0.76	1.04
Philippines	2,092	1,921	0.68	1.80
Peru	2,258	1,234	0.41	0.93
Malaysia	3,772	2,690	0.70	0.86
Sri Lanka	749	695	0.94	1.01
Morocco	2,480	1,915	0.58	1.92
Jordan	1,670	1,084	0.55	1.01
Colombia	2,588	2,438	0.57	1.21
Mauritius	2,890	2,103	0.82	0.78
Tunisia	3,466	2,451	0.54	1.80
El Salvador	2,110	1,039	0.69	1.24
Bolivia	1,336	1,381	0.49	1.61
Brazil	4,084	1,765	0.44	0.93
South Africa	4,375	2,778	0.49	1.24
Nepal	445	693	1.17	2.12
African countries				
Gabon	3,414	1,634	0.31	0.86
Cote d'Ivoire	4,220	3,031	0.66	6.39
Senegal	608	528	0.20	1.07
Cameroon	2,593	2,244	0.85	4.25
Zambia	1,327	951	0.69	3.69
Nigeria	1,423	1,548	1.09	5.93
Zimbabwe	2,125	2,299	0.47	3.48
Kenya	1,070	1,134	0.69	3.34
Ethiopia	479	719	0.60	4.79

Notes: 1. Wage data for Bangladesh, Cambodia and Gambia are from 1995; data for Vietnam and Botswana are from 1998.
2. Real wages are calculated over purchasing power in Pakistan.
Source: UNIDO (United Nations Industrial Development Organization) (2005a, b); World Bank (1998).

each country are used. For comparison, the table also shows data for African countries, although they are not major exporting countries. As described later, Pakistan shares specific features with African countries. Wage data later than 1986 for the Chinese garment sector do not exist in the UNIDO database. Table 3.4(b) contains the same items found in Table 3.4(a), but they are based on data from 1986 for

Table 3.4(b) Wages in the garment sector (1986): comparison with GNP per capita (US$)

	Wage in garment sector (nominal)	*Wage in garment sector (real)*	*Ratio of wage in garment sector to average wage in manufacturing sectors*	*Ratio of wage in garment sector to GNP per capita*
China	346	457	0.92	1.15
Pakistan	1,322	1,322	0.92	3.78

Source: UNIDO (2005a); World Bank (1988).

both Pakistan and China. Since these data are quite old, Table 3.4(b) is provided solely for reference in order to suggest, given its level of per capita income, that the wage level in the Pakistani garment sector tends to be high.

Table 3.4(a) shows that the wage level of the Pakistani garment sector is quite dissimilar from its GNP per capita when compared with other major knitwear-exporting countries. The wage level in the garment sector is four times that of the GNP per capita in Pakistan but twice that of GNP per capita in direct competitors such as India and Bangladesh. Hirano points out that 'there are exceptionally few countries other than African countries' in which the average manufacturing wage is so far different from its GDP per capita (Hirano 2005: 137). Pakistan is one of those 'exceptional' countries. Hirano also concludes that 'African countries generally do not have a competitive advantage in low labour costs'. Thus, African countries are excluded from the formula of economic development that begins in labour-intensive industries, a phenomenon experienced by Asian countries (Hirano 2005: 131–7). This implies that Pakistan, as well as many African countries, is not competitive in labour costs and thus faces difficulty in following a development process that begins in labour-intensive industries (experienced by East Asian countries and also followed by South East Asian countries).

3.3.3 Comparison of current wage levels

Wage levels of Pakistan, India and Bangladesh may be compared using data obtained from original surveys. Sections 3.4.2 and 3.5.2 contain details of the wage level of Pakistan. Wage levels of India are taken from the survey reported in Chapter 2, and those of Bangladesh are obtained from Murayama (2006). Values were calculated at the August 2006 price level and then converted into US dollars using the average exchange rate of August 2006.[13] For the same reason mentioned in note 12, real wages of India, Bangladesh and China are shown in parentheses, and these were calculated at an adjusted exchange rate relative to purchasing power in Pakistan. The average wage for all garment production workers in Pakistan is $US102, and the average for the subgroup of sewing operators is $US107. The average wage of sewing operators in India is $US59 ($US81). The average wage of all garment workers in Bangladesh is $US31 ($US38). The study survey reveals a relatively high wage level in the Pakistani garment industry.

Wages actually paid in China may be less than those reported in the official data. A survey conducted by the suppliers of a major US retailer suggests that the actual wage may be around 25 cents per hour, less than half the official minimum wage rate of 59 cents per hour (Saxena and Wiebe 2005: 61–2). According to the survey, the monthly wage in China, even with the assumption of having work time of 10 hours per day and 30 days per month, may be only about $US75 ($US81).

These comparisons are approximate, but the wage level in the Pakistani garment industry appears to be higher than in China, India or Bangladesh. Thus, labour costs may be one of the factors preventing the Pakistani garment industry from being competitive in the international market. Factual evidence for this is found in interviews with managers in the Pakistani garment industry.

3.4 Survey of managers in the garment industry

3.4.1 Survey outline

In the post-MFA era, competition is expected to increase further, and the issue arises as to whether or not the Pakistani garment industry can survive in the international market given this trend. As discussed above, it seems that the Pakistani garment industry has both a high wage level and a lack of quality labour. Both of these can pose a threat to survival amidst intensifying competition. In order to confirm wage levels and labour quality, and to further determine the indigenous factors contributing to the problems of higher wage levels and labour quality, interviews with 10 knitwear and 5 denim wear[14] manufacturers in Lahore were conducted in November 2005. Respondents were chief executives of the companies as well as their delegated financial and human resource managers. Companies interviewed were not randomly chosen from the population of all the garment manufacturer-exporters.[15] Rather, interviewed companies were carefully selected so that the sample would represent the dispersion of the population. An exception was the inclusion of one foreign-owned knitwear company. Foreign-owned companies are very rare in the Pakistani garment industry.

Table 3.5 presents an outline of the interviewed companies. Even the oldest company started its operation after 1990; this reveals that the garment industry in Pakistan is relatively young when compared with the upstream textile industry. There was only one listed company among the interviewees, and this also reflects the characteristic that the garment industry in Pakistan is comprised of relatively small and medium-size enterprises (SMEs) when compared with the upstream textile industry. There was only one company with an organized labour union, and this is another difference relative to the textile companies. As described in detail in Sections 3.4.2 and 3.4.3, most companies employed 90 per cent of their sewing operators at piece rates.[16] All of their products were for export. Destinations were almost exclusively US or EU countries. A separate category C* was set up for the one foreign-owned company which has different characteristics from other companies. Its distinctive feature was that most of its production workers are female and hired at fixed rates.

Table 3.5 Outline of interviewed garment manufacturing companies

		Number of employees including piece rate	Number of companies	Year production started				Legal status					Labour union	Average unit product price (US$)	Average annual sales in 2005[1]	Average % of exports to US among total exports
				1990–92	1993–95	1996–98	1999–2001	Listed	Quoted (unlisted)	Private limited	Partnership	Sole proprietor				
A	Knitwear	>1,000	5	4	0	1	0	0	2	3	0	0	1	4.7	17,776,000	76.0
B	Knitwear	501–1,000	2	1	1	0	0	0	0	1	0	1	0	3.9	7,527,601	40.0
C	Knitwear	100–500	2	1	1	0	0	0	0	1	0	1	0	3.3	6,189,360	79.0
C*[2]	Knitwear		1	0	0	0	1	1	0	0	0	0	0	3.5	2,007,360	0.0
D	Denim wear	501–1,000	2	2	0	0	0	0	0	2	0	0	0	5.9	6,660,960	0.0
E	Denim wear	100–500	3	0	0	1	2	0	0	2	1	0	0	5.5	1,112,776	3.3

Notes: 1. Estimated, since the figures are for the calendar year, not the fiscal year.
2. One company is classified separately in category C* because it has totally different characteristics from the other companies and is not comparable; it hires mainly female workers at fixed rates and is 100% foreign invested.
Source: Survey conducted by the author in November 2005.

3.4.2 Wage levels in the garment industry

Interviewees think that the cost of labour is one of the major factors making Pakistan uncompetitive, especially against China and Bangladesh. The common factors that drive down labour costs in China and Bangladesh are, according to the interviewees: (1) the availability of female workers, (2) higher labour productivity, and (3) lower wages. This section focuses on wage levels.

Table 3.6 shows monthly wages of the Pakistani garment manufacturing companies that were interviewed. All companies except the one in category C* employed sewing operators at piece rates. Some piece rate workers were employed in the finishing department, but interviewees generally used the term 'piece rate worker' to refer to sewing or ironing operators. Since piece rate workers are discussed in detail in the next section, only wages are given here. Table 3.6 shows that the monthly wage is higher for piece rate workers than for fixed rate workers. The average monthly wage of all production workers was calculated using the ratio of the number of piece rate workers to fixed rate workers. Except for that of C*, all categories show that the wages of piece rate workers raise the average wage to a large degree. Comparing competitor wage levels shown in Section 3.3.3, the wage level obtained in the interviews indicates relatively high wages for the Pakistani garment industry.

3.4.3 Bottleneck for garment manufacturing companies

According to the interviews, common factors resulting in higher labour costs in Pakistan include low labour productivity, the lack of female workers, and a high wage level. Interviewees were asked what they viewed as bottlenecks for their companies in competing in export markets.[17] Labour quality was ranked as highest for competing in export markets. Concretely, this bottleneck implies a lack of high-quality sewing operators. The quality of sewing operators is important because out of all the processes it is sewing in which labour quality matters the most. The sewing process involves more than 50 per cent of the total production workers in a factory. The lack of high-quality labour (or low labour productivity) together with the lack of female workers and high wage levels seems to be closely related to one distinctive feature of the Pakistani garment industry, namely that sewing operators are mostly males hired at piece rates. According to interviews, there are few highly skilled workers but many 'skilled'[18] workers, those who do not need basic training. Characteristics of Pakistan's sewing operators and how these characteristics may be related to the lack of quality labour and high labour costs are examined next.

According to the interviews, it is customary practice to hire 'skilled' sewing operators at piece rates. One of the negative effects of a piece rate system is that manufacturers cannot control turnover rates. Given the nature of the piece rate worker system, it is difficult for manufacturers to keep highly skilled workers. Thus, manufacturers cannot help but raise wages. Further, the difficulty of recruiting piece rate workers adds premiums to the wages of highly skilled workers. Six out of nine knitwear manufacturers, excluding the one in category C*, and all five denim wear manufacturers said that it is difficult to recruit piece rate workers. It is possible that excess demand for highly skilled sewing operators eventually leads to raising

Table 3.6 Monthly wages[1] in Pakistan garment manufacturing companies (US$)

		Number of employees including piece rate	*Number of companies*	*Average monthly wage of full-time production workers*	*Average monthly wage of piece rate workers*	*Ratio of the number of piece rate workers to the number of fixed rate workers*	*Average monthly wage of all production workers*	*Ratio of labour cost to total operation cost*
A	Knitwear	>1,000	5	82.8	170.4	0.53	113.1	0.20
B		501–1,000	2	85.8	139.9	2.86	125.9	0.15
C		100–500	2	74.5	176.1	1.85	140.5	0.24
C*			1	72.2	–	0.00	72.2	0.15
D	Denim wear	501–1,000	2	85.8	175.6	0.72	123.4	0.13
E		100–500	3	84.7	126.6	1.13	106.9	0.18

Note: 1. Figures are calculated at the price level of August 2006. Currency is converted at the average exchange rate of August 2006, $US1 = 60.33 Pakistan rupees (*Source: IFS*, IMF).
Source: Survey conducted by the author in November 2005.

the overall wage level. Another negative effect is that the piece rate system is likely to cause lower product quality. This is because piece rate workers by definition only care about how many pieces they produce and do not have quality incentives such as being promoted. Interviewees said that highly skilled piece rate workers are not willing to accept full-time status such as that of a supervisor, because they can earn more as a piece rate worker.[19]

Given these negative effects, why do manufacturing companies not shift from a piece rate to a fixed rate payment system with full-time workers? The interviewees indicated that it is a matter of custom, and they cannot do anything to change it. Is there any positive reason for a company to hire sewing operators at piece rates? Interviewees said that they can respond to seasonal or other sudden fluctuations in orders by hiring sewing operators at piece rates. However, response to fluctuations in orders does not fully explain the hiring of the sewing operators at piece rates. It was observed in many factories that about one-third of the piece rate operators were idle away from their working time, even during peak season. This may indicate that Pakistani manufacturers cannot make annual production plans and arrange for proper placement of production workers. Another positive reason for having a piece rate system is that manufacturers do not have to provide basic training, because piece rate workers are already basically 'skilled'. Hiring 'skilled' workers at piece rates seems more profitable in the short run; companies do not have to assume the risk of keeping on idle workers when orders decline, nor do they have to provide any official training. However, it would still appear to cost less to shift from piece rate workers to fixed rate workers in the long run. Table 3.6 shows the annual average of monthly wages, and the wage level of piece rate workers seems high even after averaging out seasonal fluctuation.

Recognizing that it costs less in the long run to hire workers at fixed rates, the one manufacturer in category C* employs only female workers as sewing operators at fixed rates. In addition, a few manufacturers have started to provide training on sewing machine operation for female workers in an attempt to shift their payment system from piece rates to fixed rates.[20] According to the interviews, manufacturers perceive that it is difficult to control male workers, even those hired on a full-time, fixed rate basis, but that it is relatively easy to control female workers in terms of turnover rates and training. Female workers are thought to do more careful sewing, and this may lead to higher-quality products. In reality, however, most of the sewing operators in Pakistan are male piece rate workers[21] (Table 3.7). This contrasts markedly with China where 80–90 per cent of sewing operators are female workers, or with Bangladesh where more than 60 per cent are such. In Pakistan, it is difficult to shift from male to female workers. Hiring female workers is itself difficult due to social norms in Pakistan. For example, companies hiring female workers are required to arrange a suitable working environment such as a working floor exclusively for female workers. Further, when evaluating labour productivity, some managers tend to focus on how many pieces a worker can complete per minute rather than how carefully the work is done. These managers believe that female workers are less productive because their sewing speed is slow. They further indicated that they are planning to shift to hiring only male workers for sewing

Table 3.7 Percentage of female sewing operators in Pakistan garment manufacturing companies

		Number of employees including piece rate	*Number of companies*	*Percentage of female workers among sewing operators*
A	Knitwear	>1,000	5	15.9
B		501–1,000	2	3.5
C		100–500	2	0.0
C*			1	100.0
D	Denim wear	501–1,000	2	7.7
E		100–500	3	0.0

Source: Survey conducted by the author in November 2005.

operators. It should be noted that a technical advisor of the Japan International Cooperation Agency (JICA) who teaches sewing techniques in such factories has recommended a shift to female sewing workers because it is easier to provide training for them and to maintain the quality of products, something necessary in order to survive in the export market.

3.5 Survey of production workers in the garment industry

3.5.1 Survey outline

On the basis of the interviews with managers, 315 production workers in knitwear and denim wear factories were interviewed in August 2006. The author attended 93 per cent of these interviews. In the sample, 82 per cent of the workers were employed at companies noted in Table 3.5. The remainder worked for similar exporting manufacturers. The objective of the interviews was to confirm wage levels from the worker point of view and to examine whether or not managerial perceptions of the bottleneck (lack of quality labour and high labour cost resulting from piece rate employment) are reasonable. Workers were chosen randomly in each factory, with some conditions. The first condition was that 60 per cent of the sample be from knitwear manufacturing companies that have already started to show stagnant performance under intensifying international competition. The second condition was that 60 per cent of the sample be sewing operators. Sewing operators constitute 60 per cent of all production workers in the companies that were interviewed, and they engage in the most quality-sensitive work. The third condition was that no more than 30 workers from any one company be interviewed. Interviews were conducted at both the workplace and at the interviewee's residence. This was done to assess how honestly the interviewee responded at the workplace. It should be noted that there were no remarkable differences in answers between the two places. One reason may be that at the workplace, the influence of the interviewees' colleagues and supervisors was minimized by secluding the interviewee from others and by assuring interviewee confidentiality.

Table 3.8 shows the number of interviewed production workers in each category. As in Table 3.5, category C* includes the one distinctive company which mainly hires female workers at fixed rates. As discussed earlier, except in category C*, production workers in the Pakistani garment industry are predominantly male. Further, except in category C*, the payment system is primarily determined by the type of work. Sewing and ironing operators are largely paid at piece rates.

3.5.2 Wages of production workers

In order to confirm wage levels reported by managers, interviewees were asked about their wages. Table 3.9 shows the wages in August 2006 and in December 2004 obtained from the employee interviews. Piece rate workers were also asked about annual wages in 2004 and 2005. Piece rate wages reported for August 2006 may be more accurate than the annual average because they are the amount actually paid at the time of the interview. However, they may not be comparable with fixed wages if there are large seasonal fluctuations. Therefore, both figures are shown in the table. Nevertheless, there are no significant differences between the wage level in August 2006 and the annual average wage level in 2005.[22]

Wage levels provided by the managers seen in Table 3.6 do not deviate from those given by production workers, although managers tend to reveal wage levels in the peak season rather than the average. Specifically, the wage level of piece rate sewing operators in the knitwear sector in 2004 reached $US166 (Table 3.9). Perceptions of managers that wages paid to piece rate workers raise overall wage levels can thus be understood.

Although the wage level is higher for piece rate workers, changes between 2004 and 2005 or 2006 seem to be less favourable for them. In fact, with few exceptions, only wages of piece rate workers decreased. However, piece rate status still seems to be preferred by most workers. Piece rate workers were also asked how they regard their payment system and specifically whether or not they would be willing to be hired at fixed rates. Table 3.10(a) shows that more than 70 per cent of piece rate workers wished to retain their piece rate status. The main reason given was that they can earn more at piece rates than at fixed rates (Table 3.10(a)). This supports perceptions of managers that piece rate workers raise the overall wage level. However, opinions of those who are willing to be hired at fixed rates should be noted (Table 3.10(b)). They said that as long as orders are coming in, they prefer to be hired at piece rates; but when orders are stagnant, they prefer to be hired at fixed rates. This seems consistent with the fact that as competition has increased since the end of 2004, only the wages of piece rate workers have decreased. This indicates that, although in a minority, some workers have begun to feel the effects of intensifying competition in the post-MFA era. Although significant effects of phasing out the MFA have not yet been seen, opinions of most piece rate workers may change if orders drastically decrease after the end of 2008.

3.5.3 Factors in raising the wage level

What factors may raise wage levels? Generally speaking, the Minimum Wages Act, labour unions, and efficiency wages can be regarded as reasons for the downward

Table 3.8 Number[1] of production workers interviewed

		Number of employees including piece rate in the company	*Type of work and payment system*																		*Total*
			Sewing		*Cutting*[2]		*Packing*		*Ironing*		*Supervisor, coordinator*		*Quality controller/checker (including Finishing Dept.)*		*Mechanic, electrician*		*Helper*		*Others*[3]		
			Fixed rate	*Piece rate*	*Fixed rate*	*Piece rate*	*Fixed rate*	*Piece rate*	*Fixed rate*	*Piece rate*	*Fixed rate*	*Piece rate*	*Fixed rate*	*Piece rate*	*Fixed rate*	*Piece rate*	*Fixed rate*	*Piece rate*	*Fixed rate*	*Piece rate*	
A	Knitwear	>1,000	9 (0)	56 (0)	8 (0)	0	3 (0)	1 (0)	0	4 (0)	9 (0)	0	13 (2)	0	1 (0)	0	8 (2)	0	2 (0)	0	114 (4)
B		501–1,000	–	–	–	–	–	–	–	–	–	–	–	–	–	–	–	–	–	–	–
C		100–500	0	25 (0)	0	0	2 (0)	0	0	3 (0)	2 (0)	0	3 (0)	0	0	0	3 (0)	0	0	0	38 (0)
C*			20 (20)	0	1 (1)	0	1 (0)	0	0	0	4 (4)	0	1 (1)	0	0	0	8 (8)	0	0	0	35 (34)
		Subtotal	29 (20)	81 (0)	9 (1)	0	6 (0)	1 (0)	0	7 (0)	15 (4)	0	17 (3)	0	1 (0)	0	19 (10)	0	2 (0)	0	187 (38)
D	Denim wear	>1,000	–	–	–	–	–	–	–	–	–	–	–	–	–	–	–	–	–	–	–
E		501–1,000	1 (1)	22 (3)	2 (0)	0	1 (0)	0	0	1 (0)	1 (0)	0	4 (0)	0	0	0	1 (0)	0	2 (0)	0	35 (4)
F		100–500	5 (0)	50 (0)	6 (0)	0	2 (0)	0	0	7 (0)	5 (0)	0	8 (0)	0	1 (0)	0	6 (0)	2 (2)	1 (0)	0	93 (2)
		Subtotal	6 (1)	72 (3)	8 (0)	0	3 (0)	0	0	8 (0)	6 (0)	0	12 (0)	0	1 (0)	0	7 (0)	2 (2)	3 (0)	0	128 (6)
		Total	188 (24)		17 (1)		10 (0)		15 (0)		21 (4)		29 (3)		2 (0)		28 (12)		5 (0)		315 (44)

Notes: 1. Figures are the total number of production workers interviewed in the category. The number of female workers is shown in parentheses.
2. 'Cutting' includes all the operators in the cutting department such as laying, shaping and measuring operators.
3. 'Others' includes printing, dyeing, and washing (denim) operators, and also storekeepers.
Source: Survey conducted by the author in August 2006.

Table 3.9 Average monthly wages[1] of production workers by type of work and payment system (US$)

		Fixed rate worker[2]						Piece rate worker											
		Aug. 2006		Dec. 2004		% change		Aug. 2006		Dec. 2004		% change		Annual average[3]					
														2005		2004		% change	
		Male	Female	Male	Female	Male	Female	Male	Female	Male	Female	Male	Female	Male	Female	Male	Female	Male	Female
Knitwear	Sewing	109.0	75.7	100.9	57.6	8.0	31.5	121.1	–	166.2	–	–27.1	–	117.4	–	132.5	–	–11.4	–
	Cutting	97.7	59.3	87.0	–	12.3	–	–	–	–	–	–	–	–	–	–	–	–	–
	Packing	81.9	–	67.3	–	21.8	–	116.0	–	115.3	–	0.6	–	125.5	–	120.1	–	4.4	–
	Ironing	–	–	–	–	–	–	116.5	–	135.2	–	–13.8	–	121.9	–	131.1	–	–7.0	–
	Supervisor, coordinator	145.2	86.0	124.8	–	16.3	–	–	–	–	–	–	–	–	–	–	–	–	–
	Quality controller/checker (including Finishing Dept.)	103.8	67.3	97.1	86.5	6.9	–22.2	–	–	–	–	–	–	–	–	–	–	–	–
	Mechanic, electrician	74.6	–	74.0	–	0.8	–	–	–	–	–	–	–	–	–	–	–	–	–
	Helper	74.8	59.8	64.5	55.8	15.9	7.2	–	–	–	–	–	–	–	–	–	–	–	–
	Other	79.6	–	73.8	–	7.8	–	–	–	–	–	–	–	–	–	–	–	–	–
Denim wear	Sewing	103.4	90.3	80.9	76.9	27.8	17.5	100.8	99.5	114.3	100.9	–11.8	–1.4	103.6	102.3	104.8	96.1	–1.2	6.5
	Cutting	78.5	–	61.0	–	28.7	–	–	–	–	–	–	–	–	–	–	–	–	–
	Packing	91.7	–	64.1	–	43.1	–	–	–	–	–	–	–	–	–	–	–	–	–
	Ironing	–	–	–	–	–	–	93.9	–	90.1	–	4.2	–	84.3	–	82.8	–	1.8	–
	Supervisor, coordinator	151.0	–	134.5	–	12.2	–	–	–	–	–	–	–	–	–	–	–	–	–
	Quality controller/checker (including Finishing Dept.)	96.2	–	79.9	–	20.4	–	–	–	–	–	–	–	–	–	–	–	–	–
	Mechanic, electrician	69.6	–	57.7	–	20.7	–	–	–	–	–	–	–	–	–	–	–	–	–
	Helper	63.3	–	51.1	–	23.9	–	–	43.9	–	50.9	–	–13.8	–	–	–	–	–	–
	Other	82.8	–	70.4	–	17.6	–	–	–	–	–	–	–	–	–	–	–	–	–

Notes: 1. Wages are calculated at the August 2006 price level and converted into US dollars at the average exchange rate in August 2006, $US1 = 60.33 Pakistan rupees.
2. Wages for the workers paid at fixed rates include: basic wages and salaries, cost-of-living allowances and other guaranteed and regularly paid allowances as well as averaged-out overtime payments, bonuses and gratuities, and other irregularly paid allowances.
3. Annual average is calculated as annual wages divided by 12. The intention is to see the seasonal fluctuation of piece rate workers' wages.
Source: Survey conducted by the author in August 2006.

Table 3.10(a) Reasons for preferring piece rate status

	Number of piece rate workers
Total (sewing operator)	171 (153)
Willing to stay at piece rate status	122
Reasons (one choice)	
Higher earnings	96
Freedom	23
Shorter working hours	2
On-time payment	1

Source: Survey conducted by the author in August 2006.

Table 3.10(b) Reasons for preferring fixed salary status

	Number of piece rate workers
Total (sewing operator)	171 (153)
Willing to be hired at fixed salary status	47
Reasons (multiple choices)	
Higher earnings	20
Shorter working hours	1
Better working environment	2
Job security	31
Other[1]	11

Note: 1. 'Other' includes: less workload at fixed rate (1, = the number of respondents), desire to use paid holidays (3), predictability and stability of income (5), protection from minimum wage 4000 Pakistan rupees (1), desire to be a supervisor, who is usually hired at fixed rates (1).
Source: Survey conducted by the author in August 2006.

rigidity of wages (Higuchi 1996). In the context of the Pakistani garment industry, the former two reasons may not be applicable because piece rate workers are not in reality protected by the Minimum Wages Act, and labour unions do not exist in most companies. Hypotheses based on efficiency wages as a factor include several explanations such as securing subsistence costs of workers or controlling turnover rates (Higuchi 1996: 294–5). Since the official price of subsistence commodities is not high in Pakistan,[23] turnover rates become the primary focus.

The annual turnover rates of piece rate and fixed rate sewing operators were calculated based on their working experience (Table 3.11). The difference between fixed rate and piece rate workers is ambiguous. This is counter-intuitive because the piece rate workers can move to other factories whenever they want.[24] It is difficult to judge whether or not the turnover rates shown here are high or low.

Table 3.11 Turnover rate of sewing operators

	Fixed rate (35)[1]		*Piece rate (153)*	
	Male (14)	*Female (21)*	*Male (150)*	*Female (3)*
Average years of total working period in the current company	6.3	2.7	4.9	7.5
Annual turnover rate	0.33	0.04	0.35	n.a.[2]

Notes: 1. Numbers in parentheses indicate the total number of workers falling into each category.
2. 'n.a.' means that no worker in the category had job experience in the garment industry before joining the current company.
Source: Survey conducted by the author in August 2006.

However, there is one interesting feature in the length of continuous employment. The annual turnover rate can be interpreted as the probability of one randomly chosen worker leaving a company in one year. Using this probability as a basis for comparison, the average number of years in the working period of the current company is relatively long. For example, piece rate sewing operators in the knitwear sector have worked in their current company for five years on average. In a way, this is surprising for piece rate workers. It seems that most of the interviewees tend to stay for a relatively long time in their current company. It may be that companies for which the interviewees work are relatively successful in the face of intensifying competition. These companies may thus keep workers motivated to stay in the same company by paying piece rates that are higher than market rates. 'Higher earnings' was in fact given as the main reason for workers to shift from their previous to their current company (Table 3.12).

That the labour market is one for sellers (workers) is supported by the fact that 64.4 per cent of workers perceived that there are many jobs in the market and 85.9 per cent thought that it is not difficult to find a job. Worker perceptions are consistent with those of managers with regard to recruiting workers as seen in Section 3.4.3. Table 3.13 shows how workers find a job. Friends appear to be the main source for workers when it comes to finding their current job. Since friends are generally more skilled than the workers they introduce, skilled workers seem to have bargaining power not only in their skills, but also in the network of workers. Piece rates are considered to reflect worker productivity (Shearer 1996), but piece rates can cause wage levels to rise higher than worker productivity when such bargaining power is very strong. In the knitwear industry, the maximum monthly wage of a piece rate worker is $US365, and 16 out of 81 (19.8 per cent) piece rate workers earn more than the average of supervisors. In the denim wear industry, the maximum monthly wage of a piece rate worker is $US199, and the number of

Table 3.12 Reason for shifting from the previous company to the current company

	Number of workers	
	All (both piece/non-piece rate) workers	*Piece rate workers*
Possess working experience in the garment company (out of 315)	199	127
Reason for shifting to the current company (one choice)		
Higher earnings	64	34
Nearer location	29	22
Closure of the previous company	24	16
Better working environment	20	17
Relationship (followed teachers, supervisors, or friends)	20	13
Layoff	11	3
Less workload (in the current company)	9	3
Delayed payment	7	6
No or less work in the previous company	6	6
Other	9	7

Source: Survey conducted by the author in August 2006.

Table 3.13 Information sources: how a job was found

	Number of workers
Responses (out of 315)	312
Information sources[1] (one choice)	
Friends	115
Relatives	69
Manager or supervisor in the factory	58
Worker in the factory	28
Teacher	16
Noticeboard in front of the factory	13
Own visit	8
Contractor (labour intermediary agent)	5

Note: 1. Answer options included formal sources such as 'job-placement advertisement' and 'job-placement agency', but no one selected those answers.
Source: Survey conducted by the author in August 2006.

piece rate workers who earn more than the supervisors' average is 5 out of 72 (6.9 per cent). Especially in the knitwear sector, it seems evident that wages of highly skilled piece rate workers are higher than those of supervisors.

Information in Table 3.13 shows the probabilities that labour intermediary agents have bargaining power, or that they can lift overall wage-related costs, to be quite low. Out of 315 workers, only 13 (4.1 per cent) were contract workers whose direct employer was not a manufacturing company but rather a labour intermediary agent. Workers were also asked whether or not they have to pay commission to someone such as a supervisor or labour intermediary agent. Only 22 workers (7.0 per cent) indicated that they had to pay commission to someone. The rate of commission ranged from 3.3 to 25.0 per cent, and the average rate was 11.2 per cent. The types of workers who paid commission were sewing operators, ironing operators, or helpers; and all of them were hired at piece rates. The percentage of ironing workers who paid commission was relatively high for the sample. Four out of 15 ironing operators were hired by a labour intermediary agent and thus had to pay commission to an agent.

3.5.4 Labour and product quality

The difficulty of controlling product quality is often seen as a primary disadvantage of the piece rate system (Lazear 1986; Freeman and Kleiner 1998; Baland et al. 1999). The priority for piece rate workers is more likely to be speedy work (counting the number of acceptable pieces made) rather than meticulous work. According to the Japanese technical advisor of JICA mentioned earlier, the level accepted by supervisors or quality checkers is low in the Pakistani garment industry, so manufacturers face difficulty in shifting to a 'high-end' market. According to 83.7 per cent of workers, supervisors value meticulous rather than speedy work in their evaluations. This may simply reflect workers' tendency to be confident in their own skills. So workers themselves subjectively believe that their supervisors evaluate them for their meticulous rather than speedy work. The methodology of the study may not have adequately dealt with this ambivalence.

In the survey, 70 out of 109 workers who perceived a lack of jobs in the market believed that they have skills and that it will not be difficult to find a job. This is also their subjective perception. Therefore education levels may actually be more relevant for the real production quality of garment workers in Pakistan. Table 3.14 shows these education levels. In urban Punjab, where Lahore is located, male and female worker illiteracy rates are 28.7 and 43.8 per cent respectively (GoP 2004). The education level of the study sample, especially that of piece rate sewing or ironing operators, was no higher than the official Pakistani level which has been seen to be low for the level of per capita income (Easterly 2003).

Table 3.15 shows the type of training they had received before joining their current company. Most workers indicated that they had obtained their skills informally on the job. Only three females and one male mechanic responded that they had received training in formal institutions. The question included the response 'formal training in previous garment companies', but no worker chose this option.

Table 3.14 Education level of the workers interviewed[1]

	Sewing				*Ironing (all piece rate)*	*Supervisor, coordinator (all fixed rate)*		*Helper*		*Others*[2]	
	Fixed rate		*Piece rate*								
	Male	*Female*	*Male*	*Female*	*Male*	*Male*	*Female*	*Male*	*Female*	*Male*	*Female*
Knitwear											
Illiterate	0	0.25 (5)	0.26 (21)		0.71 (5)	0.09 (1)	0	0.22 (2)	0.80 (8)	0.09 (3)	0
Literate											
<5 yrs	0	0	0.05 (4)		0	0	0	0	0	0	0
5 yrs (primary completed)	0.11 (1)	0.15 (3)	0.09 (7)		0	0	0.25 (1)	0	0	0	0.25 (1)
8 yrs (middle completed)	0.44 (4)	0.25 (5)	0.40 (32)		0.14 (1)	0	0.50 (2)	0.44 (4)	0.10 (1)	0.31 (10)	0
>8 yrs	0.44 (4)	0.35 (7)	0.21 (17)		0.14 (1)	0.91 (10)	0.25 (1)	0.33 (3)	0.10 (1)	0.59 (19)	0.75 (3)
Subtotal	1.00 (9)	1.00 (20)	1.00 (81)		1.00 (7)	1.00 (11)	1.00 (4)	1.00 (9)	1.00 (10)	1.00 (32)	1.00 (4)
Denim wear											
Illiterate	0.20 (1)	0	0.43 (30)	0	0.38 (3)	0.17 (1)		0.43 (3)	1.00 (2)	0.07 (2)	
Literate											
<5 yrs	0	0	0.06 (4)	0	0	0		0	0	0	
5 yrs (primary completed)	0.20 (1)	1.00 (1)	0.19 (13)	0	0	0		0	0	0	
8 yrs (middle completed)	0.40 (2)	0	0.14 (10)	0.33 (1)	0.38 (3)	0.50 (3)		0.14 (1)	0	0.37 (10)	
>8 yrs	0.20 (1)	0	0.17 (12)	0.67 (2)	0.25 (2)	0.33 (2)		0.43 (3)	0	0.56 (15)	
Subtotal	1.00 (5)	1.00 (1)	1.00 (69)	1.00 (3)	1.00 (8)	1.00 (6)		1.00 (7)	1.00 (2)	1.00 (27)	

Notes: 1. Figures are the percentage (100% = 1.00) falling into each education level in the subtotal of workers. The number of workers in the category is in parentheses.
2. 'Others' include cutting operators, packing operators, quality controllers/checkers and mechanics/electricians.
Source: Survey conducted by the author in August 2006.

Table 3.15 Training type before joining this company[1]

	Sewing				Ironing (all piece rate)	Supervisor, coordinator (all fixed rate)		Helper		Others[2]	
	Fixed rate		Piece rate								
	Male	*Female*	*Male*	*Female*	*Male*	*Male*	*Female*	*Male*	*Female*	*Male*	*Female*
Knitwear											
Formal training institution	0	0.15 (3)	0		0	0	0.25 (1)	0	0	0.03 (1)	0
Informal on the job training	0.56 (5)	0.20 (4)	0.80 (65)		0.57 (4)	0.55 (6)	0	0.33 (3)	0.30 (3)	0.59 (19)	0.25 (1)
Never trained	0.44 (4)	0.65 (13)	0.20 (16)		0.43 (3)	0.45 (5)	0.75 (3)	0.67 (6)	0.70 (7)	0.38 (12)	0.75 (3)
If never: Average days of training at this company	105	24	111		48	16	30	15	0	97	23
If never: At least a month of training in this company?[3]	4	4	9		2	2	1	2	0	6	1
Subtotal	1.00 (9)	1.00 (20)	1.00 (81)		1.00 (7)	1.00 (11)	1.00 (4)	1.00 (9)	1.00 (10)	1.00 (32)	1.00 (4)
Denim wear											
Formal training institution	0	0	0	0	0	0		0	0	0	
Informal on the job training	0.80 (4)	1.00 (1)	0.72 (49)	0.33 (1)	0.88 (7)	0.83 (5)		0.14 (1)	1.00 (2)	0.44 (12)	
Never trained	0.20 (1)	0	0.28 (19)	0.67 (2)	0.13 (1)	0.17 (1)		0.86 (6)	0	0.56 (15)	
If never: Average days of training at this company	30	n.a.	73	15	10	0		3	n.a.	51	
If never: At least a month of training in this company?	1	n.a.	19	1	0	0		0	n.a.	5	
Subtotal	1.00 (5)	1.00 (1)	1.00 (68)	1.00 (3)	1.00 (8)	1.00 (6)		1.00 (7)	1.00 (2)	1.00 (27)	

Notes: 1. Figures are the percentages (100% = 1.00) falling into each previous training level in the subtotal of workers. The number of workers in the category is in parentheses.
2. 'Others' include cutting operators, packing operators, quality controllers/checkers, and mechanics/electricians.
3. This row shows (among the workers who had never been trained before joining this company) the number of workers who have received training on each designated skill in this company for at least a month.
Source: Survey conducted by the author in August 2006.

Although the questionnaire did not include an item related to occupational caste, a large number of male sewing operators were found to be from the tailor caste. These males had learned how to use sewing machines as they grew up among relatives in the same tailor caste. Many sewing operators in the piece rate system have 'skills' to make an entire piece of clothing rather than just one part, but these 'skills' are not required in the assembly-line system adopted by exporting manufacturers. Female sewing operators in category C* have only enough skill to make a specific part assigned to them in the line. It seems that most companies (except the one in category C*) cannot adjust to the demands of rapid globalization. These demands include hiring and/or training workers in order to match the assembly-line system. Consequently, these companies will probably fail to save labour costs.

3.6 Conclusion

This chapter included an examination of possible factors that lower the competitiveness of the Pakistani garment industry in the post-MFA international market. Focus centred on distinctive features of sewing operators in the Pakistani garment industry. Two phenomena were confirmed: (1) the relatively high wage level in the Pakistani garment industry and (2) the labour quality problem faced by the industry. Possible factors related to these phenomena were examined by conducting a survey of managers and production workers in the garment industry.

Managers in the Pakistani garment industry were interviewed with regard to both wage levels and the bottleneck in international competition. In the perception of the managers, one competitive disadvantage for Pakistan is labour costs which are higher than those of competitors such as China, India and Bangladesh. Managers further think that labour quality is the bottleneck for competing in the international market.

Based on the survey with managers, production workers in the garment industry were interviewed in order to confirm wage levels and to examine factors affecting wage level and labour quality. Results of the survey support the idea that one factor explaining higher wage levels and the lack of labour quality is the fact that most sewing operators are male workers hired at piece rates. Wages in a piece rate system are considered to reflect worker productivity, but results of the survey suggest that the piece rate system in Pakistan may raise wages to a higher level than productivity or the market rate. Highly skilled workers can have more bargaining power with their skills and their networks by being hired at piece rates rather than at fixed rates because at piece rates, they can shift to any company at will. In the knitwear sector, 20 per cent of highly skilled workers earn more than supervisors. Thus, they may contribute to raising the overall wage level of the industry. Another negative aspect of the piece rate system may be the tendency toward a lack of incentive to focus on the quality of goods produced.

There are also other factors that may potentially increase wage levels and reduce product quality. The gap between demand and supply in the labour market may explain the high wage level, not only in the garment industry, but also in all formal manufacturing industries in Pakistan (as seen in Table 3.4(a)). The gap in the labour market can be explained by the lack of education that is needed to become qualified in the formal sector, the lack of female workers, labour segregation based on occupational caste, and the lack of training institutions necessary to overcome such segregation. Without training opportunities in formal training institutions or manufacturing companies, especially for female sewing operators, the gap in the labour market of the Pakistani garment industry will remain. As long as manufacturers continue to depend on workers from the tailor caste who receive informal training from family members, they will have no choice but to hire sewing operators at piece rates because of customary practice and the willingness of these workers to be hired at piece rates.

For the Pakistani garment industry to survive intensifying international competition, results of the survey indicate that it will be necessary to shift the payment system from piece rate to fixed rate with full-time workers. Of course, further study is needed on the effect of different payment systems on overall labour costs, worker productivity,[25] profitability and labour segregation in order to support views presented in this chapter. Freeman and Kleiner (1998) have shown that advantages of fixed wage over piece rate systems include among others, lower monitoring costs, lower wages, and flexibility in introducing new styles of products. The piece rate system makes it easier to deal with seasonal fluctuations, but hiring full-time workers at fixed rates seems to cost less in the long term. In order to shift to a fixed rate system, it will probably be more realistic to hire female sewing operators at fixed rates and to provide them with training, rather than to shift existing piece rate workers who prefer to remain with piece rate status. In order to achieve this objective, it will be necessary to establish and manage effective training institutions to expand the pool of sewing operators. In addition, the shift to a fixed rate system should improve the quality of products since female workers are thought to be more careful in sewing operations. Shifting from piece rate male operators to fixed rate female operators will be one of the ways to survive in an international market that has intense competition both in price and quality. Since there are few female sewing operators in Pakistan at this time, the shift represents a future potential for the Pakistani garment industry rather than a present reality.

Notes

* Tariq Munir, Sana Ullah and the author conducted the field survey for this study.

1. 'Textile industry' generally refers to the upstream textile industry (including spinning and weaving), the home textile industry and the garment industry. In the classification of the CMI (Census of Manufacturing Industries) in Pakistan, the textile industry and the garment industry both fall into the primary classification category of the 'textile industry'. The 'textile industry' as a secondary classification includes home textile as well as upstream industries, but not the garment industry. The CMI secondary classification is followed in this chapter, i.e. the term 'textile' means upstream industries and the home textile industry and does not include the garment industry.
2. Before reaching an agreement with China on export restrictions, the US invoked safeguard measures on textile and garment imports from China. WTO member countries

have the right to impose safeguard measures on imports from China until the end of 2008. This was an interim measure developed in exchange for accepting Chinese accession to the WTO. By safeguard measures, WTO member countries can limit the yearly quantity-wise growth rate of imports from China below 7.5 per cent (WTO 2001; US GAO 2005).

3. Some knitwear manufacturers argue that this tendency began before 2005. A study by the SMEDA (Small and Medium Enterprise Development Authority) (2005) indicates that knitwear stagnation can be attributed largely to the Afghan War that broke out after the 9/11 event of 2001. Manufacturers also argue that, after 9/11, international buyers of major brands such as GAP and Banana Republic temporarily left the Pakistani market due to a fear of transportation delays, and this caused a decrease in demand and consequently in prices by 17–40 per cent. Buyers came back to the Pakistani market later, but the bargaining power of Pakistani manufacturers has remained weak since that time.
4. From an international buyer is point of view, transactions in Pakistan can be substituted by those in India or Bangladesh, and the switching cost among these South Asian countries is not high.
5. Pakistan's fiscal year is from July to June. In this chapter, a term such as '2005/6' reflects data on the Pakistani fiscal year basis. A term such as '2005' reflects data on a calendar year basis.
6. 'Bedwear' is the term used in Pakistani statistics. It means bedlinens such as sheets, quilt covers and pillow covers.
7. The latest available version of CMI in Pakistan is 1995/96, while the latest version of the summary of CMI 2000/1 is available on the website of the Federal Bureau of Statistics (http://www.statpak.gov.pk/depts/index.html).
8. For Pakistan, men's knit shirts are the main export products in the knitwear category, and men's trousers are the main export products in the woven wear category. They constitute 40.2 and 10.7 per cent, respectively, of total garment exports from Pakistan to the US market.
9. The US Department of Commerce implemented safeguard measures on the imports of cotton knit shirts, cotton trousers and other commodities from China on 23 May 2005 (OTEXA 2005).
10. The US and China signed a memorandum of understanding on 18 November 2005, to limit Chinese textiles and clothing exports to the US over the period 2006–8.
11. Referring to the same method used in Makino (2006a), the labour-to-capital endowment ratio is assumed in this chapter to be higher in Pakistan than in China or India.
12. Both nominal and real wages are shown and are calculated relative to purchasing power in Pakistan. Nominal wages are used in comparisons of international competitiveness since nominal wages determine price competitiveness in the international market. On the other hand, real wages are used to assess whether the wage level is high in terms of price level in each country.
13. The following average exchange rates in August 2006 in IMF *International Financial Statistics* are used: $US1 equals 60.33 Pakistani rupees, 46.54 Indian rupees, and 69.66 Bangladeshi taka. Secondary data for China are used and are already denominated in US dollars.
14. Denim wear is the major woven wear in Pakistan.
15. According to the Pakistan Hosiery Manufacturers Association (PHMA), composed of knitwear manufacturer-exporters, the number of large knitwear manufacturing units hiring more than 100 workers in Pakistan is around 175 out of a total of 3500 units. According to the Pakistan Ready-made Garments Manufacturers and Exporters Association (PRGMEA), composed of woven wear manufacturer-exporters, the total number of members is 1183.
16. Sewing operators hired at piece rates in the Pakistani garment industry are described as follows. Each piece rate, usually determined by some skill test, corresponds to the

level of a designated operation that is a part of the assembly line of the sewing operation. Piece rate operators do not necessarily have incentives to make as many pieces as possible since the number of pieces an operator can make per day is subject to the productivity of other operators in the same line as well as the number of pieces assigned to the line.

17. Interviewees were asked to choose only one response from the following options: labour, utility costs, taxes, transportation infrastructure and costs, government other than tax authorities, and others. The answer 'others' included responses such as the difference in governmental policy (export rebate or refinance rate) and lack of joint-venture opportunities with foreigners.
18. In accordance with customary usage by the interviewees, 'skilled' (with use of quotation marks) piece rate workers refer to sewing operators who know how to operate sewing machines without training. Thus, 'skilled' workers are not necessarily highly skilled workers.
19. Full-time workers can get benefits that piece rate workers cannot, such as social insurance, a pension and medical insurance. However, these benefits are not enough to induce piece rate workers to accept full-time status since the social security system in Pakistan is not well established, and full-time workers cannot really benefit from the system. Thus, workers generally tend to make a decision based on short-term benefits.
20. Siegmann (2005: 411) also shows one unit, among 10 textile/clothing units interviewed in Faisalabad, that completed this shift due to quality concern.
21. Murayama (2006: 62) points out that the female labour participation rate is lower in Pakistan than in Bangladesh and India. According to a qualitative study on textile/clothing companies done by Siegmann (2005), the share of female workers ranged from 1 to 50 per cent in 10 textile/clothing units in Faisalabad where interviews were conducted, with about 20 per cent in 5 of the 10 units.
22. The difference in average monthly wages of sewing operators between August 2006 and the year 2005 is not statistically significant for both the knitwear ($t=1.022$, $p=0.310$) and denim wear ($t=-1.230$, $p=0.223$) sectors.
23. Hirano (2005) seeks to explain the reason for high wages in African countries in light of high commodity prices in those countries.
24. Lazear (2000: 1354) shows that the turnover rate increases under the piece rate system, but the difference is not statistically significant.
25. Worker productivity is generally thought to increase under a piece rate compensation system. For example, see Lazear (2000) and Shearer (2004). On the other hand, Freeman and Kleiner (1998) argue that the advantages brought by the shift from a piece rate system to a fixed rate one, such as lower monitoring costs and higher quality output, more than offset reduced productivity.

References

Baland, Jean-Marie, Jean Dreze and Luc Leruth (1999) 'Daily Wages and Piece Rates in Agrarian Economies'. *Journal of Development Economics* 59(2): 445–61.

Bhattacharya, Debapriya and Mustafizur Rahman (2001) 'Bangladesh's Apparel Sector: Growth Trends and the Post-MFA Challenges'. In Pratima Paul-Majumder and Binayak Sen (eds), *Growth of Garment Industry in Bangladesh: Economic and Social Dimensions*. Dhaka: Bangladesh Institute of Development Studies, pp. 2–26.

Easterly, William (2003) 'The Political Economy of Growth without Development: a Case Study of Pakistan'. In Dani Rodrik (ed.) *In Search of Prosperity*. Princeton: Princeton University Press, pp. 439–72.

Freeman, Richard B. and Morris M. Kleiner (1998) 'The Last American Shoe Manufacturers: Changing the Method of Pay to Survive Foreign Competition', NBER Working Paper Series, no. 6750. Cambridge, Mass.

Fukunishi, Takahiro (2005) 'Competitiveness of the Apparel Industry in Kenya: Comparison with Bangladesh'. In Katsumi Hirano (ed.) *Empirical Analysis of African Economies*. Chiba: Institute of Developing Economies, pp. 235–63 (in Japanese).

GoP (Government of Pakistan) (2004) *Pakistan Labour Force Survey 2003–2004*. Karachi: Statistics Division, Federal Bureau of Statistics.

Higuchi, Yoshio (1996) *Labour Economics*. Tokyo: Toyokeizai (in Japanese).

Hirano, Katsumi (2005) 'Poverty Linkage between Agriculture and Industry'. In Katsumi Hirano (ed.) *Empirical Analysis of African Economies*. Chiba: Institute of Developing Economies, pp. 131–90 (in Japanese).

Krugman, Paul and Maurice Obstfeld (eds) (2000) 'Resources and Trade: the Heckscher–Ohlin Model'. In *International Economics: Theory and Policy*, 5th edn. Reading; Mass.: Addison-Wesley, pp. 66–91.

Lazear, Edward P. (1986) 'Salaries and Piece Rates'. *The Journal of Business* 59(3): 405–31.

—— (2000) 'Performance Pay and Productivity'. *The American Economics Review* 90(5): 1346–61.

Makino, Momoe (2006a) 'Pakistan Labour-Intensive Industries Struggling with Cheap Products from China: Footwear Case'. *Ajia Keizai* 47(6): 55–82 (in Japanese).

—— (2006b) 'Competitiveness of the Apparel Industry in Pakistan in the post-MFA Era'. In Hiroshi Sato (ed.) *Globalization in South Asia: Its Impact on Employment and Labour Issues*, Research Report Series 2005-IV-08. Chiba: Institute of Developing Economies, pp. 55–105 (in Japanese).

Murayama, Mayumi (2006) 'Globalization and Female Employment in Bangladesh: Ready-Made Garment Workers in Post-MFA Era'. In Mayumi Murayama (ed.) *Employment in Readymade Garment Industry in Post-MFA Era: the Cases of India, Bangladesh and Sri Lanka*, JRP Series no. 140. Chiba: Institute of Developing Economies, pp. 53–101.

Nordås, Hildegunn K. (2004) 'The Global Textile and Clothing Industry post the Agreement on Textiles and Clothing', WTO Discussion Papers no. 5. Geneva: World Trade Organization.

OTEXA (Office of Textiles and Apparel) (2005) 'Announcement of Request for Bilateral Textile Consultations with the Government of the People's Republic of China', OTEXA Federal Register Notices, 20 May 2005, Office of Textiles and Apparel, US Department of Commerce (http://otexa.ita.doc.gov/fr2005.htm, accessed January 2006).

—— (2006) *Trade Data – U.S. Imports and Exports of Textiles and Apparel* (http://otexa.ita.doc.gov/msrpoint.htm, downloaded January 2006).

Raffaelli, Marcelo (1998) 'Bringing Textiles and Clothing into the Multilateral Trading System'. In Jagdish Bhagwati and Mathias Hirsch (eds) *The Uruguay Round and Beyond*. Berlin: Springer, pp. 51–9.

Saxena, Sanchita B. and Franck Wiebe (2005) 'The Phase-Out of the Multi-Fiber Arrangement: Policy Options and Opportunities for Asia'. San Francisco: Asia Foundation.

SBP (State Bank of Pakistan) (2006) *Statistical Bulletin*. State Bank of Pakistan (http://www.sbp.org.pk/reports/stat_reviews/bulletin/2006/index.htm, downloaded December 2006).

Shearer, Bruce (1996) 'Piece-Rates, Principal–Agent Models, and Productivity Profiles: Parametric and Semi-Parametric Evidence from Payroll Records'. *The Journal of Human Resources* 31(2): 275–303.

—— (2004) 'Piece Rates, Fixed Wages and Incentives: Evidence from a Field Experiment'. *Review of Economic Studies* 71(2): 513–34.

Siegmann, Karin Astrid (2005) 'The Agreement on Textiles and Clothing: Potential Effects on Gendered Employment in Pakistan'. *International Labour Review* 144(4): 401–21.

SMEDA (Small and Medium Enterprise Development Authority) (2005) 'Pakistan's Textile Garments: the Exports Growth Engine'. Lahore: Small and Medium Enterprise Development Authority, Ministry of Industries, Production and Special Initiatives, Government of Pakistan.

UNIDO (United Nations Industrial Development Organization) (2005a) *INDSTAT3 ISIC Rev.2* (CD-ROM). Vienna: United Nations Industrial Development Organization.

—— (2005b) *INDSTAT4 ISIC Rev.2&3* (CD-ROM). Vienna: United Nations Industrial Development Organization.

United Nations. *COMTRADE Database*, Statistics Division (http://unstats.un.org/unsd/comtrade).

US GAO (Government Accountability Office) (2005) 'U.S.–China Trade: Textile Safeguard Procedures Should Be Improved'. Report to Congressional Committees, GAO-05-296 (http://www.gao.gov/new.items/d05296.pdf, accessed January 2006).

World Bank (1988) *World Tables 1987 The Fourth Edition*. Washington, DC: World Bank.

—— (1998) *World Development Indicators 1998*. Washington, DC: World Bank.

World Bank and SMEDA (2003) 'Improving the Investment Climate in Pakistan: an Investment Climate Assessment'. Mimeo.

WTO (World Trade Organization) (1996) 'Textiles', Press Brief, Singapore WTO Ministerial 1996 (http://www.wto.org/english/thewto_e/minist_e/min96_e/textiles.htm, accessed January 2006).

—— (2001) 'WTO Successfully Concludes Negotiations on China's Entry', WTO News: 2001 Press releases, Press/243. 17 September 2001 (http://www.wto.org/english/news_e/pres01_e/pr243_e.htm, accessed January 2006).

Yamagata, Tatsufumi (2006) 'Textile Goods Trade: Consequence of Liberalization'. *Ajiken World Trend* no. 125, February: 20–3 (in Japanese).

Zaidi, Akbar S. (1999) *Issues in Pakistan's Economy*. Karachi: Oxford University Press.

Part II

Employment: Law and Policy Reforms

4
Economic Liberalization and Labour Law Reform in India[1]

Hitoshi Ota

4.1 Introduction

This chapter deals with the labour reforms in India, mainly focusing on labour legislation, the reform of which has been much discussed during the past decade. It is well known that, in the post-independence period, the policymakers in India attempted for a long time to build a nation characterized by a 'socialistic pattern of society', where the emphasis was placed on economic and social equality as well as social justice rather than on economic efficiency. With the resource constraints and the inward-looking economic administration, market competition was curbed and the efficiency that competition could have engendered was compromised. However, the situation began changing gradually in the 1980s when the government initiated partial economic liberalization, and then dramatically after the announcement of the New Economic Policy (NEP) in 1991. Especially due to the NEP and the subsequent economic and industrial policies in the 1990s, the structural adjustments of the Indian economy have proceeded, and ever since, market competition has been intensified by the gradual but substantial deregulations and the abolition of the restrictions on entry to the market. Nonetheless, one of the areas where the reforms by government initiatives did not moved forward greatly was that of labour.

The legislative measures in the domain of labour taken in India have often been described as excessive and have been considered responsible for slowing down the growth of employment by discouraging investment and economic growth (Deshpande et al. 2004: 40). Also, when the goal of economic reforms is to achieve higher economic growth, the labour reforms are not unrelated to the policies to enhance competitiveness of the economy. Proponents of the market principle of the economy argue that what should be highly emphasized is realization of allocative efficiency, which is essential to achieve high growth as well as to generate employment by measures like deregulation. To them, the rigidity, or inflexibility, especially that caused by the institutional factors of the labour market, is to be considered as having harmful effects. The proponents of labour reforms, therefore, urge the central government to reform labour laws that they charge are archaic and the main cause of the rigidity in the labour market, hampering high economic growth such as that being achieved by the powerful neighbouring country of China. Whether the argument is true or not, there is no doubt that labour law reform is a requisite part of economic reforms.

As may be seen from the above argument, one of the viewpoints that is most frequently quoted in respect of the study on labour reforms is 'flexibility'. There are many who classify the types of labour flexibility. Standing (1999), for instance, classifies the types into four: organizational or production flexibility, wage system flexibility, employment or numerical flexibility, and work process (functional) flexibility. Door (2005) classifies them broadly into qualitative flexibility and numerical flexibility, with the former being internal and the latter external flexibility. Imano and Sato (2002), quoting Atkinson's (1985) flexible firm model, classify them into four types of flexibility: numerical, functional, financial and temporal flexibilities.[2] However, though the viewpoint of flexibility may well be useful for grasping the contour of labour law reform and is used as a reference here too, we should duly recognize that there are certain areas of labour law reform where the flexibility argument should never be applied. It should also be pointed out that the flexibility which is discussed by management and that which is discussed by workers/trade unions may differ, and that these different versions may have effects in opposite directions. Flexibility, therefore, is not the absolute guiding principle for labour law reform.

With this backdrop, a close look at labour law reform is indispensable for a better and clearer understanding of the issues at stake in the domain of labour as well as labour policies that are relevant in the discussions on economic liberalization in India. In the next section, we first observe the government initiatives in labour reforms of the past decade while placing the discussion in the context of the economic liberalization launched in 1991. Then, the nature of the Indian labour law regime is reviewed in the third section, where an outline of the main labour laws at the central level is presented. We will see there that labour laws in India are protective of labour as well as restrictive. Some of the issues at stake for the labour law reforms are made clear. Section 4.4 deals with the labour law reform, focusing on the issues at stake there. The most contentious issue is related to numerical flexibility, and it involves whether, for instance, the employer has the freedom to dismiss employees at his/her will. It also has to do with the type of employment, such as on a temporary or contract basis, as well as with whether the employment relation is direct or indirect. It is shown that the related labour laws have not been amended so far at the central level, and that those that have been reformed may not be quite as contentious as those regarding numerical flexibility, at least for their stakeholders. In Section 4.5, we look at some of the important judicial cases that relate to the labour legislation and its reform, as it is sometimes argued that the judiciary leads the state in the subject of labour in India.

4.2 Background of the labour reforms of the past decade and government initiatives

After the economic liberalization of 1991, while efforts had certainly been made prior to the second term of the National Democratic Alliance (NDA) government with respect to the labour reforms such as the National Renewal Fund institutionalized in 1992 as countermeasures for workers affected by industrial restructuring and such as the Central Pay Commission that made the fifth recommendation in 1997 on pay and personnel management for central government employees, the situation started to appear to take on a more market-oriented tune in the late 1990s. Just around the time of the 13th National Election in 1999, the policymakers of the NDA government, under the leadership of Prime Minister Atal Bihari Vajpayee of the Bharatiya Janata Party (BJP), initiated a debate on launching the 'Second Generation Economic Reforms' for further, accelerated economic growth. One can see from Figure 4.1, which summarizes the annual growth rates of real GDP since fiscal year 1990/91, that the growth rate in the mid-1990s was more than 7 per cent but declined to around 5 per cent in the latter half of the 1990s. Employment generation was also stagnant in the mid- and late 1990s. According to the National Sample Survey (NSS), the pace of employment growth slowed from 2.7 per cent between 1983 and 1993/94 to 1.07 per cent between 1993/94 and 1999/2000 (Government of India 2002b: 141). Under the slogan of 'Second

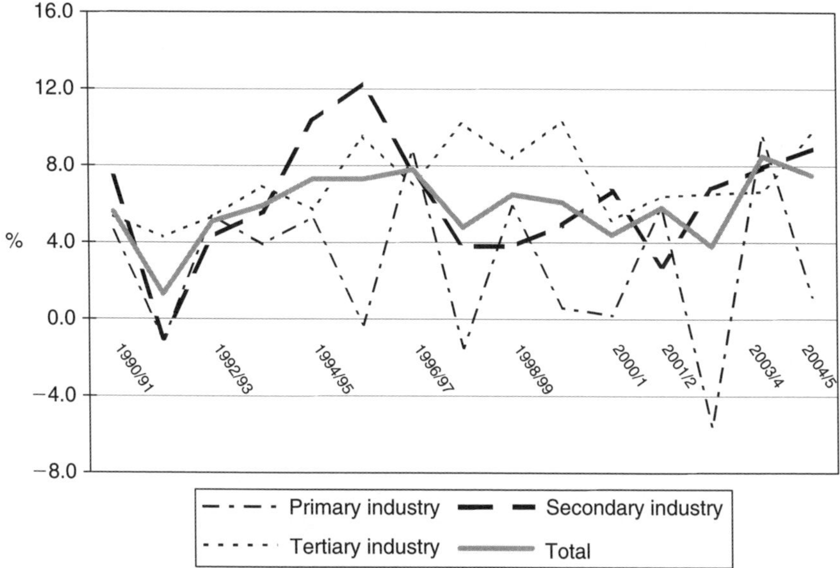

Figure 4.1 Annual growth rates of real GDP at factor cost by industry of origin

Notes: 1. Industry classification is as follows: Primary industry: agriculture, forestry and fishing, mining and quarrying. Secondary industry: manufacturing, construction, electricity, gas and water supply. Tertiary industry: three sectors consisting of 'trade, hotels, transport and communications', 'financing, insurance, real estate and business services' and 'public administration and defence and other services' combined. The growth rate was derived in terms of a geometric mean of the above three sectors.

2. Growth rates of real GDP are at 1993/94 prices up to 1999/2000, and at 1999/2000 prices from 1999/2000 onward.

3. Figures for 2003/4 are provisional, and figures for 2004/5 a quick estimate.

Source: Government of India (2006: S10 (Table 1.6)) (http://indiabudget.nic.in/es2005-06/chapt2006/tab16.pdf).

Generation Economic Reforms', the re-elected NDA government tried to achieve high growth and generate employment, especially in the organized sector,[3] by initiating reforms in the areas where liberalization and structural adjustments had not moved forward. Labour reforms were one of the most important reforms in the 'Second Generation Economic Reforms', along with the reforms regarding finances, PSUs (public sector units) and subsidiaries, as well as further induction of the FDIs.[4]

It may be more comprehensible as to why the issue of labour reforms attracted rather intense attention around the late 1990s if one takes into account the relative slowdown of the manufacturing sector at that time, in terms of both the pace of growth and employment absorption. The manufacturing and the secondary sectors are generally expected to be the driving force of economic growth, especially for developing countries, and this applies to India as well. It is also true that the export of manufactured goods is a very important source of foreign-exchange earnings. It was around 1997 that the slowdown of India's manufacturing sector became apparent (Uchikawa 2003), and the growth rate for the secondary sector became stagnant (see Figure 4.1). Regarding manufacturing activities, India in the late 1990s, and even presently, too, was no doubt outshone by China, which had become the global manufacturing base by that time. The share of the manufacturing sector in the Indian economy was less than 20 per cent in 2000, and its employment share just above 10 per cent. Whether the charges are true or not, the archaic labour legislation, which did not conform to the economic liberalization and bound management decision-making, was made the culprit for the slowdown of the manufacturing sector, leading to the claim that it was necessary to reform labour legislation in order to revive manufacturing activities and, by so doing, to generate employment in the sector.

The NDA government, after being re-elected in October 1999, constituted the Second National Commission on Labour (SNCL) in order to usher in labour reforms. The terms of reference of the SNCL were to suggest rationalization of existing laws relating to labour in the organized sector, and to suggest umbrella legislation for ensuring a minimum level of protection to workers in the unorganized sector (Sundar 2000). The SNCL appointed six study groups on, namely, globalization and its impact, labour laws, skills development, umbrella legislation for unorganized labour, female and child labour, and social security, with the task of suggesting policy direction in each subject. However, unlike the First National Commission on Labour appointed in 1966 which focused on the labour market and conditions of labour, the SNCL focused on the product market and the need to adjust labour policies and laws to meet the competitive requirements of the product market in the wake of globalization (Venkata Ratnam 2002). In the context of the 'Second Generation Economic Reforms' of the NDA government, therefore, the main emphasis was placed on the reorganization of labour legislation in terms of labour reforms.

Though suggestions and recommendations for the reform of certain labour laws had been actively made since the 1980s especially from among industrialists, reforms rarely occurred in the manner that the proponents desired.[5] There were also announcements and reports made by government officials supporting labour law reform under the NDA government. For instance, the Finance Minister, going beyond his jurisdiction in his budget speech of 2001, suddenly suggested an amendment of the Industrial Disputes Act and the Contract Labour (Regulation and Abolition) Act. In the same year, the report of the Task Force on Employment Opportunity headed by Montek Singh Ahluwalia, who became the deputy chairman of the Planning Commission in 2004 under the United Progressive Alliance (UPA) government, also proposed an amendment of the Industrial Disputes Act for employment generation, which was later set aside, due to its controversial nature, by another report of the Planning Commission's Special Group on targeting 10 million employment opportunities (Datt 2003: 182–213). The impression given by the initiatives on labour law reform under the NDA government is that they have been conducted in an ad hoc manner.

What about the policy stance of the UPA government towards labour law reform? It has been reported that Prime Minister Manmohan Singh, who was the Finance Minister at the time of the New Economic Policy (NEP) in 1991, and the Union Ministers have repeatedly stated the need for labour reforms. For instance, at the fortieth meeting of the Indian Labour Conference held in December 2005, the Prime Minister urged trade union leaders to understand the needs of the changing times and the simultaneous need for changing labour-related legislation. He pointed out the problem of a multiplicity of labour laws leading to a confusion of definitions, the problem of excessive regulatory legislation which had possibly contributed to the relative lack of growth of the organized industrial sector, and the problem of the 'Inspector Raj', i.e. an excess of administrative procedures for inspections under various Labour Acts, while at the same time paying due attention to the difficulties that workers in the unorganized sector face (*Hindu Business Line*, 10 December 2005). *Economic Survey 2005–06* says that Indian labour laws are highly protective of labour. It adds that the laws apply only to the organized sector, and consequently, the laws have restricted labour mobility, have led to capital-intensive methods in the organized sector and have adversely affected the sector's long-run demand for labour (Government of India 2006: 209). It should also be added that the Planning Commission which is drafting the Eleventh Five-Year Plan favours more flexibility in labour laws. Its deputy chairman is reported to have stated that more flexibility would attract greater investment and create more jobs, while ruling out the 'hire-and-fire policy' on the government's agenda (*Hindu Business Line*, 15 November 2006). The UPA government is not unwilling to reform labour laws for more flexibility.[6]

4.3 Nature of the Indian labour law regime

In this section, we review the main features of the Central Labour Acts in India.[7] It is often claimed that labour laws in India are protective of labour and at the same time are restrictive (Sharma 2006). The state has considered labour–management relations as a matter of law and order and has actively intervened in them by way of adjudication (Doshi 1993; Punekar et al. 1994; Ota 2001, 2005). Frequent state intervention has hampered the construction of a harmonious and mature bipartisan relationship based on mutual understanding between labour and management.

The author thinks that labour legislation in India is not one that seeks to foster independence and initiatives of the actors' own. Making light of such initiatives may not actually be compatible with the concept of protection.

4.3.1 The constitutional background [8]

The Preamble of the Constitution of India states that the people of India resolved to constitute India into a sovereign socialist secular democratic republic, and secure to all its citizens justice, liberty and equality, and to promote among them all fraternity.[9] Amplifying and elaborating the Preamble, the Constitution specifies 'Directive Principles of State Policy' in Part IV of the Constitution, where Article 38 states that the state shall promote the welfare of the people by securing and protecting a social order in which justice, social, economic and political, shall inform all institutions of national life. The state is also directed to secure the following: equal pay for equal work for men and women, and the health and strength of workers (Article 39), the right to work, the right to education and to public assistance in cases of undeserved want including unemployment (Article 41), just and humane conditions of work and for maternity relief (Article 42), a living wage and a decent standard of life for labourers (Article 43), and the participation of workers in management of undertakings or industrial establishments by suitable legislation or otherwise (Article 43A).

The Constitution enumerates the fundamental rights in Part III of its text, where the rights to equality and freedom, among others, are articulated. Article 16 guarantees equality and opportunity in matters of public employment. Article 19 guarantees the right to freedom of speech and expression, to assemble peacefully and without arms, to form associations or unions, to acquire, hold and dispose of property, and to practise any profession or to carry on any occupation, trade or business. Article 24 prohibits the employment of children in factories, etc., such that no child below the age of 14 years shall be employed to work in any factory or mine or engaged in any other hazardous employment.[10]

In this connection, it is worth noting the observation of the SNCL that the government recognizes the following rights of workers as inalienable so that they must, therefore, accrue to every worker under any system of labour laws and labour policy (Government of India, 2002a: 315–16). These are (a) the right to work of one's choice, (b) the right against discrimination, (c) the prohibition of child labour, (d) just and humane conditions of work, (e) the right to social security, (f) protection of wages, including the right to guaranteed wages, (g) the right to redress of grievances, (h) the right to organize and form trade unions and the right to collective bargaining, and (i) the right to participate in management.

Article 246 of the Constitution stipulates that labour is a concurrent matter designated in List III: Concurrent List of the Seventh Schedule to the Constitution, such that both the central government and state governments can enact laws with respect to labour subjects. The areas relevant to labour in the list are:

- No. 22: Trade union; industrial and labour disputes
- No. 23: Social security and social insurance; employment and unemployment

- No. 24: Welfare of labour including conditions of work, provident funds, employers' liability, workmen's compensation, invalidity and old age pensions, and maternity benefits
- No. 36: Factories

In practice, the main Labour Acts such as those regarding gratuities, bonuses, provident funds, and employees' state insurance are uniform all over India, while some of the labour laws are amended by the states to suit their own requirements.[11] There are cases where the implementation of an Act enacted by the central government is undertaken by the state government authorities (Taxmann 2005: I-5).

4.3.2 Labour laws regulating industrial relations

The major laws regulating labour–management relations are namely the Trade Unions Act, 1926, the Industrial Employment (Standing Orders) Act, 1946 and the Industrial Disputes Act, 1947.

4.3.2.1 The Trade Unions Act, 1926

The Act mainly seeks to confer a legal and corporate status on registered trade unions. It provides immunity from civil and criminal liability to trade union executives and members for bona fide trade union activities. Though the Act provides for registration of trade unions, it does not contain provisions regarding their recognition by management.

The Trade Unions Act was amended in 2001. Prior to the amendment, it provided that any seven or more members of a trade union could apply for registration, and at least half the total number of the office bearers of a registered union had to be persons actually engaged in the industry to which the union belonged. With the amendment of 2001, no trade union of workmen shall be registered unless at least 10 per cent or 100, whichever is less, subject to a minimum of seven workmen engaged or employed in the establishment or industry with which it is connected, are members of such trade union on the application date of the registration. A registered trade union of workmen must at all times continue to meet the above requirement. Regarding office bearers, all those of a registered trade union, but not more than one-third of the total number of office bearers or five, whichever is less, shall be persons actually engaged or employed in the establishment or industry with which the trade union is connected. A provision for filing an appeal before the Industrial Tribunal/Labour Court in case of non-registration/restoration of registration is also provided.[12]

4.3.2.2 The Industrial Employment (Standing Orders) Act, 1946

The Industrial Employment (Standing Orders) Act, 1946, provides service rules to workmen. The major aims of the Act, among others, are to regulate the standards of conduct of the employers and employees so that labour–management relations can be improved, and to maintain proper discipline and harmonious working conditions and to achieve higher productivity by providing satisfactory employment and working conditions (Mamoria et al. 1997: 711–28). The Act extends to every industrial establishment where 100 or more workmen are employed in a 12-month period, while the central or state governments can extend its provision to any industrial establishment. The Act provides that, to carry out its purposes, the appropriate government, i.e. either the central or state government, can after prior publication, by notification in the *Official Gazette*, make rules, one being the Industrial Employment (Standing Orders) Central Rules, 1946.

4.3.2.3 The Industrial Disputes Act, 1947

The objective of the Act is to make provisions for investigation and settlement of industrial disputes. The Act introduced the principle of compulsory arbitration, and it prohibited strikes without at least 14 days' notice in public utility services. The Act provides works committees consisting of representatives of employers and employees in undertakings employing 100 or more workmen. Under the Act, discharge, dismissal, retrenchment or otherwise terminating the employment of an individual workman is deemed to be an industrial dispute. There is also a provision regarding a change in the conditions of service. An employer cannot effect any change in the conditions of service applicable to any workman without giving 21 days notice (Section 9-A), while this is not required if there is a settlement or award by the Labour Court or Tribunal. In addition to the above provisions, the Act prohibits unfair labour practices.

The most contentious issue regarding the Industrial Disputes Act concerns the regulation of layoffs, retrenchment and closure of establishments. If the number of workmen employed at an establishment is 100 or more, prior permission of the appropriate government is necessary for layoffs, retrenchment, or closure of the undertaking (Chapter V-B).

4.3.3 Labour laws related to wages and bonuses

4.3.3.1 The Payment of Wages Act, 1936

The Act regulates payment of wages to a certain class of employed persons. Under the Act, every employer is primarily responsible for payment of wages to employees and should make timely payment of wages. The wage ceiling for eligibility was raised from 'not more than Rs.1600' to 'not more than Rs.6500' by the amendment of 2002.

4.3.3.2 The Minimum Wages Act, 1948

The Minimum Wages Act, 1948, requires the appropriate government to fix minimum rates of wages payable to employees in various industries and trades as well as in the agricultural sector. The appropriate governments can refrain from fixing minimum rates of wages with respect to any scheduled employment in which there are less than 1000 employees engaged in the entire state.

4.3.3.3 The Payment of Bonus Act, 1965

The purpose of the Act is to provide for the payment of a bonus, and it is applicable to any factory using power and employing 10 or more persons, or other establishments employing 20 or more persons. The minimum bonus payable is 8.33 per cent and the maximum is 20 per cent of the salaries and wages earned by the employee. The bonus is payable to all employees whose salaries or wages do not exceed Rs.3500 per month.

4.3.4 Laws related to conditions of service, employment and training

The service and employment conditions are regulated by multiple laws for different industries and sectors such as factories, docks, plantations, mines, motor transport, buildings and construction, etc.

4.3.4.1 The Factories Act, 1948

The main objectives of the Factories Act are to regulate working conditions in factories to ensure that the basic minimum requirements for the safety, health and welfare of the factory workers are met, and to regulate working hours, leave, holidays, overtime and employment of children, women and young persons. The Act applies to all establishments carrying out a manufacturing process and employing 10 or more workers where power is used, or employing 20 or more workers where power is not used. By the amendment introduced in 2005, women workers can now work in night shifts at factories under certain conditions (*Economic and Political Weekly*, 14 October 2006).

4.3.4.2 The Shops and Commercial Establishments Acts (Central and State Acts)

The objective of the Act is to regulate the service conditions of persons employed in shops, commercial establishments, residential hotels, restaurants and eating houses, and theatres, etc. Usually, information technology (IT) and allied industries such as ITES (IT enabled services) and BPO (business process outsourcing) are covered by this Act. The state governments have the authority to make these laws, and they have enacted the Acts applicable to specified shops and commercial establishments within the states.

4.3.4.3 The Contract Labour (Regulation and Abolition) Act, 1970

The purpose of the Act is to regulate the employment of contract labour and to provide for abolition of contract labour in certain cases. The main provisions of the Act relate to, among others, registration of establishments employing contract labour, licensing of contractors, and welfare and health of contract labour. The Act applies to every establishment in which 20 or more workers are employed as contract labour or were so employed any time during the preceding 12 months. The Act does not apply to establishments where work of an intermittent or casual nature is performed.

The appropriate government can prohibit, by notification in the *Official Gazette*, employment of contract labour in any process, operation or other work in any establishment (Section 10(1)). Before issuing such notification, the government will consider aspects of conditions of the work and benefits provided for the contract labour, including (a) whether the process, operation or other work is incidental to, or necessary for, the industry, trade, business, manufacture or occupation that is carried on in the establishment, (b) whether it is of perennial nature, (c) whether it is done ordinarily through regular workmen in that establishment or an establishment similar thereto, and (d) whether it is sufficient to employ a considerable number of whole-time workmen (Section 10 (2)).

4.3.4.4 The Employment Exchanges (Compulsory Notification of Vacancies) Act, 1959

The Act provides for the compulsory notification of vacancies to employment exchanges by every establishment in the public or private sectors before filling up any vacancy. 'Establishment in the private sector' means an establishment where ordinarily 25 or more persons are employed to work for remuneration. Though the establishments to which the Act applies shall give notification of the vacancies to the employment exchanges, they are not obligated to hire through them.

4.3.4.5 The Apprentices Act, 1961

The main purpose of the Act is to provide practical training to technically qualified persons. Every employer is under an obligation to take on apprentices in a ratio prescribed by the central government that reflects the number of skilled workers in his/her employment in different trades. An apprentice is not a workman during apprentice training, and basically the provisions of labour laws are not applicable to him/her. However, the provisions of the Factories Act regarding health, safety and welfare apply. Though trade unions sometimes demand that an employer hire the apprentices as regular workers once the training period is over, it is not the employer's obligation to do so.

4.3.5 Laws related to social security

We briefly present some of the major laws related to social security in this subsection. We do not present those related to welfare funds.

4.3.5.1 The Workmen's Compensation Act, 1923

The beginning of social security in India was effected with the passing of the Workmen's Compensation Act (Sarma, 1994: 218). This Act makes it obligatory for employers to pay compensation to their workers for injury by accident, arising out of and in the course of employment, resulting in death or disablement under the Act. While there is no wage limit for coverage, the Act does not apply to workers covered by the Employees' State Insurance Act, 1948, and those employed in clerical capacities.

4.3.5.2 The Employees' State Insurance Act, 1948

The Act was enacted to provide certain benefits to employees in case of sickness, maternity, or employment injury and to make provisions for certain other related matters. The Act applies to power-using factories employing 10 or more workers and non-power-using factories employing 20 or more, as well as shops, theatres, cinemas, hotels, restaurants, motor transport undertakings and newspaper establishments employing 20 or more persons in a number of states. The Act covers persons employed directly or indirectly as clerical staff but does not apply to members of the armed forces or to persons whose remuneration in aggregate exceeds Rs.7500 a month.

In April 2005, an unemployment allowance for workers who lose employment due to retrenchment, outsourcing, or closure of the undertaking, etc., was introduced under the ESI Scheme.

4.3.5.3 The Employees' Provident Fund and Miscellaneous Provisions Act, 1952

The objective of the Act is to provide for the institution of compulsory provident funds. The Act covers three schemes, namely the Employees' Provident Fund Scheme (EPF Scheme), Employees' Pension Scheme, and Employees' Deposit Linked Insurance Scheme. The EPF Scheme provides for financial assistance by allowing partial withdrawals by subscribers in situations such as illness, invalidism, etc., and provides funds to enable them to discharge their social responsibilities, such as those related to marriage of their siblings.[13]

4.3.5.4 The Maternity Benefit Act, 1961

The Act regulates employment in certain establishments for a certain period before and after childbirth and provides for maternity and other benefits. There is no wage limit for coverage under the Act. The Act has been amended and enforced since 1996 with a view to encouraging planned parenthood.

4.3.5.5 The Payment of Gratuity Act, 1972

The gratuity is a lump-sum payment that an employee receives when she/he retires or leaves service. An employment period of at least five years at an establishment is required to qualify for the gratuity. The Act applies to every factory, mine, oilfield, plantation, port and railway company, as well as to every shop and establishment where 10 or more persons are employed or were employed on any day during the preceding 12 months.

4.3.6 The features of India's labour legislation

As pointed out at the beginning of this section, it is observable that labour laws in India are protective of labour as well as restrictive. Apart from this, labour legislation in India has the following features. First, as mentioned in subsection 4.3.1, matters regarding labour are concurrent according to the Constitution so that both the central and state governments are entitled to enact labour laws. The states are generally expected to make amendments in favour of workers, but the recent trend is that this is not always the case. The states' initiatives in labour nowadays are more and more related to their industrial policy,[14] and labour standards are tending to become a subject of competition among states to attract domestic and foreign direct investments, which may lead to worsening of working conditions. Another current tendency also appears to be for central government to allow state governments to take initiatives related to labour first and observe the outcome rather than being the first to take difficult steps. The central trade unions oppose this move towards decentralization. Furthermore, the issue sometimes arises as to whether the 'appropriate government' refers to the centre or the state, especially in the case of the central PSUs.

Second, some of India's main labour laws are old. They have been amended from time to time, but there is criticism that labour legislation does not appropriately fit the present fast-changing economic environment.

Third, there are more than 50 labour laws in the central sphere and more than 150 if one includes those at state level. In addition, the definition of certain terms such as 'workmen' and 'industry' varies from one to the other. This makes administration of labour legislation cumbersome, and it is therefore argued that it is necessary to rationalize labour laws.

Fourth, the criteria for determining whether the laws apply or not are usually the size of the establishment (the number of workers employed there) and/or the wage level of the workers. As to the former criterion, it is applied to the establishment (and/or workers employed there) whose employment size is *above* the stipulated threshold, while as to the latter, it is applied to the workers whose earnings are *below* the stipulated threshold. In terms of the size criterion, this means that the laws are not applied to small and micro-scale industries, that is, the unorganized sector, and thus the number of those who benefit from labour laws in India is very small, much less than 10 per cent of the workforce. In addition, as the working conditions of workers in the unorganized sector are usually less attractive, this raises the serious question of whether the very purpose of the labour legislation to protect workers is realized. In terms of the wage criterion, this certainly does not mean that those who earn more than the threshold do not require the benefits of the law. Under the wage criterion, some workers in the unorganized sector are also covered, though in a very limited way.

Another issue regarding the applicability of labour laws is that those in managerial positions and certain white-collar employees are not covered by the legislation. Just because a person is a manager does not necessarily mean that better working conditions are automatically guaranteed to him/her.

Fifth, regarding labour administration, supervision of the implementation of the legislation is far from satisfactory. This is due to, among others, budgetary constraints and an insufficient number of labour inspectors. The remote locations of some establishments make inspection of the implementation status difficult. It has also been pointed out that some labour inspectors perform their duties with malicious intent.

Finally, labour laws are applicable in the Export Processing Zones (EPZs) and the Special Economic Zones (SEZs) in India. The Special Economic Zones Act enacted in 2005 did not incorporate flexibility into labour laws there either. Industries demand an exemption from labour laws in these zones. The SNCL has also suggested an exemption (Government of India 2002a).

4.4 Labour law reform at stake

We now discuss the labour law reform presently at stake in India. We first observe the major reforms in labour laws up to now. Then, we briefly review the recommendations of the SNCL regarding labour legislation. The most contentious issue of labour law reform, relating to numerical flexibility, will be discussed in the third subsection.

4.4.1 Major central labour laws reformed

As we have seen in the previous section, certain labour laws have been amended so far. The most important change is the amendment made to the Trade Unions Act, 1926, under the NDA government in 2001. The amendment aimed at reducing the multiplicity of trade unions, promoting internal democracy, and facilitating orderly growth and regulation of the unions (*Hindu*, 3 August 2001). As a result of the amendment, however, a trade union cannot now be registered if it is formed at an establishment with less than 100 employees. This, the author believes, is a drawback to the trade union movement in India, and he wonders why this amendment was passed considering the fact that the central trade unions are still capable of flexing their muscles. It would be safe to assume that the amendment does not harm the existing unions. In fact, the SNCL recognized the problem created by the amendment and suggested that a specific provision be made to enable workers in the unorganized sector to form trade unions and get them registered even where an employer–employee relationship does not exist or is difficult to establish and that the proviso stipulating 10 per cent of membership not apply in their case (Government of India 2002a: 335–6). In any case, since management decisions are more or less affected by the trade union if one exists, the change in the Trade Unions Act can be considered to relate to functional flexibility. In terms of employment size, the amendment would especially encourage ancillary industries.

Another important reform made in recent years was the one regarding nightshift work by women under certain conditions in the Factories Act, implemented in 2005 under the UPA government.[15] In terms of the flexibility classification, nightshift work by women workers is part of temporal flexibility. There are several factors behind this change. Regarding cost considerations, the labour cost of women workers is generally less than that of men, and employers would prefer women workers if there were no difference in the productivity between the genders. There may also be some advantages in hiring women for certain types of work. In addition, changes in the perception and the roles of women in Indian society are under way, and these changes are closely entwined with globalization and information technology. More and more women in India are now enrolled in higher education and get jobs with relatively handsome incomes, as an example of a change in society. Another factor one may add is that, in contrast to the past, the emphasis has shifted globally more towards equality of opportunity and empowerment of women while at the same time balancing the need for consideration of maternity, and India is no exception.[16]

A welcome reform was made relating to fundamental human rights. In August 2006, the central government banned employment of children as domestic servants or workers, and as helpers in *dhabas* (i.e. roadside eateries), restaurants, hotels, motels, teashops, resorts, spas and other recreational centres. The ban was imposed under the Child Labour (Prohibition and Regulation) Act, 1986, and became effective from 10 October 2006. Fundamental rights is a concept that is far superior to the flexibility argument that is used for the sake of the discussion here. The implementation of the Act and the subsequent supervision not only by administrative offices but also by society are key to improving child welfare.[17]

Overall, one may conclude that the major central labour laws that have been reformed may not be quite as contentious regarding numerical flexibility as we will see later, at least for their stakeholders. This may be the exact reason that the amendments could be made.

4.4.2 Recommendations of the Second National Commission on Labour

The report of the SNCL was presented to the public in September 2002. Since the SNCL was constituted under the NDA government, it is not certain whether the current policymakers of the UPA government with the support of the leftist parties are serious about making reforms along the lines of the recommendation. In addition, the recommendation was largely to provide the greater flexibility desired by employers, and the final report was even submitted with a note of dissent by the Bharatiya Mazdoor Sabha (BMS), which is one of the two central trade unions that participated in the commission and is the trade union wing of the Rashtriya Swayamsevak Sangh (RSS), with which the BJP has a close tie. The author has some reservations about implementing the labour law reforms just as the committee recommended. Nonetheless, it is worth reviewing them to understand the issues at stake in the labour law reforms. Therefore, we briefly review some of the recommendations regarding labour laws.[18] The controversial issue of layoffs, retrenchment and closure under the Industrial Disputes Act, 1947, is dealt with in the next subsection.

4.4.2.1 Rationalization of labour laws

The SNCL recommends that the existing set of labour laws be broadly grouped into four or five groups of laws pertaining to industrial relations, wages, social security, safety, and welfare and working conditions. They also recommend that the central laws relating to the subject of labour–management relations should be judiciously consolidated into a single law, covering all establishments employing 20 or more. Moreover, a separate labour law for establishments employing 19 or fewer should also be enacted.

4.4.2.2 Definition of the terms

It is recommended that the definitions of certain terms, the issue of which was pointed out in subsection 4.3.6, should be rewritten. For example, there is need for a uniform definition of the term 'workman' in all groups of laws. The SNCL suggested, as an alternative, that all those drawing up to Rs.25,000 per month be treated as workers, while all the supervisory personnel, irrespective of their wage/salary, be kept outside the rank of worker. There is no need to define 'industry' if the laws cover all establishments employing 20 or more. There should be uniformity and consistency in the definition of 'appropriate government' under all groups of laws.

4.4.2.3 Industrial action

It is recommended to allow a strike to be called if 51 per cent or more of union membership supports the decision through a strike ballot. In essential services, once a 14-day notice is given, a strike could be deemed to have occurred and the dispute must forthwith be referred to compulsory arbitration. A union which leads an illegal strike must be derecognized and debarred from applying for registration or recognition for a period of two or three years.

4.4.2.4 Negotiating agent

One of the problems regarding the trade union movement in India is their fragmentation and multiplicity. For recognition of trade unions, therefore, the SNCL recommends that unions be selected for recognition as negotiating agents on the basis of the check-off system, with 66 per cent entitling a union to be accepted as a single negotiating agent. If no union has 66 per cent support, the unions that have the support of more than 25 per cent should be given proportionate representation. The validity of the check-off, the tenure of union recognition, and wage settlement should all be four years.

4.4.2.5 Prior notice under Section 9-A of the Industrial Disputes Act, 1947

The recommendations say that there need be no statutory obligation for the employer to give prior notice. Notice given under Section 9-A should not operate as a stay under Section 33, though such a decision by the management is justifiable under Section 33A.

4.4.2.6 Workers' participation in management

Article 43A of the Constitution directs the state to secure workers' participation in management, as we have seen in subsection 4.3.1, and the Industrial Disputes Act, 1947, provides works committees. The Joint Management Councils were also introduced in 1958 to have administrative responsibility over various matters relating to welfare, safety and vocational training, etc. There have been other attempts in the past to institutionalize workers' participation in management, but with little success. The SNCL favours providing a legislative scheme for workers' participation in management, initially in establishments employing 300 people or more.

4.4.2.7 Minimum wages

The minimum wage payable to any employed person, in whatever occupation, should be such as would satisfy the needs of the worker and his/her family (consisting in all of three consumption units) arrived at on the Need-Based Formula of the Fifteenth Indian Labour Conference.

4.4.3 Amendments passed to enhance numerical flexibility?

The most controversial issue of labour law reform is related to numerical flexibility which appears in two labour laws, the Industrial Disputes Act, 1947, and the Contract Labour (Regulation and Abolition) Act, 1970.

As to the Industrial Disputes Act, the controversy concerns the provisions in Chapter V-B of the Act regarding prior permission from the appropriate government for retrenchment, layoffs and closure of the units if the establishment employs 100 or more employees. There are studies, Fallon and Lucas (1991) and Besley and Burgess (2004) among others, which show that the labour market rigidity arising from these provisions hampers employment generation. Some argue that the entire Chapter V-B should be deleted, and others suggest that the threshold be raised from 100 employees to 1000. The most frequently proposed, and possibly the most conceivable change if it should come to pass, would be to raise the threshold to 300, though the trade unions fervently oppose any such move. However, we may need to see that layoffs, retrenchment, or closure of an establishment per se are not completely prohibited under the Act, but that the Act provides procedures to follow in such cases. Frequent mention is made of the fact that obtaining approval from the appropriate government is difficult and requires time; however, if approval could be obtained more smoothly, amendment of the clauses in Chapter V-B may become unnecessary. The fact is that companies do reduce their excess workforce through voluntary retirement schemes (VRS) and other measures. There may be alternatives to this part of the reform.

Regarding the Contract Labour (Regulation and Abolition) Act, the proponents of change argue that it should be amended to provide flexibility to engage contract labour in core activities.[19] Though the central government has not made any changes in the Act as of yet, the state of Andhra Pradesh did so in 2003 (Government of Andhra Pradesh 2003). The Contract Labour (Regulation and Abolition) (Andhra Pradesh Amendment) Act, 2003, redefines the core activities of an establishment as any activity for which the establishment is set up, including any activity which is essential or necessary to the core activity, but excluding sanitation, guard and security services, canteen, loading and unloading, running of hospitals and educational institutions, courier services, civil and other constructional works, gardening, housekeeping, and transport, etc. The Act also prohibits contract labour in core activities in Section 10 but provides that the principal employer may engage contract labour or a contractor for any core activity, if (a) the activity is ordinarily done through contractors, (b) the activities are such that they do not require full-time workers for the major portion of the working hours in a day or for longer periods as the case may be, or (c) there is any sudden increase of volume of work in the core activity which needs to be accomplished in a specified time. One of the factors leading to the amendment was that the state chief minister at the time was very enthusiastic about the industrial development of the state. Also, one cannot overlook the fact that, historically, there has been more contract labour, as a percentage of the total number of workers in the manufacturing sector in Andhra Pradesh, than in most other states (Government of India 2002c). There may be some economic as well as social factors rather specific to Andhra Pradesh in this situation (Ota 2006: 148). Several states have now been contemplating amending the Contract Labour Act in a similar manner.

Another law that relates to numerical flexibility is the Industrial Employment (Standing Orders) Act, 1946. In 2003, the NDA government made an amendment to the Industrial Employment (Standing Orders) Central Rules, 1946, and introduced a fixed term of employment for which workers may be engaged on the basis of contract of employment for a fixed period. It has been reported, however, that this change was withdrawn by the UPA government, possibly under pressure from the leftist parties. Fixed-term employment may still be possible under the Industrial Disputes Act, though this may only be with respect to temporary jobs (*Hindu Business Line*, 15 June 2005).

Although the key labour laws related to numerical flexibility have not been amended in the central sphere, one can at least observe that the direction of the labour law reform is to increase numerical flexibility.[20]

4.5 Judicial cases

It is widely thought that central government lacks initiatives in labour reforms for various reasons, and some even claim that it is the judiciary that has been leading the state on certain issues regarding the subject of labour (Sen 1996; Datt 2003: 303). In this section, we look into two such recent landmark cases where judicial judgment has made a strong impact on the industrial relations situation in India. One is a case regarding the Contract Labour (Regulation and Abolition) Act, and the other is a case regarding the right of government employees to strike.

4.5.1 Case concerning the Contract Labour (Regulation and Abolition) Act [21]

As has already been seen, matters related to contract labour are regulated by the Contract Labour (Regulation and Abolition) Act, 1970. The major defect of the Act is that no procedure or direction is provided for the absorption of contract labour following the prohibition of employment of contract labour under Section 10 of the Act, and in most cases the workers lost their contract jobs when the abolishment of contract labour was announced by the government.[22] In this regard, two judgments were made by the Supreme Court, one in the case of *Gujarat State Electricity Board (GSEB)* vs *Union of India* in May 1995 and one in the case of *Air India Statutory Corporation Ltd. & Others* vs *United Labour Union & Others* in December 1996 (Datt 2003: 301).

In the case of *GSEB* vs *Union of India*, the Supreme Court recommended that all public sector undertakings should discontinue the usage of contract labour that satisfies Section 10(2) of the Act and absorb as many as feasible as their direct employees. In the case of *Air India Statutory Corporation Ltd. & Others* vs *United Labour Union & Others*, the Supreme Court held that the central government would be the appropriate government in all undertakings in which it has a deep and pervasive interest, and in such cases where contract labour has been prohibited, such contract labour would automatically become the employees of the principal employer.[23] It also held that the principal employer is under statutory obligation to absorb the contract labour, and so the linkage between the contractor and the employees was dissolved and a direct relationship stood restored between the principal employer and contract labour as its employees.

Subsequently, there was a major development in August 2001. In the case of *Steel Authority of India (SAIL) & Others* vs *National Union of Waterfront Workers & Others*, the Supreme Court overruled the above judgment in the Air India Statutory Corporation Ltd case, and held that there is no automatic obligation on the part of the principal employer to absorb all the contract labour working on its behalf, in the event that the government prohibits the type of contract labour engaged in by it.[24] The industries in the public sector in particular naturally welcomed the judgment. However, the court stated that the judgment would not apply retroactively and those contract labourers who had already been absorbed by the PSUs would not be affected. Therefore, the industries claim that it is necessary to amend the Act for greater flexibility in view of such measures as outsourcing, among others (*Economic Times*, 31 August and 5 November 2001).

4.5.2 The right to strike [25]

There was a shocking judgment by the Supreme Court in August 2003 on the right to strike by government employees. The state government employees of Tamil Nadu went on strike in July 2003 against the curtailment of their pension benefits due to them from the state government. The Tamil Nadu government, drawing its authority from the Tamil Nadu Essential Services Maintenance Act (TESMA), 2002, as amended *post facto* by Ordinance No. 3 of 2003, carried out summary dismissal of all the employees on strike, who numbered more than 170,000. The employees went to the High Court to challenge the ordinance, and eventually the entire matter was shifted to the Supreme Court. While the issue before the court was not the right to strike but the constitutional validity of TESMA and the ordinance, the court held that the government employees have no fundamental, statutory or equitable/moral right to go on strike (ISLE & IHD, 2004).

Trade unions vehemently condemned the verdict, and experts in the field of industrial relations study and labour law strongly criticized the judgment and expressed their deep concern over its possible consequences. Even the Attorney General of India spoke up against the apex court's observation, saying that it was uncalled for and beyond comprehension. The International Labour Organization (ILO) also asked the government of India to take urgent steps to reaffirm trade union rights and restore industrial relations in Tamil Nadu (*Hindu*, 13 and 25 August 2003).

In the end, most of the dismissed employees were reinstated, some with demotion, not unconditionally but upon submission of an apology and undertaking not to indulge in similar activities in the future. It has also been reported that the Supreme Court judgment was under review by the court. The author has yet to follow up the possible review, but unless some measures were taken against the Supreme Court judgment, it would still be considered effective as a precedent and would have negative ramifications for the trade union movement in India. The judgment of the Supreme Court in this case may be the biggest misjudgment in the history of industrial relations in India in the post-independence period.

It is true that some of the actions taken by trade unions in the past have only served to senselessly disturb the daily life of ordinary citizens, and it was the author's impression that the citizens were not as sympathetic as might have been expected when the Tamil Nadu government dismissed all the employees who resorted to striking in the above case. However, while the yardstick of judicial judgments may be expected to shift from time to time in accordance with changes in the norms of a society, this should never be a reason to justify infringement on workers' rights and especially fundamental rights. Nonetheless, it may well be conceded that, all in all, the recent trend of the judgments of the court are not as pro-labour as they had been at least prior to the NEP in 1991, and rather may well conform to economic liberalization.

4.6 Concluding remarks

In this chapter, labour law reform has been discussed in the context of economic reforms in India. The author is well aware that the labour reforms have many dimensions at macro, micro and even meso levels, and that a discussion just on labour legislation is limited in its perspective.[26] Yet, the author believes that this aspect is as important as the matters that are not covered here since labour legislation affects the outcome and the function of the labour market and of organizations, as well as how people are employed and how they work.

Labour legislation is frequently claimed to be the cause of labour market rigidity and is indirectly made the culprit for economic stagnation; therefore, it is argued that it needs to be reformed. However, India's labour market is quite flexible despite the so-called restrictive labour laws (Sharma 2006). In spite of all the 'protective' labour legislation, a remarkable recovery of the economy has been recorded from 2003/4 up to now. India's labour market can be considered quite flexible partly because companies do reduce redundant workforces by resorting to VRS as well as by making use of contract labour. Nonetheless, there may be a certain truth in the statement by the proponents of labour law reform that labour legislation in India is archaic and does not conform to the current economic environment undergoing globalization. The present UPA government does not seem unwilling to make changes in labour legislation.

In any event, it is important to recognize that it is not legislative reform alone that will make a difference. The focus should be on people, harmonious relations among them, and 'decent work', not on laws and regulations (Venkata Ratnam 2000). It is hoped that the direction of labour law reform will be to foster mutual understanding, independence and initiatives of the actors' own, placing emphasis on dialogue based on the concept of 'inclusion'. Flexibility is not the absolute guiding principle for the labour reform.

Finally, it is regrettable that the amendment in 2001 to the Trade Unions Act, 1926, was made in the manner in which it was. Even if the objective of the amendment was to reduce the multiplicity of trade unions, promote internal democracy, and facilitate orderly growth and regulation of the unions, the fact should not be ignored that India has not ratified the ILO Convention 87 regarding freedom of association and Convention 98 regarding freedom to organize and bargain collectively, which are two of the Conventions of the Core Labour Standards. The ratification of these conventions would involve granting to government employees specific rights, among them the right to strike (Swamy 2000: 59), and this was the exact issue raised by the Tamil Nadu summary dismissal case. Compliance with international standards is also necessary to play in the global arena.

Notes

1. This chapter was written as of December 2006, and Sections 4.3 and 4.4 especially reflect the best of the author's knowledge at that time.
2. As a reference for the discussion here, we use the classification of flexibility adopted by Imano and Sato (2002: 267–9). Their classification is as follows. Numerical flexibility is related to the capability for making adjustments to quantitative changes in labour demand, by recruiting/retrenching permanent employees, making use of fixed term employment, resorting to contract labour and outsourcing, and employing temporary staff, etc. Numerical flexibility is, therefore, associated with the type of employment, but the centre of the controversy concerns the regulation on 'hire and fire' since it is argued to be the major cause of rigidity by the proponents of labour law reforms. Functional flexibility relates to the capability for making adjustments to qualitative changes. This would be realized, for instance, by retaining employees who possess multiple skills, or by having employees trained with such. Financial flexibility is related to the firm's capability for adjusting its labour costs according to its financial situation. It is said to be realized by such measures as 'pay for performance' and 'profit-sharing systems'. Finally, temporal flexibility relates to working hours and their allocation. Systems such as flexible and variable working hours are some of the measures applied to enhance temporal flexibility. Restrictions on overtime work and nightshifts also fall into this category of flexibility.
3. The organized sector includes all the establishments in the public sector and non-agricultural establishments employing 10 or more persons in the private sector.
4. The economic reforms from the late 1990s onwards are sometimes termed 'institutional reforms' since the institutions needed to be reorganized to conform to the fast-changing economic environment.
5. As stated in Sections 4.3 and 4.4, the Trade Unions Act, 1926, was amended under the NDA government.
6. We should duly add that employment generation and social security for the unorganized sector are other important agenda items relating to labour and labour reforms for the UPA government. The UPA government enacted the National Rural Employment Guarantee Act (NREGA) in February 2006 that guarantees 100 days of wage employment in a fiscal year in 200 districts in rural areas. Also, the Unorganised Sector Workers Bill 2004, which aims at providing social security for workers in the unorganized sector and which received approval from the former Union Cabinet of the NDA government in 2004, was redrafted by the National Commission for Enterprises in the Unorganized Sector (NCEUS/Arjun Senguputa Commission) under the UPA government.
7. The outline of the labour laws in Section 4.3 relied heavily on Taxmann (2005). References are also made to Saxena (1996), Government of India (2004) and the website of the Ministry of Labour and Employment.

8. This subsection is mainly indebted to Srivastava (1994).
9. The Constitution of India came into force in 1950. As to its Preamble, 'socialist secular' was inserted by the Constitution (Forty-Second Amendment) Act of 1976.
10. The main laws related to fundamental rights are the Equal Remuneration Act, 1976, the Bonded Labour System (Abolition) Act, 1976, and the Child Labour (Prohibition and Regulation) Act, 1986. The fundamental right of freedom of association is associated with the Trade Union Act, 1926, which is mentioned in the next subsection.
11. Amendments by the states require approval by the centre for enactment. Venkata Ratnam (1996) describes the diversity of labour laws at the state level.
12. Provisions regarding the minimum rate of subscription and setting up of separate political funds are also contained in the amendment.
13. Advance withdrawal is regarded as a problem in certain cases, considering the purpose of the EPF Scheme. Another problem is the fixed interest currently payable on EPF deposits. Reform of the pension system in India is urgently needed due to the financial burden to the exchequer, and the New Pension Scheme (NPS), a defined contributory scheme for government employees, was launched in January 2004 under the NDA government.
14. As a related example, there is a demand in West Bengal that IT and ITES industries including BPO, which are considered key for economic growth, be designated as essential services so that they are kept out of the purview of strikes.
15. The author has not been able to independently confirm this amendment. It was quoted in the 14 October 2006 issue of *Economic and Political Weekly*.
16. India ratified Convention 89 of the International Labour Organization (ILO) regarding nightshift work by women workers in 2003.
17. In addition to what we have seen here, it was reported in May 2005 that the Union Cabinet approved the introduction of a bill amending the Labour Laws (exemption from furnishing returns and maintaining of registers by certain establishments) Act, 1988, in Parliament so as to simplify the forms of returns and registers prescribed under certain labour laws.
18. The review of the SNCL recommendation here is based on Government of India (2002a) and Venkata Ratnam (2002). The coverage of the recommendation regarding labour laws here is not comprehensive for each issue. Concerning the view of employers' organizations on labour reforms, see FICCI/AIOE (2004), for instance.
19. We will take up this Act again in Section 4.5 where judicial cases are discussed.
20. There are expectations and fears that initiatives in the textile, garment and allied industries may lead labour reforms in India in view of their high potential for export and employment generation.
21. The description of the cases in this subsection is based on Datt (2003: 291–308).
22. The question of appropriate government has also been disputed, but that dispute is not presented here.
23. This part of the judgment concerning the automatic absorption of contract labour was, however, referred to a large bench for hearing by the judgment in another case.
24. The problem of determining 'appropriate government' for the central PSUs was also said to be resolved by this judgment.
25. ISLE and IHD (2004) offers both a summary and a profound analysis on the issue.
26. For instance, Ota (2005) deals with the labour reforms at the shop floor level by focusing on work organizations.

References

Atkinson, J. (1985) *Flexibility, Uncertainty, and Manpower Management*, IMS Report no. 89. Brighton: University of Sussex, Institute of Manpower Studies.

Besley, Timothy and Robin Burgess (2004) 'Can Labour Regulation Hinder Economic Performance? Evidence from India'. *Quarterly Journal of Economics* 119 (1): 91–134.

Datt, Ruddar (2003) *Economic Reforms, Labour and Employment*. New Delhi: Deep & Deep Publications.

Deshpande, Lalit K., Alakh N. Sharma, Anup K. Karan and Sandip Sarkar (2004) *Liberalisation and Labour: Labour Flexibility in Indian Manufacturing*. New Delhi: Institute for Human Development.

Door, Ronald P. (2005) *Hataraku to Iukoto: Global-ka to Roudou no Atarashii Im*. Tokyo: Chukoushinsho (in Japanese. The original title is *New Forms and Meanings of Work in an Increasingly Globalising World* published by the International Labour Organization in 2004).

Doshi, Kokila (1993) 'India'. In Miriam Rothman, Dennis R. Briscoe and Raoul C.D. Nacamulli (eds) *Industrial Relations around the World, Labor Relaions for Multinational Companies*. Berlin/New York: Walter de Gruyter, pp. 173–86.

Economic and Political Weekly (2006) Editorial ('Women and Work: After the Law'). 14 October, 41 (41).

Fallon, Peter R. and Robert E.B. Lucus (1991) 'The Impact of Changes in Job Security Regulations in India and Zimbabwe'. *The World Bank Economic Review* 5(3) (Sept.): 395–413.

FICCI-AIOE (2004) *Core Group on Restructuring Labour Policy: Report*. New Delhi: FICCI.

Government of Andhra Pradesh (2003) 'Notifications by Government, Labour, Employment Training and Factories Department (Lab-I) Bringing into Force the Contract Labour (Regulation and Abolition Act) (Andhra Pradesh Amendment) Act 2003, (Andhra Pradesh Act No. 10 of 2003) [G.O.Ms. No. 48, Labour Employment Training and Factories (La-I), 18th August 2003].' *The Andhra Pradesh Gazette*, 22 August, Hyderabad.

Government of India, Ministry of Labour (2002a) *Second National Commission on Labour Report*. New Delhi.

Government of India, Planning Commission (2002b) *10th Five Year Plan (2002–2007)*. New Delhi.

Government of India, Ministry of Labour (2002c) *Annual Survey of Industries: Summary Report on Absenteeism, Labour Turnover, Employment and Labour Cost in the Census Sector*. Shimla/Chandigarh.

Government of India (2004) *Indian Labour Year Book*, Ministry of Labour. Shimla/Chandigarh.

Government of India, Ministry of Finance (2006) *Economic Survey 2005–2006*. New Delhi.

Imano, Koichiro and Hiroki Sato (2002) *Jinji Kanri Nyumon* (Introduction to Human Resources Management). Tokyo: Nihon Keizai Shinbun-sha (in Japanese).

Indian Society of Labour Economics and Institute for Human Development (ISLE and IHD) (2004) *Workers and the Right to Strike: Report of Four Consultations*. New Delhi: Institute for Human Development.

Mamoria, C.B., Satish Mmoria and S.V. Gnakar (1997) *Dynamics of Industrial Relations*. Mumbai: Himalaya Publishing House.

Ota, Hitoshi (2001) 'Indo ni okeru Roushi-kankei no Kinnen no Doukou: Miro-data wo Mochiita Seizougyou no Bunseki' (The Recent Trend of the Industrial Relations in India: an Analysis on the Indian Manufacturing Sector Using Micro-Data). *The Bulletin of the Graduate School of Commerce*, no. 53. Tokyo: Graduate School of Commerce, Waseda University, pp. 169–82 (in Japanese).

—— (2005) 'Flexible Work Organisation, Human Resource Practices and Worker Perception in India: a Case Study of Bangalore City'. *Indian Journal of Labour Economics* 48(1) (January–March): 115–29.

—— (2006) 'Indo no Roudou-keizai to Roudou-kaikaku no Dainamizumu' (Labour and Economy in India and its Dynamism of Labour Reforms). In Shuji Uchikawa (ed.) *Yakudou Suru Indo Keizai* (The Dynamic Indian Economy). Chiba: The Institute of Developing Economies, JETRO, 126–67 (in Japanese).

Punekar, S.D., S.B. Deodhar and Saraswathi Sankaran (1994) *Labour Welfare, Trade Unionism and Industrial Relations*, 4th edn. Mumbai: Himalaya Publishing House.

Sarma, A.M. (1994) *Aspects of Labour Welfare and Social Security*. Bombay: Himalaya Publishing House.

Saxena, R.C. (1996) *Labour Problems and Social Welfare*. Meerut: K. Nath & Co.

Sen, Ratna (1996) 'Emerging Issues in Industrial Relations in Transition'. *Indian Journal of Labour Economics* 39(4): 1047–53.
Sharma, Alakh N. (2006) 'Flexibility, Employment and Labour Market Reforms in India'. *Economic and Political Weekly* 41(21) (27 May): 2078–85.
Srivastava, Suresh C. (1994) *Industrial Relations and Labour Laws*, 3rd edn. Delhi: Vikas Publishing House Pvt Ltd.
Standing, Guy (1999) *Global Labour Flexibility: Seeking Distributive Justice*. London: Macmillan Press Ltd.
Sundar, K.R. Shyam (2000) 'Second National Commission on Labour: Not up to the Task'. *Economic and Political Weekly* 35(30): 2607–11.
Swamy, Subramaniam (2000) *India's Labour Standards and the WTO Framework*. New Delhi: Konark Publishers Pvt Ltd.
Taxmann (2005) *Taxmann's Labour Laws 2005*. New Delhi: Taxmann Allied Services (P.) Ltd.
Uchikawa, Shuji (2003) 'Employment in the Manufacturing Organized Sector in India: the Rise of Medium Scale Units'. In Shuji Uchikawa (ed.) *Labour Market and Institutions in India: 1990s and Beyond*. New Delhi: Manohar, pp. 39–63.
Venkata Ratnam, C.S. (1996) 'Industrial Relations in Indian States – an Overview'. In C.S. Venkata Ratnam (ed.) *Industrial Relations in Indian States*. New Delhi: Global Business Press.
Venkata Ratnam, C.S. (2000) 'Competitive Labour Policies and Labour Laws in Indian States'. *Indian Journal of Labour Economics* 43(4) (October–December): 1049–60.
Venkata Ratnam, C.S. (2002) 'Report of the 2nd National Commission on Labour – a Critique', mimeo.

Journals

Economic Times (http://economictimes.indiatimes.com/).
Hindu (http://www.hinduonnet.com/).
Hindu Business Line (http://www.thehindubusinessline.com/).

Periodical

Economic and Political Weekly (http://www.epw.org.in).

Website URL

Ministry of Labour and Employment, Government of India:(http://labour.nic.in/).

5

Labour Law Reform in Sri Lanka: Revision of the Termination of Employment of Workmen Act and its Implications

Etsuyo Arai

5.1 Introduction

Sri Lanka, known for its welfare-oriented policies, is characterized by the presence of an educated labour force, which strongly distinguishes it from other South Asian countries. In the sphere of economic management, it has followed public sector-dominated policies. However, when the country changed its course in the late 1970s towards economic liberalization, placing emphasis on private sector initiatives, the labour problem became one of its most formidable tasks. The labour protection and employment practices in the public sector affected the private sector as well, and strong opposition was raised against any move that would diminish the existing privileges of workers. After economic liberalization, Sri Lanka achieved an average economic growth rate of 5.4 per cent during the first half of the 1980s, 3.2 per cent in the second half of the 1980s, 5.3 per cent in the 1990s and 4.8 per cent between 2000 and 2006, in spite of ethnic conflict and natural disaster (Central Bank 2006). Nevertheless, it is argued that the growth is lower than its potential (Jayawardena 2004). Besides the decades-long ethnic conflict, distortions in the labour market are pointed out as one of the impediments to high economic growth (Yatawara 2004).

In spite of calls for labour law reform from business circles, the government has avoided implementation of drastic reforms in labour laws due to political considerations in the face of pressures from trade unions and frustration among the unemployed youth. As a consequence, the distortions in the labour market created chiefly by the wide gap in employment conditions between the formal sector (including the public sector and relatively large-scale private sector) and the informal sector remained up to the end of the 1990s. However, after the turn of the century, Sri Lanka's deeper integration into the globalized economy as well as imperatives to meet the requirements set by international agencies compelled the government to finally take extensive measures for labour law reform.

The Central Bank of Sri Lanka once enumerated as many as 50 labour laws (Central Bank 2000). Most of them were enacted during the period when the public sector dominated the country's economy. Among them, the Industrial Dispute

Table 5.1 Difficulty of firing and firing costs

Region or economy	*Difficulty of Firing Index*	*Firing costs (weeks of wages)*
East Asia and Pacific	19	41
Europe and Central Asia	39	26
Latin America and Caribbean	27	61
Middle East and North Africa	33	57
OECD	27	31
Sub-Saharan Africa	45	70
South Asia	38	72
Sri Lanka	60	178
India	70	56
Bangladesh	40	51
Pakistan	30	90

Note: Difficulty of Firing Index is difficulty and expense of dismissing a redundant worker and firing cost (weeks of wages) is the cost of dismissal of redundant worker after 20 years of employment expressed in weeks of wages.
Source: Compiled from World Bank, *Doing Business 2007*, Indicator Tables.

Act (IDA) (No. 43, 1950) and the Termination of Employment of Workmen Act (TEWA) (No. 45, 1971) are the main targets for reform by business concerns as well as international agencies. TEWA, which is to be addressed in this chapter, restricts termination of employees in private sector enterprises with 15 or more employees on a permanent basis, for non-disciplinary reasons. *Doing Business*, a publication compiled by the World Bank, compares the flexibility of labour regulations of various countries (World Bank 2006a). Table 5.1 indicates the very high firing costs in Sri Lanka. Among the South Asian countries, Sri Lanka is next to India in terms of difficulty in firing employees, but the firing costs far exceed those of India. In fact, among 177 countries covered, Sri Lanka ranks in fourth place, along with Ghana and Zambia, following Zimbabwe (446), Sierra Leone (329) and Egypt (186). This clearly shows that deregulation of termination, in other words amendment of TEWA, is an urgent need of the day from the perspective of 'doing business'.

Two reasons are discerned behind the recent amendment of TEWA. First, the conventional belief is that rigid labour law has distorted the labour market in Sri Lanka. TEWA has been perceived as overprotecting existing workers employed in the formal sector. It is challenged as an impediment to healthy development of the labour market, preventing the private sector from adjusting to the globalized economy.

Second, apart from the need for removing constraints on growth of the private sector, the country is plagued with a prevalence of unemployment on a large scale. Thus, labour law reform has been addressed from the viewpoint of coping with chronic unemployment, especially among the educated youth.

In this regard, a point missing in the debates in favour of labour law reforms is that the jobs favoured by educated youths should be taken into account. As will be discussed later, there is a strong orientation among educated youths towards white-collar and protected jobs, which is the result of public sector dominance as well as implementation of protective legislation including TEWA, in the private sector. This has created a mismatch of labour demand (high security) and supply (low security). It is a matter of serious concern whether this gap can be narrowed merely by changes in the labour law.

This chapter investigates the legislation process of TEWA and the problems brought about by its implementation. Moreover, after delineating the debates concerning amendment of TEWA and its implemented reforms, I will elucidate the extent to which the recent amendments restructured the existing regime of labour protection. Lastly, the implications of the amendments especially on the fundamental question of unemployment in Sri Lanka will be examined.

The essay is structured as follows. In the next section, the structure of the economy and the labour market is described. In the third section, the political and economic background of TEWA is discussed. The fourth section shows the protection provided by TEWA. In the fifth section, proposals and policies of international institutions, the government of Sri Lanka, and employers and investors are investigated. Section 5.6 will examine the amendment of TEWA in order to investigate the effect of the amendment in light of the anticipated results. The seventh section will sum up the discussion.

5.2 Sri Lankan economy and the labour market

Before going into the discussion about TEWA, let us overview the structure of the economy and labour market in Sri Lanka.

5.2.1 Structural change in the economy and labour market

When Sri Lanka attained independence in 1948, plantation agriculture was the major component of the economy. The first industrialization policy was implemented in 1956, and it was a state-led industrialization and import substitution policy. Expansion of the public sector continued until the mid-1970s due to the nationalizing of private companies and plantations. The public sector accounted for 24 per cent of GNP in 1977 (Kelegama 1993: 5).

Sri Lanka changed its policy stance to liberalize the economy in 1977. An export-oriented industrialization policy was introduced to develop the economy. Export from Free Trade Zones increased greatly, and furthermore, privatization began in the 1990s.[1]

Tables 5.2 and 5.3 show the contributions to GDP and employment by each sector since 1980. Like many other countries, Sri Lanka has experienced a structural shift from agriculture to non-agriculture. The share of agriculture in GDP and employment decreased from 24.3 to 17.2 per cent and from 51.6 to 30.7 per cent, respectively, between 1980 and 2005. In its place, the industry and service sectors expanded their share. A few points should be noted from the tables. First, with respect to employment, the structural shift from agriculture to non-agriculture took place quite rapidly. Second, the reduction of agricultural employment was replaced by the rapid expansion of service sector employment. Although job

Table 5.2 Share of GDP by sector (%)

Sector	*1980*	*1985*	*1990*	*1995*	*2000*	*2005*
Agriculture	24.3	25.9	23.2	20.0	20.5	17.2
Industry	23.7	25.6	28.5	31.2	27.6	27.0
Manufacturing	13.7	14.8	17.4	20.4	17.4	16.3
Services	51.9	48.5	48.3	48.7	52.0	55.7

Source: Central Bank of Sri Lanka, *Annual Report, Economic and Social Statistics of Sri Lanka*, various issues.

Table 5.3 Share of employment by sector (%)

Sector	*1980*	*1985*	*1990*	*1995*	*2000*	*2005*
Agriculture	51.6	49.3	47.7	36.7	36.0	30.7
Industry	21.8	18.4	20.6	22.2	23.6	24.5
Manufacturing	19.3	12.6	14.1	14.7	16.6	18.4
Services	26.5	32.3	31.7	41.1	40.3	44.8

Source: Central Bank of Sri Lanka, *Annual Report, Economic and Social Statistics of Sri Lanka*, various issues.

opportunities in such well-organized sectors as communication, banking and insurance increased, the service sector contains a significant amount of informal employment. Third, while employment in the industrial sector increased slightly, employment in the manufacturing sector decreased during 1985–95 and almost recovered to the 1980s level in 2005. It was construction sector employment, included in the industrial sector, which compensated for the decrease. This testifies to the stagnation of manufacturing employment.

Looking at the public–private division of the economy as a whole, the private sector accounts for a major portion of economic activities. More than 96 per cent of value added in the industrial sector is derived from the private sector. Although one-quarter of chemical, petroleum, rubber and plastic products were produced by public enterprises in 2006 (Central Bank 2006), most of the products were supplied by the private sector. Other important sectors for the sake of employment are public administration, other government services and defence. However, their contribution to GDP is as low as 4 per cent in 2006 (Central Bank 2006). Therefore, it should be mentioned that the economic development of Sri Lanka largely depends on the growth of the private sector, and labour issues in that sector also have an important bearing for the welfare dimension of the country.

5.2.2 Labour market in the private sector and TEWA coverage

In this section, I will analyse the structure of the labour market in more detail and identify the extent to which TEWA is applied.

As mentioned above, TEWA is applied to private sector units which employ 15 employees or more. In Sri Lanka, no statistics are collected concerning the number of firms and employees that are protected by labour law in the private sector. Instead, the active number of companies which participate in the Employees' Provident Fund (EPF[2]) account is often cited as a proxy (Central Bank 1985). Here, I will estimate the scale of the protected private sector through a residual method by way of subtracting the sectors outside the purview of the law.

The Quarterly Labour Force Survey (QLFS) data issued by the Department of Census and Statistics (DCS) are used. QLFS is a household survey and does not include the non-household population, such as those in barracks, hostels and large boarding houses.[3] In this format, members of the armed forces who are in operational areas[4] and factory workers who stay in hostels are excluded. Though armed forces that are out of the labour market statistics are not important for our purposes, factory workers who stay in hostels should be examined separately.

Since only 'employees' are protected by law, employers, own-account workers and unpaid family workers are first subtracted from total employed. Table 5.4 shows the labour force status of the household population. It should be noted that coverage of the data for 2003, 2004 and 2005 is larger than that of other data and includes the area which had been involved in the ethnic war. Therefore, it is not strictly comparable with the figures of previous years, but it does show the rough trend over 15 years. As the total number of employed[5] increased, the total number of employees also increased from 1990. However, the share of employees in the total employment does not exceed the 62.4 per cent recorded in 1991 when privatization started in full swing. In contrast, own-account workers who are not covered by the protection of labour law increased both in absolute numbers and percentage.

The second step is to subtract public sector employees. The public sector consists of government, local government, state corporations, statutory boards and state authorities. The public sector was downsized from the early 1990s due to privatization which was implemented on tea estates and state corporations. The Voluntary Retirement Scheme (VRS) was also implemented to reduce public employees. As Table 5.4 shows, employees in semi-government employment were reduced to 3.1 per cent of the total employed in 2004, from 12.5 per cent in 1990. State owned estate labourers were also reduced dramatically from 7.7 to 0.2 per cent during the same period. The reduction of the number and the share of public employees, however, is not as large as that recorded by the semi-government and estate sectors. To paraphrase, the government sector remains an important employment absorber. However, its function as an employment absorber is unstable because government policy changes frequently. For example, the government minimized new hiring and promoted VRS in 2002 and 2003, but then introduced a special recruitment programme for university graduates and hired more than 42,000 graduates (Central Bank 2004). The private sector seemed to increase in the early 1990s, but this was due to the shift of estate labourers and state corporation workers to the private sector. After the large-scale privatization of the estate sector in 1992 and 1996, the growth of the private sector was not high.

Table 5.4 Labour force status of the household population (10 years of age and over) ('000) (percentage of total employed)

	Total employed	Employee					Employer worker	Own-account family worker	Unpaid
		Total	Public			Private			
			Total	Semi-government	Estate				
1990[1]	5,047	2,786	1,085	629	387	1,701	91	1,474	697
	100	55.2	21.5	12.5	7.7	33.7	1.8	29.2	13.8
1991[1]	5,016	3,130	1,149	616	376	1,981	110	1,274	502
	100	62.4	22.9	12.3	7.5	39.5	2.2	25.4	10
1992[1]	4,962	2,982	992	466	266	1,985	79	1,345	556
	100	60.1	20	9.4	5.4	40	1.6	27.1	11.2
1993[1]	5,201	3,121	905	541	313	2,226	104	1,425	541
	100	60	17.4	10.4	6.0	42.8	2.0	27.4	10.4
1994[1]	5,281	3,206	866	543	301	2,340	121	1,437	518
	100	60.7	16.4	10.3	5.7	44.3	2.3	27.2	9.8
1995[1]	5,357	3,204	836	503	261	2,373	134	1,516	504
	100	59.8	15.6	9.4	4.9	44.3	2.5	28.3	9.4
1996[1]	5,537	3,367	831	364	122	2,536	127	1,484	554
	100	60.8	15.0	6.6	2.2	45.8	2.3	26.8	10.0
1997[1]	5,608	3,331	847	356	117	2,484	129	1,615	527
	100	59.4	15.1	6.3	2.1	44.3	2.3	28.8	9.4
1998[1]	6,049	3,363	877	368	120	2,492	115	1,748	823
	100	55.6	14.5	6.1	2.0	41.2	1.9	28.9	13.6

(Continued)

Table 5.4 (Continued)

	Total employed	*Employee*					Employer worker	Own-account family worker	Unpaid
		Total	Public			Private			
			Total	Semi-government					
					Estate				
1999[1]	6,083	3,498	876	373	116	2,622	122	1,721	742
	100	57.5	14.4	6.1	1.9	43.1	2.0	28.3	12.2
2000[1]	6,310	3,553	846	383	102	2,707	145	1,792	820
	100	56.3	13.4	6.1	1.6	42.9	2.3	28.4	13
2001[1]	6,236	3,654	867	370	94	2,787	143	1,777	661
	100	58.6	13.9	5.9	1.5	44.7	2.3	28.5	10.6
2002[1]	6,519	3,775	874	272	21	2,901	183	1,865	698
	100	57.9	13.4	4.2	0.3	44.5	2.8	28.6	10.7
2003[2]	7,013	4,060	947	244	19	3,114	182	2,076	694
	100	57.9	13.5	3.5	0.3	44.4	2.6	29.6	9.9
2004[3]	7,394	4,392	961	232	17	3,431	214	2,093	695
	100	59.4	13.0	3.1	0.2	46.4	2.9	28.3	9.4
2005[4]	7,518	4,458	1,000			3,466	233	2,233	594
	100	59.3	13.3			46.1	3.1	29.7	7.9
2006[1]	7,081	3,916	949			2,967	227	2,238	701
1st quarter	100	55.3	13.4			41.9	3.2	31.6	9.9

Notes: [1]Excluding northern and eastern provinces.
[2]Including eastern provinces but excluding northern provinces.
[3]Excluding Mulathivu and Kilinochchi districts.
[4]All districts are included.
Source: Compiled from DCS, *The Report of the Sri Lanka Labour Force Survey*, First Quarter 2006, Tables 1 and 5. Data for semi-government sector and state owned estate labourers are from *Bulletin of Semi Government Sector Employment 2004*, Tables 1 and 2.

The final step is to remove the private sector which is not covered by TEWA, i.e. small-scale units with less than 15 employees. However, there are no statistics readily available concerning the exact number of workers employed in units with more than 14 workers. Therefore, I will make a rough estimate by subtracting the informal sector. The LFS is scheduled to collect information relating to the informal sector, which is defined in terms of (i) registration of the organization, (ii) accounting practices of the organization, and (iii) total number of regular employees of the organization (DCS, first quarter 2006).[6] According to the DCS, employment in 2006 by the formal, non-agricultural sector was 2.22 million. Subtracting the public sector from this, we have a rough estimation of about 1.28 million workforce to which TEWA is applied in present-day Sri Lanka. This is about 40 per cent of workers in the private sector.

An important section outside the purview of TEWA is the Board of Investment (BOI) companies. They are registered under the BOI and ensure several investment incentives. Most of the employees who work in BOI companies in and around Colombo live in hostels or boarding houses provided by the companies[7] since they are from rural areas distant from Colombo. As mentioned before, LFS is a household survey and does not cover workers living in boarding houses and hostels. Therefore, since the labour statistics of DCS do not include workers in hostels, DCS underestimates the number of employed persons in that sector. It is estimated that 1.5 per cent of the total employed are in this category (Nanayakkara 2004). There were 121,780 employees in EPZ enterprises, which are a part of BOI companies, as of the end of December 2004, of which 70 per cent were female (Department of Labour 2004).

It is pointed out that most of the formal employment generated in Sri Lanka since the introduction of the free enterprise era, according to Central Bank reports, seems to be in BOI companies (Amerasinghe 1998). There are several reasons for the expansion of BOI companies. Exemption from the labour law is one of the most important reasons among the various incentives given to investors. It is well known that the original bill which set up the Greater Colombo Economic Council (GCEC, which is now the BOI) envisaged that the labour laws would not apply in the areas covered by GCEC. This was vehemently opposed by trade unions; however, in reality the zones developed on the basis of what could be termed 'special arrangements'. GCEC appeared to be an intermediary for settling disputes. Ordinary labour disputes are investigated by the Labour Department and applications are placed before the Labour Tribunals. However in the case of BOI companies, the BOI attempts to contain any problem within its boundaries. Within the zones, the likelihood of unions successfully taking root is minimal. This is because of the lack of access to the zones, which maintain a high degree of security and also because of the fact that employees work on a shift basis, round the clock. Since access by trade unions to the zones is limited, management believes that it is operating in an oasis cut off from the rest of the island. The companies operate on the assumption that all industrial relations are handled for them by the BOI's industrial relations division.

To sum up, I will state two points; first, the workforce outside the purview of TEWA, thus without much protection, is quite large, i.e. 80 per cent of the total employed, and second, the effects of TEWA, however, are also substantial since 40 per cent of the employed in the private sector which is expected to play an important role in economic development is not a negligible share. It is therefore important to examine precisely what kind of protection TEWA has provided and how it has been changed in order to see the nature of the 'distortions' TEWA has created.

5.3 Political and economic background of TEWA

Before going into the contents of TEWA, let us reflect first of all on why TEWA was enacted and remained as it was, except for minor amendments in favour of workers, until the end of the 1990s.

5.3.1 Introduction of TEWA

The Mahajana Eksath Peramuna (MEP) government (a coalition led by the Sri Lanka Freedom Party (SLFP)) adopted import-substitution industrialization as an economic policy from the mid-1950s. Importation of non-essential goods was reduced by a high tax barrier and quantitative restrictions starting in 1960 because of a foreign exchange problem. The imported materials were forwarded to priority industries. By 1965, the Sri Lankan economy was effectively isolated from the rest of the world. With a change of the government to the United National Party (UNP) in 1965, the economy was liberalized to some extent. However, SLFP allied with leftist parties and returned to office as the United Front (UF) government in 1970. They campaigned for a socialist welfare state. The UF government started to extend the role of public corporations in the economy for the purpose of raising employment, output growth and national savings. In addition to nationalization of industry, they introduced a stricter licensing system for all imports.

Soon after the UF government came into office, a heavy blow hit Sri Lankan politics as well as its economy in 1971. In April 1971, the UF government suffered an attempted *coup d'état* led by the Janatha Vimukthi Peramuna (JVP), an organization composed mostly of educated but unemployed rural Sinhalese youths who thought the new government had betrayed them. However, JVP lacked wide support in the community. Its uprising was crushed by the government with the help of military support from both Western and communist countries. The insurgency, though it was abortive, cost Sri Lanka heavily. Because the insurgency interrupted economic activities for a few months, the government decided to increase the defence budget, and the economy also deteriorated. The government found it necessary to reduce foreign exchange allocations for imports of raw materials by the private sector. Several firms were faced with the problem of layoff or retrenchment of workers as a result of a marked decline in the volume of business, consequent to a reduction in import quotas and a shortage of raw materials (Ministry of Employment and Labour 2002a).

However, when retrenched workers turned to obtain relief under the IDA, they had to wait for a long period of time as inquiries before the Labour Tribunals and Arbitrators appointed under the IDA were prolonged and took time to be resolved. The resultant atmosphere of social tension hampered production and development. The Labour Minister at the time said in Parliament that workers' jobs were terminated by reason of lack of raw materials, which he called a 'false premise' (*Hansard*, 3 June 1971). It was thought that widespread unemployment would bring about another insurgency. The low level of economic activity could not create enough employment opportunities to absorb the increasing newcomers in the labour market. By 1960, the age cohorts that had benefited from the low death rate finished their free education[8] and came in flocks into the limited labour market (Central Bank 1979). Unemployment became one of the most urgent economic problems for the Sri Lankan government. Unemployment worsened further in the 1970s due to economic depression and the threat of insurgency.

Therefore, the increasing retrenchment and unemployment figures pushed the government to quickly enact legislative measures to safeguard workers. The Act was preceded by Emergency Regulations[9] under the Public Security Ordinance which contained the main provisions of the Act and which was regularized as TEWA in October 1971.[10] As a consequence of the new legislation, employees were guaranteed employment security in the private sector even if the employer faced loss of business or lack of raw materials. The Act was amended in 1976 and 1988 in order to provide wider security to employees.

5.3.2 TEWA after the liberalization of economy

As mentioned above, TEWA was enacted to provide employment security for vulnerable workers in a sluggish economy. However, it remained intact even after the liberalization of the economy was initiated in 1977, despite repeated requests from business circles.

The government also took the opportunity to issue proposals to change the labour law to better fit the economy. The Department of Labour published a *White Paper on Employment Relations* in January 1978. This White Paper suggested that bills be proposed to repeal and modify several existing statutes, such as old statutes like the Service Contracts Ordinance of 1875 and the Estate Labour (Indian) Ordinance of 1889. The White Paper also suggested the replacement of TEWA with less stringent controls on dismissals. Consequently, some parts of the proposals were implemented, such as Workers' Councils which were introduced in Free Trade Zones.[11] The Gratuity Act and the Employees Trust Fund Act were introduced by the bill. In business circles, this White Paper was considered to be an improvement on the existing labour law. The Employers' Federation of Ceylon (EFC[12]) welcomed its removal of the need for prior permission from the Commissioner of Labour for non-disciplinary dismissal. However, the proposal was strongly opposed by the unions, and in the end, it was not realized.[13]

Table 5.5 Economic indicators before and after liberalization in Sri Lanka

	GDP growth rate (%)	*Exports (US$million)*	*Direct investment (US$million)*
1970	4.3	338.7	−0.3
1971	0.2	325.4	0.3
1972	3.2	317.9	0.3
1973	3.7	366.4	0.5
1974	3.2	511.2	1.4
1975	2.8	563.4	−0.1
1976	3.0	558.8	0.0
1977	4.2	767.1	−1.0
1978	8.2	845.1	1.5
1979	6.3	981.4	47.0
1980	5.8	1064.7	42.9
1981	5.8	1065.5	50.2
1982	5.1	1013.7	63.6
1983	5.0	1064.1	37.5
1984	5.1	1462.3	32.6
1985	5.0	1315.3	24.4

Source: Compiled from Central Bank of Sri Lanka, *Annual Report 2000*, Tables 7 and 18.

In addition to the opposition by trade unions, amendment of TEWA was set aside due to the favourable turn of the economy. The GNP increased 8.2 and 6.3 per cent in 1978 and 1979, respectively (Table 5.5). By the end of 1979, a dozen factories in the Free Trade Zones started operation and export, mainly of ready-made garments. Also the unemployment rate decreased from 19.7 per cent in 1975 to 14.8 per cent in 1978/79 (Table 5.6). A growth-oriented package of new policies generated employment in rural areas as well as in urban areas. An IPZ (Investment Promotion Zone, the name used for Free Trade Zones at that time) and the Urban Renewal and Housing Construction Programme absorbed urban unemployment, and the Mahaveli Development Project[14] absorbed rural unemployment.[15] This was quite a relief for the government. Once the unemployment problem ameliorated and social unrest eased due to the spate of investments (Table 5.5) and the development programme, the debates about the labour law were shelved.

The privatization that started in the 1990s did not entail labour reforms. Privatization was associated with labour retrenchments in many cases. Rather than revising TEWA, a Cabinet decision offered a voluntary retrenchment package amounting to approximately Rs.250,000 per person on average (Kelegama 1993).[16]

In addition to protection under the labour law, political decisions also provide security for workers. There are two main political parties in Sri Lanka. Each has strong linkage with trade unions. Support from trade unions is fundamental for mobilizing people at election rallies. Once one party comes into office, the trade union which has linkage with the governing party vehemently demands rights, whether the demands are reasonable or not. They have staged radical strikes so often that they are called 'militant'.[17] This shows that workers were protected

Table 5.6 Unemployment rates in Sri Lanka

Year	*Source*	*Unemployment rate*		
		Total	*Male*	*Female*
1959	ILO Survey	10.5 (low estimate) 12.8 (high estimate)		
1963	Population Census	16.6	15.3	20
1968/69	Socio-economic Survey	14.3	11.2	20.1
1971	Population Census	18.7	14.3	31.1
1973	Survey of Labour Force Participation Rates	18.3	13.7	26.8
1975	Land and Labour Utilization Survey	19.7	14.3	33.1
1978/79	Consumer Finances and Socio-economic Survey	14.8	9.2	24.9
1981	Population Census	17.9	13.3	31
1981/82	Consumer Finances and Socio-economic Survey	11.7	7.8	21.3
1985/86	Labour Force and Socio-economic Survey	14.1	10.8	20.8
1990	Quarterly Labour Force Survey	15.9	7.6	20.2
1995	Quarterly Labour Force Survey	12.3	9	18.7
2000	Quarterly Labour Force Survey.	7.6	5.8	11
	Quarterly Labour Force Survey	7.7	5.5	11.9

Sources: Central Bank of Sri Lanka (1979: 95). Central Bank of Sri Lanka (2000) *Annual Report*. Special Statistical Appendix Table 4. DCS (2005: 4–5).

politically as well as by the labour law. From the viewpoint of employers, a system for the protection of employers was lacking.

The reason why the demands of the employers in the private sector were not realized is that other sectors were more important to the government from the viewpoint of employment absorption. The agriculture and public sectors absorbed employment up to the 1960s. In the 1970s, however, agriculture ended its role as an absorber because educated youth preferred white-collar jobs. Since insufficient white-collar jobs were created in the private sector, the government expanded the public sector through nationalization and more hiring to secure employment in the 1970s.[18] The government expected the public sector to create employment as it did in the 1970s. Regarding the private sector, the government expected it to retain its existing workforce rather than to promote business and generate new employment. This was the reason why TEWA was enacted. As a result, the public sector as well as the private sector was forced to make staff redundant in many cases.

In the 1980s, the BOI-registered companies in the FTZ, large-scale public works in Mahaveli and Housing projects, absorbed large numbers of job seekers for a while. The pressure on the government to produce employment was temporarily sufficiently reduced, and so proposals for more revisions to TEWA ceased. In this way, the government did not touch the labour laws and avoided conflict with trade unions.

The government first issued an emergency regulation to establish TEWA. As employment pressure increased, the government issued a Cabinet decision for emergency relief measures to defuse social unrest caused by unemployment.

A timely economic boom temporarily created employment and helped the government to cope with the unemployment without repealing TEWA, in spite of requests from the business community and some recognition by the government that repeal was due.

5.4 The protection provided by TEWA

Let us now turn to the contents of TEWA; what kind of 'protection' or 'shortcomings' from the viewpoints of employers are entailed in the legislation?

5.4.1 The coverage of TEWA

The coverage of TEWA is quite wide. Employees are given abundant opportunities to exercise their rights based on TEWA. The law covers all non-disciplinary reasons for dismissal, including as a consequence of closure of business as well as inefficiency and chronic absence of employees. The Act was amended in 1976 by Act No. 4 to include non-employment of workers arising out of closures. This amendment was introduced as the original Act did not cover dismissals arising out of closures, and many employers were circumventing the provisions of the Act by closing down their establishments and reopening later with a new set of employees. Section 6A (1) of the Act empowers the Commissioner to order an employer to pay to a worker whose services have been terminated in contravention of the provisions of the Act, in consequence of closure of any trade, industry or business by him/her on or before a specified date, any sum of money as compensation, as an alternative to reinstatement of such worker. 'Non-disciplinary reason' was expanded from the original law to benefit employees more by including inefficiency and chronic absence of employees[19] after a court of appeals stated that inefficiency and incompetence are not misconduct for which punishment by way of disciplinary action may be imposed. The wider the coverage of 'non-disciplinary reason' expands, the greater the number of the employees that are protected by TEWA.

There is no provision which excludes chief executives from protection by the law. Even if they have responsibility in times of financial crisis of the company, they can draw compensation when they are made redundant, although the law is intended to protect vulnerable employees who have been made redundant and have lost their source of income. Moreover, it might be easier for ex-executives to find another job because they have professional knowledge and social status.

Mass retrenchments and layoffs were a concern of the government at the time of the establishment of the law, and these seriously affected the lives of the workers. TEWA applies even to cases in which an employer is firing only one employee on grounds other than disciplinary reasons. The process required by law compels employers to fulfil a heavy duty in their day-to-day management.

Furthermore, the Act was amended in 1988 by Act No. 51 which stipulated a six-month period from the date of termination of employment within which the dismissed employee can seek relief from the Commissioner, and so workers are allowed a long period of time to claim their rights. As a result, employers find it extremely difficult to dismiss their employees for non-disciplinary reasons because TEWA covers a wide variety of workers over a long time period.

5.4.2 Implementation of TEWA

Implementation of the law was disadvantageous to employers. Employers are required to seek approval of the Commissioner of Labour for a non-disciplinary dismissal, in cases where the employee has not given written consent to the termination of his service. Section 2 (2) (c) requires the Commissioner to grant or refuse approval within three months from the date of receipt of an application from an employer. In many cases, however, inquiries take a longer time, and the average is six months. The employer must continue paying basic salary to the employee until the employer receives the result.

The Labour Commissioner is vested to order an employer to reinstate a worker to his/her original position when the Commissioner has identified the dismissal as unjustified and is also vested to order an employer to pay compensation as a severance allowance in case the dismissal is accepted at the closure of business. Though unlimited and absolute discretionary power is vested in the Commissioner of Labour under Section 2 (2) (e), there is no legal provision that requires the reasons for his/her decision to be stated in writing. The Commissioner is also not required to explain the criteria s/he followed to determine any particular compensation package. Therefore, an employer is unable to predict how long it would take and how much it would cost to dismiss an employee for a non-disciplinary reason.

5.4.3 No formula for compensation

Most important is the fact that there are no guidelines for the computation of compensation and no ceiling on compensation. The Act stipulates in Section 6A (1) that when employment of a worker is terminated in contravention of the provisions of this Act in consequence of the closure of business, the Commissioner may order the employer 'to pay to such workman ... any sum of money as compensation as an alternative to the reinstatement of such workman and any gratuity or any other benefit payable to such workman'.

Several conditions should be considered to determine the amount of compensation, such as the nature of the employer's business, its capacity to pay, the workers' ages, the nature of employment, length of service, seniority, salary at the time of termination and opportunities of obtaining similar alternative employment. In most countries, severance payments to workers made redundant on economic grounds are calculated on the basis of years of service. In general, most of the redundant workers receive a payment worth several months' pay. In Sri Lanka, dismissed workers receive a larger amount of payment as compensation than workers in other countries which are at the same level of development. Frequently, the Labour Commissioner orders compensation payment beyond the capacity of the employer to pay.

5.5 Contesting approaches to the revision of TEWA

Although TEWA was always under criticism from private employers, some sections of the government also acknowledged its shortcomings. The call for its revision became more vocal in the 1990s when international agencies joined the chorus. In this section, we delineate the debates and different approaches presented by these three actors.

5.5.1 International institutions

So-called structural adjustments initiated by the IMF/World Bank started in 1989 in Sri Lanka. Those international institutions suggested that Sri Lanka should reform its public sector in order to reduce its budget deficit. At the same time, they expected the government to take measures to improve the business environment by way of eradicating impediments for the private business community. The main issue in public sector reform was reduction of redundant officers, adjustment of salary and privatization or restructuring of public enterprises. Deregulation[20] was assumed to revitalize the private sector and improve the balance of payments with export expansion. The reforms, though they succeeded in reducing the budget deficit and improving the balance of payments and the inflation rate, were stalled due to institutional impediments (World Bank 1995). Consequently, the World Bank focused on labour market rigidity as one of the constraints.[21] It recognized that the high unemployment rate remained unchanged in spite of the reforms and that this should be addressed in order to attain poverty reduction. The World Bank recommended amendment of TEWA to create employment in the long run.

In the 2000s, the rhetoric used by the international institutions shifted to poverty reduction through employment. They have asserted that a social protection programme, social dialogue, and assurance of equal access to job opportunities should be developed. Amendment of TEWA was considered to be a prerequisite for reducing excessive job security for formal sector workers and also for improving job prospects of vulnerable groups of society.

The international institutions have taken serious note of unemployment problems in Sri Lanka which were triggered by TEWA itself. The ILO (1971) pointed out the mismatch of skills as a reason for unemployment. Though Sri Lanka provides free education and the dropout rate is low, young people are not trained to become part of the workforce with the skills required by businesses. The schools are academic-oriented rather than business-oriented. The youths who receive higher education prefer white-collar jobs to agriculture or working in factories. As a result, the unemployment rate among the highly educated is higher than average.

Dickens and Lang (1991) state that employment practices by the government are the cause of unemployment. Public sector jobs are usually characterized by more security, higher benefits, lower effort and more prestige than their private sector counterparts. Thus, unemployment may be generated by queuing for government jobs.

In the 1990s, rigid labour laws became the target for criticism. The World Bank (1993) discussed the generosity of severance payments and how TEWA prohibits the growth of the private sector and contains the creation of employment. The World Bank (2006b) analysed the number of employees of firms by using the Employees' Provident Fund (EPF) data. It focused on firms with 15 employees because TEWA covers firms of that size. Its analysis indicates that firms with 15 employees are particularly 'unstable', while firms with 14 employees are stable. It is assumed that employers are trying not to expand the scale of their firms by keeping their workforce below 15 and thus benefiting from TEWA exclusion.

5.5.2 Government of Sri Lanka

Largely following the approaches initiated by the international institutions, the Government of Sri Lanka (GOSL) put forward *Regaining Sri Lanka* as a Poverty Reduction Strategy Paper in 2002. This paper proposed a wide variety of reforms to realize high growth. *Regaining Sri Lanka* suggested several goals to be attained and one of the main ones was to create 'high-productivity jobs with higher incomes' (GOSL 2002: Part I, 2), It is expressed 'sufficient productive, desirable employment opportunities' in another way (GOSL 2002: Part I, 4).[22] GOSL believes that 'flexibility in the movement of people between jobs is a prerequisite to achieve this' (GOSL 2002: Part I, 2). Reform of the labour market is supposed to be one of the tools to realize this.[23] GOSL also considers its labour market to be 'highly distorted due to outdated laws and regulations, which are impeding investment growth, job creation and business expansion' (GOSL 2002: Part II, 44) and proposes to enact a new Employment and Industrial Relations Act[24] which will enhance the flexibility of the labour market, promote the upward mobility of labour, and increase labour productivity (GOSL 2002: Part II, iii). Revising TEWA is one of the measures taken to deregulate the labour market.

The government view, however, is not uniform. The Ministry of Employment and Labour (MEL) also recognized productivity growth as the highest requisite for raising the standard of living of all Sri Lankans in its report on the private sector (MEL 2002b: III). MEL proposed seven initiatives to improve productivity. Its third initiative is to improve labour market flexibility. MEL anticipates that labour market flexibility will enable workers to move out of low-productivity sectors, or sectors facing increased competition, and move into higher-productivity ones (MEL 2002b: 31). Notwithstanding, MEL considers the shortage in employment opportunities to be the greatest barrier to job mobility in Sri Lanka, rather than restrictive labour law (MEL 2002b: 31). The Ministry points out that 'it is not clear that just removing TEWA would make a significant difference in the creation of new jobs' and developing an unemployment insurance system to provide a safety net is considered more effective for promoting labour market flexibility (MEL 2002b: 33).

MEL also issued *Draft National Employment Policy for Sri Lanka* and put forward seven initiatives to realize its vision for the development of human capital. Its sixth initiative is called 'Partnerships Realigned'. MEL said that the rigidities and inappropriateness of laws have been a hindrance to the growth of industry and hence to the creation of employment opportunities. The amendments to IDA and TEWA are expected to be implemented 'with the overall objective of strengthening national economic growth, stability and competitiveness, which will result in new employment opportunities for our people' (MEL 2002c: 53).

5.5.3 Requests from business circles

The Employers' Federation of Ceylon (EFC) continuously proposed modifications of the law to promote Sri Lanka as a country striving to be part of the globalized economy. The EFC suggested the following (Amerasinghe 1994):

1. Create transparency regarding the compensation payable and the right to reorganize or restructure business;
2. Remove executives drawing more than a prescribed amount, e.g. Rs.15,000, from coverage by TEWA;
3. Remove inefficiency and incompetence from the jurisdiction of the Act;
4. Remove the coverage of persons over a specified age, e.g. 60 years.

The EFC repeatedly made requests to each government to review the labour law for the sake of greater flexibility and consistency with the new open economic environment. The EFC firmly believed that the changes they advocated in TEWA would not discriminate against employees, but rather would benefit them by ensuring the smoother functioning of the labour market. The EFC expected that the revisions would strengthen the relationship between employers and employees while retaining protection for workers (Central Bank 2002).

Though employers continued to request modification of TEWA, the restrictions remained as they were. Therefore, private sector employers cannot resort to hiring and firing in order to restructure their organization. The Act covers not only retrenchments and layoffs but also dismissal on account of inefficiency and absence. Under such constraints, employers tend to maintain a minimum number of workers and abstain from employing permanent workers, even if the employers feel that they could expand their businesses by employing permanent workers. Investors also identify Sri Lanka as a difficult place to a start business, though the quality of workers is high and the government offers quite good incentives for investment. Since the law has several serious shortcomings that are disadvantageous for employers, they have devised their own methods for coping with the situation. Many employers, in situations of restructuring, closure, retrenchment or any other non-disciplinary dismissal, offer voluntary retirement compensation packages. Employers are often compelled to offer huge packages, especially where restructuring has to be done quickly. Some foreign investors just close down business overnight and flee the country, without fulfilling fundamental employer obligations such as payment of wages and termination benefits, etc. Moreover, some employers have adopted various methods to circumvent the law. Subcontracting of manpower and the creation of satellite enterprises are practices some employers adopted to avoid TEWA.

5.6 The revision of the Termination of Employment of Workmen Act in the 2000s

5.6.1 Revision of TEWA

It was observed in the preceding section that TEWA remained in effect for a long period despite strong criticism from business circles and investors, while the government used ad hoc Cabinet decisions and was blessed with a timely economic boom which reduced the unemployment rate and criticism against government. As a result, TEWA caused several distortions in the economy in Sri Lanka.

However, the situation began to change in the early 1990s. As the result of structural adjustment programmes, the public sector was compelled to start reducing its size. Since the public sector could no longer play a role as a stable employment absorber, the private sector came to be a source of employment. Globalization and recession in the economy also caused Sri Lanka to revise the long-standing rigidity of its labour law. External and domestic shocks hit the Sri Lankan economy heavily. In 2001 Sri Lanka experienced a negative growth rate of 1.4 per cent for the first time since independence. The excessively rigid labour law began to be blamed for causing sluggish economic recovery. TEWA prevented enterprises from restructuring by reducing their workforce despite the contraction in their activities during 2001. Hence, enterprises had to bear the entire cost of maintaining the excess labour, thereby reducing their productivity and discouraging future investment in labour-intensive industries. The long-felt need to review existing labour legislation to support achievement of higher growth performance in the economy was further heightened by the country's economic performance in 2001.

The unemployment rate rose marginally, to 7.8 per cent, in the third quarter of 2001, compared to the 7.6 per cent in 2000, due to contraction in the economy. However, the unemployment rate in 2001 was actually worse than the official figure, which sent the wrong signals to policymakers. This was because many enterprises were compelled to downsize their activities due to lack of demand, but employees were advised to stay at home on payment of their minimum monthly salary, excluding allowances, in order to minimize costs and avoid closure of business. In the hotel sector, although it was expected that the number of redundant workers would rise to about 40,000 after the 9/11 terrorist attacks, TEWA prevented such layoffs. Accordingly, the forced maintenance of employment levels prevented a clear reflection of the effects of the economic slowdown on employment in the affected sectors (Central Bank 2001).

In 2001, the government issued the *Sri Lanka Labour Gazette*, Vol. 52, No. 1,[25] with the aim of reducing long delays in delivering redundancy orders. First, the inquiring officer was required to make a determination within a period of three months from the date of receipt of the application/complaint. This simply restated Section 2 (2) (c) of TEWA. Second, a recommended compensation formula was introduced, calling for '2 to 3 months of salary per each year of actual service, or full salary for the remaining period denied (service) up to retirement, whichever is less, subject to a maximum of 50 months salary'. This decision was made to provide a rough formula, and so it still was not the mandatory but only the recommended compensation formula.

The Sri Lankan government introduced labour law reform legislation in July 2002, along with another 30-plus pieces of legislation. The purpose of the reform was to bring the labour laws in line with the times, expedite the process taken by the Labour Commissioner, and improve transparency in decision making. Revisions to TEWA were intended to make it easier to fire workers.[26] However, opposition by the trade unions and opposition parties was able to weaken the legislation, and the Labour Minister agreed not to implement the reforms until such time as an adequate social protection scheme was in place to deal with the resulting increase in unemployment. The amendments to TEWA were finally passed by Parliament on 8 January 2003, incorporating the changes proposed by the opposition parties during the committee stage (Central Bank 2002).

The determination of a clear compensation formula by the Commissioner, which was expected to be published in the Gazette shortly, with a safety net for the displaced workers, is one of the main highlights of the TEWA amendments. In addition, the Act was amended to grant employees the right to be heard before a determination is made by the Commissioner in cases of dismissal (Central Bank of Sri Lanka 2002).

(Special Provisions) Act No. 13 of 2003 (certified on 20 March 2003) amended both IDA and TEWA. It requires the Labour Commissioner to respond to applications from employers for termination of employment within two months of receipt of the application or complaints.[27] The Act also requires the Commissioner to respond to complaints from employees for relief within two months.

Act No. 12 of 2003 (certified on 20 March 2003) gives workers the opportunity of being heard when applications for dismissal are made by employers. The new Act also provides for the Commissioner to call upon the workers within three days of an application to receive submission of their responses to such application. The new provision took away the excessive powers of the Commissioner, who had been vested with powers to proceed with an application without informing the worker. Without this new provision, the workers may never have known of an impending threat to their employment.[28]

Act No. 12 of 2003 also amended Section 6B (1) of TEWA. Section 6B (1) required employees to apply for relief within six months of their dismissal. The words 'six months' were altered to 'three months', making the time frame for employees to claim relief or compensation shorter. Section 6D, which provides a compensation formula, was newly introduced by Act No. 12 of 2003 (EFC 2004). The compensation formula was set out in the *Gazette Extraordinary* dated 31 December 2003. The formula was generous and gives more benefits to employees than similar formulas in other Asian countries (World Bank 2006b). Furthermore, the formula adopts a rather complex structure related to the employees' age at dismissal (as of the last birthday). For example, compensation paid to an employee over 50 years old is less than that paid to young employees.

However, the UPFA government which assumed office in April 2004 suspended the formula through a Cabinet decision on 26 May (Central Bank 2004). The UPFA consists of the Peoples' Alliance (PA) and the JVP, which are socialist rather than capitalist. The National Labour Advisory Council (NLAC), which comprises the Ministry of Employment and Labour, trade unions and representatives of employers, began working to review the entire labour market reform programme in June. The main task of the NLAC was to establish a safety net (i.e. Unemployment Benefit Insurance Scheme) to provide income support and other benefits that promote the employability of displaced workers in parallel with the compensation formula (Central Bank 2005).

Following the discussion in the NLAC, a new formula was drawn up by October 2004 and gazetted on 15 March 2005 (Central Bank 2004, 2005). The new compensation formula linked the amount of severance pay to the workers' length of service (as is common in other countries) (see Figure 5.1) and thus reduced the non-transparency and arbitrariness in the firing process. The maximum compensation as computed according to the new formula is 1.25 million rupees (Rs.1,250,000).

There was another reversion in 2006. The above-mentioned 2003 amendment reduced to three months the time period for a dismissed employee to make an application to the Commissioner. However, it was decided to amend the law to restore the period for making the application to the original six months. It was decided to reinstate the original period because three months was not considered sufficient for a dismissed worker to apply due to potential practical difficulties such as potential ambiguities in termination, delays in making the application by the worker or trade union, and postal delays, etc.

5.6.2 TEWA revisions examined

The amendment of 2003 introduced the compensation formula which had been requested by the business community. Though transparency in the process was increased by the amendment, the business community still found it overprotective of workers. The amount of compensation payment is generous when the new compensation formula is compared with those of other countries. It has to be emphasized that, in addition to TEWA compensation, in Sri Lanka there is another severance payment gratuity (Gratuity Act No. 12 of 1983). This payment must be paid by employers (with 15 or more employees) to all workers upon termination of their employment, provided that they have more than five years of service with the employer. The amount paid is one month of salary for each two years of service. Note that the gratuity is paid regardless of the reason for the termination of employment (so, for the workers qualifying under TEWA, this is an additional benefit).

When we compare the 2003 formula and that of 2005, it is clear that generosity is retained. Figure 5.1 shows the relationship between years of service and compensation payment. The 2003 formula is used for employees who are under age 50 to avoid complication. Retrenched workers whose service is less than 10 years receive almost same amount of compensation. Workers who worked more than 10 years receive more generous compensation under the new 2005 formula. An analysis of 44 case studies based on ILO (2001), the Labour Commissioner's decision on compensation payments, shows that the average amount of payment is not far from

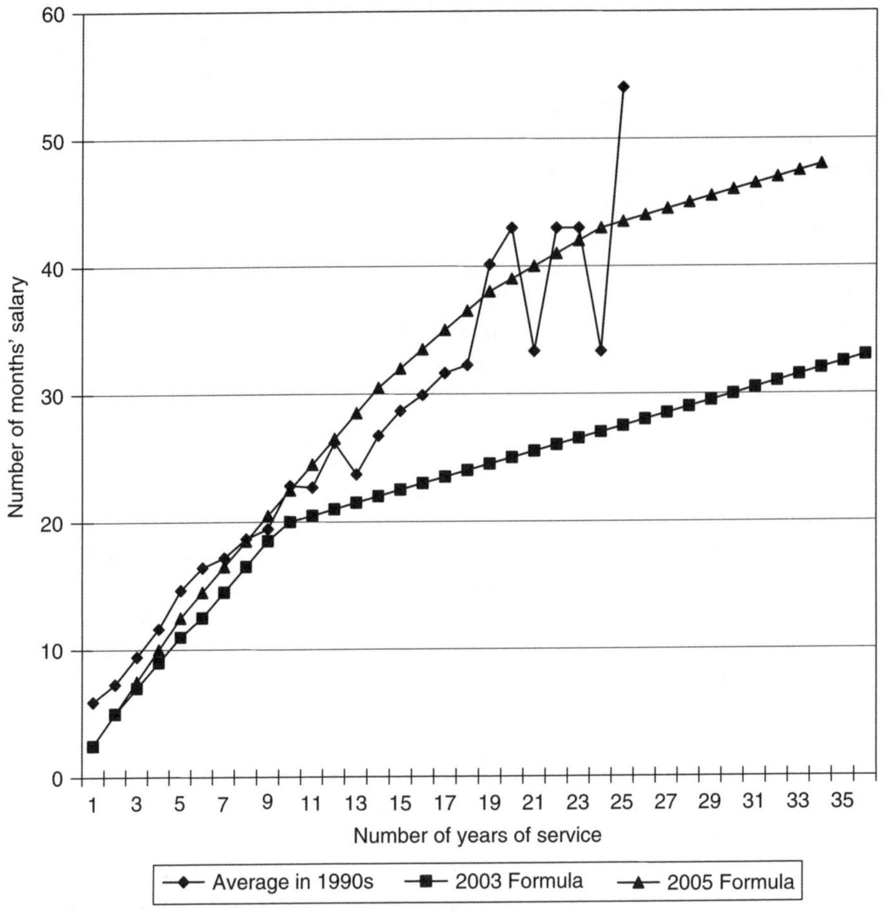

Figure 5.1 Compensation calculated by formula
Notes: Prepared by the author based on the formulas of 2003 and 2005. The 1990s average is calculated using ILO (2001).

the result of the 2005 formula, though there are fluctuations in cases of longer service. So, the employer's financial duty at the time of retrenchment has not been reduced in spite of the continuous requests from business circles.

Regarding issues other than the compensation formula, the process of dismissal was expedited and was made clearer to the employers, but they still have to provide expensive severance pay to employees. In addition, the process still involves prior approval by the Labour Commissioner, and thus it is not free of non-transparency. From the viewpoint of workers' welfare, trade union activists were dissatisfied that an adequate safety net was not introduced as promised in January 2003.[29]

In opposition to the business circles, trade unions insisted that the upper limit was too low for compensation. If a retrenched worker received 1.25 million rupees for compensation, he/she was supposed to earn salary at the time of retrenchment in the highest deciles.[30] Considering employers' request to remove executives and management from the protection, the revised TEWA remained overprotective of workers.

5.7 Conclusion

Let us summarize the findings from the perspectives of the two major issues concerned.

First, to what extent has the protective regime been transformed as the result of the recent revisions of TEWA? What we have found is that the amendment was not sufficient for employers because it requires employers to have the prior permission of the Labour Commissioner in document form. The Labour Commissioner still has considerable discretion. The law still ensures protection for workers at the time of closure of a company, for inefficient employees and for executive-level employees. On the other hand, a new formula was stipulated by law and transparency in the process of paying compensation was secured. Further, expeditiousness was emphasized. These changes are what the employers most eagerly requested. Therefore, the revision is considered to be a halfway revision at most.

The second issue of importance is whether the revised TEWA will contribute to mitigation of the distortions in the labour market and to reduction of unemployment. This question is related to what type of jobs will be created as the result of TEWA revisions. It is beyond the scope of this chapter to investigate this question. However, what is certain is that new jobs provide less employment security compared with those currently available.

As we have already seen, discussions on the high unemployment in Sri Lanka have often viewed the problem as lying in the mismatch of education and industry needs, the expectation of availability of public sector jobs, and the security provided by TEWA. In addition to these factors, job seekers' behaviour should also be considered in an analysis of the labour market. Alailima (1991) and Glewwe (1987) pointed out that the higher the household income, the higher the unemployment rate of the family members. Bowen (1990) showed that during a long period of unemployment, job seekers received financial support from family members rather than government social aid. The World Bank (2006b) emphasized that some jobless persons choose to stay unemployed because the jobs available in the market are not acceptable to them. That is, since some of the job seekers prefer the formal private and public sectors which offer employment protection, they remain unemployed even if there is an employment opportunity available in the informal sector. The Labour Market Information (LMI) Unit in the Ministry of Employment and Labour checks job advertisements in the Sunday papers both in Sinhala and English and summarizes them in the *LMI Bulletin*.[31] The LMI divides the job demand and supply into formal and informal. The *LMI Bulletin* (Table 5.7) shows that more than half of the demand in the labour market is in the informal sector. It is clearly stated in the first issue of the *LMI Bulletin* that 'unemployed persons are not willing to accept the employment opportunities readily available in the labour market'. This shows an acute imbalance between labour supply and demand.

Table 5.7 Job demand in newspapers, Jan.–Oct. 2005

	Public	*Private*	*NGO*	*Informal*	*Total*
Skilled agricultural and fishery workers	2	52	2	276	332
Craft and related workers	21	2,848	6	10,596	13,471
Elementary occupation	42	2,914	40	12,703	15,699
Management trainees and other trainees	17	1,484	20	444	1,965
Sales and service clerks	54	6,436	140	9,208	15,838
Plant and machine operators and assemblers	48	1,887	46	6,176	8,157
Clerks	275	4,778	232	5,286	10,571
Senior officials and managers	390	3,091	307	768	4,556
Professionals	732	8,146	360	2,337	11,575
Technicians and associate professionals	4,656	3,436	451	1,929	10,472
Others	69	2,561	295	832	3,757
Total	6,306	37,633	1,899	50,555	96,393
	7%	39%	2%	52%	100%

Source: *LMI Bulletin*, Vol. 1, Nos. 1 and 2.

Therefore, while relatively well-to-do job seekers can afford to wait until they finally find an appropriate formal sector job, socially weak job seekers have very few opportunities to access the protected formal sector. Even if TEWA were revised to be less restrictive, the formal sector would remain more protected and attractive than the informal sector, which has no official protection at all. Therefore, job seekers' behaviour is likely to remain unchanged unless new job opportunities which meet their expectations are created.

It is unlikely, at least in the short run, that new formal employment will be increased as a result of the TEWA amendment. In the meantime, there will remain a large gap in the working conditions between those protected by TEWA and those without protection. It is, therefore, necessary to set out to develop approaches other than amendment of TEWA for the sake of revitalizing the private sector, while retaining the welfare orientation which Sri Lanka has proudly upheld.

Notes

1. Though the Act for privatization was enacted in 1987, privatization started in the 1990s.
2. All registered firms are required to pay contributions for their permanent workers. The EPF offers a joint action plan by which the employer and the employees save for the future retirement of the employees in the corporate and private sectors. The aim of the EPF is to prudently manage the Fund to ensure a better return for its members at retirement (http://www.epf.lk/).
3. Those who leave the country for employment abroad are also excluded from the labour force estimate.
4. The Central Bank's Annual Public Sector Employment Survey (APSES) includes the field staff of the armed forces and the police.

5. The total number of employed is the sum of the number of employees, employers, own-account workers and unpaid family workers. Employees consist of public and private sector.
6. The definition of formal sector worker in the income and expenditure survey is 'persons engaged in paid employment and having one of the following principal occupations: legislators, senior managers, and officials; technicians and associate professionals; clerks; and plant and machine operators and assemblers' (World Bank 2006b). The large informal sector is estimated in another way, such that about half of the workforce is engaged in the informal sector. (Based on total employment from the labour force survey, employment in the government sector, and the number of EPF contributors, it is estimated that this share amounted to 53 per cent in 2002.) (*Sri Lanka Labour Gazette*, 55(4) 25).
7. Seventy-five per cent of workers in garment factories in and around Colombo live in hostels (Arai 2006).
8. Public education up to university level was provided free of charge.
9. *Government Gazette* 14965/12, 6 July 1971.
10. The Act was retroactive from 21 May 1971.
11. In the Free Processing Zone, companies have joint consultative committees set up on the instructions of the Greater Colombo Economic Commission (now the Board of Investment). In companies where such committees exist, there do not seem to be trade unions though workers in the zone have also been allowed to organize trade unions since 1999.
12. The Employers' Federation of Ceylon (EFC) is the principal organization of employers dealing with labour and social issues in Sri Lanka.
13. Trade unions opposed the bill strongly. Dr Colvin de Silva, an activist, criticized the White Paper, saying that it was not in the workers' best interest in his paper 'White Paper – Black Law'. *An Analysis of the White Paper on Employment Relations*, published by the Ceylon Federation of Labour (1978), criticized the policy issued by the new government, saying that it was completely different from their election platform.
14. The Mahaveli Project is a large-scale irrigation programme in northern and eastern Sri Lanka.
15. Though the unemployment rate decreased in 1978/79, the Central Bank pointed out that employment generated in rural areas was not remunerated employment but was in the category of unpaid family workers.
16. Ten per cent of shares was also given to employees free of charge.
17. The labour movement lost its power after the government repressed public officers' strikes in 1980.
18. Public sector employment more than tripled from 1970 to 1979. On the other hand, private sector employees increased 24 per cent from 1972 to 1980 (Central Bank 1981).
19. In case of *St. Anthony's Hardware Stores, Ltd.* vs *Kumar & Another 1978–79 2 SLR 06*).
20. Deregulations lower tax and expand the role of the private sector in distribution in the local market.
21. Other areas indicated were rationalization of the structure of public expenditure such as health, education, water supply and transfer programmes, deepening of the privatization of public enterprises, deepening of the deregulation of foreign direct investment, and pursuit of reforms for tackling land market rigidities and reforms in agriculture.
22. Two million jobs will be needed to achieve the goal set by *Regaining Sri Lanka*. Considering the total number of the labour force, 2 million is quite a large figure.
23. Education, training and provision of information follow labour market reform.
24. It was still not enacted as of 2007.
25. A quarterly journal published by the Ministry of Labour Relations and Foreign Employment, Sri Lanka.

26. The changes to IDA were supposed to allow for faster resolution of labour disputes. The reform of the EPF was to provide a greater private sector role in administering these accounts.
27. The IDA-related rule is that the arbitrator makes a decision on disputes within 3 months and that the labour tribunal makes a decision within 4 months.
28. *The Island*. 9 January 2003.
29. *The Daily News*. 5 January 2004.
30. Retrenched employees who cannot claim the full amount of compensation as calculated by the 2005 formula due to the upper limit of Rs.1.25 million would not be numerous. In such cases, the employee's salary at the time of retrenchment would be, for example, Rs.250,000 (2 years of service at the date of termination), Rs.100,000 (10 years), Rs.39,000 (15 years), Rs.32,000 (20 years) and Rs.27,000 (30 years). These salaries belong to highest household income decile according to *Household Income and Expenditure Survey* 2002.
31. According to staff at the Ministry of Labour, nearly 80 per cent of companies in the private sector use Sunday papers for recruitment advertising. Jobs Net, which was created in 2003, also provides information on labour demand in Sri Lanka (see Central Bank of Sri Lanka 2003).

References

Alailima, Patricia (1991) 'Education–Employment Linkages: the Macro Profile'. Colombo: Department of National Planning (unpublished).

Amerasinghe, Franklyn (1994) *The Employers' Federation of Ceylon 1929–1994*. Colombo: Aitken Spence Printing (pvt) Ltd.

—— (1998) *Employee Relations and Industrial Law in Sri Lanka*. Colombo: Aitken Spence Printing (pvt) Ltd.

Arai, Etsuyo (2006) 'Readymade Garment Workers in Sri Lanka: Strategy to Survive in Competition'. In Mayumi Murayama (ed.) *Employment in Readymade Garment Industry in Post-MFA Era: the Case of India, Bangladesh and Sri Lanka*. Joint Research Programme Series no. 140. Chiba: Institute of Developing Economies.

Bowen, Alex (1990) 'The Unemployment Problem in Sri Lanka'. Working Paper. Washington, DC: World Bank.

Ceylon Federation of Labour (1978) *An Analysis of the White Paper on Employment Relations*. Colombo.

Dickens, William and Kevin Lang (1991) 'An Analysis of the Nature of Unemployment in Sri Lanka'. NBER Working Paper 3777. Cambridge, Mass.: National Bureau of Economic Research.

Employers' Federation of Ceylon (2004) *Handbook of Industrial Relations*. Rajagiriya Sri Lanka.

Glewwe, Paul (1987) 'Unemployment in Developing Countries: Economist's Models in Light of Evidence from Sri Lanka'. *International Economic Journal* 1 (4) (winter): 1–17.

ILO (1971) *Matching Employment Opportunities and Expectations*. Geneva: ILO.

—— (2001) *Report on the Operation of the Termination of Employment of Workmen (Special Provisions) Act, 1971*. Geneva: ILO.

Jayawardena, Lal (2004) 'Understanding Reforms: 1960–2000'. In Saman Kelegama (ed.) *Economic Policy in Sri Lanka*. New Delhi: Sage Publications Pvt Ltd.

Kelegama, Saman (1993) *Privatization in Sri Lanka: the Experience during the Early Years of Implementation*. Colombo: Sri Lanka Economic Association.

Nanayakkara, A.G.W. (2004) *Employment and Unemployment in Sri Lanka – Trends, Issues and Options*. Colombo: Department of Census and Statistics, Sri Lanka.

World Bank (1993) 'Sri Lanka Private Sector Assessment, White Paper Draft'. Washington, DC: World Bank (September).

—— (1995) *Sri Lanka Poverty Assessment*. Washington, DC: World Bank (January).

—— (2006a) *Doing Business 2007*. Washington, DC.
—— (2006b) *Sri Lanka: Strengthening Social Protection*. Washington, DC.
Yatawara, Ravindra A. (2004) 'Labour Productivity Growth and Employment Generation'. In Saman Kelegama (ed.) *Economic Policy in Sri Lanka*. New Delhi: Sage Publications Pvt Ltd.

Government publications

Central Bank of Sri Lanka. *Annual Report*. Each year.
—— (1979) *Review of the Economy*.
Department of Census and Statistics (DCS) (2005) *Sri Lanka Labour Force Survey*.
—— (2006) *Report of Sri Lanka Labour Force Survey (LFS)*. First Quarter.
Department of Labour, Ministry of Employment and Labour Relations and Foreign Employment. 2004. *Statistics Sri Lanka*.
Government of Sri Lanka (2002) *Regaining Sri Lanka: Vision and Strategy for Accelerated Development*.
Hansard Department. *Hansard* (official report of Parliament's proceedings).
Labour Market Information Unit, Ministry of Employment and Labour, Sri Lanka. *LMI Bulletin*.
Ministry of Employment and Labour, Sri Lanka. *Sri Lanka Labour Gazette*.
—— (2002a) *Understanding Labour Law*.
—— (2002b) *The Draft National Productivity Policy for Sri Lanka (Private Sector Component)*.
—— (2002c) *Draft National Employment Policy for Sri Lanka*.

Newspapers

The Daily News
The Island

6

Social Dimension of Employment Policy in India: Indian Debate on Employment Reservation in the Private Sector

Hiroshi Sato

6.1 Introduction: origin of the debate

Reservation of public sector employment for certain classes of discriminated or segregated sections of the people proportional to their share of the population has been one of the major tools of affirmative action (henceforth 'AA') in independent India. It has also formed the very backbone of the national employment policy for the underprivileged. This has been one of the varied instruments of the state to provide protection for employment. Regulations in favour of small-scale industries that bar competitive entry by large-scale enterprises constitute another policy for employment protection, although these have been largely dismantled under economic liberalization measures since the 1990s.[1] However, the direct AA measures to ensure employment for the underprivileged are more resistant to economic reform initiatives.[2] AA has largely survived the dominant discourse of market-friendly reforms since the 1990s, though more extensive application is expected to quickly invite resistance, as in the recent case where 27 per cent of the seats at institutions of higher education were reserved for the 'Other Backward Classes' (OBC) applicants.[3] However, one point to be noted is that all these measures taken by the Indian government have been confined to public institutions, either under central or state control.[4] The topic discussed here differs from the earlier topics in India's experiences with AA, in that the proposed AA is intended to apply to the private sector.[5] A brief account of the background of the new proposal would be helpful.

On assuming office in May 2004, a ruling coalition led by the Indian National Congress (INC) party publicized a policy manifesto to start dialogue on that issue, and it triggered a debate that aroused a wide range of public opinion. The United Progressive Alliance (UPA), the coalition so named, formed the government, and in its National Common Minimum Programme (NCMP), pledged its readiness to initiate dialogue on extending affirmative action in favour of Scheduled Castes (SCs) and Scheduled Tribes (STs) to private sector industries. NCMP states,

> The UPA Government is very sensitive to the issue of affirmative action, including reservations in the private sector. It will immediately initiate a national dialogue with all political parties, industry and other organizations to see

how best the private sector can fulfill the aspirations of Scheduled Castes' and Scheduled Tribes' youth. (*The Hindu*, 28 May 2004)

NCMP cautiously chose phrases such as to 'initiate a national dialogue' on 'the issue of affirmative action, including reservation', so as not to give an immediate impression that it is firmly committed to 'reservation'. However, this pledge was largely understood to express a government preference for the introduction of 'reservation' into the private sector. Before any further government's initiative, there ensued a fierce debate on the pros and cons of the 'reservation' that may be applied to the private sector.

This chapter tries to elucidate the background and rationale of this new proposal for state intervention in the labour market, which runs counter to the market-oriented reforms. Our concern is twofold. One is to focus on the main lines of arguments for and against 'reservation' in the private corporate sector, ranging from those from political parties, human rights bodies and intellectual society to industrialists, in order to identify their respective concerns and the divergence and convergence of their contentions. Not all the points raised here are necessarily new,[6] but close analysis of the arguments will highlight the unique context in which the demand for reservation in the private corporate sector has been raised only in recent years.

Another concern is to broaden the scope of our discussion without limiting it only to the issue of for or against *reservation* in the private sector. Preferential policy for the underprivileged sections of Indian society, the SCs and the STs, need not be limited to the form of *reservation*, which is more or less equal to an employment quota. AA encompasses much wider options of preferential treatment. Furthermore, this aspect is more crucial when AA is applied to the private sector, which has to be more flexible and well designed to fit in the diverse texture of private sector enterprises. The actual debate often tends to be conducted around the alternative of 'reservation or not', but a more fruitful debate would allow wider options and designs of public policy.

The initial reaction on the business side was less flexible, almost amounting to an outright rejection and condemnation without few alternative suggestions. They regarded this proposal as a veiled threat to impose 'reservation' on the private corporate sector, and counterpoised 'merit and efficiency' to rebut the proposal. Their 'feverish' reaction may have been due to their lack of familiarity with any kind of AA, as they have long been safeguarded against the intrusion of any public policy aimed at AA in the corporate world. As we shall see, they later adjusted their reaction to accommodate a more progressive policy for AA, and if any positive proposal on their part is not meant just for 'gaining time', the debate must have served even the private corporate sector as a new opportunity for them to become more 'sensitized' to the societal aspects of employment as well as to develop a more 'inclusive' strategy to reach the underprivileged section of society.

This chapter, with its focus on the reservation debate, will surely assist the search for any meaningful public intervention to make economic globalization more inclusive and sustainable.

In Section 6.2, a compact review will be presented of the economic background of the policy initiatives. Particular attention will be given to the employment situation during the process of economic reforms in the 1990s. Section 6.3 situates this proposal in a broader historical perspective. A kind of genealogy of the idea of AA in the economy as a whole is presented. Section 6.4 is an analysis of the main lines of arguments for and against the reservation in the private corporate sector. Section 6.5 will focus on an action plan jointly formulated by two major business chambers in reaction to the demand for reservation. The final section discusses the relevance of the debate with regard to positive policy options to promote employment opportunities among the underprivileged in Indian society.

6.2 Socio-economic background of the debate

Expansion of the market economy, which is the main thrust of economic liberalization, has two major orientations with respect to employment. One is that it creates new economic opportunities in the form of increased employment mainly within the private sector, and the other is that it brings a contraction of public intervention that reduces or caps employment in the public sector. Demand for reservation for private sector employment is related to both orientations.

The first point raises the question of whether expanded opportunities are equitably enjoyed by socially and economically marginalized societies such as SCs and STs, while the second point definitively aggravates their employment opportunities by substantially diminishing the size of reserved employment in public sector. Apart from these rather direct and more obvious consequences in the domain of employment, pervasive retreat of public intervention in such areas as education and medical services tends to further marginalize less privileged sections of the population by reducing their opportunities to enjoy public services. Highly sensitive concerns over disparity as well as exclusion are the direct consequence of the market-friendly reforms. There remains a plausible question as to whether 'reservation' serves to actually alleviate these concerns, and that is a question to be addressed critically. However, a widely shared apprehension of increasing disparity and exclusion is no doubt a major force behind the demand for expansion of reservation in the private sector.

Although this chapter is much more concerned with discursive issues than empirical analysis of the vast statistical information supplied by National Sample Surveys and decennial census data, a brief observation is in order for a fuller understanding of the background of the debate.

6.2.1 Social implications of poverty and disparity

In terms of the headcount ratio of the population under the poverty line, it is widely held that there was observed to be a significant decrease in the ratio during the 1990s, under the economic liberalization regime, though an exact count is still subject to debate, especially on the readings of findings in results of the 55th round (1999–2000) (Drèze and Sen 2002).[7]

What could be underlined in this context is that the decreasing ratio of the poverty index goes hand in hand with the increasing ratio of concentration of poverty among certain classes of the people, SCs and STs in particular.[8] This somewhat optimistic observation on the decreasing trend of the poverty ratio has to be critically analysed in relation to the social composition of the poor, along with the absolute size of the poor which appears not to have decreased substantially. The irony is that the more the poverty ratio decreases, the more it would be evident that SCs and STs form the core or the bedrock of poverty in Indian society.[9] This situation can easily convey a message to the more informed among the SCs and STs as well as equity-conscious people to the effect that economic liberalization would end up leaving out the marginal classes of society. Demand for reservation in the private sector is not unrelated to this perception.

No doubt this concern as well as the reasoning based on it has serious lacunae in its logic. We can point out two of them. First, it overlooks inner differentiation among the underprivileged communities. The so-called issue of the 'creamy layer' is related to this differentiation. The fact that the 'reservation' has so far benefited this layer among the SCs and STs[10] casts serious doubt on the efficacy of 'reservation' as a means of poverty eradication/alleviation. Also, this doubt on the operational side of 'reservation' leads to a more fundamental question of whether 'reservation' is a proper instrument to cope with poverty. Concerns can be justified, but the instrumental appropriateness is a separate matter to be discussed. The debate on the introduction of 'reservation' into the private corporate sector could be harnessed beneficially only if it leads to exploration into the appropriate strategy to cope with disparity and exclusion in the process of economic liberalization.

In any case, the social implications of poverty reduction are quite important as they raise the question of whether economic liberalization includes or excludes the marginal strata in society, and this question is to be addressed not only in terms of aggregated figures but also in terms of social and economic interactions. Its political implications are also highly sensitive.

6.2.2 Employment situation since the 1990s

The immediate background of the reservation debate is no doubt a particular situation surrounding employment both in the public and private sectors. We shall have a brief overview to relate the main issue with the dynamics of change in the employment situation in the 1990s.

In contrast to the growth of such service sectors as the IT industry which created mainly middle-class jobs in several cities in India, the widely shared view with regard to the growth of employment since the 1990s is rather gloomy. A task force organized by the Planning Commission, in its review of the employment situation in the 1990s, found the growth too tardy to cope with the growing labour force population (Government of India (Planning Commission) 2001).[11]

A basic feature in the employment situation is termed 'growth without employment expansion'. In the public sector, reduction of total employment is quite visible, and in the private sector, especially in the so-called 'organized sector', total employment is more or less stagnant at the level of 8 million employees. To cite recent figures on the organized sector, employment in the public sector decreased from 19.057 million to 18.580 million between 1991 and 2003, which shows a net decrease of 477,000 employees.[12] The central government started reducing the number of employees from the early 1990s, and it was followed by public enterprises. The state governments have followed suit since 2000. On the other hand, the private sector employed 7.677 million workers in 1991, and the figure went up to 8.421 million, i.e. a net growth of 144,000. Within the private sector, the service sector, which includes finance, insurance, real estate and other social services, showed a remarkable increase, while in the manufacturing sector, the number of employees decreased from the late 1990s (Government of India 2005: S-49–50).

So far, as we discuss employment in the organized sector, the overall picture is almost a stagnant one. However, either in loss or growth, the 'net' figure tells us little about the dynamic nature of the labour market, where new employment is created while simultaneously old employment is 'destroyed'. As the net loss or growth is only the result of addition and deduction, it does not show us the dynamism of employment, particularly in the private sector.

It is quite hard to find an aggregate figure for all of India on this addition and deduction, but a partial reference to Maharashtra state will give some idea of the total picture, as the state's economy is one of the most vibrant ones. In Maharashtra, public sector employment decreased from 2.26 million to 2.17 million (less 90,000) between 2000 and 2003, while private sector employment decreased from 1.43 million to 1.39 million (less 40,000). These are net figures. Still, the same document reports that 22,701 industrial enterprises, large, medium and small, closed during the same period (between 2000 and 2003). The total loss of employment in these industries (both in the public and private sectors) amounted to 292,372. Put these figures together, and we reach the conclusion that, in Maharashtra between 2000 and 2003, the net loss of 130,000 in employment was the result of a loss of 292,000 jobs, offset by 160,000 newly created jobs, which is almost on the same scale as the net loss of employment.[13]

This simple calculation tells us that 'stagnation' may not be the proper way of describing what is going on in the labour market. If we presume that newly created jobs are only in the private sector (as in the public sector we can expect little growth of employment), jobs are simultaneously lost as well as created. Some of the pro-reservationists support the need for applying reservation to the private sector by insisting that the private sector 'actively generates new employment'. Such people rightly point to one side of the truth (Thimmaiah 2005: 745).

6.2.3 Decay in the activities in the public sector

In the process of economic liberalization, the public sector suffers from two-way pressure from the market economy. Downsizing of the public sector, which directly affects the employment capability of the public sector, is only one aspect of this process. Another is increasing competition with market forces which filter into a new arena of activity due to opening up the fields so far restricted to the public sector. Under these competitive conditions, pressure by the private sector renders the public sector less active or economically viable. This process of decay takes place in such wide sectors as education (even in primary education) or medical services. Once the public sector is trapped in the process of decay, it becomes quite difficult to maintain the standard of services. It caters to the less privileged sections of the population and a vicious cycle of ever-lowering standards comes to stay.[14]

Gaps in the service standard between the public and private sectors compound the feeling of disparity and exclusion. The immediate outcome of this feeling is the demand for more liberal access to better standards of services, with the instrumentality of the state. As we pointed out earlier (Section 6.1), there has been a series of initiatives on the part of the UPA government to introduce reservation into public and private sector education, especially into higher professional training including management, technology and medicine. Though the issue is somewhat different from our present focus, i.e. employment reservation in the private sector, the nature of the debate as well as its background is identical in these two issues.

6.3 Genealogy of the debate

To fully understand the meaning and relevance of the recent debate on employment reservation in the private sector, the somewhat earlier history of similar demands has to be taken into consideration.

6.3.1 Ambedkar and 'the untouchables in the market economy'

Many of the supporters of introducing reservation into the private sector trace the demand to the ideas enunciated by B. R. Ambedkar in his various documents addressing the constitutional issues in the pre- and post-independence period (Thorat 2005). He did not limit his argument to the realm of public employment or representation, but placed the problems of the untouchables in a much wider framework of socio-economic segregation. He had a clear view of the discriminated being alienated from the market economy due to basic handicaps originating from lack of property endowment. In his *States and Minorities* (1947), the cruellest form of market exclusion by the Hindu caste against the untouchables in the form of *boycott* is severely blamed. However, in even milder forms, he demonstrated, they were always subject in many ways to discrimination or segregation in day-to-day market transactions. Any proportionate preference in employment or public representation might find a solution to these forms of exclusion from the market, but empowering the untouchables as market actors in some form or other would entail a prescription of something other than these preferential treatments.

Ambedkar's perception is quite relevant to avoidance of limiting the issue of AA within the narrow range of reservation. Although the current demand for introducing reservation into the private sector does not originate from Ambedkar's idea, his comprehensive view of the helpless position of the SCs in the market economy certainly helps to locate the debate in a much wider perspective.

6.3.2 Early demands for reservation in the private sector

The immediate forerunner of the current demand is traced back to 1991 when the MP (Members of Parliament) Forum of SCs and STs put forth its resolution to introduce reservation in the private sector. The Forum issued another demand for a promotion quota (in public employment) for the SCs and STs in 1995. The demand was accepted by the then INC government with an amendment (77th) inserted in clause (4A) in Article 16 of the Indian Constitution.

The next significant step, taken by a state government, was to put forward a charter of demands to improve the socio-economic condition of the SCs and STs. The initiative was taken by the Madhya Pradesh (MP) government, which was ruled by the INC, in 2001–2. The charter was christened the 'Bhopal Declaration' to 'chart a new course for Dalits'. 'Dalit' here denotes SCs and STs combined. The MP government formed a task force in 2001 whose members included ministers, public officials, experts and intellectuals.[15]

Deliberation by the task force clearly reflects the consciousness among the members that the Dalits face a fresh challenge in the age of economic liberalization (Mehta 2005b: 268). Reservation, so far restricted to the public sector, is increasingly losing its relevance as an instrument for improving their status. 'Unless the Dalits make a formidable foray into areas of pure sciences, management, technologies, and in particular the emerging newer branches of IT, they cannot find a respectable place in the evolving global economy' (Government of Madhya Pradesh 2002b: 107). Though the task force strongly recommends the introduction of reservation into the private sector, at the same time it points out the limitation of reservation, as a vast number of Dalits remain left outside the purview of the reservation. In order to cover those Dalits in the unorganized sector, more effective policies or tools have to be explored *beyond reservation* (Government of Madhya Pradesh 2002b: 57–9, italics added).

In line with the comprehensive agenda propounded by Ambedkar, the Bhopal Declaration included such redistribution programmes as the distribution of common agricultural and grazing lands, as well as reservation in the private sector. The most unique part of the declaration is the proposal of 'supplier diversity' or 'dealer diversity', taking a cue from the practice in the United States, to promote Dalit entrepreneurship. The government and private corporate sectors are called on to distribute a certain portion of their procurement and supply to their Dalit counterparts.

In the evolution of public policy towards SCs and STc, the Bhopal Declaration needs attention because of its comprehensive scrutiny of the issues involved. It is also important in that the members of the task force are active participants in the ensuing debate on the reservation in the private sector.

6.3.3 The 2004 Lok Sabha election and its aftermath

On the eve of the fourteenth Lok Sabha (People's House) election in 2004, two major political parties, the INC and the BJP, made public that they were positive about introducing reservation in the private sector. First, the INC, in its 'conclave' of ruling chief ministers held in July 2003 at Shimla, launched this demand as a part of its manifesto for the coming election. Then, on behalf of the BJP, Prime Minister A.B. Vajpayee, who led the ruling coalition of the National Democratic Alliance (NDA), was sympathetic to the demand in his address to the meeting of the MPs Forum of SCs and STs on 16 December 2003. When the NDA lost the election and the alternative UPA government was formed with the INC and its allies, the UPA pledged to 'initiate the debate on AA, including reservation in the private sector'.[16]

Concrete steps began in July 2004. In Lok Sabha, Ajaya Kumar, a member of the Communist Party of India (Marxist) [CPIM], proposed a resolution to the debate on reservation in the private sector. In the concluding statement of the debate, Meira Kumar, the Minister in charge of Social Justice and Empowerment, expressed agreement with the demand for reservation and promised government action. Meira Kumar, an SC minister in the UPA cabinet and another SC minister, Ram Vilas Paswan (Minister of Chemicals, Fertilizer and Steel) were the main proponents of the demand.

In late August, the government appointed a Group of Ministers (GOM) to deliberate on the issue. The GOM was chaired by Sharad Pawar (Agriculture) and joined by the above two ministers as well as the Finance Minister (P. Chidambaram), Commerce Minister (Kamal Nath), Railway Minister (L.P. Yadav) and Communications Minister (Dayanidhi Maran) (*Indian Express*, 1 Sept. 2004). Prime Minister Manmohan Singh also appeared positive about the move.

However, appointment of the GOM triggered strong opposition from private business circles. Major industry associations and individual entrepreneurs scathingly criticized reservation in the private sector in various forums. An industrialist, Rahul Bajaj, who was one of the most vocal opponents of reservation, wrote an article entitled 'Reservation: Devoid of Merit' in the *Times of India* (10 September 2004). He emphasized that quality is vital for private sector enterprises, and in the age of severe competition, lack of 'merit' would seriously compromise 'efficiency'. He went on to allude to the fact that the 'inefficiency' in the public sector was due to the system of employment reservation.

However, Bajaj perceptively noticed the nuanced expression in the NCMP phrase as well as the GOM agenda stating 'AA including reservation' and suggested his willingness to talk about 'AA without reservation'. He even disclosed that, among the 11,000 employees in his Bajaj Auto Company, 3800 (34 per cent) were recruited from the SCs, STs and OBCs (Bajaj 2005).[17]

This opposition from private business blunted the approach of the government. In October, the Prime Minister urged private business to understand the problem, and he denied making any unilateral decision on the issue. Meira Kumar herself tried to pacify the opposition in the Rajya Sabha (Upper House) debate, saying that the government was thinking of some AA measures including reservation but they had to be taken voluntarily by the private sector. Business circles appreciated this stand by the government, as shown by the submission of a memorandum signed by 22 industrialists. Bajaj himself maintained a strict stance that no reservation was permissible in the private sector.

However, the reaction of industrialists was not so uniform. For example, Ratan Tata was more emphatic about the private sector's 'social responsibility' (Thimmaiah 2005: 747), and the rising electronics manufacturer Videocon was not averse to the legislation.[18] Some leaned upon the formula of 'AA without reservation' as a palliative, but others were intent on exploring real alternative proposals. It was left to major business organizations to sort out the opinions of businesses and put forward some alternative proposals (see Section 6.5).

However, the immediate negative reaction by the private enterprises based on 'merit and efficiency' gave the debate an acrimonious colour.

6.3.4 'Delhi Declaration' of the 'National Summit'

Meanwhile, organizations and movements which demand reservation in the private sector formed an all-India body named the National Organizing Committee (NOC) and under its aegis organized the 'National Summit on Reservation in the Private Sector' on 8–9 August 2005, in Delhi. The summit adopted a document entitled 'Delhi Declaration' on the second (and final) day.[19]

The document first of all focused on 'persistent and perpetuating caste-based discrimination' and violence against the SCs and other oppressed communities. It expressed a high appreciation of the 'multi-dimensional approach' of Ambedkar and formulated a fairly comprehensive list of demands. The reservation policy for the private sector was to be based on the following four principles:

1. It should apply to multiple spheres, namely employment, markets, private capital markets, agricultural land, private education and housing, access to inputs and services, products and consumer goods;
2. Legal safeguards in the form of Equal Opportunity Laws should be included;
3. Quotas in proportion to population to ensure fair participation should be included;
4. A monitoring mechanism in the form of the Equal Opportunity Commission should be set up.

We can readily note that the reservation in this document has very broad implications. It connotes any sort of quota as reservation, and if we sort out this complication, various AA measures beside employment reservation would fit into this formula, including 'supplier diversity' or 'dealer diversity' as proposed in the Bhopal Declaration.

What is significant from a political perspective is the sharing of the platform by the Ambedkarites and the Marxists.[20] Besides the two factions of the Republican Party of India (Ramdas Athavale and R. S. Gavai), not only the two major communist parties but also ex-Prime Minister V. P. Singh joined the National Summit. Singh expressed little hope for voluntary cooperation on the part of the private sector and urged state legislation for reservation in the private sector (*People's Democracy*, 14 August 2005).

We have examined the diachronic process of the debate on reservation in the private sector. We shall not be off the mark if we conclude that, between the two extremities of immediate introduction of reservation and its outright rejection, there is a wide spectrum of views on AA which so far have been left out of the serious discussion and which merit exploration to achieve more inclusive treatment of marginal communities in the market economy.

6.4 Main lines of argument

Throughout the debate, major forums for the debate were offered by Parliament and the mass media, including TV, newspapers and journals. Among the journals, *The Economic and Political Weekly* (*EPW*) and *The Seminar* (No. 549, May 2005) were instrumental in disseminating diverse views for dialectical interaction. There is also an edition of these views by several concerned scholars (Thorat et al. 2005).

In this section, these diverse views will be grouped into five lines of argument. These are the battle lines of clear demarcation between sympathetic and antipathetic views in the debate. They are: (1) reservation and 'merit', (2) recruitment and caste discrimination, (3) 'talent pool', (4) globalization and AA, and (5) AA and reservation. However, it does not imply that all battle lines are new or recent. Rather, most of them may be as old as the reservation system which was comprehensively introduced after independence.[21] However, at least one of them, that is the fourth point which is related to the background of the debate (see Section 6.2), signifies the most important facet of the ongoing debate. It illustrates the particular context of the current debate which has much to do with the globalization and liberalization of the Indian economy (Shah 2005: xi).

6.4.1 Reservation and merit

In principle, reservation and merit belong to different domains of the argument. However, as the idea of reservation in India originated as compensation for 'historical injustice', because of the condescending treatment of SCs and STs, people outside the orbit of reservation tend to regard the institution as something like a 'historical evil' which is in conflict with the principle of equal competition on the basis of 'merit'.

Although the basic principle of reservation underwent a slight shift from 'historical injustice' to 'social representation' in the wake of the OBC claim for reservation, 'reservation' and 'merit' are still supposed to be mutually exclusive principles. R. Bajaj's unrestrained contention against reservation made 'merit' the central issue of the debate.

However, the centrality of 'merit' works against its logic, as 'merit' is not so self-evident as Bajaj would like others to believe. Apart from the fact that education, which is very much relevant to providing 'merit', is largely influenced by the socio-economic background of individuals, 'merit' itself is not a simple concept to be defined or valued unambiguously. Uncritical assertion of 'merit' eventually leads to neglect of the underprivileged sections of the population as well as denial of the potential and diverse capabilities of human beings.[22] Such a deeply flawed concept cannot pilot the debate to a more accommodating conclusion. It only makes the debate more acrimonious between the parties involved, as we have witnessed.

The concept of 'merit' also suffers from some lack of empirical validity. As V. P. Singh asserted in the case of the Mandal debate in the early 1990s, the southern states of India as a whole, where reservation policy for depressed and backward classes started much earlier and remains more pervasive than in northern India, in no way suffer from lack of 'merit', say, in terms of overall growth or efficiency.

To be more exact, there is found no proof to show the public sector in these states to be less 'efficient' or 'viable' due to reservation (Singh 1996).[23] Evidently with wide diversity in performance, the public sector as a whole cannot be condemned as inefficient only due to the 'merit-less' recruitment of employees under the reservation policy.

An alternative to the 'merit-less' application of reservation, as suggested by Bajaj, is the promotion of 'employability' among the SCs and STs. Bajaj expresses readiness to cooperate with the government to provide them with education and technical training to promote 'employability'. Similar advice is also given by the FICCI representative (Mitra 2005). The prevailing view in the private sector is to relieve private businesses of any legal obligation to employ SC and ST recruits and to offer an alternative facility to enhance 'employability' with 'joint' effort through public–private coordination. This view is clearly reflected and reiterated in policy notes jointly formulated by CII and ASSOCHAM in 2006, which we shall discuss in the following section.

6.4.2 Discrimination in recruitment

The current debate raised another important question as to whether private enterprises had actually paid much effort to recruit employees who were meritoriously the best available in the labour market. The question is closely related to the need to scrutinize the ways and manners of recruitment prevalent among private companies.

Leaders in private companies claim that they base their recruitment choice only on 'merit' and there is no room for them to resort to any social discrimination in recruitment. They do not take note of the communal identity of the recruits, it is claimed.

This claim can be scrutinized both empirically (what actually are the ways and manners of private recruitment) and logically (what is the inherent logic of their denial of discrimination).

Empirical scrutiny is a bit difficult without a large sample of recruitment practices, which is generally absent except in a few pioneering studies. Of course, there are many sporadic cases reported to prove discrimination in recruitment. The Bhopal Document we dealt with in the last section focuses on the case of an SC engineering student of excellent 'merit' who had been continuously rejected by private employers and eventually got a job as soon as he erased his community identity from his biodata (Government of Madhya Pradesh 2002b: 11). However, a better explanation of the cause for exclusion, in contrast to the wilful and explicit one, as supported by labour market studies, is the closed nature of the recruitment process. Private companies seldom refer their recruitment information to the Employment Exchange, and recruitment information is highly informal. Rather than an open invitation or public announcement, what is called 'employee referral' is the more general practice.[24] The closed nature of recruitment, which actually limits the access to recruitment information, excludes those unrelated to the employees or employers. The recruitment procedure tends to be structurally exclusive, and it raises a barrier against new entrants.

When exclusion is structural, few people working in the process feel explicit exclusion. As employers do not apply a 'caste yardstick' to recruiting, they feel themselves free from any social injustice. Bajaj clearly denies his caste prejudice in recruitment. It looks as if the market never discriminates. A commentator accuses private enterprises of wearing a 'veil of ignorance' (not exactly in the same context as Rawls uses his well-known phrase) (Guru 2005).

Mehta comments that '[T]here is a widespread impression that, for all the talk of merit, recruitment in the private sector is not fair, open and transparent. ... Indian industry could use this occasion to have a dialogue over its own recruiting practices, and to ask whether the labour market is genuinely open from its side' (Mehta 2005a: 210). In the next section of this chapter, we shall see how major industrial associations address this issue in their policy papers on reservation.

6.4.3 'Talent pool'

Shortage in the 'talent pool' is another variation of the 'merit' discourse. The argument focuses on the 'non-availability' of proper candidates for recruitment in spite of a willingness to employ on the part of private companies. In support of this contention, the public sector's failure to make full use of the reserved allocation of employment, especially in the upper grades offices, is often invoked.[25] This contention sounds very unpersuasive in the light of the exclusive and closed nature of private recruitment practice, as we have just pointed out. Louis (2005) refuted this charge by quoting from education statistics which show that nearly 300,000 SC and ST students graduate annually. He contends that there is a large enough 'pool' to exploit among the SC and ST graduates (Louis 2005: 148).[26] We are familiar with the allegation against the practice of reservation that it has benefited only a tiny privileged section, a 'creamy layer', in the SC and ST communities, and in fact, the 'talent pool' discourse is quite in line with this 'creamy layer' allegation against reservation.

To the extent that reservation, whether in the public or private sector, only benefits a miniscule section of people, Jhunjhunwala (2005: 244) argues that a better policy would be to prepare an environment for the private sector to enhance opportunities for more employment (rather than to distribute scarce resources under reservation). Even if we accept this argument, a problem remains as to whether private sector enterprises would be willing to employ more recruits from SCs and STs in response to the enhanced opportunities. Enhanced opportunity does not automatically increase the share of the underprivileged among the recruits. In other words, a crucial issue is whether the private sector would be ready to positively engage with the social dimension of employment.

6.4.4 Globalization and reservation

Whereas anti-reservationists uncompromisingly reject any consideration other than 'merit' for recruitment due to the fiercely competitive conditions under economic globalization, pro-reservationists contend, by citing various cases (from the United States, Malaysia and South Africa), that many countries in the world under the same conditions adopt AA in one form or another.

Among the many cases, the US is most favoured by pro-reservationists as an example of implementation of AA as it is undoubtedly a showcase of a market economy. They urge people to learn from the US about how AA actions coexist with high competition and meritocracy. We shall look into what this argument suggests as to the relevance of AA in the competitive economy.

Pro-reservationists prefer to invoke a recent judgment by the US Supreme Court on the case of entrance into the Law School at Michigan University (June 2003) to support their contention. The judgment allowed application of AA for the sake of promotion of 'diversity', which has been a ruling principle in the US for introducing AA measures. No doubt the judgment itself was a fairly big surprise for many, especially for those concerned with the future of AA in the US, as recent public opinion had supposedly been very much against such liberal measures as AA.[27] It was a 'surprising outcome' (Weisskopf 2004: xv). Weisskopf's interpretation of the background of the judgment is very suggestive. He assumes that a very wide coalition of elites, including world-class entrepreneurs in the US, has internalized the principle of 'diversity' as a part of their market strategy. Their support for AA is not from sympathy for social justice or equality but rather is due to economic interest (Weisskopf 2005: 264). Comparing the situation in India with that in the US, he points out that the effect of globalization on support for racial/ethnic preference in the US is quite the opposite of its effect on support for such policies in India. Most Indian business, military and educational leaders – especially those representing the most elite institutions – line up firmly against reservation policies in higher education and employment. They argue that these policies weaken India's ability to compete in a globalized world, because they provide opportunities to typically underprepared and culturally deprived members, at the expense of well-prepared and culturally sophisticated members of mainstream groups, who are primed for success on the world stage. From this perspective, preferential policies are seen as a costly luxury rather than a good investment (Weisskopf 2005: 265).

Weisskopf's perceptive observation is shared by Omvedt (2005: 132). Gail Omvedt also highlights a similar contrast between India and the US and proceeds to assert that such marginal communities as SCs and STs are highly excluded from, and have less power to exert influence in, the market (Omvedt 2005: 132). One crucial observation in the ongoing debate is that such marginalized communities are not regarded as agents in the market economy. Omvedt (2005: 136) warns:

> In fact, today as India is 'going global' faster than many sections of the society want, it is important to realize that a truly modern society requires the conscious creation of opportunities for all citizens, and a truly competitive society cannot afford to waste any talent . . .
>
> If liberalisation is to be successful, the private corporate sector cannot remain an island of upper caste privilege.

6.4.5 Affirmative action and reservation

Contrasting India with the US brings forth another important point of discussion. Both in India and abroad, reservation is often used interchangeably with

AA, which is no doubt a more inclusive term. They involve different principles as well as different means and instruments as public policy. As regards the principles, Indian reservation is based primarily on the principle of compensation for 'historical injustice' in the 'Hindu' society (at least in case of SCs and STs). The principle of 'proportional representation' has also been invoked in the case of reservation for OBCs. However, the AA in the US bases its principle on 'diversity' and no quota-like allotment of entitlement is allowed, in contrast to Indian reservation.

As a means of public policy, reservation has a much narrower scope than AA. Reservation in India applies only to representation, employment and education (including scholarship), whereas AA has a much wider range of application such as 'dealer diversity' or 'supplier diversity'. Indian debates on reservation so far, including one in the case of the OBC reservation in the early 1990s and another recently in 2006, could never enlarge the scope of debate on affirmative measures. One relevant point in the current debate is that this is the first time that such enlarging of the domain of argument on AA took place. One of the participants in the debate clearly put forth this point by titling his article 'Affirmation without Reservation' (Mehta 2005b). Omvedt points out that the social justice programme in India has become stereotyped around the theme of 'reservation' in the public sector (Omvedt 2005: 133). If the current debate helps to broaden the domain of affirmative measures to include licence distribution, 'supplier diversity', or 'dealer diversity' as suggested by the Bhopal Declaration, it will break through the blind alley of uncompromising antagonism. The wide variety of measures taken in the name of AA in other countries could be harnessed, coupled with the principles of fairness and transparency.

6.5 A business plan for affirmative action

In April 2006, a chamber of commerce of major importance, the Confederation of Indian Industries (CII), in collaboration with the Associated Chambers of Commerce (ASSOCHAM), appointed a task force to look into possible alternative actions to reservation. J. J. Irani, former Managing Director of Tata Steel, chaired the task force and submitted in July a comprehensive plan to propose concrete steps on AA for the SCs and STs.[28]

General concern with marginalization of less privileged groups of people in the rapidly globalizing economy is shared by Irani as well. He observes,

> Given the country's projected population dynamics, marginalization of any sections of society will seriously impact India's overall competitiveness and economic prospects. In our rapid march towards economic prosperity, *inclusiveness and competitiveness are interdependent and one cannot be achieved without the other.* (*Indian Express*, 29 July 2006, italics added)

The Action Plan proposed several concrete steps, with full awareness of 'centuries-old social discrimination' and the need to uplift less privileged sections of the society. The plan states that 'inclusiveness' could ultimately be achieved through universal access to quality education. However, it further states, 'Industry believes that competitiveness of enterprise and economy is not negotiable and must be achieved and maintained through knowledge and competence in the rapidly developing Indian economy.' So, the report categorically denied reservation, saying 'private sector industry is against any legislation that would compromise the sanctity of its non-negotiable freedom of choice in employment'.

Within the above framework, the report urges private sector industry to commit to several concrete steps which are totally voluntary in nature, but at the same time companies are required to disclose the steps they have undertaken in their annual reports. Individual companies will have counsel to oversee the company's practice of these steps, and CII will appoint an ombudsman to watch these initiatives.

Some of the salient features of the concrete steps are as follows.

6.5.1 Workplace

Industry will endeavour to reflect greater representation of SCs and STs in its new recruitment at all levels, and it is expected that its efforts will become visible within the next year. Companies will also strengthen their human resource systems for enhancing access and opportunity for applicants from SCs and STs. Obviously this step is meant to ensure more open recruitment practices. Companies will be encouraged to provide more executive positions through appointments/promotions from these classes.

Note has to be taken of the fact that the task force includes only SCs and STs, and includes neither OBCs nor the so-called 'creamy layer' even among the SCs and STs, in their steps.[29]

6.5.2 Entrepreneurship development

This proposal is unique in the sense that it is addressed to a far wider 'informal' sector than the workplaces which are mentioned in the step in Section 6.5.1 above. The report says, 'as 93 per cent of the aggregate workforce is engaged in agriculture, small and tiny businesses, and the self-employed sectors, Concrete Steps for the creation of entrepreneurs from Scheduled Castes and Scheduled Tribes are necessary for more inclusive economic growth'.

Larger companies are to mentor and create at least one entrepreneur among SCs and STs a year to build business partnerships in the supply and distribution value chain. CII and ASSOCHAM companies will maintain a database of such entrepreneurs promoted by them.

6.5.3 Employability

For expanding the pool of employable personnel from among SCs and STs, industries are ask to commit to coaching programmes and scholarships to facilitate their studies in superior management and technical training. In the first year, 10 universities will be identified for coaching programmes covering 10,000 students with the objective of increasing to 50 cities and 50,000 students by 2009. A supply of scholarships to enable at least 100 students to study at the Indian Institutes of

Technology, the Indian Institutes of Management and other superior institutions is the first year's target.

6.5.4 Education

The report also underlines high-quality universal education as being important to achieving the objective of building an inclusive and integrated society. Also, industry can supplement and complement the efforts of government and other providers of education services (NGOs) through such means as promoting quality schools, improving the level of primary education, and providing other financial aid, particularly in the 104 districts with a pronounced population that is socially and economically backward among SCs and STs.

In the proposed comprehensive steps, reservation is categorically excluded. Also, the report carefully avoids any mention of obligation to employ recruits from SCs and STs. However, the steps include several fresh initiatives, especially those related to creating entrepreneurs among the SCs and STs, which so far have received little attention (except by the Madhya Pradesh government's Bhopal Declaration).

So far as the concrete steps are voluntary and individual companies are left to exercise these steps, positive engagement by apex organizations is crucial for the promotion of the steps in the agenda. Also, we are at least inclined to believe that the Indian private corporate sector is determined to engage with the social implications of the exclusion of the less privileged people in the labour market.[30]

6.6 Conclusion: relevance of the debate

After all, what is the new element of argument in the current reservation debate? We shall first address this question and then summarize the salient points in the debate. It is quite obvious that concern with the widening disparity and further exclusion from the market economy is the motive force for demanding reservation in the private sector. As far as SCs and STs are concerned, there has been an overall convergence of public opinion advocating reservation in public sector employment as a compensatory measure.[31] This argument is beyond dispute so far as its application is limited to (1) public employment and representation and (2) narrow sections of marginalized communities, including SCs and STs. On this assumption, Indian private capitalists fully supported protective discrimination in spite of its inherent contradiction with the ideology of free enterprise. So far as it is applied only to the public sector, private corporate leaders found themselves safely outside the scope of the nuisance. Also, as a commentator discusses, as the private sector itself has long been under the protective shield of the government in the form of subsidies and an insulated market, it was in no position to oppose this kind of state intervention on behalf of the marginalized communities. Only when the private sector found itself more independent and free to act did it start raising its voice against reservation. So what is 'new' in the recent debate is the active participation of the private corporate sector in the debate (1) as a possible 'victim' as well as (2) as a more vocal agent in the age of economic liberalization. Also, in so far as this new element has been added to the debate, the edge of the opposition has become much sharper and less restrained. The principles of 'competition', 'efficiency' and 'merit' mixed with thinly veiled prejudice against the capability of the underprivileged people has freely appeared on the stage of public debate. The recent debate is no doubt a product of the 'globalized' Indian economy.

Finally, we shall summarize what the current debate on reservation in the private sector could contribute to the future formulation of employment policy, particularly with regard to the search for an 'inclusive' model of employment creation.

First, we observe that in a liberalized and globalized economy in India, private sector leaders are yet to become attuned to a more accommodating employment policy for the less privileged sections of Indian society. The contrast is evident if we compare the attitude of the major US businesses which have established a more elaborate AA policy on the basis of the 'diversity' formula. At the root of the contrast lies the absolute lack of socio-economic and even political power of the marginalized communities. However, the 'inclusive' strategy cannot be left to the natural process of the market economy. This is the domain where the social dimension of employment is to be taken into full account.

Second, problems remain if reservation is the optimal policy to redress the marginalization of the less privileged classes in Indian society. Debate on AA in India has so far been overly centred on the issue of reservation, but overcoming the multitude of disadvantages in the market economy requires measures that are more comprehensive than reservation. The scope of the current debate on reservation in the private sector needs to be more comprehensive.

Finally, it is evident that the private sector cannot remain insulated from social responsibility. The market economy itself is based on social consent or 'legitimacy' of the system. Total neglect of the marginal communities on the plea of free competition, meritocracy and efficiency jeopardize the stability of system. The authors of the CII–ASSOCHAM formula appear to be very conscious of this basic nature of the market. The proposed steps are a good example of a proactive and positive reaction on the part of Indian private enterprises, provided that they are carried into practice. The current debate on reservation in the private sector has contributed to the projection of a growing awareness and recognition that the social dimension of employment certainly needs to be addressed.[32]

Notes

1. The textiles and garment sectors are typical examples of sectors which have undergone deregulation since the late 1980s, as some other chapters in this volume illustrate.
2. Hodges-Aeberhard (1999) reviews the judicial cases of AA across the world in the 1990s and observes that the trend of court decisions is not uniform but mixed, which is described as 'variously reflecting hostility, lukewarm acceptance and full endorsement' (p. 249). As illustrated by her quotes of the decisions on the so-called Mandal case, i.e. the reservation case for Other Backward Classes (OBC), the Indian cases must be ones of 'full endorsement'. For OBC, see note 3.

3. The government of India in the spring of 2006 announced its plan to reserve 27 per cent of places in highly esteemed educational institutions, including the Indian Institute of Technology, Indian Institute of Management and All India Medical Institute. This aroused a violent reaction from those who opposed the move, but a law to that effect was enacted in December the same year. OBC is the administrative term for the socially and educational backward classes of people. It is generally understood as the people of castes which are positioned between forward castes and Schedule Castes (SC). It also includes those who converted from SC into religions other than Hinduism (including Buddhists, Sikhs and Jains). As for employment in the central government, OBC are already allotted 27 per cent of the new positions, as confirmed by the 1992 Supreme Court decision in the so-called Mandal case.
4. Reservation in education is now extended into purely private (unaided) institutions, following the constitutional amendment (the 104th amendment) of Article 15 in December 2005.
5. It should be remembered that the 'private sector' in the context of this debate actually implies the 'private corporate sector' because self-employed industry and owner-operated agricultural households can in no way be an appropriate field of 'reservation' although they belong to the 'private sector'. In the debate, it is also presumed that 'reservation' applies only to the 'organized sector' in contrast to the 'unorganized sector'.
6. The most authentic Galanter (1984) and the more recent Weisskopf (2004) are two resourceful works which probe the rationale for, and the discontent with, reservation policy in the Indian context.
7. In March 2007, the result of the 61st round of National Sample Survey on the Below Poverty Line (BPL) population was announced by the Planning Commission. It revealed further decline in percentages of the BPL population from 36.0 per cent in 1993–94 to 27.5 per cent in 2004–5 (figures are for the total population as well as for the 'uniform recall period', i.e. period of 30 days preceding the investigation) (*Indian Express*, 22 March 2007).
8. Sundaram and Tendulkar (2003) give a clear picture of poverty in terms of communities and occupation. Mohanty (2006) links caste differences (SC, ST and OBC) with several socio-economic indicators (e.g. household expenditure, literacy and education, and employment) available in the 1999–2000 National Sample Survey.
9. The concurrence of deprivation in diverse forms including economic poverty and social discrimination at the bottom of the strata ('underdogs') is focused on by Sen (2005) in his Essay 10 on 'Class in India'.
10. In applying reservation, the concept of a 'creamy layer' has been effective only in the case of OBC employment reservation for central institutions. However, in October 2006, an opinion handed down by the Supreme Court of India expressed the desirability of excluding 'creamy layers' even in the case of SC and ST reservation (*Indian Express*, 20 October 2006).
11. 'The rate of growth of employment declined sharply from 2.04 per cent per year in the period from 1983 to 1993–94 to only 0.98 per cent per year in the period 1993–94 to 1999–2000. This sharp deceleration in the growth of employment has naturally been the focus of much attention and comment, raising fears that economic growth in the 1990s has been of a "jobless" variety' (Government of India (Planning Commission) 2001: 18 and Table 2.3). The latest comparable figure is given by the National Sample Survey result for the 61st Round 2004–5. It showed notable recovery of the employment growth rate, which registered 2.89 per cent per annum between 1999–2000 (the year of the previous 'large sample' survey) and 2004–5 (for more details, see Introduction of this volume, note 15).
12. Louis (2005: 146) states that 110,000 SC jobs were lost in central government during 1992–97.
13. *Economic Survey of Maharashtra 2003–4*, and *2004–5* (Internet edition).

14. Aryama (2005: 99) notes this decay has already penetrated into primary education. Earlier, Drèze and Sen (2002) also warned against the same process, quoting the miserable state of primary education based on the Public Report on Basic Education (PROBE), which was based on a survey in several northern Indian states.
15. Some of the experts in the task force are Chandra Bhan Prasad (Convenor), Teesta Setalvad (Editor, *Communalism Combat*), S. K. Thorat (School of Social Sciences, JNU University Grant Commission since February 2006), Gail Omvedt (Government of Madhya Pradesh 2002a, b), and also http://www.mp.nic.in/tribal/taskforce/English/capter1.htm.
16. For the pledge by the UPA, see Section 6.1.
17. Rahul Bajaj was elected Member of the Parliament in the Rajya Sabha (Upper House) in August 2006, drawing on the support given by the BJP and Nationalist Congress Party.
18. But strangely enough, Videocon officials profess not to induct women into their management cadres (Parthasarathy 2005: 195).
19. The document is from http://www.dalits.org/delhideclaration.htm. The list of organizations that have joined includes the National Campaign on Dalit Human Rights, National Conference of Dalit Organization, National Dalit Forum, Indian Institute of Dalit Studies, Indian Social Institute (New Delhi), National Federation of Dalit Women, All India Confederation of SC and ST Organizations, Dalit Solidarity Peoples, Buddha Smriti Samsthan, Samata Sainik Dal, All India Defence SC and ST Employees Federation, National Coordination Committee of Dalit Christians, Indian Catholic Union, All India Christian Council, Buddhist Society of India, National Safai Karmachari Andolan, Social Justice Front, All India Vidyut Employees Association and many other state-level organizations.
20. The support by communist parties of the 'Delhi Declaration' is politically significant as it is an explicit coordination between Ambedkarites and Marxists. Also, if it does not remain only as a strategic alliance but involves any fresh theoretical exploration, the implications with regard to the political alliance would be far-reaching for social science theory on 'class and caste'.
21. See note 6 in this chapter.
22. In the US, there is extensive literature on the empirical studies which proved AA measures are not always associated with lower merit among AA recruits. See the review by Fugazza (2003).
23. Sachar (2005: 158) states that in Tamil Nadu state, the cut-off point in medical education is 95 per cent for general applicants and 93 per cent for SCs and others, which shows there is little difference. On the south–north contrast, see also Parthasarathy (2005: 200).
24. The most informed scholar on recruitment practices in the private sector is T.S. Papola (Papola 2005). Parthasarathy (2005: 196) states that even such progressive enterprises as Infosys's (IT giant) practice of recruitment is not much different. Narayana Murthy, CEO of Infosys, supports reservation based on economic criteria, not caste criteria (Thimmaiah 2005: 747). The recruitment practice of utilizing 'employee referral' in other IT companies such as Abode India or MAQ Software is described in Kumar (2005: 805).
25. Even in the public sector, among the four ranks of employees from D to A, for the two upper echelons of A and B, SC people are not employed up to the prescribed proportions.
26. Kumar (2005: 804) estimates a much larger 'talent pool' and claims that estimates so far have been vastly underestimated.
27. One of the recent surges against AA was the popular initiative against AA in the state of California in November 1996.
28. Confederation of Indian Industries and Associated Chambers of Commerce, *CII-ASSOCHAM Action Plan, Proposed Concrete Steps by Indian Industry on Affirmative Action for Scheduled Castes and Scheduled Tribes*, accessed on CII website on 10 September 2006. Another apex business body, the Federation of Indian Chambers of Commerce and Industries, made public a similar policy paper in June 2006 (*FICCI's Agenda for Affirmative Action*). Its appendix shows the result of interviews of member companies. One interesting result is that opinion is equally divided for and against AA (though the

content of the opinions is not clear). This underlines the importance of 'entrepreneurial development' just like the CII–ASSOCHAM paper, but it is less operative than the latter, as it does not talk either about a 'code of conduct' or a target or roadmap for implementation of its proposals. For a totally negative view of the CII–ASSOCHAM agenda from the trade union side, see M. K. Pandhe, 'Why to Legislate for Reservation in Private Sector'. *People's Democracy*, XXXI(1), 7 January 2007.

29. See note 10 above. The judiciary appears to share the view of the business leaders on the 'creamy layer' of the SCs and STs.
30. Government and major business associations met on 15 November 2006 to exchange views on reservation in the private sector. Government asked business associations to clarify their agenda on such issues as roadmaps and the nature of 'codes of conduct', and both sides agreed to make ready by March 2007 the current employment profile as of 1 January 2007 (*Indian Express*, 16 November 2006).
31. Historically, this convergence was the 'gain' by Mahatma Gandhi's fast against the British plan to introduce a separate electorate system for the SCs during the debate on revision of the Government of India Act in the early 1930s. With the compromise move on the part of Ambedkar, reservation for SCs (and STs) was acknowledged as a safety measure so as not to isolate these communities from mainstream Hindu society. It may be called a kind of 'national' consensus for a limited application of reservation.
32. As a sort of postscript, our attention may be drawn to the subsequent move by the UPA government and concerned parties to advocate extension of AA to a major religious minority (Muslims). In November 2006, a government-appointed commission (Sachar Commission) compiled a comprehensive national report on the socio-economic status of the Muslim community in India. The importance of the 'social dimension' in the liberalized economy is hard to miss.

References

Ambedkar, B.R. (1947) *States and Minorities: What are their Rights and how to Secure them in the Constitution of Free India.* Bombay: Thacker.

Aryama (2005) 'Public–Private Divide and Affirmative Action in India'. In Sukhadeo Thorat et al. (eds) *Reservation and Private Sector: Quest for Equal Opportunity and Growth.* New Delhi: Institute of Dalit Studies and Rawat Publications, pp. 89–100.

Bajaj, Rahul (2005) 'Reservation: Devoid of Merit'. In Sukhadeo Thorat et al. (eds) *Reservation and Private Sector: Quest for Equal Opportunity and Growth.* New Delhi: Institute of Dalit Studies and Rawat Publications, pp. 248–50.

Drèze, Jean and Amartya Sen (2002) *India Development and Participation.* New Delhi: Oxford University Press.

Fugazza, Marco (2003) 'Racial Discrimination: Theories, Facts and Policy'. *International Labour Review* 142(4): 508–41.

Galanter, Marc (1984) *Competing Equalities: Law and Backward Classes in India.* Berkeley: University of California Press.

Government of India (Ministry of Finance) (2005) *Economic Survey 2004–05*. New Delhi.

Government of India (Planning Commission) (2001) *Report of the Task Force on Employment.* New Delhi.

Government of Madhya Pradesh (2002a) *The Bhopal Declaration, Charting a New Course for Dalits for the 21st Century*. Bhopal.

—— (2002b) *The Bhopal Document, Charting a New Course for Dalits for the 21st Century*. Bhopal.

Guru, Gopal (2005) 'Corporate Classes and its "Veil of Ignorance"'. *Seminar* 549 (May): 36–9.

Hodges-Aeberhard, J. (1999) 'Affirmative Action in Employment: Recent Court Approaches to a Different Concept'. *International Labour Review* 138(3): 247–272.

Jhunjhunwala, Satish Kumar (2005) 'Job Reservation in Private Sector'. In Sukhadeo Thorat et al. (eds) *Reservation and Private Sector: Quest for Equal Opportunity and Growth*. New Delhi: Institute of Dalit Studies and Rawat Publications, pp. 242–7.

Kumar, Vivek (2005) 'Understanding the Politics of Reservation. A Perspective from Below'. *EPW* 26 February: 803–6.

Louis, Prakash (2005) 'Affirmative Action in Private Sector: Need for a National Debate'. In Sukhadeo Throat et al. (eds) *Reservation and Private Sector: Quest for Equal Opportunity and Growth*. New Delhi: Institute of Dalit Studies and Rawat Publications, pp. 140–56.

Mehta, P. B. (2005a) 'New Agenda for the Dalits'. In Sukhadeo Thorat et al. (eds) *Reservation and Private Sector: Quest for Equal Opportunity and Growth*. New Delhi: Institute of Dalit Studies and Rawat Publications, pp. 267–73.

—— (2005b) 'Affirmation without Reservation'. In Sukhadeo Thorat et al. (eds) *Reservation and Private Sector: Quest for Equal Opportunity and Growth*. New Delhi: Institute of Dalit Studies and Rawat Publications, pp. 207–18.

Mitra, Amit (2005) 'Is Reservation in Private Sector Warranted?' In Sukhadeo Thorat et al. (eds) *Reservation and Private Sector: Quest for Equal Opportunity and Growth*. New Delhi: Institute of Dalit Studies and Rawat Publications, pp. 239–41.

Mohanty, Mritiunjoy (2006) 'Social Inequality, Labour Market Dynamics and Reservation'. *EPW* (2 September): 3777–89.

Omvedt, Gail (2005) 'Reservation in the Private and the Corporate Sector'. In Sukhadeo Thorat et al. (eds) *Reservation and Private Sector: Quest for Equal Opportunity and Growth*. New Delhi: Institute of Dalit Studies and Rawat Publications, pp. 129–39.

Papola, T. S. (2005) 'Social Exclusion and Discrimination in Hiring Practices: the Case of Indian Private Industry'. In Sukhadeo Thorat et al. (eds) *Reservation and Private Sector: Quest for Equal Opportunity and Growth*. New Delhi: Institute of Dalit Studies and Rawat Publications, pp. 101–8.

Parthasarathy, D. (2005) 'Reservations, Towards a Larger Perspective'. In Sukhadeo Thorat et al. (eds) *Reservation and Private Sector: Quest for Equal Opportunity and Growth*. New Delhi: Institute of Dalit Studies and Rawat Publications, pp. 193–202.

Sachar, Rajindar (2005) 'Is Reservation in Private Sector Warranted?' In Sukhadeo Thorat et al. (eds) *Reservation and Private Sector: Quest for Equal Opportunity and Growth*. New Delhi: Institute of Dalit Studies and Rawat Publications, pp. 157–9.

Sen, Amartya (2005) *The Argumentative Indians: Writings on Indian History, Culture and Identity*. London: Penguin.

Shah, Ghanshyam (2005) 'Foreword'. In Sukhadeo Thorat et al. (eds) *Reservation and Private Sector: Quest for Equal Opportunity and Growth*. New Delhi: Institute of Dalit Studies and Rawat Publications, pp. ix–xii.

Singh, V. P. (1996) 'Affirmative Action in India'. *Mainstream* 18 May: 7–13.

Sundaram, K. and Suresh D. Tendulkar (2003) 'Poverty among Social and Economic Groups in India in the 1990s'. *EPW* 13 December: 5263–76.

Thimmaiah, G. (2005) 'Implications of Reservation in Private Sector'. *EPW* 19 February: 745–50.

Thorat, Sukhadeo (2005) 'Caste System and Economic Discrimination: Lessons from Theories'. In Sukhadeo Thorat et al. (eds) *Reservation and Private Sector: Quest for Equal Opportunity and Growth*. New Delhi: Institute of Dalit Studies and Rawat Publications, pp. 66–88.

Thorat, Sukhadeo, Aryama and Prashant Negi (eds) (2005) *Reservation and Private Sector: Quest for Equal Opportunity and Growth*. New Delhi: Institute of Dalit Studies and Rawat Publications.

Weisskopf, Thomas E. (2004) *Affirmative Action in the United States and India. A Comparative Perspective*. London: Routledge.

—— (2005) 'Globalization and Affirmative Action'. In Sukhadeo Thorat et al. (eds) *Reservation and Private Sector: Quest for Equal Opportunity and Growth*. New Delhi: Institute of Dalit Studies and Rawat Publications, pp. 263–6.

Part III

Employment: Assessing the Regulatory Effects

7
Labour Demand in India's Textile and Garment Industries: a Comparative Analysis of the Organized and Informal Sectors

Takahiro Sato

7.1 Introduction

In 2005, the international textile and garment product markets entered a new stage, towards a more liberalized trade regime. Until that year, under the Multi-Fibre Arrangement (MFA), export quotas for textile and garment products from the developing countries had been allocated by the advanced countries. With the end of the MFA on 31 December 2004, India's textile and garment industries came to face new challenges, but also with chance to stimulate growth momentum.

The textile and garment industries make up one of the largest and most important sectors in India in terms of industrial production, export earnings and employment generation. Moreover, the international market share of cotton yarn exports from India is 20 per cent, and its international share of looms is 58 per cent.[1] India's textile industry is one of the largest in the world.

However, whether India's textile and garment industries utilize their capability fully is dependent on the economic policy regime and domestic market structure. Given that the textile and garment industries can absorb much labour, especially among disadvantaged groups and women, the chronic poverty and unemployment problem in India could be alleviated by the faster growth of these industries. Thus in this chapter, we examine the issues relating to the effects of economic regulation on employment in the textile and garment industries in India.

We focus on the Industrial Dispute Act as a job security regulation which requires any firm employing more than 100 workers to receive government permission before retrenching or laying off even a single worker. We provide a new estimate of the labour demand function in the textile and garment industries in order to determine the impact of job security regulation on employment in these industries. We find that on one hand, job security regulation in the organized sector depresses labour demand in that sector, and on the other hand, raised wage elasticity of labour demand in both the organized and the informal sectors.

This chapter is divided into the following five sections. Following this introduction, Section 7.2 explains the institutional background of this subject, focusing on the textile and garment industries and the IDA as a job security regulation. Section 7.3 examines the theoretical arguments regarding a profit-maximizing firm's demand for labour. Section 7.4 presents a statistical analysis of the determinants of a firm's labour demand. Section 7.5 concludes with some remarks.

7.2 Institutional background

7.2.1 Overview of India's textile and garment industries

The textile and garment industries are quite large and important sectors in India in terms of output, export and employment. These industries accounted for 12 per cent of industrial production and about 20 per cent of total export earnings in 2003, and absorbed about 8 per cent of employment in non-primary industries in 1999. In the post-MFA regime that has been in place since 2005, these industries face new challenges and opportunities to stimulate growth momentum.

Table 7.1 shows the average annual growth rate in the registered, unregistered and combined sectors.[2] The performance of these industries in the registered sector is inferior to that of all other manufacturing industries. However, the achievement of these industries in the unregistered sector is comparable with that of all industries in the unregistered sector. In the recent period of 1991–2003, the growth rate of the registered textile and garment industries was 4.8 per cent and that of the unregistered was 5.7 per cent. As seen in Table 7.2, in the period for 1951–60, the output share of these industries was about 25 per cent, which is remarkably high. Therefore, we can see that while these industries are traditional and old,

Table 7.1 Average annual growth rates of the textile and apparel industries in different sectors (%)

Period	*Registered sector*		*Unregistered sector*		*Combined*	
	Textile/ apparel	*All manufactures*	*Textile/ apparel*	*All manufactures*	*Textile/ apparel*	*All manufactures*
1951–60	3.3 ***	7.7 ***	5.5 ***	4.8 ***	4.1 ***	6.3 ***
1961–70	2.0 ***	5.2 ***	1.8 *	3.2 ***	1.9 **	4.3 ***
1971–80	5.8 ***	4.7 ***	7.3 ***	4.7 ***	6.4 ***	4.7 ***
1981–90	5.8 ***	8.2 ***	3.1 ***	6.1 ***	4.7 ***	7.4 ***
1991–2000	5.5 ***	7.5 ***	6.8 ***	7.0 ***	6.0 ***	7.3 ***
1991–2003	4.8 ***	6.7 ***	5.7 ***	6.3 ***	5.1 ***	6.6 ***
1951–2003	4.0 ***	6.3 ***	4.4 ***	4.7 ***	4.2 ***	5.7 ***

Notes: Textile and apparel industries include 'cotton textiles', 'wool, silk, etc', 'just textiles', and 'textile products'. 'Annual growth rate' is the estimated coefficient of the time trend in the semi-log trend equation by OLS.
***, **, * mean statistically significant at the 1, 5 and 10% level, respectively.
Source: Compiled from Central Statistical Organization, *National Account Statistics Back Series 1950–51 to 1992–93*, statements 43 and 45, and *National Account Statistics 1993–94 to 2003–04*, statements 60 and 62.

they still continue to grow. Table 7.2 shows that while the decline in the share of these industries from 1951–60 to 1961–71 was large, it has been modest since then.

Textile industries include the spinning, weaving and processing sectors. We use the weaving and knitting sectors as examples for understanding the structure of the textile industries. Table 7.3 shows the production of fabrics in different sectors, e.g. the mill sector, handloom sector, powerloom sector, hosiery (knitting) sector and Khadi, etc., in 1993–2004. Fabrics production in the mill sector decreased, and that of the handloom sector was stagnant. Fabrics production of the powerloom sector was the largest, increasing from 15,994 million sq. metres in 1993 to 28,325 million sq. metres in 2004, and that of the hosiery sector also grew remarkably in same period. Fabrics production of Khadi, wool and silk remained small, but increased in 1993–2004. Looking at all sectors, it is noted that 100 per cent non-cotton approach cotton fabrics in the period for 1993–2004. We confirm that the textile industries may be understood as a complex of various sectors and fibre users.

Table 7.4 shows the export performance of the textile and garment industries. Export earnings increased from less than US$1 billion in 1970 to about US$13 billion in 2004. The export share of these industries decreased in the mid-1970s and then increased to maintain a level of roughly 20 per cent or more since the mid-1980s. In Table 7.5, we take 'cotton yarn, fabrics, made-ups, etc.' and 'ready-made garments' as examples of the export direction of textile and garment products. India's principal export destinations are the US and EU. It is noted that 'cotton yarn etc.' increased remarkably from about US$4 billion in 1998 to about US$16 billion in 2004. However, 'ready-made garments' showed only a small increase from about US$2.7 billion to US$3.2 billion in the same period. This implies that the global competitiveness of the garment industries is relatively lower than that of the textile industries due to the reservation policy for small-scale industries and the lack of modernization.[3]

Table 7.2 Sector-wise share of value added generated by textile and apparel industries (%)

Period	*Registered sector*	*Unregistered sector*	*Combined*
1951–60	30.7	18.6	24.5
1961–70	20.3	17.8	19.2
1971–80	16.7	16.6	16.7
1981–90	13.9	16.5	14.8
1991–2000	11.8	16.4	13.3
1991–2003	11.4	16.0	12.9
1951–2003	18.5	17.0	17.5

Notes: Textile and apparel industries include 'cotton textiles', 'wool, silk, etc.', 'jute textiles' and 'textile products.' The figures are the ratio of value added of the textile and apparel industries in the sector to that of all manufacturing industries in the sector.
Source: Compiled from Central Statistical Organization, *National Account Statistics Back Series 1950–51 to 1992–93*, statements 43 and 45, and *National Account Statistics 1993–94 to 2003–04*, statements 60 and 62.

Table 7.3 Production of fabrics in different sectors (million sq. metres)

	1993	*1994*	*1995*	*1996*	*1997*	*1998*	*1999*	*2000*	*2001*	*2002*	*2003*	*2004*	*2005**	*2005***
Mill sector														
Cotton	1,356	1,262	1,159	1,222	1,238	1,111	1,105	1,106	1,036	1,019	969	1,049	521	1,042
Blended	575	746	602	488	466	444	379	332	296	263	253	243	121	242
100% Non-cotton	59	263	258	247	244	230	230	232	214	214	212	211	105	209
Total	1,990	2,271	2,019	1,957	1,948	1,785	1,714	1,670	1,546	1,496	1,434	1,503	747	1,493
Handloom sector														
Cotton	5,241	5,429	6,239	6,441	6,699	5,861	6,376	6,577	6,698	5,098	4,519	4,792	2,589	5,178
Blended	2	13	18	52	69	111	119	111	95	118	117	146	81	162
100% Non-cotton	608	738	945	963	835	820	857	818	792	764	857	784	373	747
Total	5,851	6,180	7,202	7,456	7,603	6,792	7,352	7,506	7,585	5,980	5,493	5,722	3,043	6,087
Decentralized powerloom sector														
Cotton	7,836	7,021	7,014	7,238	6,652	5,856	6,291	6,584	6,473	6,761	6,370	7,361	4,263	8,526
Blended	2,425	2,640	3,137	3,948	4,481	4,356	4,613	5,071	5,025	4,695	4,688	4,526	2,332	4,663
100% Non-cotton	5,733	6,315	7,050	8,166	9,818	10,478	12,283	12,148	13,694	14,498	15,889	16,438	8,219	16,438
Total	15,994	15,976	17,201	19,352	20,951	20,690	23,187	23,803	25,192	25,954	26,947	28,325	14,814	29,627
Decentralized hosiery sector														
Cotton	3,357	3,307	4,488	4,940	5,403	5,121	5,217	5,451	5,562	6,422	6,182	7,430	4,078	8,155
Blended	153	262	268	400	735	788	802	837	871	800	1,010	1,117	576	1,152
100% Non-cotton	127	179	282	193	256	367	355	408	634	659	655	565	261	523
Total	3,637	3,748	5,038	5,533	6,394	6,276	6,374	6,696	7,067	7,881	7,847	9,112	4,915	9,830
All sectors														
Cotton	17,790	17,019	18,900	19,841	19,992	17,949	18,989	19,718	19,769	19,300	18,040	20,632	11,451	22,901
Blended	3,155	3,661	4,025	4,888	5,751	5,699	5,913	6,351	6,287	5,876	6,068	6,032	3,110	6,219
100% Non-cotton	6,527	7,495	8,535	9,569	11,153	11,895	13,725	13,606	15,334	16,135	17,613	17,998	8,958	17,917
Total	27,472	28,175	31,460	34,298	36,896	35,543	38,627	39,675	41,390	41,311	41,721	44,662	23,519	47,037
Khadi wool and silk	426	431	431	540	545	584	581	558	644	662	662	693	331	693
Grand total	27,898	28,606	31,891	34,838	37,441	36,127	39,208	40,233	42,034	41,973	42,383	45,355	23,850	47,730

Notes: * From April to September. ** Anticipated.
Source: Compiled from Ministry of Textiles, *Annual Report 1999–2000*, Chapter 3; *Annual Report 2002*, Table 3.5; *Annual Report 2005–06*, Table 3.6.

Table 7.4 Exports of textile and textile products

Year	*Textile and textile products*		*Textile and textile products (including raw cotton)*	
	US$ million	*Export share (%)*	*US$ million*	*Export share (%)*
1970	512.5	25.2		
1971	639.3	29.7		
1972	685.2	26.7		
1973	859.9	26.6		
1974	962.4	23.0		
1975	906.4	19.5		
1976	1,094.5	19.1		
1977	1,110.5	17.6		
1978	1,228.9	17.7		
1979	1,722.6	21.7		
1980	1,985.5	23.4		
1981	1,640.5	18.8		
1982	1,301.5	14.3		
1983	1,399.9	14.8		
1984	1,615.1	16.4		
1985	1,574.5	17.7		
1986	1,915.6	19.7		
1987	3,013.8	24.9	3,098.3	25.6
1988	3,037.7	21.7	3,052.5	21.8
1989	3,746.5	22.6	3,823.6	23.0
1990	4,342.6	23.9	4,814.0	26.5
1991	4,693.1	26.3	4,816.8	27.0
1992	5,007.4	27.0	5,070.2	27.4
1993	5,472.3	24.6	5,680.7	25.5
1994	7,117.7	27.0	7,162.2	27.2
1995	8,031.6	25.3	8,092.4	25.5
1996	8,635.8	25.8	9,079.3	27.1
1997	9,050.4	25.9	9,271.5	26.5
1998	8,866.3	26.7	8,915.5	26.8
1999	9,822.1	26.7	9,839.9	26.7
2000	11,285.0	25.3	11,333.4	25.4
2001	10,206.5	23.3	10,215.5	23.3
2002	11,617.0	22.0	11,627.4	22.1
2003	12,791.5	20.0	12,996.6	20.4
2004	12,614.0	15.9	12,695.1	16.0

Note: Figures from 1970 to 1986 and 1987 to 2004 are not comparable due to the change of industrial classification.
Source: Compiled from Reserve bank of India, *Handbook of Statistics on Indian Economy 2004–05*, Table 131.

In Table 7.6, we see that it is principally non-primary industries that are absorbing labour. Textile industries ranked third, employing about 9.5 million workers in 1993 and about 8 million in 1999. The share of the textile industries was 8.3 per cent in 1993 and 6 per cent in 1999. Garment industries ranked eighteenth, employing

Table 7.5 Exports of textile and apparel products to principal countries (%)

	1987	*1988*	*1989*	*1990*	*1991*	*1992*	*1993*	*1994*	*1995*	*1996*	*1997*	*1998*	*1999*	*2000*	*2001*	*2002*	*2003*	*2004*
Cotton yarn, fabrics, made-ups, etc.																		
Bangladesh	4.2	3.2	4.0	4.0	2.7	2.7	2.8	4.4	4.7	4.2	3.0	2.8	2.6	3.0	3.9	2.6	3.6	1.9
Germany	3.3	2.6	2.4	3.0	3.8	3.8	3.2	4.5	4.7	3.5	4.0	5.0	4.1	4.2	4.2	4.2	4.2	4.2
Hong Kong	1.0	1.0	0.7	0.8	1.1	1.5	1.9	2.2	3.2	2.6	2.5	2.7	3.4	3.3	1.7	1.8	1.4	1.3
Italy	0.8	1.3	0.9	1.0	3.0	2.9	1.1	1.6	1.7	1.8	3.1	2.7	2.9	2.9	2.5	2.5	2.9	3.8
Malaysia	1.0	1.4	1.5	2.4	3.1	2.4	2.8	2.5	3.0	4.1	3.6	1.6	3.0	3.6	4.0	1.6	1.9	1.5
Singapore	6.1	3.3	3.9	6.9	4.6	6.9	6.0	6.3	6.4	5.3	5.1	3.8	4.3	4.6	5.1	4.1	3.5	4.5
Sri Lanka	2.6	2.6	1.1	2.7	2.8	3.9	3.8	4.5	3.4	3.1	3.1	3.7	3.2	3.2	2.3	2.9	3.1	2.7
UAE	1.8	1.6	2.9	2.6	4.5	5.6	6.9	6.6	6.2	6.6	5.2	7.0	7.1	6.5	6.6	6.6	7.7	6.6
UK	5.5	4.8	4.4	4.7	5.2	5.1	5.4	6.2	7.3	7.3	6.4	6.5	6.5	6.3	5.2	4.9	5.9	5.3
USA	10.2	10.6	9.2	9.7	10.0	11.3	12.1	14.0	13.7	18.5	16.8	17.3	18.1	17.9	16.3	16.9	13.9	16.3
Others	63.5	67.6	69.1	62.0	59.4	53.8	54.0	47.3	45.7	43.0	47.3	46.9	44.7	44.6	48.2	51.9	52.0	51.9
Total (US$ million)	1,152.3	1,601.3	1,997.7	2,250.4	2,253.1	2,480.8	3,038.1	3,508.0	4,391.0	4,962.7	5,336.2	4,463.9	5,152.1	6,818.6	6,957.8	9,033.0	12,405.4	16,440.6
Ready-made garments																		
Bangladesh	5.7	8.6	11.6	10.1	9.6	12.4	11.4	11.4	10.8	10.8	8.4	4.5	5.1	5.1	5.4	4.1	5.1	6.3
Germany	7.7	6.8	7.5	8.3	6.9	7.2	7.4	6.1	6.3	5.5	4.9	4.9	4.2	4.1	3.8	4.1	4.3	4.1
Hong Kong	2.3	1.8	2.3	3.0	3.7	2.2	1.9	2.9	4.6	7.4	7.7	7.6	5.5	5.9	4.0	3.1	3.6	2.8
Italy	7.3	5.0	5.0	6.2	5.1	4.8	4.2	4.9	5.1	3.5	4.3	5.5	4.2	4.4	5.3	4.6	5.1	5.4
Japan	3.0	5.5	3.9	2.9	3.7	3.3	3.9	4.4	3.7	3.4	3.9	2.9	3.4	3.1	3.6	3.5	2.9	2.6
Korea, Republic of	3.6	1.5	2.0	1.1	4.6	1.4	1.4	3.7	3.6	3.7	3.7	3.0	6.1	3.8	4.3	5.3	6.3	5.1
Mauritius	1.1	1.0	1.2	1.6	1.6	1.7	2.3	2.7	3.1	2.8	3.1	3.1	3.0	2.9	2.5	2.0	2.3	1.9
UAE	2.0	4.0	4.5	3.6	5.4	4.3	4.6	3.6	3.1	3.2	2.8	3.3	3.2	3.2	2.5	2.8	2.6	3.3
UK	13.6	10.1	8.6	12.0	11.3	11.3	12.3	10.4	9.1	7.4	7.3	7.0	6.3	5.7	5.6	4.6	4.8	4.5
USA	14.8	13.1	12.1	10.6	13.0	14.1	12.7	11.7	12.5	14.2	12.3	13.8	14.5	15.4	16.0	18.6	16.3	17.6
Others	38.9	42.7	41.3	40.6	35.2	37.3	37.9	38.3	38.2	38.1	41.7	44.4	44.6	46.5	49.5	47.2	46.7	46.3
Total (US$ million)	882.8	797.6	905.1	1,170.3	1,299.3	1,350.5	1,537.1	2,233.8	2,576.6	3,121.7	3,264.3	2,771.9	3,089.6	3,460.7	3,072.9	3,351.0	3,394.8	3,202.5

Note: 'Jute, manufactures, including floor coverings' and 'carpets' are excluded from the figures.
Source: Compiled from Reserve Bank of India, *Handbook of Statistics on Indian Economy 2004–05*, Table 135.

Table 7.6 Principal non-primary industries employing workforces

Ranking	*Industry*	*1999*		*1993*	
		No. of workers	*Share (%)*	*No. of workers*	*Share (%)*
1	Retail trade	30,039,860	22.5	23,580,558	20.5
2	Education + Coaching centre + Activities of the individual providing tuition	8,586,361	6.4	6,640,500	5.8
3	*Spinning, weaving and finishing of textile + Other textiles + Knitted and crocheted fabrics and articles*	8,021,979	6.0	9,529,942	8.3
4	Manufacture of wood and of products of wood and cork except furniture, manufacture of articles of straw and planting materials	5,334,786	4.0	4,077,628	3.5
5	Manufacture of tobacco products	4,635,640	3.5	4,404,066	3.8
6	Restaurants, bars and canteens	4,442,200	3.3	3,182,474	2.8
7	Manufacture of other non-metallic mineral products	4,008,775	3.0	3,742,609	3.2
8	Funeral and related activities	3,909,391	2.9	2,266,123	2.0
9	Freight transport other than by motor vehicles	3,825,074	2.9	2,109,707	1.8
10	Wholesale trade except of motor vehicles + Auctioning activities	3,791,647	2.8	3,990,919	3.5
11	Manufacture of fabricated metal products + Manufacture of machinery and equipment n.e.c + Office, accounting and computing machinery	3,739,000	2.8	3,505,658	3.0
12	Other non-scheduled passenger land transport + Freight transport other than by motor vehicles	3,736,727	2.8	3,563,219	3.1
13	Repair of personal and household goods	3,373,966	2.5	2,747,534	2.4
14	Non-scheduled passenger land transport by motor vehicles	2,938,835	2.2	1,689,665	1.5
15	Manufacture of grain mill products, etc. and animal feeds	2,760,601	2.1	1,603,452	1.4
16	Human health activities + Veterinary activities	2,738,635	2.0	2,092,550	1.8
17	Manufacturing of medical, precision and optical instruments, watches and clocks + Manufacturing n.e.c.	2,705,017	2.0	2,333,487	2.0
18	*Wearing apparel, except fur apparel and tailoring*	2,584,668	1.9	1,205,356	1.0
	Total*	133,658,289	100.0	115,228,967	100.0

Note: * Excluding 'agriculture, hunting and forestry' except for 'cotton ginning, cleaning and baling', 'fishing', and 'mining and quarrying'.
n.e.c. = not elsewhere classified.
Source: Compiled from Central Statistical Organization, *Report of the Working Group on Workforce Estimation for Compilation of National Accounts Statistics with Base Year 1999–2000*, Appendix 4.3.

Table 7.7 Principal industries employing women workers

Ranking	*Industry (two-digit classification of NIC-1998)*	*Code*	*(1) (%)*	*(2) (%)*
1	Hotels and restaurants	55	75.8	0.0
2	*Manufacture of wearing apparel, etc.*	18	54.6	12.4
3	Manufacture of tanning and dressing of leather, etc.	19	42.8	6.6
4	Wholesale trade and commission trade	51	38.1	0.3
5	Agriculture, hunting and related service activities	1	37.3	3.3
6	Manufacture of tobacco products	16	35.3	1.2
7	Manufacture of radio, television and communication equipment and apparatus	32	27.1	2.3
8	Other service activities	93	24.9	0.1
9	Manufacture of chemicals and chemical products	24	23.1	18.2
10	Manufacture of office, accounting and computing machinery	30	22.8	0.3
11	Manufacture of furniture, etc.	36	21.3	1.8
12	Manufacture of food products and beverages	15	19.5	18.5
13	Manufacture of medical, precision and optical instruments, watches and clocks	33	14.9	0.6
14	All	–	14.7	100.0
15	*Manufacture of textiles*	17	13.6	15.7

Notes: (1) indicates female employment share of the industry and (2) means the industry's share of total female employment.
Source: Compiled from Labour Bureau, *Statistics of Factories 2001*, Table 2.13.

about 1.2 million workers in 1993 and 2.6 million in 1999. The share of the garment industries was about 1 per cent in 1993 and about 2 per cent in 1999. The total number of workers in the textile and garment industries is about 10 million. Table 7.7 shows major non-primary industries employing female workers. More than half of the total workers in the garment industry are women, and in the textile industry, the figure is about 14 per cent. Approximately 12 per cent of total female employment is in the garment industry, and 16 per cent is in the textile industry. Thus, for women workers, the textile and garment industries make up one of the largest employment sectors. Therefore, we find that the textile and garment industries in India have a considerable ability to absorb huge surpluses of labour, including many women.

In concluding this subsection, we may hypothesize that the industry will be able to respond more quickly to the worldwide growth of international trade in textile and garment products following the expiration of the MFA at the end of 2004, if the present labour laws are rationalized to allow a more flexible labour market. It is also noted that export-led growth in textiles and garments will be possible if large investments, especially in garment industries, are complemented by a flexible labour market. In addition, progress in the textile and garment industries will alleviate poverty and unemployment and contribute to the social participation of many women in India.[4]

7.2.2 The Industrial Dispute Act as job security regulation

According to Datta Chaudhuri (1996), the Industrial Dispute Act (IDA), 1947, is 'the single most important piece of legislation that governs the relationship between the worker and his employer' and 'the most onerous provision of IDA is chapter V-B'.

The Industrial Disputes Act was enacted in 1947.[5] The IDA has provisions for the investigation and settlement of industrial disputes and for providing certain protections to workers. It comprises 7 chapters and 40 sections. Chapter I contains definitions. Chapter II deals with the various authorities under the Act including Conciliation Officers, Labour Courts and Tribunals. Chapter III relates to the reference of disputes to Labour Courts and Industrial Tribunals. Chapter IV contains the provisions on the procedure and the power and duties of the related authorities. Chapter V comprises provisions prohibiting strikes and lockouts, declaration of strikes and lockouts as illegal, and provisions relating to layoff, retrenchment and closure. Chapter VI deals various penalties under the Act. Chapter VII has miscellaneous provisions.[6]

Chapter V-B of the IDA contains special provisions relating to layoffs, retrenchments and closures in enterprises employing not less than 100 workers. This chapter of the Act aims to moderate the serious trouble caused by such situations in large-scale enterprises. When the chapter was inserted in 1976, large-scale enterprises were regarded as enterprises employing 300 or more workers. In 1982, the criterion was reduced to 100 workers. Under the chapter, industrial enterprises employing 100 or more workers are required to get prior permission from the state government before laying off or retrenching workers or closing down. In fact, this permission has seldom been given to any employers by any state government. Therefore, Chapter V-B provides strong job security to existing workers in the large, organized sector.

Needless to say, the intention behind this job security regulation is to protect employment. However, it may have resulted in slow growth of new employment in the organized sector in the 1980s. Moreover, India's industrial firms have faced strong competition from rival MNCs since economic liberalization started in 1991. They need the flexibility to restructure, but may be unable to deal with the new and much more competitive environment due to the job security regulation. Several scholars believe that job security regulation may make the Indian labour market highly rigid.

Recently, the government of India suggested amendment proposals to the IDA. For example, the Montek Singh Ahluwalia Committee recommended making Chapter V-B of IDA applicable only to units with more than 1000 employees, or more radically and preferably, deleting Chapter V-B entirely.[7] In addition, in the 2001–2 budget speech, the Minister of Finance made the following suggestion:

> Along with these changes, it is also necessary to address the contentious issue of rigidities in our labour legislations. Some existing provisions in the Industrial Disputes Act have made it almost impossible for industrial firms to exercise any labour flexibility. The Government is now convinced that some change is

> necessary in this legislation. Chapter VB of the ID Act stipulates that employers in specified industrial establishments must obtain prior approval of the appropriate government authority for effecting layoff, retrenchment and closure, after following the prescribed procedure. It is proposed that these provisions may now apply to industrial establishments employing not less than 1,000 workers instead of 100.[8]

The Indian government set up the Second National Labour Commission. The commission reviewed the IDA and made suggestions as follows:[9]

1. Enterprises should have the option to close down. The best and more honest and equitable course will be to allow closure, provide for adequate compensation to workers, and in the event of an appeal, leave it to the Labour Relations Commission to find ways of redress through arbitration or adjudication.
2. Prior permission is not necessary in respect of layoff and retrenchment in an establishment of any employment size. Workers will, however, be entitled to two months' notice or pay in lieu of notice, in case of retrenchment. In the case of an establishment employing 300 or more workers where layoff exceeds a period of one month, such establishment should be required to obtain *post facto* approval of the appropriate government authority. The provisions of Chapter V-B pertaining to permission for closure should be made applicable to all the establishments to protect the interest of workers.

7.2.3 Earlier studies on the relationship between the IDA and labour demand

In this context, several scholars have studied the magnitude of the effect of job security regulations on the demand for labour. Fallon and Lucas (1993) use a dummy variable which is unity if the year is 1976 or after 1976, and zero otherwise, to investigate the labour demand of the organized manufacturing industries in 1959–81 period. Their data are drawn from CSO's *Annual Survey of Industries*. They state: 'In India, the weighted average drop in long-run demand for employees, at given output levels, is estimated to be 17.5 per cent' (p. 269).

Hasan et al. (2003) show that labour-demand elasticities are higher for states with less job security regulation and are also affected to a larger extent by trade reforms. They employ the variation of state-level amendment of IDA to identify the impact of the job security regulation, using data drawn from the *ASI* data in the 1980–97 period. The measure of job security regulation which they use is based on the measure constructured by Besley and Burgess (2004).

Besley and Burgess find that states which amended the IDA in a pro-worker direction experienced lower employment in the 1958–92 period. They use both state domestic product data and the *ASI* data. Recently, Aghion et al. (2006) confirmed the results of Besley and Burgess (2004). Badri Narayanan (2005) covers the textile and garment industries in the 1973–97 period. He uses the state-level measure of the IDA and finds that job security regulation depresses demand for labour.

Table 7.8 State-level Job Security Regulation (JSR) Index

	Besley and Burgess (2004)	*Hasan et al. (2003)*	*JSR Index (this chapter)*
Andhra Pradesh	Flexible	Flexible	Flexible(−1)
Assam	Neutral	Inflexible	Neutral(0)
Bihar	Neutral	Inflexible	Neutral(0)
Gujarat	Inflexible	Flexible	Flexible(−1)
Haryana	Neutral	Inflexible	Neutral(0)
Karnataka	Flexible	Flexible	Flexible(−1)
Kerala	Flexible	Inflexible	Inflexible(+1)
Madhya Pradesh	Flexible	Inflexible	Neutral(0)
Maharashtra	Inflexible	Flexible	Flexible(−1)
Orissa	Inflexible	Inflexible	Inflexible(+1)
Punjab	Neutral	Inflexible	Neutral(0)
Rajasthan	Flexible	Flexible	Flexible(−1)
Tamil Nadu	Flexible	Flexible	Flexible(−1)
Uttar Pradesh	Neutral	Inflexible	Neutral(0)
West Bengal	Inflexible	Inflexible	Inflexible(+1)

Contrary to popular perception, Roy (2004b) finds that the impact of job security regulations is minimal, using data from 1960 to 1993. In his study, dummy variables which indicate before or after 1976 and 1984 are employed.

It should be noted that, under the Constitution of India, the subject of 'labour' is registered on the 'concurrent list'. Thus, not only central government but also state governments have a responsibility to implement labour policy. In particular, state governments are able to amend the IDA, 1947, by themselves. For this reason, the labour regulation regime in India varies across the states. Besley and Burgess (2004) utilize the amendments of IDA at state level to identify exogenous policy change, and then categorize each amendment as pro-worker, pro-employer or neutral.

The first and second columns of Table 7.8 show the state-level indices of job security regulation constructed by Besley and Burgess (2004) by interpreting all state-level amendments to the IDA, and modified by Hasan et al. (2003) by changing the status of Gujarat, Kerala and Maharashtra in Besley and Burgess (2004). In this chapter, we adjust these indices as seen in the last column of Table 7.8. We regard Gujarat and Maharashtra as flexible, e.g. less regulated states, Kerala as an inflexible state, and Madhya Pradesh as a neutral state, taking into account the two existing indices.

The original index by Besley and Burgess (2004) is based on the mechanical scoring of state-level amendments to the IDA. Therefore, it does not exploit the implementation of the law and labour administration regime in each state. Hasan et al. (2003) take into account the *Investment Climate Survey* by the World Bank, and then identify Gujarat and Maharashtra as flexible states and Kerala as an inflexible state. Basically, we agree with their modification of the original index except for the following two minor points: first, since as the job security index, they use a dummy variable which takes a value of 1 or 0 they do not utilize the variations of state-level amendments to the IDA. Therefore we use a variable which takes a value of −1, 0, or 1 to show the state-level variation. Second, they regard Madhya Pradesh as an inflexible state. After once amending IDA in a pro-worker direction, it quickly made the IDA neutral by amending it in the opposite direction. Thus, we see Madhya Pradesh as a neutral state rather than an inflexible one.

In a later section, we will use our index as one of the main variables of job security regulation. In addition, as another index of job security regulation, we will use a dummy variable which is 1 if the year is 1984 or after 1984, and zero otherwise, since the IDA, 1982, came into force in 1984.

In concluding this subsection, we can summarize that earlier studies focus mainly on the organized sector. Therefore, this will be the first attempt to use firm-level data of the informal sector to investigate the regulatory effect on labour markets.

7.3 A model of a firm's demand for labour

The main purpose of this section is to explain a profit-maximizing firm's demand for labour à la Blanchard and Fischer (1989: Chapter 2) and Romer (1996: Chapter 6). We assume a firm cannot adjust the employment level without cost. Because of the IDA, as mentioned earlier, a firm employing more than 100 workers must get prior permission from the state government before laying off or retrenching even a single worker or closing down. For this reason, a firm must expend firing costs in restructuring its own business. In addition, a firm cannot avoid disbursing hiring costs despite the existence of surplus labour since its demand for workers is usually specific in terms of required ability and skill.

We assume that the labour adjustment cost function is $C = C(\dot{L})$ and that $C(\dot{L})$ is shaped as follows: C is zero if there is no change of labour, otherwise positive, and the greater the change of labour the greater C becomes ($C(0) = 0$, $C'(0) = 0$, $C'(\dot{L}) > 0$ for $\dot{L} > 0$, $C'(\dot{L}) < 0$ for $\dot{L} < 0$, $C''(\dot{L}) > 0$ for $\dot{L} > 0$, $C''(\dot{L}) > 0$ for $\dot{L} < 0$), where C is total adjustment cost, $\dot{L}$ is a unit change of labour ($= \mathrm{d}L/\mathrm{d}t$, L is labour). In other words, the adjustment cost function is continuous, strictly convex and twice differentiable with respect to $\dot{L}$. Therefore, the marginal hiring (or firing) cost becomes C'. A firm at time 0 maximizes the intertemporal profit subject to transitional equations of labour as follows:

$$\text{Max } v_0 = \int_0^{\infty} (F(L_t) - wL_t - C(l_t))\, \mathrm{e}^{-rt}\, \mathrm{d}t$$

where r is the interest rate. We can deal with this dynamic profit-maximization problem by using Pontryjagin's Maximum Principle. The present value of the Hamiltonian is defined as follows:

$$\begin{aligned} H_t &= [F(L_t) - wL_t - C(l_t)]\, \mathrm{e}^{-rt} + \mu_t l_t \\ &= [F(L_t) - wL_t - C(l_t) + \lambda_t l_t]\, \mathrm{e}^{-rt} \end{aligned}$$

where $\lambda_t = \mu_t \, e^{rt}$. μ_t is the marginal value of labour at time t evaluated at time 0 and λ_t is the same but evaluated at time t. The first-order conditions (FOC) for the maximization are as follows:

$$H_l = 0$$
$$\frac{d\mu_t}{dt} = -H_L$$

The transversality condition is given by

$$\lim_{t\to\infty} \mu_t L_t = 0$$

From the first FOC we have

$$-e^{-rt}\, C'(l_t) + \mu_t = 0 \rightarrow C'(l_t) = e^{rt}\,\mu_t = \lambda_t$$

That is

$$C'(l_t) = \lambda_t \tag{7.1}$$

From the second FOC we have

$$\begin{aligned} e^{-rt}(F'_t - w) &= -\dot{\mu}_t \rightarrow F'^{rt}\,(e^{-rt} r\lambda_t - e^{-rt}\,\dot{\lambda}_t) \\ &= r\lambda_t - \dot{\lambda}_t \end{aligned} \tag{7.2}$$

The first FOC implies that a firm hires new workers or dismisses old workers so that the shadow price of labour λ_t equals the marginal cost of new employment. The second FOC is regarded as a first-order linear differential equation in λ. Using the transversality condition we can solve this differential equation as follows:

$$\lambda_t = \int_{s=t}^{\infty} e^{-r(s-t)}(F'_s - w)\, ds \tag{7.3}$$

This condition implies that the shadow price of labour λ_t is the same as the discounted present value of the future marginal profit stream.[10] λ means an increase in the discounted preset value of future profit raised by hiring additional labour. Hence a firm hires labour when λ is high, otherwise it fires labour.

To understand a firm's dynamic response to an exogenous shock such as the introduction of Chapter V-B into the IDA, we present a phase diagram of the dynamic system in Figure 7.1.[11] From Equation (7.1), a firm hires or fires workers in order to make the value of labour equal to the marginal cost of labour. Since $C'(l)$ is an increasing function of l, l is an increasing function of λ. Given $C'(0)$ is zero, when $\lambda = 0$, l is zero. Thus, we get following relationship:

$$\dot{L} = f(\lambda), \qquad f(0) = 0, \qquad f'(\lambda) > 0$$

where $f(\lambda) = C'^{-1}(\lambda)$. From the above equation, when $\lambda > 0$, L increases and when $\lambda < 0$, L decreases. L is constant when $\lambda = 0$. From the above reasoning, we can draw

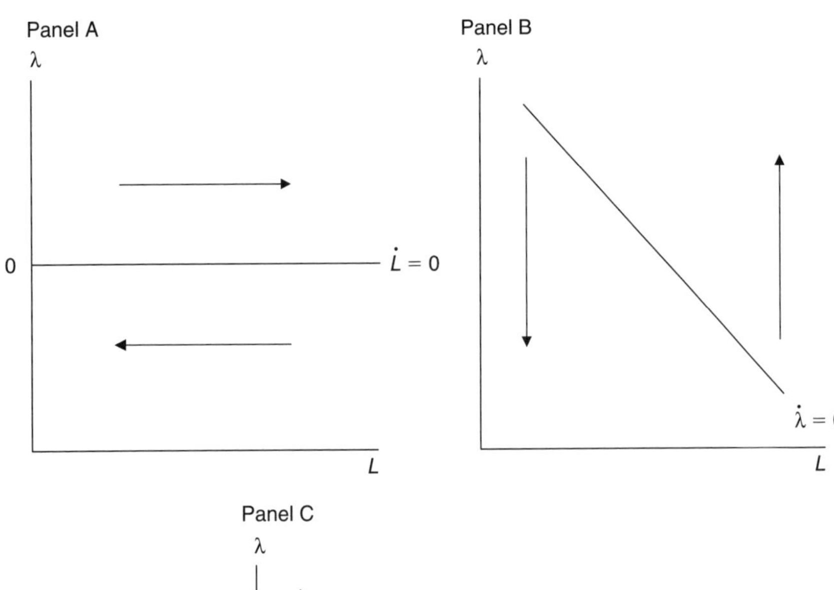

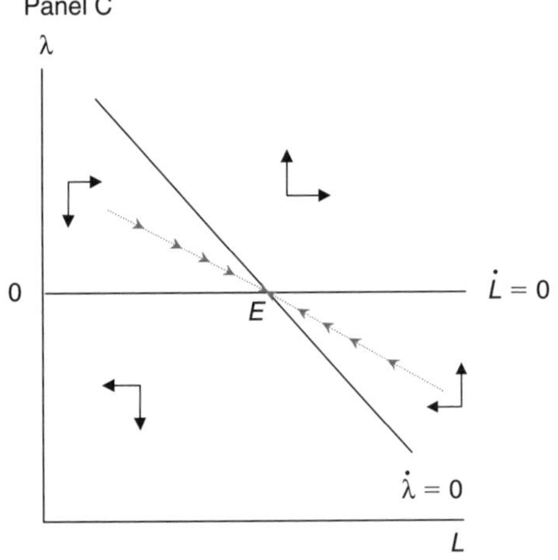

Figure 7.1 Phase diagram

the $\dot{L} = 0$ schedule in Panel A of Figure 7.1. We rearrange the terms of Equation (7.2) to get

$$\dot{\lambda} = r\lambda - [F'(L) - w]$$

From this equation we find that when $r\lambda = F'(L) - w$, or $\lambda = [F'(L) - w]/r$, λ is constant. Since $F'(L)$ is a decreasing function of L, we can depict the $\dot{\lambda} = 0$ schedule in Panel B of Figure 7.1. From Equation (7.2) $\dot{\lambda}$ is an increasing function of L. This implies that in the region in the right side of the $\dot{\lambda} = 0$ schedule, $\dot{\lambda} > 0$ and in the region of its left side, $\dot{\lambda} < 0$. In Panel C of Figure 7.1, the point E represents a long-run equilibrium point satisfying both $\dot{L} = 0$ and $\dot{\lambda} = 0$.

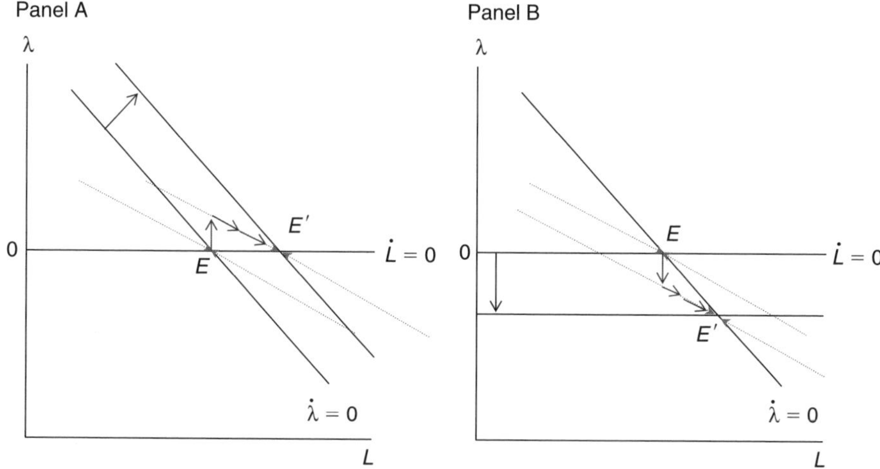

Figure 7.2 The effect of the permanent change in exogenous variables on labour demand and shadow price of labour

Next we consider the impact of (1) a permanent decline of the wage rate, (2) permanent rise of aggregate demand and (3) permanent decline of labour adjustment cost on labour demand L and shadow price of labour λ.

1. *Decline of the wage rate*: This problem is illustrated in Panel A of Figure 7.2. Noting that $\lambda = [F'(L) - w]/r$, a decline of the wage rate shifts the $\dot{\lambda} = 0$ schedule to the right. As the shadow price of labour λ is discounted present value of the future profit stream, a rise in λ stimulates labour demand L but with the adjustment cost, L cannot be instantly increased. Thus, firstly λ jumps to the saddle path and then, the higher λ stimulates a firm's labour demand resulting in an increase in L. As L increases, the marginal productivity of labour decreases (e.g. marginal profit decreases), therefore λ also decreases.
2. *Permanent rise of aggregate demand*: This stimulates the demand for a firm's product. Although our model does not incorporate the price of a firm's product, we can define a firm's profit as $pF(L) - wL - C(l)$. Then, it is easy to find that the $\dot{\lambda} = 0$ schedule means $\lambda = [pF'(L) - w]/r(\dot{L} = 0$ schedule does not change). If a permanent rise of aggregate demand increases p, it shifts the $\dot{\lambda} = 0$ schedule to the right. Therefore, the dynamics in this case are the same as those of a decline in the wage rate.
3. *Permanent decline of labour adjustment cost*: Panel B shows this case. We recall the FOC of Equation (7.1): $C'(l_t) = \lambda$. The left-hand side shows the marginal cost of new employment (or new dismissal). Now we regard a decline of adjustment cost as a decrease of C' by $\bar{c}$. Therefore, $C'(l_t) - \bar{c} = \lambda$ becomes the new FOC. Then, it shifts the $\dot{L} = 0$ schedule down (the $\dot{\lambda} = 0$ schedule does not change). Since the marginal cost of new employment decreases, new employment increases. This

implies that a firm's marginal profit decreases and then the shadow price of labour declines. As L cannot increase instantly, first λ jumps to the saddle path with a decline of the adjustment cost. Then, λ decreases and L increases towards a new long-run equilibrium point E'.

The previous assumption concerning the adjustment cost function is a simplified one. Actually, however, the adjustment cost function may be more complex.

Thus, à la Abel and Eberly (1994), we assume an augmented adjustment cost function $C^A(l)$ which is continuous, strictly convex and twice differentiable with respect to l everywhere except at $l=0$. In this case, $C^A(l)$ is not only kinked at $l=0$ but discontinuous. Then, we define $C^A(0)^+$ and $C^A(0)^-$ as the left and right-hand partial derivatives, respectively, of $C^A(l)$ with respect to l evaluated at $l=0$.

According to Equation (7.1), the firm equates the marginal cost of new employment (or dismissal) and the marginal benefit of new employment (or dismissal) which is measured by λ. Assuming that λ is given, Equation (7.1) is equivalent to the FOC in the following profit-maximization problem:

$$\max_{l} \lambda l - C^A(l)$$

It is natural that the FOC in the above static profit-maximization problem is also a necessary condition for original intertemporal profit maximization, and it is natural to assume that the augmented adjustment cost function does not change the second FOC of Equation (7.2).

We denote l^* as the value of l that maximizes the profit. Then, the FOC are

$$\lambda = C^{A'^*} \quad \text{for } \lambda > C^A(0)^- \quad \text{or} \quad \lambda > C^A(0)^+ \tag{7.4}$$

$$l^* = 0 \quad \text{for} -C^A(0)^- \leq \lambda \leq C^A(0)^+ \tag{7.5}$$

Thus, with the augmented adjustment cost function, the firm neither hires nor fires workers when $C^A(0)^- \leq \lambda \leq C^A(0)^+$. In other words, there is a range of values of λ for which $\dot{L}=0$.

Panel A of Figure 7.3 shows the phase diagram. The $\dot{\lambda}=0$ schedule is the same as in the previous model.

However, the $\dot{L}=0$ schedule is replaced by the $\dot{L}=0$ region from $-C^A(0)^-$ to $C^A(0)^+$. L_1 denotes the value of L where the $\dot{\lambda}=0$ schedule enters the $\dot{L}=0$ region from the left-hand side and L_2 means the level of L where the $\dot{\lambda}=0$ schedule crosses the $\dot{L}=0$ region from the right-hand side.

We can consider two types of textile and garment industries for an economic interpretation of this augmented model. One is the textile sector, especially the mill sector, whose initial level of L^M, $L(0)^M$ is larger than L_2, and the other is the garment (clothing) industry whose initial value of L^C is smaller than L_1. In the former case, $\lambda(0)^M$ is smaller than $-C^A(0)^-$ and there is a dismissal of workers. The economy moves through the saddle path to the point E^M. In the latter case, $\lambda(0)^C$ is larger than $C^A(0)^+$ and there is employment of workers. The economy moves down the saddle path to the point E^C.[12]

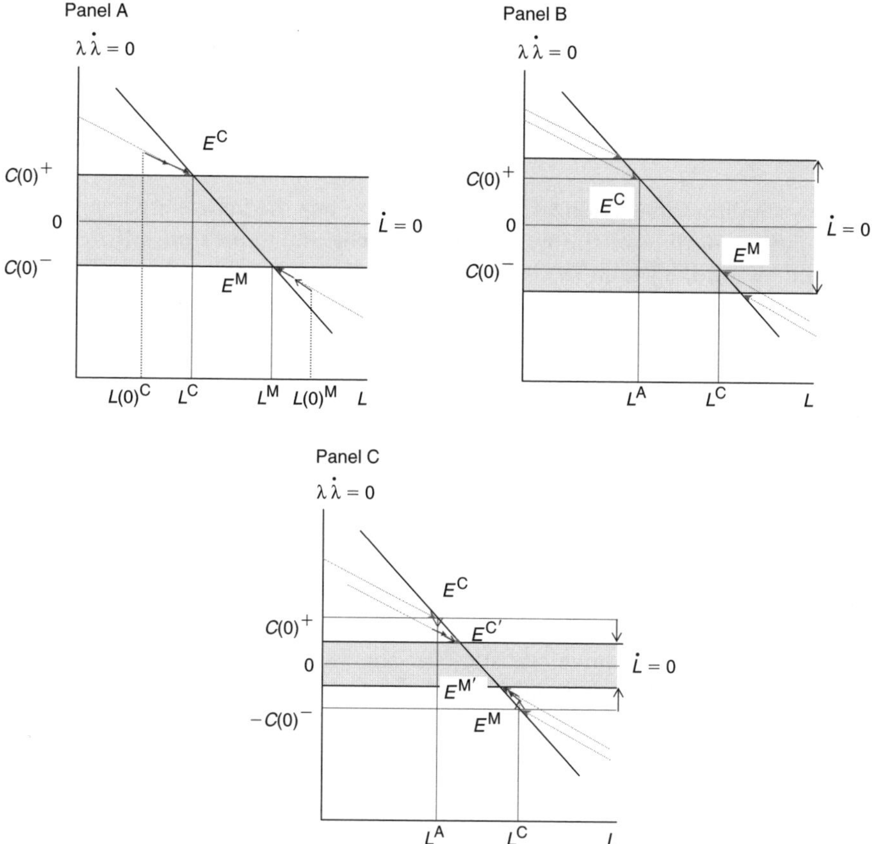

Figure 7.3 The effect of the permanent change in adjustment cost on labour demand and shadow price of labour

Next we consider the impact of a permanent change of the labour adjustment cost on labour demand L.[13]

4. *Permanent change of labour adjustment cost*: We can regard the rise of the adjustment cost as an incremental increase from $C(0)^+$ and $C(0)^-$, respectively. Panel B of Figure 7.3 shows the case of a cost increase. The rise of the adjustment cost expands the $\dot{L}=0$ region and the $\dot{\lambda}=0$ schedule is not changed. In the cases of both the clothing and mill sectors, employment does not change and both equilibria remain at the original points E^C and E^M, respectively, since both E^C and E^M are on the $\dot{\lambda}=0$ schedule and within the new expanded area of $\dot{L}=0$. Panel C of Figure 7.3 shows the case of a cost decrease, which is an interesting one. We assume the decline of the adjustment cost to be an incremental one from $C(0)^+$ and $C(0)^-$. Similarly, the decline of the adjustment cost depresses the $\dot{L}=0$ region. In the case of the clothing sector, employment increases and

reaches a new equilibrium point $E^{C'}$ from E^{C}. In the case of the mill sector, employment decreases and the equilibrium changes from E^{M} to $E^{M'}$. Therefore, the net effect of a cost decrease on labour demand is ambiguous, depending on the balance between the positive impact in the clothing sector and negative impact in the mill sector.

In concluding this section, we can summarize our theoretical argument as follows. First, a decline in the wage rate has a positive impact on a firm's labour demand. Second, a rise in demand for the goods produced by a firm encourages labour demand by the firm. Third, taking both the simplified adjustment cost function model and augmented adjustment cost model together, an increase of the adjustment cost of labour that raises the marginal cost of new employment (or dismissal) has a negative impact on labour demand. Fourth, the evidence is inconclusive as to whether or not a decrease of the adjustment cost of labour stimulates labour demand as a whole. Therefore, we will empirically investigate the impact of job security regulation on employment in the next section.

7.4 Empirical evidence

7.4.1 Organized sector

Table 7.9 shows descriptive statistics for the variables used in our regression analysis. We use data on the textile and garment industries from EPW Research Foundation's *Annual Survey of Industries 1973–74 to 1997–98* at the two-digit industry level in the 15 main states for the period from 1979 to 1997. The data cover 'Manufacture of Cotton Textiles', 'Manufacture of Wool', 'Silk and Manmade Fibre Textiles', 'Manufacture of Jute and Other Vegetable Fibre Textiles (except Cotton)', and 'Manufacture of Textile Products (including wearing apparel)'. The original data are from CSO's *Annual Survey of Industries*.

The definitions of the main variables are as follows:[14]

- Labour input (L): We use the number of employees in *ASI* as labour input.
- Real wage rate (W): Nominal wage rate is defined as total emolument divided by the number of employees. We obtain the real wage rate by deflating nominal wage by the wholesale price of the corresponding segment of the textile and garment industries.

Table 7.9 Descriptive statistics of main variables in organized sector

Variable	*NOB*	*Mean*	*SD*	*Min*	*Max*
L: Employees	855	32,339	51,315	44	295,424
W: Real wage rate (Rs.) at 1973 price	855	4,775	2,004	861	12,627
VGO: Real value of gross output (Rs. lakhs) at 1973 price	855	16,003	24,515	5	221,432
K: Real capital stock (Rs. lakhs) at 1973 price	855	7,717	14,875	5	139,326

- Real value of gross output (VGO): The depreciation in *ASI* is not necessarily a real one since it is linked to a firm's tax obligation and accounting practices. Thus, the gross term including depreciation as the measure of output is better than the net term excluding depreciation. Real gross value of output is deflated by its wholesale price.
- Capital stock (K): The fixed capital in *ASI* is evaluated at the end of the reference year and does not contain the value of the accumulated depreciation. We employ the perpetual inventory accumulation method for making the figure of capital stock. Real gross fixed capital formation (I) is defined as $I_t = (B_t - B_{t-1} + D_t)/P^I_t$, where D is depreciation, B is fixed capital and P^I_t is the implicit deflator of gross fixed capital formation. Then, we make a time series of real gross capital stock (K^G) as $K^G_t = K^G_{t-1} + I_t = K^G_0 + \sum_{i=1}^{t} I_t$, where K^G_0 is the base year capital stock and is regarded as $B_0 + D_0$ in *ASI*. Finally, assuming that the depreciation ratio per year is 5 per cent, real net capital stock K is set as $K_t = (1-\delta)K^G_t$.
- Relative price (P): We define the relative price as the ratio of output price to input price. Output price is the wholesale price of the corresponding segment of the textile and garment industries. We construct the input price series of each segment. Input price is the weighted average of fuel price, material price and other input prices, and its weights are drawn from fuel consumed, material consumed and other input in *ASI*. Fuel price, material price and other input prices are also constructed using wholesale prices, implicit deflator of national account statistics and weight from the input–output table.[15]

First, we estimate the labour demand function of the following form:[16]

$$\begin{aligned}\ln L_{ist} &= \alpha_{is} + \beta_1 \ln W_{ist} + \beta_2 \ln VGO_{ist} + \beta_3 \ln K_{ist} + \beta_4 \ln P_{ist}\\ &\quad + \gamma_1 \text{JSR dummy}_t + \gamma_2(\ln W_{ist})(\text{JSR dummy}_t)\\ &\quad + \mu(\ln W_{ist})(\text{JSR index}_s) + \theta\ \text{Trend} + e_{ist}\end{aligned}$$

where L_{ist} is the number of employees in state s at time t, W is the real wage rate, VGO is output, K is capital stock, P is the input price, JSR dummy is a dummy variable which takes the value of unity in 1984 or after 1984 and zero before 1984, JSR index is the state-level job security regulation index (see Table 7.8), Time is time trend, and α_{is} is state-industry fixed effect. The variable e is a stochastic error.[17]

With this specification, we can see the impact of job security regulation not only on labour demand itself but also on labour demand elasticity with respect to wages. We are interested in investigating the degree to which the introduction of job security regulation affects a firm's labour demand activity.[18]

We use the fixed effect model known as least squares dummy variables (LSDV) model for empirical investigation. Column (1) of Table 7.10 shows the estimation of the simplest firm's labour demand. The estimated coefficient on the JSR dummy is not significant. The estimated coefficients of the main variables are significant with the expected signs. That is, wage, output and capital elasticities are −0.40, +0.63 and +0.20, respectively. The sign for the relative price is positive and statistically

Table 7.10 Estimated labour demand equations of textile and apparel industries in organized sector (dependent variable: log(employees))

	(1)		*(2)*		*(3)*		*(4)*		*(5)*	
	Coefficient	*t-value*	*Coefficient*	*t-value*	*Coefficient*	*t-value*	*Coefficient*	*t-value*	*Coefficient*	*t-value*
ln W: log(real wage)	−0.398	−5.06 ***	−0.266	−3.12 ***	−0.246	−2.79 ***	−0.389	−4.91 ***	−0.381	−4.85 ***
ln W_1984: log(real wage)*JSR dummy			−0.154	−3.06 ***	−0.133	−2.6 ***				
ln W_Index: log(real wage)*JSR index					0.178	2.84 ***				
ln W_1984 Index: log(real wage)*(JSR dummy)(JSR index)							−0.014	−4.10 ***	−0.012	−3.68 ***
ln VGO: log(real value of gross output)	0.637	14.27 ***	0.638	14.19 ***	0.630	13.92 ***	0.632	14.14 ***	0.624	14.57 ***
ln K: log(real capital stock)	0.200	4.15 ***	0.192	3.98 ***	0.208	4.35 ***	0.219	4.63 ***	0.228	4.93 ***
JSR dummy: 1 If year is 1984 or after 1984, 0 otherwise	0.010	0.30	−1.210	−3.06 ***	−1.045	−2.61 ***	0.046	1.40		
ln P: log(relative price)	0.671	4.63 ***	0.608	4.15 ***	0.588	4.08 ***	0.660	4.58 ***	0.649	4.51 ***
Time trend	−0.037	−7.62 ***	−0.036	−7.46 ***	−0.036	−7.49 ***	−0.039	−8.31 ***	−0.038	−8.21 ***
State-industry fixed effect	Yes		Yes		Yes		Yes		Yes	
F-value	1248.34 ***		1307.14 ***		1250.53 ***		1382.73 ***		1362.11 ***	
R^2	0.98		0.98		0.98		0.98		0.98	
NOB	855		855		855		855		855	

Notes: ***, ** and * indicate significant at 1, 5 and 10%, respectively. White's robust standard error is employed.

significant. This result suggests that an increase of relative price measured by the ratio of output price to input price stimulates labour demand. The sign of the time trend is negative and statistically significant. In our reference period from 1979 to 1997, labour demand has a downward trend.

In columns (2) and (3), we employ the slope dummies in order to examine the impact of job security regulation on labour demand elasticity with respect to wages. In column (2), the estimated coefficients on the interaction of wages with the JSR dummy are negative and statistically significant. This suggests that job security regulation allows the wage sensitivity of labour demand to be higher than it would otherwise be. However, in column (3) the interaction of wage with the JSR index is positive and statistically significant although that of the JSR dummy is still significantly negative. To confirm the impact of job security regulation on wage elasticity, we employ the product of the JSR dummy and the JSR index. Columns (4) and (5) show that the interaction of wage with the composite JSR variable is negative and statistically significant. Thus, we can conclude that job security regulation raises the wage elasticity of labour demand.

Columns (2) and (4) show the JSR dummy is negative and highly statistically significant although columns (1) and (5) show that it is insignificant. This suggests the possibility that introduction of that regulation contributes to the depression of the employment in organized textile and garment industries.

Next, we run the following regression:

$$\begin{aligned}\ln L_{ist} &= \alpha_{is} + \beta_1 \ln W_{ist} + \beta_2 \ln \mathrm{VGO}_{ist} + \beta_3 \ln K_{ist} + \beta_4 \ln P_{ist} \\ &\quad + \gamma \mathrm{JSR\ dummy}_t + \mu \ln L_{ist-1} + e_{ist}\end{aligned}$$

In this specification, we include the lagged dependent variable $\ln L_{ist-1}$, implying that the coefficient on $\ln L_{ist-1}$ will be biased if the above equation is estimated by OLS since the unobserved α_{is} must be correlated with the lagged dependent variable $\ln L_{ist-1}$. Then, we employ the generalized method of moment (GMM) proposed by Arellano and Bond (1991) to generate a consistent estimate on the coefficient of the lagged dependent variable.[19] Such a dynamic labour demand equation with a lagged dependent variable is consistent with the theoretical model with a labour adjustment cost function as described in Section 7.3. Thus, we can test the adjustment cost hypothesis by running the above regression.

Table 7.11 shows the results of the estimates of the dynamic labour demand equation. Column (1) presents the two-step GMM estimator, which is asymptotically more efficient than the one-step GMM estimator. Sargan test statistics are distributed according to a chi-square distribution under the null hypothesis that over-identification exists. This test confirms whether or not the instruments for identification are valid. The result shows that the instruments for identification are valid. AR(1) and AR(2) are tests for the first- and the second-order serial correlation in the residuals. If the null hypothesis of absence of the second-order serial correlation is rejected, the coefficient of the lagged dependent variable will be inconsistent. However, even when the null hypothesis of absence of the first-order serial correlation is rejected, the coefficient will be inefficient but still consistent.

Table 7.11 Estimated dynamic labour demand equations of textile and apparel industries in organized sector (dependent variablc: log(employees))

	(1)		*(2)*	
	Coefficient	*t-value*	*Coefficient*	*t-value*
ln $L(-1)$: lagged log(hired labour)	0.135	13.98 ***	0.344	14.74 ***
ln W: log(real wage)	−0.469	−34.37 ***	−0.404	−13.50 ***
ln $W(-1)$			0.159	5.32 ***
ln VGO: log(real value of gross output)	0.586	47.07 ***	0.626	69.92 ***
ln VGO(−1)			−0.198	−11.65 ***
ln K: log(real capital stock)	0.215	13.58 ***	0.235	9.09***
JSR dummy: 1 If year is 1984 or after 1984, 0 otherwise	−0.005	−0.67	−0.027	−3.64 ***
ln P: log(relative price)	−0.055	−1.15	0.221	2.61 ***
Constant	−0.037	−14.29 ***	−0.038	−10.49 ***
Sargan test statistics	42.75		41.83	
AR(1)	−2.65 ***		−2.95 ***	
AR(2)	−0.36		0.12	
Wald statistics	15,831.79		30,818.24	
NOB	765		765	

Notes: ***, ** and * indicate significant at 1, 5 and 10%, respectively.
Column (1): Two-step estimation of difference GMM.
Column (2): Two-step estimation of difference GMM when ln W and ln VGO are regarded as endogenous variables.

In column (1), the estimated coefficient is consistent as the null hypothesis of absence of the second-order serial correlation is accepted, although the null hypothesis of absence of the first-order serial correlation is rejected. The Wald test is about zero-slope restrictions. The result tells us that the null hypothesis of zero-slope restrictions is rejected. All variables except the JSR dummy and relative price have the expected sign, which is statistically significant. The JSR dummy is negative but not significant. The lagged dependent variable is positive and highly statistically significant. This suggests the adjustment cost hypothesis is appropriate.

In column (2), we find the same pattern in the Sargan test, AR(1) test, AR(2) test and the Wald test as the result of column (1). Column (2) presents the two-step GMM estimator when wage and output are regarded as endogenous variables. We find that all variables are statistically significant and also confirm that the job security regulation depresses a firm's demand for labour. We can calculate the short- and long-run elasticities of labour demand with respect to explanatory variables as follows: short-run elasticities with respect to wage, output and capital are −0.40, +0.63 and +0.23 respectively, and the long-run elasticities are −0.61 (= −0.40/(1 − 0.34)), +0.95 (= 0.63/(1 − 0.34)) and +0.35 (= 0.23/(1 − 0.34)) respectively.

7.4.2 Informal sector

The enterprise survey of the NSSO's 55th round covers informal enterprises in the non-agricultural sector. The survey classifies enterprises in the informal sector into

Table 7.12 Descriptive statistics of main variables in informal sector

Variable	*NOB*	*Mean*	*SD*	*Min*	*Max*
L: Hired labour	3,153	2.54	2.68	1	41
W: Wage rate per year (Rs.)	3,153	13,233	9,648	360	147,600
VGO: Value of gross output (Rs.)	3,153	210,391	663,668	1,920	12,200,000
K: Own fixed asset (Rs.)	3,153	68,983	199,433	100	6,300,000

two types, e.g. 'Own Account Enterprises', which do not hire any workers on a regular basis, and 'Establishments', which make up all the remaining enterprises. All unincorporated enterprises that operate on either a proprietary or partnership basis are considered to constitute the informal sector.

It is noted that the definition of the informal sector is different from the concept of the unorganized sector. The unorganized sector consists of not only proprietary or partnership enterprises but also cooperative societies, trusts, and private and public limited companies. The informal sector is regarded as a subset of the unorganized sector. It is noted that all manufacturing units of the proprietary or partnership type which covered by *ASI* are not considered informal enterprises.

Table 7.12 shows the descriptive statistics for the variables used in our regression analysis. The data we use cover 'Manufacture of Textiles' (17) and 'Manufacture of Wearing Apparel; Dressing and Dyeing of Fur' (18) of the two-digit code of NIC 1998 for the 15 main states in 1999. The data unit is business firms.

The definitions of the main variables used in our regression are as follows:

- Labour input (L): We employ the number of hired workers as labour input. Therefore, we neglect working owners and other workers/helpers.
- Wage rate (W): Wage rate is defined as the ratio of the total emolument to number of hired workers. Looking at the data set of the 'Own Account Enterprises', total emolument is unavailable in almost all cases except a few firms. We drop the sample firms that do not employ hired labour as we are interested in labour demand response to wage rate. That is the reason why we use hired labour as a labour input in this chapter.
- Value of gross output (VGO): We use yearly total receipt in the NSS survey as value of gross output.
- Capital stock (K): We use own fixed assets as capital stock. Hired fixed assets is also available in the NSS survey, but there are many missing values. Due to their unreliability as statistics, we do not combine own fixed assets and hired fixed assets.

Then, we estimate the labour demand function of the form

$$\begin{aligned}\ln L_{is} &= \alpha_{1i} + \alpha_{2s} + \beta_1 \ln W_{is} + \beta_2 \ln \mathrm{VGO}_{is} + \beta_3 \ln K_{is} \\ &\quad + \mu_1(\ln W_{is})(\mathrm{JSR\ index}_s) + e_{is}\end{aligned}$$

where α_{1i} is an industry fixed effect and α_{2s} is a state fixed effect. It is noted that we are unable to use the JSR dummy since the NSS survey has a cross-section data set in 1999 without time series. In addition, we cannot estimate the direct effect of JSR index on employment since the JSR index can be constructed by the linear combination of the individual state dummy variables.

In Table 7.13, we present the results of the estimated equations with and without capital. Column (1) shows that wage and output variables are negative and positive, respectively, and both are statistically significant. In column (2) we use the interaction of the JSR index with wage. The wage and output remain the same as in column (1). The interaction of the JSR index with the wage is negative and statistically significant. This implies that job security regulation makes the labour market more flexible. In columns (3) and (4) we include capital, which is regarded as a superior model to an output-constrained model as capital market imperfection is a common phenomenon in the Indian context. We find basically the same pattern as in columns (1) and (2). The capital is positive and statistically significant.

In summary, job security regulation in the organized sector makes the informal labour market more flexible in the sense of increasing the wage elasticity of labour demand.

7.4.3 Labour demand and industrial disputes

So far, we have focused on the effect of the Industrial Dispute Act (IDA) on the firm's demand for labour. In this subsection, we investigate the relationship between the firms' demand for labour and actual labour conflict such as strikes and lockouts.

Using investment projects data from 1997 to 1999, Sanyal and Menon (2005) find that actual industrial disputes, such as the number of lockouts by state, percentage of unionized workers, and number of man-days lost in disputes, have a strong negative effect on new investment. However, they do not examine the impact of labour conflicts on employment. Besley and Burgess (2004) show that the job security index is strongly positively correlated with strikes and lockouts. In place of the job security regulation index, Badri Narayanan (2005) employs strikes and lockouts in order to check the robustness of his empirical results. He shows that industrial disputes have a significant impact on employment.

In this subsection, we employ the ratio of the number of strikes to the number of the lockouts as a proxy for the relative bargaining power of workers and firms. The data of strikes and lockouts at the national level are drawn from the Government of India, Ministry of Labour, *Indian Labour Statistics*, various years.[20] Strikes by workers can be seen as the degree of workers' power on the one hand, and lockouts by firms as firms' power, on the other. Therefore, the ratio of strikes to lockouts is an indicator of the relative bargaining power in industrial relations. Tentatively, an increase of this ratio depresses the labour demand by firms. Let us check this tentative statement.

Table 7.14 shows the result of the estimate equations including the strikes–lockouts ratio. All columns in Table 7.14 confirm that the strikes–lockouts ratio is negative and statistically significant. In fact, this ratio has a downward trend

Table 7.13 Estimated labour demand equations of textile and apparel industries in informal sector (dependent variable: log(hired labour))

	(1)		(2)		(3)		(4)	
	Coefficient	*t-value*	*Coefficient*	*t-value*	*Coefficient*	*t-value*	*Coefficient*	*t-value*
ln *W*: log(wage)	−0.20	−11.68 ***	−0.22	−11.76 ***	−0.20	−12.00 ***	−0.22	−12.16 ***
ln *W*_jsr: log(wage)*JSR index			−0.06	−2.79 ***			−0.04	−2.32 **
ln VGO: log(real value of gross output)	0.49	27.90 ***	0.49	27.91 ***	0.47	26.37 ***	0.47	26.38 ***
ln *K*: log(own fixed asset)					0.04	4.98 ***	0.04	4.90 ***
State fixed effect	Yes		Yes		Yes		Yes	
Industry fixed effect (5 digit)	Yes		Yes		Yes		Yes	
F-value	45.31 ***		45.31 ***		45.70 ***		45.62 ***	
adj. R^2	0.49		0.49		0.50		0.50	
NOB	3,178		3,178		3,155		3,155	

Notes: ***, ** and * indicate significant at 1, 5 and 10%, respectively. White's robust standard error is employed.

Table 7.14 Estimated labour demand equation including industrial disputes (dependent variable: log(employees))

	(1)		(2)		(3)		(4)	
	Coefficient	*t-value*	*Coefficient*	*t-value*	*Coefficient*	*t-value*	*Coefficient*	*t-value*
ln *W*: log(real wage)	−0.408	−5.25 ***	−0.406	−5.16 ***	−0.397	−5.00 ***	−0.394	−4.99 ***
ln *W*_1984Index: log(real wage)*(JSR dummy)(JSR index)					−0.014	−4.05 ***	−0.013	−3.87 ***
ln VGO: log(real value of gross output)	0.651	13.89 ***	0.649	13.63 ***	0.643	13.45 ***	0.640	13.53 ***
ln *K*: log(real capital stock)	0.183	3.53 ***	0.184	3.54 ***	0.205	3.98 ***	0.207	4.03 ***
JSR dummy: 1 If year is 1984 or after 1984, 0 otherwise			−0.013	−0.39	0.025	0.75		
ln *P*: log(relative price)	0.756	4.90 ***	0.758	4.91 ***	0.740	4.82 ***	0.745	4.85 ***
Time trend	−0.041	−8.47 ***	−0.041	−8.31 ***	−0.043	−8.84 ***	−0.042	−8.93 ***
Strikes–lockouts ratio	−0.022	−1.71 *	−0.023	−1.79 *	−0.021	−1.64 *	−0.024	−1.91 *
State-industry fixed effect	Yes		Yes		Yes		Yes	
F-value	1,241.2 ***		1,216.6 ***		1,343.9 ***		1,347.7 ***	
R^2	0.98		0.98		0.98		0.98	
NOB	855		855		855		855	

Notes: ***, ** and * indicate significant at 1, 5 and 10%, respectively. White's robust standard error is employed.

from 8.0 in 1979 to 1.5 in 1997. The firms' demand for labour might have been stimulated in this period.

7.5 Concluding remarks

We have provided a new estimate of the labour demand function in the textile and garment industries using data from CSO's *Annual Survey of Industries* and NSSO's *Informal Non-Agricultural Enterprises*. Our conclusions are as follows: first, the variable which indicates the degree of job security regulation has a negative relationship with labour demand in the organized sector. As we argued in Section 7.3, theoretically, a deregulation of labour laws in a pro-industry direction does not necessarily raise labour demand as a whole, or conversely may reduce it. Empirically we confirm that job security deregulation has a positive effect on the creation of employment in the organized sector. Second, job security regulation makes the labour market more sensitive to wage fluctuations. It raises the wage elasticity of labour demand in both the organized and the informal sectors. Third, the adjustment cost hypothesis is justified, as the lagged dependent variable is positive and statistically significant in the estimated equation. Fourth, when the bargaining power of workers is stronger than that of firms, the firms will hire fewer workers in the organized sector.

Finally, we shall refer to the policy implications. As mentioned in subsection 7.4.2, we are unable to investigate the direct effect of the job security regulation on employment in the informal sector. This means that we do not know whether or not deregulation has a positive impact on total employment in both organized and informal sectors since deregulation may result in job loss in the informal sector. Therefore, our empirical evidence that job security regulation has a negative effect on employment in the organized sector does not imply that the government should deregulate labour laws in order to absorb the huge surplus of labour. In other words, if the government deregulates labour laws in order to combat the chronic poverty and unemployment in Indian society and to alleviate the difficulties caused by transient or permanent job loss, then the government must prepare social safety nets and support employment-enhancing textile and garment firms.

7.6 Appendix

We can find the solution to a first-order linear differential equation in a textbook for mathematics. If its differential equation is $\dot{x} = bx + \phi(t)$, then the solution is as follows:

$$x = \mathrm{e}^{bt}[H(t) - H(0) + \overline{x}]$$

where $H(t) = \int \phi(t)\mathrm{e}^{-bt}\,\mathrm{d}t$ and $\overline{x} = x(0)$. We substitute $x = \lambda, b = r, \phi(t) = -(F' - w)$ into the above formula. Taking care of the endpoints of the interval, we easily obtain the following two equations:

$$\lambda_t\,e^{-rt} = H_t - H_0 + \lambda_0 = \int_{s=0}^{t} -(F'_s - w)\,e^{-rs}\,ds + H_0 + \lambda_0$$

$$\lambda_T\,e^{-rT} = H_T - H_0 + \lambda_0 = \int_{s=0}^{T} -(F'_s - w)\,e^{-rs}\,ds + H_0 + \lambda_0$$

Subtracting the second equation from the first and setting $T \to \infty$ yields

$$\begin{aligned}\lambda_t\,e^{-rt} - \lim_{T\to\infty} \lambda_T\,e^{-rT} &= \int_{s=0}^{t} -(F'_s - w)\,e^{-rs}\,ds - \int_{s=0}^{\infty} -(F'_s - w)\,e^{-rs}\,ds \\ &= \int_{s=t}^{\infty} -(F'_s - w)\,e^{-rs}\,ds\end{aligned}$$

Substitute the transversality condition $\lim_{T\to\infty} \lambda_T e^{-rT} = 0$ into this equation, finally we get

$$\begin{aligned}\lambda_t\,e^{-rt} &= \int_{s=t}^{\infty} (F'_s - w)\,e^{-rs}\,ds \\ \lambda_t &= \int_{s=t}^{\infty} (F'_s - w)\,e^{-r(s-t)}\,ds\end{aligned}$$

as seen in our text.

Notes

1. Government of India, *National Textile Policy – 2000*, 2000, paras. 11 and 12.
2. The registered sector covers all factories covered under the Indian Factory Act, 1948 which refers to factories using power and employing 10 or more workers, and those not using power and employing 20 or more workers. The unregistered sector covers all factories which are not in the registered sector. In this chapter, we use organized sector and registered sector interchangeably. It is also noted that the informal sector is a subset of the unregistered sector. In subsection 7.4.2, we give a definition of the informal sector.
3. On this point, see Verma (2002).
4. See Roy (2004a), Sastry (1984) and Uchikawa (1998) for more comprehensive treatment of India's textile and garment industries.
5. The central government enacted this Act. However, as we will note in the next subsection, both the central and state governments are able to amend it under the provision of the Constitution of India. It is noted that actually the central government introduced additional important legislation into the Act and state governments also amended it.
6. Ministry of Labour website: (http://labour.nic.in/ir/Industrialdisputesacts,1947.htm). This subject is treated by Basu (2005), Debroy and Kaushik (2005) and Zagba (1999).
7. Government of India, *Report of the Task Force on Employment Opportunities*, 2001, para. 7.16.
8. Government of India, *Finance Minister's Budget Speech 2001–2*, para. 52.
9. Government of India, *Report of the Second National Commission on Labour*, 2002, paras. 6.87 and 6.88.

10. See the Appendix.
11. It is remarkably messy to solve the simultaneous differential equation. Instead, we analyse the nature of the solution by looking at the phase diagram.
12. If $L(0)$ is between L_1 and L_2, there is neither employment nor retrenchment of workers. The $\dot{\lambda} = 0$ schedule from E^C to E^M is the long-run equilibrium.
13. The impact of other parametric changes of exogenous variables is basically the same as that in the previous model. Therefore, we skip it.
14. We learn about the characteristics on the *ASI* data from Goldar (1997, 2004). We follow them as precisely as possible.
15. The data sources we use are as follows: Reserve Bank of India, *Database on Indian Economy*, and *Handbook of Statistics on Indian Economy*; CSO, *Input–Output Transaction Table 1989* and *National Account Statistics*.
16. The following specification is essentially based on a firm's cost minimization behaviour. Of course, it is consistent with a firm's profit maximization behaviour.
17. The reason we use the relative price for regression analysis is that, given output price, the movement of input price which is crucially dependent on oil price has influenced the level of output and allocation of resources by firms. If we neglected the relative price variable, explanatory variables that are correlated with relative price might become endogenous. Thus, we use relative price in order to avoid the endogeneity problem. It is also noted that we regard K as an exogenous variable in this chapter since K was strongly regulated by the government's industrial licence regime at least until 1991.
18. We are unable to estimate the direct effect of the JSR index on employment using the fixed effect model since the JSR index is a time-invariant variable. It is noted that any time-invariant variable can be constructed by the linear combination of the individual dummy variables. Therefore, the regression with time-invariant variables will fail due to perfect multicollinearity.
19. GMM is a popular estimation method in the econometric research field, used by Bhalotra (1998), Hasan et al. (2003) and Badri Narayanan (2005) to estimate the dynamic labour demand function of Indian industries. The original estimator of Arellano and Bond (1991) is called 'difference GMM', and the improved one by Arellano and Bover (1995) and Blundell and Bond (1998) is called 'system GMM'. To make the instruments matrix, while on one hand the 'difference GMM' utilizes the orthogonality condition of first difference of endogenous variables and their own lagged levels, on the other hand the 'system GMM' inserts the original level equation into the 'difference GMM' framework and utilizes the orthogonality condition of their own levels and the lags of the first difference of endogenous variables in addition to the orthogonality condition of the 'difference GMM'. The 'system GMM' estimator is considered less biased and more efficient than the 'difference GMM'. However, according to Blundell and Bond (1998), the longer the time series, the less the gap between the 'difference GMM' estimator and the 'system GMM' estimator. The time series that we use is long relative to the industry-state units. The number of the time series is 19 and that of industry-state unit is 75. Thus, in this chapter we employ only the 'difference GMM' for regression analysis.
20. The *Indian Labour Statistics* we utilize for making the bargaining power variable at the national level do not give a breakdown of industrial disputes at state level. Therefore, we are unable to employ bargaining power variables at the state level.

References

Abel, A. B. and J. C. Eberly (1994) 'A Unified Model of Investment under Uncertainty'. *American Economic Review* 84(5): 1369–84.

Aghion, P., R. Burgess, S. Redding and F. Zilibotti (2006) 'The Unequal Effects of Liberalization'. NBER Working Paper, no. 9879. Cambridge, Mass.

Arellano, M. and S. Bond (1991) 'Some Tests of Specification for Panel Data'. *Review of Economic Studies* 58(2): 277–97.

Arellano, M. and O. Bover (1995) 'Another Look at the Instrumental-Variable Estimation of Error Components Models'. *Journal of Econometrics* 68: 29–52.

Badri Narayanan, G. (2005) 'Effects of Trade Liberalisation, Environmental and Labour Regulations on Employment in India's Organised Textile Sector'. IGIDR Working Paper no. P-2005-005. New Delhi.

Basu, K. (2005) 'Why India Needs Labour Law Reform'. BBC NEWS (http://news.bbc.co.uk/1/hi/world/southasia/4103554.stm).

Besley, T. and R. Burgess (2004) 'Can Labor Regulation Hinder Economic Performance?' *Quarterly Journal of Economics* 119(1): 91–134.

Bhalotra, S. R. (1998) 'The Puzzle of Jobless Growth in Indian Manufacturing'. *Oxford Bulletin of Economics and Statistics* 60(1): 5–32.

Blanchard, O. J. and S. Fischer (1989) *Lectures on Macroeconomics*. Cambridge, Mass.: The MIT Press.

Blundell, R. and S. Bond (1998) 'Initial Conditions and Moment Restrictions in Dynamic Panel Data Models'. *Journal of Econometrics* 87: 115–43.

Datta Chaudhuri, M. (1996) 'Labor Markets as Social Institutions in India'. IRIS-India Working Paper no. 10. College Park, Md.

Debroy, B. and P. D. Kaushik (eds) (2005) *Reforming the Labour Market*. New Delhi: Academic Foundation.

Fallon, P. R. and R. E. B Lucas (1993) 'Job Security Regulations and the Dynamic Demand for Industrial Labour in India and Zimbabwe'. *Journal of Development Economics* 40: 241–75.

Goldar, B. (1997) 'Econometrics of Indian Industry'. In K. L. Krishna (ed.) *Econometric Applications in India*. New Delhi: Oxford University Press.

—— (2004) 'Indian Manufacturing'. *Economic and Political Weekly* 20 November.

Hasan, R., D. Mitra and K. V. Ramaswamy (2003) 'Trade Reforms, Labor Regulations and Labor–Demand Elasticities'. NBER Working Paper no. 9879. Cambridge, Mass.

Romer, D. (1996) *Advanced Macroeconomics*. New York: McGraw-Hill.

Roy, S. D. (2004a) 'Employment Dynamics in Indian Industry'. *Journal of Development Economics* 73: 233–56.

Roy, T. (2004b) 'The Textile Industry'. In S. Gokarn, A. Sen and R. R. Vaidya (eds) *The Structure of Indian Industry*. New Delhi: Oxford University Press.

Sanyal, P. and N. Menon (2005) 'Labour Disputes and the Economics of Firm Geography'. *Economic Development and Cultural Change* 53: 825–54.

Sastry, D. U. (1984) *The Cotton Mill Industry in India*. New Delhi: Oxford University Press.

Uchikawa, S. (1998) *Indian Textile Industry*. New Delhi: Manohar.

Verma, S. (2002) 'Export Competitiveness of Indian Textile and Garment Industry'. ICRIER Working Paper 94. New Delhi.

Zagba, R. (1999) 'Labour and India's Economic Reforms'. In J. D. Sachs, A. Varshney and N. Bajpai (eds) *India in the Era of Economic Reforms*. New Delhi: Oxford University Press.

8

Effects of the Minimum Wage Regulations on Employment Level and Efficiency: Evidence from the Ready-Made Garment Industry in India

Yoshie Shimane

8.1 Introduction

This chapter deals with one of the key issues in India: the consequences of the labour regulations for economic performance in the era of globalization.

In India, economic reforms aim to reduce the intervention of the state, which has sought to take a role in enhancing both economic development and social welfare. Internal reforms were initiated in the mid-1980s, and major internal and external reforms began in 1991. But even so, reforms have been piecemeal, and there is a large gap between areas where reforms are advanced and those where they are not. The labour market is the area in which reforms are lagging most noticeably.[1] Even now, according to laws and regulations, workers in the organized sector[2] are provided with job security and employee benefits such as pensions, leave of absence and other entitlements. In the private sector, large firms are not allowed to replace workers without permission from the government. Even the bankruptcy laws, which prevented non-performing companies from closing down, were directed for the sake of protecting organized labour.

Since there has been no significant deregulation there, labour market regulations are frequently cited as an explanation of India's poor growth performance.[3] The claim is that the excessive protection thus granted to organized labour discouraged employment and investment, and hence economic growth.

However, we must always pay careful attention to distinguish what is written in laws and regulations from what is actually binding upon economic practices, especially in the case of India. In a nation like India with a vast pool of potential labour, labour-related laws and regulations might not be as restrictive as they appear, or their effects might be limited to only a small formal part of the labour market. So, whenever we investigate how restrictive laws and regulations are, it is important to investigate how significant the actual effects are.

In this chapter, among various labour-related laws and regulations, we focus on the effects of minimum wage regulation on the efficiency of production. The ready-made garment industry is chosen as a case for examining such effects since efficiency matters in this industry far more now than before given the process of globalization. It is worth examining if the ready-made garment industry is subject to inefficient practices because of the minimum wage, which is imposed even now when the sector faces increased domestic as well as international competition. The period examined in this chapter is restricted to fiscal year 1993 to fiscal year 1996.

In Section 8.2, we show the general features of the labour market and the ready-made garment industry, explain the minimum wage regulations in India and in the ready-made garment industry, and survey literature on labour reform and economic performance. Section 8.3 presents methods and results of the empirical analysis of the effect of the minimum wage regulations on the efficiency of firms in the ready-made garment industry. Section 8.4 presents the summary and conclusions.

8.2 Background

8.2.1 Overview of the employment climate

At the end of fiscal 1992, the organized sector is estimated to have accounted for 8.61 per cent of total employment, and this figure declined to 8.35 per cent at the end of fiscal 1998.[4] Out of a total workforce consisting of 336.75 million in fiscal 1999, 190.84 million were in the agriculture sector, 40.79 million in the manufacturing sector and the rest in the services sector. The number employed in the organized private manufacturing sector peaked at 5.239 million at the end of fiscal 1996 and continued declining to reach 4.867 million at the end of fiscal 2001. However, this does not automatically mean that private manufacturing firms in the organized sector employ fewer workers. Contract workers, who are not counted as organized labour even if they work for firms in the organized sector, increased to 22.8 per cent in fiscal 2001. This indicates that firms are escaping from some of the labour regulations by hiring workers indirectly as contract workers. Thus, whether labour regulations are binding firms' employment practices or not is not easy to assess because some are escaping from restrictions one way or another.

8.2.2 Overview of the ready-made garment industry

The ready-made garment industry is currently exposed to more competition both internally and internationally. Reservation[5] of the ready-made garment industry for small-scale industries (SSI) was abolished in January 2001, and now firms of any size are free to enter into manufacturing. Subsequently, abolition of quantitative restrictions on imports followed shortly after, in April 2001, so that now firms are exposed to competition from imported products. Furthermore, the Multi-Fibre Agreement (MFA) expired at the end of 2005. As a result of all these deregulatory measures, the ready-made garment industry now faces more domestic as well as international competition.

The ready-made garment industry is believed to consist mainly of small manufacturers because it was reserved for SSI[6] until 1 January, 2001. Investment in plant and machinery in the SSI sector could not exceed Rs.6 million, or Rs.7.5 million in the case of export-oriented units and ancillary units, until 1997. In 1997, the limit was revised to Rs.30 million for all three categories and reduced to Rs.10

million in 1999. However, garment-manufacturing units can invest in plant and machinery beyond the limits set for SSI if they export more than 50 per cent of their total production.[7] Shimane (2005) argues from the trend of investment and production of 63 major reserved commodities that the reservation policy has not been as restrictive on non-SSI's investment as it might be seen to be from the formal policy framework.

All factories with electric power employing 10 or more workers or 20 or more workers without electric power have to be registered under the Factory Act, 1948, and firms in the registered sector are included in the Annual Survey of Industries. The National Industrial Classification 1987 (NIC1987) used for the Annual Survey of Industries was applicable throughout the period of our analysis, the fiscal years from 1993 to 1996. The NIC1987 Code 26 refers to the manufacture of all textile products, and garment manufacture is Code 265. As the data at the three-digit level of NIC1987 are not published, we show data for manufacturing of garments coded 181 for fiscal 1998 in Table 8.1. From fiscal 1998 onward, the National Industrial Classification 1998 (NIC1998) is applicable, and state-level data of three digits are available. In terms of the number of factories, number of persons employed and both gross and net value added, the major states manufacturing ready-made garments are Gujarat, Haryana, Karnataka, Maharashtra, Tamil Nadu, Uttar Pradesh and Delhi.

8.2.3 Overview of the Minimum Wages Act

The Minimum Wages Act (MWA), 1948, requires the appropriate level of government, central or state as the case may be, to fix minimum rates of wages payable to the employees defined as persons 'employed for hire or reward to do any work, skilled or unskilled, manual or clerical, etc.', in an employment specified in Part 1 or Part 2 of the Schedule appended to the Act or an employment added by either the Advisory Committee appointed by them or by notification in the official *Gazette*. The appropriate governments are also required to review the minimum rate of wages, from time to time, and revise the same, if necessary.

The MWA in India provided for statutory regulation of minimum wage rates specifically in agriculture. India is among the few countries in Asia to have fixed minimum wages in the agriculture sector. The appropriate government may refrain from fixing minimum rates of wages with respect to any scheduled employment in which there are less than 1000 employees engaged in the entire state.

Under Section 27 of the Act, the appropriate government is empowered to extend the application of the Act to any other employment with respect to which it is of the opinion that the minimum rates of wages should be fixed under the Act. The numbers of areas in which the minimum wage are fixed and the range of the minimum wages are shown in Table 8.2. We can see that there is substantial variation among states in the number of areas in which minimum wages are fixed and in the level of the minimum wage per day. States in which the minimum wages were fixed for the ready-made garment industry numbered eight in 1993 and nine from 1994 to 1996, as shown in Table 8.3. Each state revised the minimum wage every year, except Goa, Jammu and Kashmir, and Orissa.

Table 8.1 Garment industry in major states in the fiscal year 1998 (values in Rs. lakh, others in number)

	All India	*AP*	*GR*	*HR*	*HP*	*KN*	*KL*	*MP*	*MH*	*OR*	*PJ*	*RJ*	*TN*	*UP*	*WB*	*DL*
1. Number of factories	3,093	40	110	63	4	561	30	4	685	4	15	61	711	175	24	564
3. Fixed capital	199,999	918	10,363	18,942	126	38,696	1,873	899	16,975	84	2,161	5,835	37,709	16,491	678	43,132
13. Total output	1,304,957	5,596	69,053	49,965	250	314,025	3,993	324	119,118	1,559	15,537	17,201	229,090	92,304	10,765	355,454
15. Materials consumed	650,018	3,088	35,956	24,992	100	160,231	2,370	160	50,963	927	11,267	5,819	121,289	42,597	7,542	172,053
17. Gross value added	318,079	1,653	16,846	10,998	89	71,373	1,081	92	29,207	546	3,104	7,123	57,094	21,606	1,713	88,173
19. Net value added	292,669	1,571	16,025	9,562	70	65,614	946	32	27,050	533	2,828	6,341	51,867	19,949	1,600	81,808
23. Gross capital formation	37,014	136	2,581	4,042	26	5,814	–18	258	2,615	244	517	553	11,401	2,468	–271	5,694
25. Profit	157,748	261	11,391	3,205	41	23,839	–272	–153	15,478	438	1,232	4,439	25,245	11,054	1,186	55,756
A. No. of persons employed	275,540	3,955	8,935	7,269	86	111,248	2,534	407	13,381	162	4,102	2,286	78,144	11,025	552	27,494
1.0 Workers	237,242	3,389	7,631	5,804	73	100,626	2,367	353	10,114	102	3,885	1,824	70,425	8,718	364	18,067
1.1 Directly employed	226,470	3,149	5,974	5,750	73	100,451	2,367	229	9,961	102	227	1,190	67,748	7,469	294	18,059
1.2 Employed through contractors	10,772	240	1,657	54	0	175	0	124	152	0	3,659	634	2,677	1,249	71	8
2.0 Employees other than workers	38,298	566	1,304	1,464	13	10,622	167	55	3,268	60	217	461	7,719	2,307	188	9,427
B. Total man-days employed (in '000)	81,563	1,181	2,769	2,116	25	31,220	688	125	4,049	50	1,264	681	22,568	5,162	154	8,279

Note: For abbreviations of names of states and union territories, see Appendix 8.1.
Source: Complied from Central Statistical Organization, Ministry of Planning and Programme Implementation, Government of India (1995), *Annual Survey of Industries 1998–99*.

Table 8.2 Scheduled employments in central/state/union territories and the range of minimum wages as of 3/12/96

Central/state/union territories	*No. of scheduled employments with fixed/revised minimum wages*[1]	*Range of minimum wages per day*	
		Minimum (Rs.)	*Maximum (Rs.)*
CLC (Central)	40	34.56	63.09
Andhra Pradesh	58	25.96	62.85
Arunachal Pradesh	16	21.00	24.00
Assam	57	23.53	56.00
Bihar	61	27.30	44.23
Delhi	29	64.50	64.50
Goa	16	15.00	68.08
Gujarat	45	34.00	59.50
Haryana	50	54.52	55.52
Himachal Pradesh	24	26.00	45.75
Jammu and Kashmir	35	30.00	30.00
Karnataka	58	23.03	58.16
Kerala	35	30.00	114.16
Madhya Pradesh	36	26.46	49.00
Maharashtra	61	8.46	83.29
Manipur	5	27.35	56.88
Meghalaya	22	35.00	35.00
Mizoram	2	35.00	35.00
Nagaland	37	25.00	25.00
Orissa	82	30.00	30.00
Punjab	60	55.73	58.73
Rajasthan	39	32.00	32.00
Tamil Nadu	58	20.00	72.40
Tripura	9	17.70	36.00
Uttar Pradesh	65	42.02	64.21
West Bengal	35	28.34	72.73
N and N Islands	8	37.00	65.50
Dadra and N. Haveli	43	35.00	40.00
Chandigarh	42	51.95	54.95
Lakshadweep	4	42.46	41.46
Pondicherry	2	19.25	40.20

Note: 1. Numbers of areas in which minimum wage is fixed or revised.
Source: Compiled from Labour Bureau, Ministry of Labour, Government of India (2000), *Report on the Working of the Minimum Wages Act, 1948 for the Year 1996.*

8.2.4 Literature on labour reform and economic performance, and aim of this chapter

As there has been no significant deregulation in the labour market since the 1982/84 amendment, 'before and after' methodology cannot be employed for the investigation of the recent period.[8] The other method of investigating the effects of labour regulations in India is to exploit the differences in regulations among

Table 8.3 Minimum wages for the ready-made garment industry (Rs. per day)

	1993	*1994*	*1995*	*1996*
Delhi	43.04	54.61	59.45	64.5
Goa	21	21	21	21
Gujarat	31.4	35.65	39.85	43.9
Haryana	42.65	50.95	51.57	54.2
Jammu and Kashmir	–	15	30	30
Maharashtra	61.61	71.9	73.97	78.27
Punjab	41.51	44.57	53.03	55.73
Orissa	25	25	25	30
Uttar Pradesh	38.24	42.01	46.23	56.23

Source: Compiled from Labour Bureau, Ministry of Labour, Government of India (2000), *Report on the Working of the Minimum Wages Act, 1948 for the Year 1996.*

states. There are 45 labour laws in operation dealing with a range of issues with respect to minimum wages, job security, benefits, industrial safety and trade unions (Patibandla 2006: 58). Some of these laws vary among states because the state governments are entitled to make amendments and decide areas of industries to be covered by laws. One pioneering work that utilized such differences among states to investigate the effects of labour policies is Besley and Burgess (2004), which focused on the Industrial Disputes Act of 1947 (IDA1947). While the Act was passed at the central level, state governments were given the right to amend it under the Indian Constitution. They coded each amendment, 113 in all, as being pro-worker, pro-employer or neutral, and further coded, for the purposes of quantitative analysis, each pro-worker amendment as a 1, each neutral amendment as a 0, and each pro-employer amendment as a −1.

Besley and Burgess (2004) attracted high and wide attention from policymakers[9] as well as scholars. While several papers[10] that used and extended the quantitative index of regulatory measures devised by them come to conclusions along the same lines, claiming that excessively pro-worker legislation impaired industrial performance, there are also cautious views of this body of work. Among them, Anant et al. (2006) and Sharma (2006) express sceptical views on their findings providing evidence of flexibility of employment even under the pro-worker legislation. Bhattacharjea (2006) is a thorough work of critique in the sense that it criticizes both their coding for amendment and their estimation methodology.

We are also sceptical of the rather simple argument regarding the consequences of the labour regulations for economic performance and feel that the robustness of the results has to be checked in various ways and in various areas of labour regulations. So, the first motivation of this chapter was to follow the same econometrical methodology as Besley and Burgess (2004) but to utilize another aspect of labour legislation that differs among states, namely the minimum wage regulations, to

Table 8.4 Growth rate of employment and man-days

(a1) Firms not under minimum wage regulation

Variable	*Obs*	*Mean*	*Std. Dev.*	*Min*	*Max*
Numbers in employment					
1994	99	1.149248	0.533605	0.226852	4.428571
1995	81	1.068726	0.349611	0.308429	2.586345
1996	127	1.68288	1.117579	0.419255	10.25
Man-days employed					
1994	99	3.68348	25.23528	0.229769	252.1741
1995	81	1.100426	0.417338	0.304194	2.750165
1996	127	1.10402	0.600926	0.313777	5.863527

(a2) Firms not under minimum wage regulation

Variable	*Obs*	*Mean*	*Std. Dev.*	*Min*	*Max*
Numbers in employment					
1994	98	1.14865	0.536315	0.226852	4.428571
1995	80	1.069854	0.351669	0.308429	2.586345
1996	126	1.688823	1.120023	0.419255	10.25
Man-days employed					
1994	98	1.147862	0.56213	0.229769	4.458495
1995	80	1.101978	0.419736	0.304194	2.750165
1996	126	1.106585	0.602626	0.313777	5.863527

(b) Firms under minimum wage regulation

Variable	*Obs*	*Mean*	*Std. Dev.*	*Min*	*Max*
Numbers in employment					
1994	146	1.26917	0.681765	0.125984	4.888889
1995	59	1.005972	0.530483	0.150376	3.326733
1996	96	2.355457	1.260065	0.093407	6.914286
Man-days employed					
1994	146	1.29346	0.721771	0.130977	4.908615
1995	59	1.040977	0.651867	0.151628	3.875828
1996	96	1.044781	0.55011	0.043171	4.975606

Notes: 1. Shaded cells in (a1) and (a2) indicate figures are larger than corresponding figures for firms under minimum wage regulation in (b).
2. In (a2), one firm for which man-days worked data in 1995 is suspected to be a typographical error, is dropped.
3. Years are fiscal years. Obs = Observations.
Source: Author's calculation.

check the results. Although Besley and Burgess (2004) argue that 'The emphasis on central planning in India meant that state governments have had limited influence on industrial policy outside the area of industrial relations' (p. 92), minimum wage fixation is another important aspect in which state governments are entitled to exert influence. The Minimum Wages Act, 1948, empowers appropriate governments, either central or state, to fix or revise the minimum rate of wages payable to employees with respect to scheduled employment,[11] employments originally included in the schedule appended to the Act and those added to the schedule subsequently. Furthermore, the Act empowers the appropriate government to extend the application of the Act to any other employment considered proper.

Although there is no work that includes investigation of the minimum wage regulations' impact on employment or economic growth exploiting the differences among states, it is naturally an even more suitable aspect of labour regulations to be dealt with quantitatively.[12] This is because (a) constructing an index could be done less arbitrarily by utilizing the number of areas covered and the levels of wages set by the Act across states, and (b) there is far less judicial interpretation involved. However, long-term data on the minimum wage, for the period comparable to the IDA amendment data that are used in Besley and Burgess (2004), were not available to us. For that reason, we altered the strategy of investigation into a cross-section analysis of firms to see if there are any differences in employment practices and production efficiency between those firms under and those not under the minimum wage regulation.

8.3 Impact of the minimum wage on employment and efficiency of production

8.3.1 Impact on employment growth

The most well-known literature in the field of the minimum wage in labour economics is regarded as Card and Krueger (1995). Since the focus of analysis there is on the growth of employment, we first compare the growth rates of the number employed and the man-days worked. Our prediction is that, since the minimum wage is fixed per day, faced with an increased demand for labour, an employer would not increase the number of employed but would further increase the man-days worked if they were under the minimum wage restrictions.[13] The growth rate of the number of employed and man-days worked from previous years shown in Table 8.4 do not really support this prediction. Compared to firms under the minimum wage regulation, those which are not under the regulation increased man-days worked more in 1996 and 1997 and increased the number of employed less in 1995 and 1997. We cannot say anything more than that the impact of minimum wage on employment growth is mixed.

8.3.2 Possible impacts of minimum wage regulation on efficiencies[14] of production

Instead of examining the impact of minimum wage regulation on employment growth further, in the remainder of this chapter we attempt to measure the level of efficiencies and analyse whether they can be explained by the minimum wage regulations. The basic reason why we are interested in measuring efficiency is (a) a sustainable increase in employment would be more likely to be achieved when

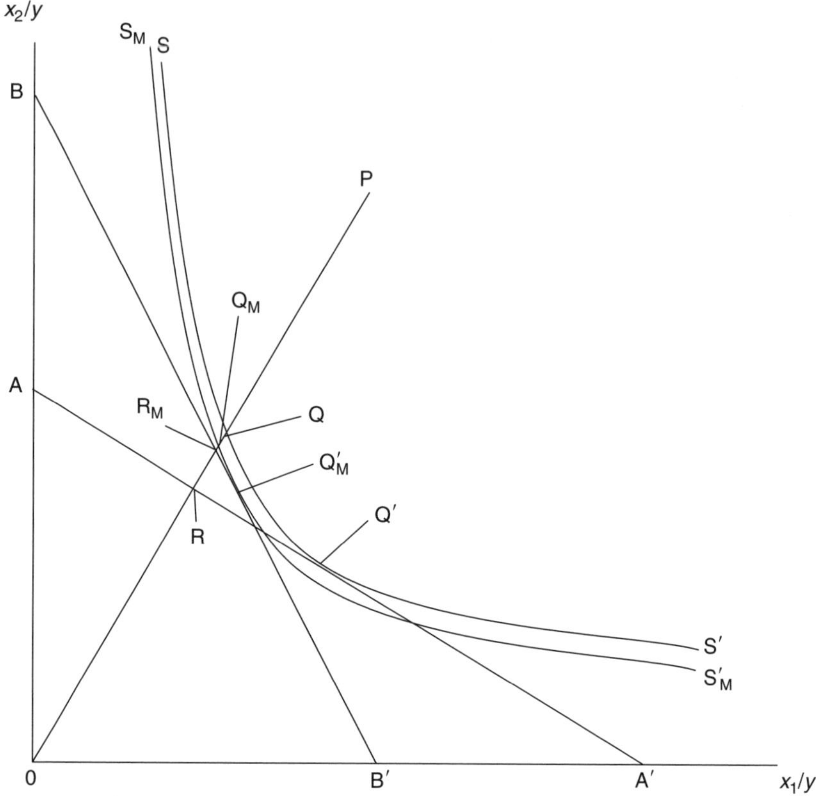

Figure 8.1 Technical and allocative efficiencies
Source: Modified from Figure 6.1 in Coelli et al. (1998)

firms are efficient in production, and (b) the minimum wage regulation is predicted to affect the level of efficiency. Besley and Burgess (2004) investigate whether pro-worker regulations cause a lower growth rate and lower per capita income. However, the effects of pro-worker or pro-employer regulations on the growth rate and per capita income are not direct, and there may be many other variables that can affect the rate of growth and the level of income. However, if there are changes in wage level caused by the minimum wage regulations, efficiencies would be affected more directly.

Here we will explain the more direct effects of the minimum wage regulations on the level of efficiency using Figure 8.1. Figure 8.1 illustrates production of firms that use two inputs, x_1 and x_2, to produce a single output, y, under the assumption of constant returns to scale. Now suppose a firm is producing at point P in the figure and also suppose the relative price of labour is made higher by the minimum wage regulation. Knowledge of the unit isoquant of fully efficient firms, represented by SS′ not under the minimum wage regulation and $S_MS'_M$ under the minimum wage regulation in the figure, permits the measurement of technical efficiency (TE). When the price ratio, represented by the slope of the isocost line, AA′, without the minimum wage and BB′ with the minimum wage, is also known, allocative efficiency (AE) may also be calculated. TE reflects the ability of a firm to obtain maximal output from a given set of inputs and AE reflects the ability of a firm to use the inputs in optimal proportions.

If wages become higher because of minimum wage regulations, the input price ratio of labour, X_1, and capital, X_2 without the minimum wage is represented by the slope of the isocost line AA′ and with the minimum wage regulation is represented by BB′. If a given firm uses quantities of inputs, defined by the point P, to produce a unit of output, the TE of a firm is measured by the ratio

$$\mathrm{TE}_i = 0\mathrm{Q}/0\mathrm{P} \quad \text{without the minimum wage and}$$

$$\mathrm{TE}_{i\mathrm{M}} = 0\mathrm{Q}_\mathrm{M}/0\mathrm{P} \quad \text{with the minimum wage}$$

which is equal to 1 – QP/0P and $\mathrm{Q_M}$P/0P respectively. It will take a value between 0 and 1, and hence it provides an indicator of the degree of technical inefficiency of the firm *i*. A value of 1 indicates the firm is fully technically efficient. For example, the points Q and $\mathrm{Q_M}$ are technically efficient because they lie on the efficient isoquant SS′ and $\mathrm{S_M S'_M}$.

AE of the firm operating at P is defined to be the ratio

$$\mathrm{AE}_i = 0\mathrm{R}/0\mathrm{Q} \quad \text{without the minimum wage and}$$

$$\mathrm{AE}_{i\mathrm{M}} = 0\mathrm{R}_\mathrm{M}/0\mathrm{Q}_\mathrm{M} \quad \text{with the minimum wage}$$

since the distance RQ to $\mathrm{R_M Q_M}$ represents the reduction in production costs that would occur if production were to occur at the allocatively (and technically) efficient points Q′ and $\mathrm{Q'_M}$, instead of at the technically efficient, but allocatively inefficient, points Q and $\mathrm{Q_M}$.

If the price of labour becomes higher under the minimum wage regulation, the isocost line AA′ is shifted to BB′, and if firms do not respond to relative prices, $\mathrm{AE_M}$, under the minimum wage, becomes larger than AE, not under the minimum wage. If firms responded to relative prices but marginal product of labour does not increase as much as it is equal to the cost of labour, $\mathrm{TE_M}$, under the minimum wage, becomes larger than TE, not under the minimum wage. Thus the minimum wage regulation is expected to have an impact either on TE or AE if the regulation is binding on a firm's practice. If the estimated results show that the minimum wage regulation is not causing inefficiency of production, we have to doubt our two assumptions. This suggests the possibility of one of two claims: either (1) the price of labour becomes higher under the minimum wage regulation, or (2) even if price of labour becomes higher, marginal product of labour increased so that it is equal to the shifted relative prices.

Since Coelli invented Frontier and DEAP, many works have been carried out to estimate inefficiencies using these software programs; however, as far as this author understands, there is neither theoretical nor empirical work to relate inefficiencies and the minimum wage regulation in the way that this chapter attempts. For the empirical work, one of the limitations might lie in difficulties in obtaining price information for individual firms.

8.3.3 Strategy of estimating inefficiencies

Our econometric analysis proceeds as follows. We measure inefficiency/efficiency using both stochastic frontiers and data envelopment analysis (DEA). Stochastic frontiers and DEA are two alternative methods for measuring inefficiency of production. Stochastic frontier analysis (SFA) is a parametric approach and involves the use of econometric methods whereas DEA is a non-parametric approach and involves the use of linear programming.[15]

There are both advantages and disadvantages in these two approaches. The largest advantage of SFA is its stochastic character. If it is deterministic, all deviations from the frontier are assumed to be the result of inefficiency, but the stochastic frontier accounts for the possible influence of measurement errors and other noise upon the frontier. On the other hand, the disadvantage of SFA is that, although the production function is never known in practice, it assumes the production function of a fully efficient firm is known. DEA avoids this disadvantage by estimating the function from sample data using a non-parametric piece-wise-linear technology. Regrettably, a stochastic method based on DEA is yet to be invented.

As Niimi (1999) pointed out, what we can best do to cover the above shortcomings of the two approaches is to conduct both of them and compare the results before drawing conclusions. So, we first analyse the level of overall efficiency based on an estimation of a stochastic frontier production function using the software Frontier Version 4.1. There the inefficiency effects are modelled in terms of other explanatory variables. Of particular interest in this chapter is the issue of whether firms under the minimum wage regulation are technically less efficient than firms not under it. Hence, the efficiency effects in the stochastic frontier production function are modelled in terms of the minimum wage dummy as well as other variables. Then we conduct DEA. The merit of DEA is that we can disaggregate overall inefficiencies into TE and AE when price information is available.

8.3.4 Stochastic frontier analysis (SFA)

8.3.4.1 Method

To begin with, a translog stochastic frontier production function is assumed to be the appropriate model for the analysis of firms in ready-made garment manufacturing from fiscal year 1993 to 1996.

$$
\begin{aligned}
\ln(Q_{it}) = {} & \beta_0 + \beta_1 \ln(K_{it}) + \beta_2 \ln(L_{it}) + \beta_3 \ln(M_{it}) + \beta_4 \ln[(K_{it})]^2 + \beta_5 \ln[(L_{it})]^2 \\
& + \beta_6 \ln[(M_{it})]^2 + 2[\beta_7 \ln(K_{it}) \ln(L_{it}) + \beta_8 \ln(K_{it}) \ln(M_{it}) \\
& + \beta_9 \ln(L_{it}) \ln(M_{it})] + \beta_{10} \ln[(K_{it})]\,t + \beta_{11} \ln[(L_{it})]\,t + \beta_{12} \ln[(M_{it})]\,t \\
& + \beta_{13} t + \beta_{14} t^2 + v_{it} - \mu_{it} \quad (i = 1, 2, \ldots, n;\ t = 1, 2, 3, 4) \qquad (8.1)
\end{aligned}
$$

where Q_{it} represents the real gross output of firm i at time t, K_{it} the real capital of firm i at time t, L_{it} the man-days employed of firm i at time t and M_{it} represents the real intermediary inputs of firm i at time t. v_{it} is assumed to be independent and identically distributed as normal random variables with mean zero and variance σ_v^2, independent of the μ_{it}, and μ_{it} is non-negative technical inefficiency of production, which is assumed to be truncated at zero of the normal distribution with mean m_i and variance σ^2, where the mean is defined by

$$\begin{aligned} m_i = {} & \delta_0 + \delta_1\,\mathrm{DUM1}_{it} + \delta_2\,\mathrm{DUM2}_{it} + \delta_3\,\mathrm{DUM3}_{it} + \delta_4\,\mathrm{DUM4}_{it} + \delta_5\,\mathrm{DUM5}_{it} \\ & + \delta_6 \ln(\mathrm{EMP}_{it}) + \delta_7\,\mathrm{DUM6}_{it} \end{aligned} \tag{8.2}$$

where $\mathrm{DUM1}_{it}$ is a dummy variable for bank loans, 1 if the loan is launched, 0 otherwise; $\mathrm{DUM2}_{it}$ is a dummy variable for rural location, 1 if the firm is located in a rural area, 0 otherwise; $\mathrm{DUM3}_{it}$ is a dummy variable for backward location, 1 if the firm is located in a scheduled backward area, 0 otherwise; $\mathrm{DUM4}_{it}$ is a dummy variable for captive power generation, 1 if the firm is equipped with a captive power generator, 0 otherwise; $\mathrm{DUM5}_{it}$ is a dummy variable for imported input, 1 if the firm utilizes imported inputs, 0 otherwise; EMP_{it} is the number of employees, including workers and staff; $\mathrm{DUM6}_{it}$ is our most interesting variable, a dummy for the minimum wage, 1 if the firm locates in states in which the minimum wage is fixed for the ready-made garment industry, 0 otherwise.

The model defined by Equation (8.1) is called the stochastic frontier production function because the output values are bounded above by the stochastic (random) variable. The random error v_{it} can be positive or negative, and so the stochastic frontier outputs vary around the deterministic part of the frontier model. This means that it accounts for the presence of measurement error in the output or the combined effects of unspecified explanatory variables in the production function.

The parameters of the stochastic frontier production function, defined by Equation (8.1), can be estimated using the maximum likelihood (ML) method, and the Frontier program automates the ML method for estimation of the parameters of stochastic frontier models.[16]

The data we used to estimate the above equation are firm-level data derived from the *Annual Survey of Industries* 1993/94, 1994/95, 1995/96 and 1996/97. Construction of variables is explained in Appendix 8.2 and a summary of major variables is shown in Table 8.5.

8.3.4.2 Primary results

A further hypothesis of interest is whether (a) the technical progress is Hicks neutral, H_0: $\beta_{10} = \beta_{11} = \beta_{12} = 0$, (b) there is no technical progress, H_0: $\beta_{10} = \beta_{11} = \beta_{12} = \beta_{13} = \beta_{14} = 0$, or (c) production function is the Cobb-Douglas, H_0: $\beta_4 = \beta_5 = \beta_6 = \beta_7 = \beta_8 = \beta_9 = \beta_{10} = \beta_{11} = \beta_{12} = \beta_{13} = \beta_{14} = 0$. Before showing the primary results of estimation, we tested these three specifications. As can be seen in Table 8.6, specification (a) cannot be rejected. Hence, we show the estimated results of original Equation (8.1) as well as the equation with the null of (a) as Equation (8.2) in Table 8.7.

Table 8.5 Summary of variables in SFA estimation

Variable	*Obs*	*Mean*	*Std. Dev.*	*Min*	*Max*
Real gross output (Q)	1964	6.81E+07	1.14E+08	114937.2	2.02E+09
Real capital (K)	1964	9006466	2.46E+07	2268.944	6.00E+08
Real intermediary input (M)	1962	3.32E+07	5.29E+07	1748.901	9.52E+08
Man-days employed (L)	1964	57438.97	64693.79	224	571978

Source: Author's calculation.

Table 8.6 Testing specifications of production function

Null hypothesis	*Log likelihood function*		*LR test statistics*	*Degrees of freedom*	$X^2_{0.01}$	$X^2_{0.05}$	*Results*
	H_0	H_1					
(a)	−806.7555	−804.4797	4.5516	3	11.3	7.81	Not rejected
(b)	−819.2003	−804.4797	29.4412	5	15.1	11.1	Rejected
(c)	−910.4715	−804.4797	211.9835	11	19.7	24.7	Rejected

Source: Author's estimation.

The most striking feature of the result shown in Table 8.7 is: the coefficient of the minimum wage dummy for the inefficiency effects is negative, which indicates that the minimum wage has an effect on firms for reducing the inefficiency. On the other hand, firms located in backward areas and firms employing more people experience higher inefficiency. Taking loans from banks, being equipped with captive power and using imported input do not have significant influence on inefficiency.

Before claiming that the minimum wage has the effect of lowering the level of inefficiency in production, it would be appropriate for us to examine two possibilities which might be behind these estimated results. One is the possibility that the minimum wage dummy acted as a proxy for the industrially advanced states. Hence, instead of the effect of the minimum wage, it is the good industrial foundation which contributed to the lower level of inefficiency. In Table 8.3, we noted that most of the states in which the minimum wages are fixed for ready-made garments are high per capita income states. Exceptions are Jammu and Kashmir, Orissa and Uttar Pradesh, among which only Uttar Pradesh has a certain presence of ready-made industry, as shown in Table 8.1. So, the natural doubt is whether the minimum wage dummy might have acted as a proxy for the advanced state dummy. In an advanced state, inefficiency could be lower not because of the minimum wage but because the infrastructure and other business climate features are better than those in other states. This point is taken care of in Section 8.3.4.3 below.

The other possibility we ought to examine is the effects of differences in factor prices. When we look at Table 8.8, which was calculated from Table 8.1, we find three groups of states classified according to characteristics. One group is states with a high value of plant and machinery per employee, such as Gujarat, Himachal

Table 8.7 Primary results of estimation

		Equation (8.1)	*Under null (a)*
β_0	constant	0.803	0.171
		(3.832)	(3.568)
β_1	$\ln K_{it}$	0.349	0.248
		(4.294)	(3.173)
β_2	$\ln L_{it}$	0.891	0.999
		(7.233)	(8.378)
β_3	$\ln M_{it}$	0.184	0.054
		(0.178)	(0.552)
β_4	$(\ln K_{it})^2$	0.001	−0.002
		(0.165)	(−0.441)
β_5	$(\ln L_{it})^2$	0.012	0.012
		(2.923)	(1.752)
β_6	$(\ln M_{it})^2$	0.056	0.053
		(12.233)	(12.169)
β_7	$2 \cdot \ln K_{it} \cdot \ln L_{it}$	0.001	0.003
		(0.258)	(0.702)
β_8	$2 \cdot \ln L_{it} \cdot \ln M_{it}$	−0.038	−0.038
		(−9.204)	(−9.144)
β_9	$2 \cdot \ln K_{it} \cdot \ln M_{it}$	−0.009	−0.006
		(−2.747)	(−1.892)
β_{10}	$\ln K_{it} \cdot t$	0.388	–
		(−4.154)	–
β_{11}	$\ln L_{it} \cdot t$	0.036	–
		(3.740)	–
β_{12}	$\ln M_{it} \cdot t$	−0.009	–
		(−1.664)	–
β_{13}	t	0.012	−0.133
		(1.582)	(−2.771)
β_{14}	t^2	0.016	0.031
		(2.486)	(3.360)
δ_0	constant	0.226	0.188
		(6.365)	(6.602)
δ_1	loan dummy$_{it}$	−0.027	0.014
		(−0.967)	(0.622)
δ_2	rural dummy$_{it}$	0.125	0.121
		(1.974)	(2.306)
δ_3	backward area dummy$_{it}$	0.182	0.163
		(2.756)	(3.094)
δ_4	captive power dummy$_{it}$	−0.056	−0.072
		(−1.591)	(−4.413)
δ_5	import input dummy$_{it}$	0.042	0.038
		(0.904)	(0.896)
δ_6	ln (No. in employment$_{it}$)	0.057	0.002
		(2.518)	(0.405)
δ_7	minimum wage dummy$_{it}$	−0.187	−0.147
		(−4.733)	(−6.946)
log likelihood function		−804.480	−806.756

Notes: 1. Figures in parentheses are *t*-ratios.
2. Shaded coefficient for Equation (8.1) is significant at 5% level.
Source: Author's estimation.

Table 8.8 Characteristics of the garment industry in major states in the fiscal year 1998

	All India	*AP*	*GR*	*HR*	*HP*	*KN*	*KL*	*MP*	*MH*	*OR*	*PJ*	*RJ*	*TN*	*UP*	*WB*	*DL*
Fixed capital per no. of factories	64.66	22.95	94.21	300.67	31.50	68.98	62.43	224.75	24.78	21.00	144.07	95.66	53.04	94.23	28.25	76.48
Gross value of plant and machinery per no. employed	0.35	0.16	0.89	1.27	1.06	0.23	0.41	0.76	0.46	0.67	0.02	1.25	0.19	0.85	0.85	0.49
Total output per no. employed	4.74	1.41	7.73	6.87	2.91	2.82	1.58	0.80	8.90	9.62	3.79	7.52	2.93	8.37	19.50	12.93
No. employed per factory	89.09	98.88	81.23	115.38	21.50	198.30	84.47	101.75	19.53	40.50	273.47	37.48	109.91	63.00	23.00	48.75
Employed through contractors per no. employed	0.04	0.06	0.19	0.01	0.00	0.00	0.00	0.30	0.01	0.00	0.89	0.28	0.03	0.11	0.13	0.00
Wages and salaries including bonus per no. employed	0.30	0.16	0.34	0.42	0.21	0.25	0.24	0.27	0.48	0.20	0.33	0.48	0.21	0.46	0.44	0.52

Note: Calculated from Table 8.1.

Source: Compiled from Central Statistical Organization, Ministry of Planning and Programme Implementation, Government of India (1995), *Annual Survey of Industries 1998–99*.

Pradesh, Haryana, Rajasthan, Uttar Pradesh and West Bengal. Among these, wages are lower in Gujarat and Himachal Pradesh than in the rest of the group. Another group is states with a very low value of plant and machinery per employee and very low average wages, such as Andhra Pradesh, Karnataka, Tamil Nadu and Punjab. Very low average wages might well be caused by contract workers in Punjab and by women workers in the rest of the states in this category. The other group is states with a medium level of value of plant and machinery per employee, such as Kerala, Madhya Pradesh, Orissa, Maharashtra and Delhi. Among these, Maharashtra and Delhi are distinguished by higher than average wage levels.

These differences simply indicate that the relative prices of labour and capital, and hence the technology to combine labour and capital, may well differ among groups of states, further among individual states and possibly among firms. Thus, what we need to examine further to accommodate relative price differences is the degree of TE and AE using capital and labour price information for each firm, and whether the minimum wage has any impact on the level of those efficiencies. This examination is conducted in Section 8.3.5 using DEA.

8.3.4.3 Accommodating time-invariant differences between the states

Here we try to accommodate the first possibility mentioned above by separating the effects of the minimum wage dummy from the effects of advanced states. One of the ways is to create an advanced states' dummy and add a cross variable of such a dummy and a minimum wage dummy. We created advanced and backward state dummies according to per capita state income in fiscal 1997, and added (minimum wage dummy$_{it}$) $*$ (advanced states dummy$_{it}$), (minimum wage dummy$_{it}$) $*$ (backward states dummy$_{it}$) as variables to explain the level of inefficiency. States and union territories with per capita income above Rs.15,000 are classified as advanced states, and those below Rs.10,000 are classified as backward states.[17]

Table 8.9 shows the result of the estimation with the additional four variables of (minimum wage dummy$_{it}$) $*$ (advanced states dummy$_{it}$), (minimum wage dummy$_{it}$) $*$ (backward states dummy$_{it}$), advanced states dummy and backward states dummy. Here, the minimum wage dummy has lost its explanatory power. Advanced state-related variables, although presumed to be significant, do not appear to have any effects on the level of inefficiency of production.

8.3.5 Data envelopment analysis (DEA)[18]

8.3.5.1 The level of efficiencies

As was discussed in Section 8.3.2, efficiency of firms consists of two components: TE, which reflects the ability of a firm to obtain maximal output from a given set of inputs, and AE, which reflects the ability of a firm to use the inputs in optimal proportions given their respective prices and the production technology. Here, by utilizing price variables, we try to disaggregate these two efficiencies by DEA. DEA involves the use of linear programming methods to construct a non-parametric piece-wise surface over the data. Efficiency measures are then calculated relative to this surface. DEA has an advantage in that it does not have to assume any

Table 8.9 Results of estimation accommodating state effects

		Equation (8.1)	*Under null (a)*
β_0	constant	0.704	0.263
		(3.412)	(4.697)
β_1	$\ln K_{it}$	0.326	0.254
		(4.022)	(3.216)
β_2	$\ln L_{it}$	1.002	0.967
		(8.411)	(8.189)
β_3	$\ln M_{it}$	−0.070	3.593
		(−0.712)	(0.357)
β_4	$(\ln K_{it})^2$	0.001	−0.005
		(0.410)	(−1.592)
β_5	$(\ln L_{it})^2$	0.010	0.009
		(1.476)	(1.340)
β_6	$(\ln M_{it})^2$	0.056	0.053
		(12.635)	(12.465)
β_7	$2 \cdot \ln K_{it} \cdot \ln L_{it}$	0.001	0.007
		(0.146)	(1.634)
β_8	$2 \cdot \ln L_{it} \cdot \ln M_{it}$	−0.035	−0.038
		(−8.645)	(−9.253)
β_9	$2 \cdot \ln K_{it} \cdot \ln M_{it}$	−0.009	−0.006
		(−2.654)	(−1.769)
β_{10}	$\ln K_{it} \cdot t$	−0.324	–
		(−3.517)	–
β_{11}	$\ln L_{it} \cdot t$	0.030	–
		(3.228)	–
β_{12}	$\ln M_{it} \cdot t$	−0.009	–
		(−1.657)	–
β_{13}	t	0.009	−0.121
		(1.257)	(−2.470)
β_{14}	t^2	0.014	0.029
		(2.298)	(3.025)
δ_0	constant	0.306	0.349
		(6.510)	(9.893)
δ_1	loan dummy$_{it}$	−0.003	0.033
		(−0.074)	(1.414)
δ_2	rural dummy$_{it}$	0.089	0.098
		(1.558)	(1.619)
δ_3	backward area dummy$_{it}$	0.226	0.199
		(4.227)	(3.620)
δ_4	captive power dummy$_{it}$	−0.140	−0.123
		(−4.283)	(−4.550)
δ_5	import input dummy$_{it}$	0.038	0.015
		(0.793)	(0.899)
δ_6	ln (no. in employment$_{it}$)	−0.001	−0.012
		(−0.080)	(−0.832)

(Continued)

Table 8.9 (Continued)

		Equation (8.1)	*Under null (a)*
δ_7	minimum wage dummy$_{it}$	0.145	0.284
		(0.229)	(0.448)
δ_8	(minimum wage dummy$_{it}$) (advanced states dummy$_{it}$)	−0.205	−0.250
		(−0.264)	(−0.322)
δ_9	(minimum wage dummy$_{it}$) (backward states dummy$_{it}$)	0.350	0.534
		(0.553)	(0.843)
δ_{10}	advanced states dummy$_{it}$	−0.205	−0.250
		(−0.264)	(−0.322)
δ_{11}	backward states dummy$_{it}$	−0.568	−0.933
		(−2.199)	(−13.013)
log likelihood function		−7790.086	−782.320

Notes: 1. Figures in parentheses are *t*-ratios.
2. Shaded coefficient for Equation (8.1) is significant at 5% level.
Source: Author's estimation.

production function and it is easy to disaggregate the overall efficiency into two kinds of efficiencies, TE and AE.

The difficult part of this analysis is obtaining price information for labour and capital. How we constructed interest rate (intrate) and wage per day (wage rate) are described in Appendix 8.2, and variables including these two are summarized in Table 8.10. Since we had to drop observations for which price variables cannot be calculated, the number of observations is decreased from when we conducted SFA analysis. What is noticeable in Table 8.10 is, compared to real gross output and real capital invested, interest rate and wage rate vary far less among firms. Firms face a surprisingly narrow range of interest rates and wage rates.

The results of various efficiencies estimated are listed in Table 8.11. CE is cost efficiency, and it consists of TE and AE, which is equivalent to efficiency estimated by SFA. Compared to the level of efficiency estimated by SFA, CE is very low. It is so low that it is difficult to explain. One of the reasons could be the large stochastic part of inefficiency, which is not included in inefficiency estimated by SFA but which is included in inefficiency estimated by DEA. Among results from DEA, TE is very low and AE is rather moderate. This indicates the tendency for firms to adjust to the relative prices of wage and interest rate rather well, leaving little room to adjust the proportion of labour and capital input. SE is scale efficiency which is calculated by TEs under the null of constant returns to scale and variable returns to scale. Larger SE means less room to increase efficiency by adjusting scales of production.

8.3.5.2 *Explaining TE and AE*

The last part of our empirical attempt is to investigate whether the minimum wage regulation has an impact on estimated TE and AE. Table 8.12 shows how the levels of TE and AE are explained by factors including the minimum wage dummy. The

Table 8.10 Summary of variables in DEA estimation

Real gross output				
Percentiles	Smallest			
1%	1,046,406	114,937.2		
5%	3,299,074	127,020.1		
10%	5,552,809	135,571.9	Obs	1688
25%	1.29E+07	188,263	Sum of Wgt.	1688
50%	3.38E+07		Mean	7.03E+07
	Largest		Std. Dev.	1.19E+08
75%	7.87E+07	8.74E+08		
90%	1.58E+08	1.37E+09	Variance	1.42E+16
95%	2.68E+08	1.48E+09	Skewness	6.342938
99%	5.28E+08	2.02E+09	Kurtosis	72.1076
Real capital invested				
Percentiles	Smallest			
1%	35,655	2268.944		
5%	183,710.2	2773		
10%	404,284.2	4824.426	Obs	1688
25%	1,358,996	10341.49	Sum of Wgt.	1688
50%	3,763,602		Mean	9,606,083
	Largest		Std. Dev.	2.62E+07
75%	9,267,573	1.76E+08		
90%	2.10E+07	4.06E+08	Variance	6.86E+14
95%	3.76E+07	5.31E+08	Skewness	14.28631
99%	8.41E+07	6.00E+08	Kurtosis	280.482
Man-days employed				
Percentiles	Smallest			
1%	1,686	224		
5%	4,242	228		
10%	7,307	660	Obs	1688
25%	16,882	869	Sum of Wgt.	1688
50%	37,862.5		Mean	58,675.64
	Largest		Std. Dev.	66,678.05
75%	74,636	495,316		
90%	132,498	512,900	Variance	4.45E+09
95%	181,106	521,469	Skewness	2.889809
99%	345,645	571,978	Kurtosis	15.03588

(Continued)

Table 8.10 (Continued)

Interest rate				
Percentiles	Smallest			
1%	0.0005532	1.17E-06		
5%	0.0038683	0.0000173		
10%	0.0094121	0.0000258	Obs	1688
25%	0.0307406	0.0000714	Sum of Wgt.	1688
50%	0.0660513		Mean	0.147201
	Largest		Std. Dev.	2.332467
75%	0.1095856	2.067629		
90%	0.1613735	2.367621	Variance	5.440401
95%	0.216016	3.722548	Skewness	40.74102
99%	0.5446243	95.67747	Kurtosis	1668.959

Wage rate				
Percentiles	Smallest			
1%	24.25953	15.15954		
5%	35.01373	16.11914		
10%	43.09439	17.16519	Obs	1688
25%	58.59753	17.44551	Sum of Wgt.	1688
50%	83.70282		Mean	104.9045
	Largest		Std. Dev.	281.2659
75%	119.1721	413.2551		
90%	163.6904	444.5654	Variance	79,110.51
95%	195.2994	6394.554	Skewness	29.01795
99%	290.0777	9539.656	Kurtosis	899.2454

Source: Author's calculation.

Table 8.11 Estimated efficiencies

Fiscal year		*1993*	*1994*	*1995*	*1996*
SFA	Equation (8.1)	0.916	0.907	0.874	0.885
	Equation (8.1) under null (a)	0.920	0.919	0.898	0.916
DEA	TE-CRS	0.082	0.156	0.167	0.059
	TE-VRS	0.122	0.203	0.223	0.117
	AE	0.607	0.757	0.726	0.795
	CE	0.073	0.156	0.169	0.088
	SE	0.672	0.768	0.749	0.504

Notes: 1. TE-CRS is technical efficiency under constant return to scale.
2. TE-VRS is technical efficiency under varying return to scale.
3. AE is allocative efficiency.
4. CE is cost efficiency.
5. SE is scale efficiency.
Source: Author's estimation.

Table 8.12 Effect of minimum wage on efficiency estimated from DEA

(a) Effect on technical efficiency							*(b) Effect on allocative efficiency*						
TE in 1993							*AE in 1993*						
				Number of obs =	*567*							*Number of obs =*	*567*
				Prob > F =	*0.0001*							*Prob > F =*	*0.0023*
				R-squared =	*0.0518*							*R-squared =*	*0.0399*
				Adj R-squared =	*0.0399*							*Adj R-squared =*	*0.0268*
te93	*Coef.*	*Std. Err.*	*t*	*P > t*	*[95% Conf. Interval]*		*ae93*	*Coef.*	*Std. Err.*	*t*	*P > t*	*[95% Conf. Interval]*	
minwage_{it}	0.0439337	0.0159974	2.75	0.006	0.0125112	0.0753561	minwage_{it}	0.0041307	0.0275391	0.15	0.881	−0.049962	0.0582234
rural_{it}	−0.0478562	0.0404598	−1.18	0.237	−0.127328	0.0316156	rural_{it}	0.1056126	0.0696502	1.52	0.13	−0.0311956	0.2424207
metro_{it}	−0.0062755	0.0162256	−0.39	0.699	−0.0381461	0.0255951	metro_{it}	−0.010352	0.0279318	−0.37	0.711	−0.0652161	0.0445122
back_{it}	−0.0560526	0.0373562	−1.5	0.134	−0.1294283	0.0173231	back_{it}	0.0098355	0.0643075	0.15	0.878	−0.1164784	0.1361494
elec_{it}	−0.0235587	0.0138043	−1.71	0.088	−0.0506734	0.0035559	elec_{it}	0.0882753	0.0237637	3.71	0	0.0415983	0.1349523
impint_{it}	−0.0041428	0.026639	−0.16	0.876	−0.0564675	0.048182	impint_{it}	0.0930208	0.0458581	2.03	0.043	0.0029455	0.1830961
init_{it}	0.0964732	0.0270665	3.56	0	0.0433087	0.1496377	init_{it}	−0.0023434	0.0465941	−0.05	0.96	−0.0938643	0.0891776
cons	0.1074738	0.015543	6.91	0	0.076944	0.1380037	cons	0.5553069	0.0267568	20.75	0	0.5027508	0.607863
TE in 1994							*AE in 1994*						
				Number of obs =	*278*							*Number of obs =*	*278*
				Prob > F =	*0.0003*							*Prob > F =*	*0.211*
				R-squared =	*0.0943*							*R-squared =*	*0.0347*
				Adj R-squared =	*0.0709*							*Adj R-squared =*	*0.0097*
te94	*Coef.*	*Std. Err.*	*t*	*P > t*	*[95% Conf. Interval]*		*ae94*	*Coef.*	*Std. Err.*	*t*	*P > t*	*[95% Conf. Interval]*	
minwage_{it}	0.1145737	0.0277215	4.13	0	0.0599959	0.1691514	minwage_{it}	0.0747594	0.0279941	2.67	0.008	0.0196449	0.129874
rural_{it}	−0.0542692	0.074996	−0.72	0.47	−0.2019204	0.093382	rural_{it}	−0.0133982	0.0757335	−0.18	0.86	−0.1625014	0.1357051
metro_{it}	0.0006062	0.0285026	0.02	0.983	−0.0555094	0.0567219	metro_{it}	−0.0673745	0.0287829	−2.34	0.02	−0.1240421	−0.010707

$back_{it}$	−0.054745	0.071325	−0.77	0.443	−0.1951688	0.0856789	$back_{it}$	−0.0046227	0.0720264	−0.06	0.949	−0.1464275	0.137182
$elec_{it}$	−0.0295907	0.0262227	−1.13	0.26	−0.0812176	0.0220363	$elec_{it}$	0.0018983	0.0264806	0.07	0.943	−0.0502364	0.054033
$impint_{it}$	−0.079321	0.0460588	−1.72	0.086	−0.170001	0.011359	$impint_{it}$	−0.0486545	0.0465117	−1.05	0.296	−0.1402262	0.0429173
$init_{it}$	−0.0101096	0.0345534	−0.29	0.77	−0.0781379	0.0579187	$init_{it}$	0.0004604	0.0348932	0.01	0.989	−0.0682369	0.0691578
cons	0.1694214	0.0285068	5.94	0	0.1132975	0.2255453	cons	0.7488956	0.0287872	26.01	0	0.6922197	0.8055714

TE in 1995							*AE in 1995*						
				Number of obs =	*237*						*Number of obs =*	*237*	
				Prob > F =	*0*						*Prob > F =*	*0.0101*	
				R-squared =	*0.2422*						*R-squared =*	*0.0767*	
				Adj R-squared =	*0.219*						*Adj R-squared =*	*0.0484*	
te95	*Coef.*	*Std. Err.*	*t*	*P > t*	*[95% Conf. Interval]*		*ae95*	*Coef.*	*Std. Err.*	*t*	*P > t*	*[95% Conf. Interval]*	
$minwage_{it}$	0.2070427	0.0287777	7.19	0	0.1503398	0.2637456	$minwage_{it}$	0.0854074	0.031198	2.74	0.007	0.0239356	0.1468792
$rural_{it}$	0.0400925	0.0553932	0.72	0.47	−0.069053	0.149238	$rural_{it}$	0.0518159	0.060052	0.86	0.389	−0.0665091	0.1701409
$metro_{it}$	0.0538147	0.0313663	1.72	0.088	−0.0079886	0.1156181	$metro_{it}$	0.0012597	0.0340043	0.04	0.97	−0.0657415	0.068261
$back_{it}$	−0.167981	0.0864801	−1.94	0.053	−0.3383795	0.0024175	$back_{it}$	0.0184298	0.0937534	0.2	0.844	−0.1662998	0.2031594
$elec_{it}$	−0.0590056	0.0297602	−1.98	0.049	−0.1176445	−0.0003668	$elec_{it}$	0.0376809	0.0322631	1.17	0.244	−0.0258896	0.1012514
$impint_{it}$	0.0063049	0.0420316	0.15	0.881	−0.0765133	0.0891231	$impint_{it}$	0.058157	0.0455666	1.28	0.203	−0.0316265	0.1479405
$init_{it}$	−0.0300973	0.0302459	−1	0.321	−0.0896932	0.0294986	$init_{it}$	0.0739708	0.0327897	2.26	0.025	0.0093627	0.1385789
cons	0.1697818	0.0317604	5.35	0	0.1072018	0.2323618	cons	0.6298106	0.0344316	18.29	0	0.5619675	0.6976538

(Continued)

Table 8.12 (Continued)

TE in 1996							*AE in 1996*						
				Number of obs =	*606*							*Number of obs =*	*606*
				Prob > F =	*0*							*Prob > F =*	*0*
				R-squared =	*0.1439*							*R-squared =*	*0.1051*
				Adj R-squared =	*0.1339*							*Adj R-squared =*	*0.0949*
te96	*Coef.*	*Std. Err.*	*t*	*P > t*	*[95% Conf. Interval]*		*ae96*	*Coef.*	*Std. Err.*	*t*	*P > t*	*[95% Conf. Interval]*	
$minwage_{it}$	0.0873217	0.0125013	6.99	0	0.0627699	0.1118734	$minwage_{it}$	0.1039162	0.0172607	6.02	0	0.0700172	0.1378152
$rural_{it}$	−0.0382015	0.0268667	−1.42	0.156	−0.0909662	0.0145631	$rural_{it}$	−0.0092239	0.0370953	−0.25	0.804	−0.0820769	0.0636291
$metro_{it}$	0.0103171	0.0133845	0.77	0.441	−0.0159692	0.0366034	$metro_{it}$	−0.0145343	0.0184801	−0.79	0.432	−0.0508281	0.0217596
$back_{it}$	0.0838902	0.0419881	2	0.046	0.0014282	0.1663523	$back_{it}$	−0.0790975	0.0579736	−1.36	0.173	−0.1929541	0.0347591
$elec_{it}$	−0.0445956	0.0119888	−3.72	0	−0.0681408	−0.0210504	$elec_{it}$	0.0586197	0.0165531	3.54	0	0.0261105	0.0911289
$impint_{it}$	−0.0346357	0.0217607	−1.59	0.112	−0.0773724	0.008101	$impint_{it}$	0.0847343	0.0300454	2.82	0.005	0.025727	0.1437415
$init_{it}$	−0.002143	0.0122662	−0.17	0.861	−0.0262329	0.021947	$init_{it}$	0.0585661	0.0169361	3.46	0.001	0.0253047	0.0918275
cons	0.0989387	0.0143581	6.89	0	0.0707402	0.1271372	cons	0.6818251	0.0198245	34.39	0	0.6428909	0.7207592

Notes: 1. Shaded coefficient is significant at 5% level.
2. Year is in fiscal year.
Source: Author's estimation.

coefficients of minimum wage dummy are significant and positive for explaining TE throughout the period and AE from fiscal 1994 to 1996. This means that the minimum wage improves the level of efficiency, except AE in fiscal 1993.

However, the minimum wage regulation might not be binding for firms paying higher wages even in states and union territories where the minimum wage is fixed, and for firms paying lower wages, the minimum wage regulation might decrease the level of efficiency. To check this possibility, we added (wage rate_{it}) and (wage rate_{it}) $*$ (minimum wage dummy_{it}) as explanatory variables. If the positive effect of the minimum wage dummy on the level of efficiency is brought mainly from high wage-paying firms for which the minimum wage regulation is not binding, and if low wage-paying firms' practice is distorted by the regulation, the coefficient of (day wage_{it}) $*$ (minimum wage dummy_{it}) would be positive and minimum wage dummy would be either non-significant or negative.

The results are shown in Table 8.13. The minimum wage dummy still has a positive impact on TE, the sign of coefficient is positive all through the estimated period and significant except in fiscal 1993, indicating that firms under the regulation are still more efficient. The sign of coefficient for wage $\text{rate}_{it} * \text{min}_{it}$, which is (wage rate_{it}) $*$ (minimum wage dummy_{it}), is negative from 1994 to 1996 and significant in 1996. This means that firms for which the minimum wage regulation is most likely to be binding are more efficient in production. For AE, the minimum wage dummy has lost explanatory power, and we may note that AE does not deteriorate because of the regulation.

8.4 Summary and conclusions

In India, even after policy reforms were accelerated from 1991, there was no significant deregulation in the labour market. Moreover, the labour market regulations are frequently cited as an explanation of India's poor growth performance. Since Besley and Burgess (2004), which focused on the Industrial Disputes Act of 1947, several papers have come to conclusions along the same lines, claiming that state-level labour regulations are also an important determinant of industrial performance, and that states which have enacted more pro-worker regulations have lost out on industrial production in general.

There are also cautious views on this body of work, and we are also sceptical of their rather simple argument regarding the negative consequences of the labour regulations on economic performance and feel that the robustness of such claims has to be checked in various ways and in various areas of labour regulations. The motivation of this chapter was to examine the impact of the minimum wage regulations, which is another important area of labour regulations in which state governments are entitled to exert influence, and to try to disprove the above claims. We chose the ready-made garment industry as a case to examine because firms there have been exposed to more domestic as well as international competition recently and efficiency matters more in this sector than ever.

Although the conventional literature on the minimum wage regulations argues more concerning the impact on employment, we focused on the efficiency of production at the firm level because (a) a sustainable increase in employment would

Table 8.13 Effect of minimum wage and wage level on efficiency estimated from DEA

(a) Effect on technical efficiency

TE in 1993

Number of obs = 567; *Prob > F* = 0; *R-squared* = 0.1105; *Adj R-squared* = 0.0961

te93	*Coef.*	*Std. Err.*	*t*	*P > t*	*[95% Conf. Interval]*	
wage rate$_{it}$ * min$_{it}$	0.0000448	0.000238	0.19	0.851	−0.00042	0.000513
wage rate$_{it}$	0.0001006	1.67E−05	6.04	0	6.79E−05	0.000133
minwage$_{it}$	0.0437621	0.026138	1.67	0.095	−0.00758	0.095103
rural$_{it}$	−0.047337	0.039385	−1.2	0.23	−0.1247	0.030024
metro$_{it}$	−0.0135051	0.015939	−0.85	0.397	−0.04481	0.017803
back$_{it}$	−0.0566498	0.036951	−1.53	0.126	−0.12923	0.015931
elec$_{it}$	−0.0273209	0.013411	−2.04	0.042	−0.05366	−0.00098
impint$_{it}$	−0.0029164	0.02586	−0.11	0.91	−0.05371	0.047878
init$_{it}$	0.0985223	0.02633	3.74	0	0.046805	0.15024
cons	0.1013714	0.015139	6.7	0	0.071634	0.131109

TE in 1994

Number of obs = 278; *Prob > F* = 0.0001; *R-squared* = 0.1145; *Adj R-squared* = 0.0848

te94	*Coef.*	*Std. Err.*	*t*	*P > t*	*[95% Conf. Interval]*	
wage rate$_{it}$ * min$_{it}$	−0.0016232	0.001048	−1.55	0.122	−0.00369	0.000439
wage rate$_{it}$	0.0020297	0.000884	2.3	0.022	0.000289	0.003771
minwage$_{it}$	0.1960586	0.07521	2.61	0.01	0.047981	0.344136

(b) Effect on allocative efficiency

AE in 1993

Number of obs = 567; *Prob > F* = 0.0028; *R-squared* = 0.0439; *Adj R-squared* = 0.0285

ae93	*Coef.*	*Std. Err.*	*t*	*P > t*	*[95% Conf. Interval]*	
wage rate$_{it}$ * min$_{it}$	0.000444	0.000423	1.05	0.294	−0.00039	0.001274
wage rate$_{it}$	3.86E−05	2.95E−05	1.31	0.192	−1.9E−05	9.66E−05
minwage$_{it}$	−0.03347	0.046333	−0.72	0.47	−0.12448	0.057539
rural$_{it}$	0.100177	0.069815	1.43	0.152	−0.03696	0.23731
metro$_{it}$	−0.01722	0.028254	−0.61	0.543	−0.07271	0.038281
back$_{it}$	0.022412	0.065501	0.34	0.732	−0.10625	0.151071
elec$_{it}$	0.086235	0.023773	3.63	0	0.039539	0.132932
impint$_{it}$	0.092136	0.04584	2.01	0.045	0.002095	0.182176
init$_{it}$	0.001802	0.046673	0.04	0.969	−0.08987	0.093478
cons	0.554345	0.026836	20.66	0	0.501632	0.607058

AE in 1994

Number of obs = 278; *Prob > F* = 0.0609; *R-squared* = 0.0583; *Adj R-squared* = 0.0267

ae94	*Coef.*	*Std. Err.*	*t*	*P > t*	*[95% Conf. Interval]*	
wage rate$_{it}$ * min$_{it}$	0.002005	0.001057	1.9	0.059	−7.5E−05	0.004086
wage rate$_{it}$	−0.00225	0.000892	−2.52	0.012	−0.004	−0.00049
minwage$_{it}$	−0.03372	0.075867	−0.44	0.657	−0.18309	0.115649

$rural_{it}$	−0.0461776	0.074504	−0.62	0.536	−0.19286	0.10051	$rural_{it}$	−0.02186	0.075154	−0.29	0.771	−0.16983	0.12611
$metro_{it}$	0.0048937	0.029371	0.17	0.868	−0.05293	0.06272	$metro_{it}$	−0.07476	0.029627	−2.52	0.012	−0.13309	−0.01643
$back_{it}$	−0.0686924	0.071841	−0.96	0.34	−0.21014	0.072753	$back_{it}$	0.014061	0.072468	0.19	0.846	−0.12862	0.156741
$elec_{it}$	−0.0317159	0.026108	−1.21	0.226	−0.08312	0.019687	$elec_{it}$	0.003413	0.026336	0.13	0.897	−0.04844	0.055264
$impint_{it}$	−0.081181	0.04591	−1.77	0.078	−0.17157	0.00921	$impint_{it}$	−0.04829	0.046311	−1.04	0.298	−0.13947	0.042894
$init_{it}$	−0.0116855	0.034326	−0.34	0.734	−0.07927	0.055897	$init_{it}$	0.002617	0.034626	0.08	0.94	−0.06556	0.07079
cons	0.0496948	0.060317	0.82	0.411	−0.06906	0.16845	cons	0.882496	0.060843	14.5	0	0.762704	1.002287

TE in 1995							*AE in 1995*						
			Number of obs =		237						*Number of obs =*	237	
			Prob > F =		0						*Prob > F =*	0.0185	
			R-squared =		0.2832						*R-squared =*	0.0827	
			Adj R-squared =		0.2547						*Adj R-squared =*	0.0484	
te95	*Coef.*	*Std. Err.*	*t*	*P > t*	*[95% Conf. Interval]*		*ae95*	*Coef.*	*Std. Err.*	*t*	*P > t*	*[95% Conf. Interval]*	
$wage\ rate_{it} * min_{it}$	−0.0005732	0.000603	−0.95	0.343	−0.00176	0.000615	$wage\ rate_{it} * min_{it}$	0.000649	0.00067	0.97	0.334	−0.00067	0.00197
$wage\ rate_{it}$	0.0006851	0.000602	1.14	0.256	−0.0005	0.001871	$wage\ rate_{it}$	−0.00067	0.000669	−1.01	0.314	−0.00199	0.000643
$minwage_{it}$	0.2374804	0.051795	4.58	0	0.135419	0.339542	$minwage_{it}$	0.041291	0.057544	0.72	0.474	−0.0721	0.15468
$rural_{it}$	0.0376696	0.054186	0.7	0.488	−0.0691	0.144441	$rural_{it}$	0.054812	0.0602	0.91	0.364	−0.06381	0.173434
$metro_{it}$	0.0454186	0.030962	1.47	0.144	−0.01559	0.106428	$metro_{it}$	0.000701	0.034398	0.02	0.984	−0.06708	0.068482
$back_{it}$	−0.1601221	0.084852	−1.89	0.06	−0.32732	0.007077	$back_{it}$	0.00979	0.09427	0.1	0.917	−0.17597	0.195547
$elec_{it}$	−0.0679482	0.029228	−2.32	0.021	−0.12554	−0.01036	$elec_{it}$	0.0418	0.032472	1.29	0.199	−0.02219	0.105785
$impint_{it}$	0.0074479	0.041061	0.18	0.856	−0.07346	0.088357	$impint_{it}$	0.058011	0.045618	1.27	0.205	−0.03188	0.1479
$init_{it}$	−0.0359148	0.030013	−1.2	0.233	−0.09505	0.023225	$init_{it}$	0.071626	0.033344	2.15	0.033	0.005923	0.13733
cons	0.1291653	0.054277	2.38	0.018	0.022214	0.236117	cons	0.677346	0.060302	11.23	0	0.558524	0.796169

(Continued)

Table 8.13 (Continued)

TE in 1996							*AE in 1996*						
				Number of obs =	*606*							*Number of obs =*	*606*
				Prob > F =	*0*							*Prob > F =*	*0*
				R-squared =	*0.1576*							*R-squared =*	*0.1067*
				Adj R-squared =	*0.1449*							*Adj R-squared =*	*0.0932*
te96	*Coef.*	*Std. Err.*	*t*	*P > t*	*[95% Conf. Interval]*		*ae96*	*Coef.*	*Std. Err.*	*t*	*P > t*	*[95% Conf. Interval]*	
wage $rate_{it} * min_{it}$	−0.0007201	0.000301	−2.39	0.017	−0.00131	−0.00013	wage $rate_{it} * min_{it}$	4.76E−05	0.000419	0.11	0.91	−0.00078	0.000871
wage $rate_{it}$	0.0003528	0.000273	1.29	0.196	−0.00018	0.000888	wage $rate_{it}$	0.00013	0.000379	0.34	0.732	−0.00061	0.000874
$minwage_{it}$	0.169373	0.031112	5.44	0	0.108271	0.230476	$minwage_{it}$	0.08742	0.043266	2.02	0.044	0.002447	0.172393
$rural_{it}$	−0.0367051	0.026711	−1.37	0.17	−0.08917	0.015755	$rural_{it}$	−0.01053	0.037147	−0.28	0.777	−0.08348	0.062426
$metro_{it}$	0.0194042	0.013615	1.43	0.155	−0.00733	0.046143	$metro_{it}$	−0.01764	0.018934	−0.93	0.352	−0.05482	0.019549
$back_{it}$	0.0728755	0.041908	1.74	0.083	−0.00943	0.15518	$back_{it}$	−0.0772	0.058279	−1.32	0.186	−0.19166	0.037258
$elec_{it}$	−0.0410559	0.012146	−3.38	0.001	−0.06491	−0.0172	$elec_{it}$	0.055351	0.016891	3.28	0.001	0.022179	0.088524
$impint_{it}$	−0.0339187	0.021885	−1.55	0.122	−0.0769	0.009062	$impint_{it}$	0.081114	0.030435	2.67	0.008	0.021342	0.140887
$init_{it}$	−0.0025576	0.012224	−0.21	0.834	−0.02657	0.02145	$init_{it}$	0.05964	0.017	3.51	0	0.026253	0.093027
cons	0.066322	0.02545	2.61	0.009	0.01634	0.116304	cons	0.674446	0.035392	19.06	0	0.604937	0.743954

Notes: 1. Shaded coefficient is significant at 5% level.
2. Year is in fiscal year.
Source: Author's estimation.

be achieved when firms are efficient in production, and (b) the minimum wage regulation is presumed to affect the level of efficiency of production.

We estimated the level of efficiency both by SFA, a stochastic and parametric method, and DEA, a deterministic and non-parametric method. First, primary results from the SFA approach indicate that the dummy variable for the minimum wage regulation reduces the level of inefficiency. However, when we separated the effects of the minimum wage dummy from time-invariant differences between states, the minimum wage dummy lost its explanatory power.

Second, the results from the DEA approach indicate that (a) the minimum wage regulations enhance the level of efficiency for most of the period estimated, and (b) firms under the minimum wage regulation paying lower wages, in other words firms for which the minimum wage regulation is presumed to be binding, experience a higher level of efficiency, although this claim is not statistically significantly supported, except in fiscal 1993 and 1994.

Based on our empirical exercises, we can safely conclude that there is no evidence to show that the minimum wage regulation decreases the efficiency of production of ready-made garment manufacturers in India. Under the political and social climate in India, deregulating the minimum wage might incur large political as well as social costs. Moreover, our study suggests the possibility of economic gain from the regulation. Unless harm from the regulation is proven to be evident, we have to be cautious of claims regarding the need for deregulation.

Our aim in this chapter was to disprove Besley and Burgess (2004)'s argument regarding the negative consequences of the labour regulations on economic performance. We have not yet examined the background of our empirical results, but would only like to point out two possibilities here. One is that the effectiveness of the minimum wage regulation is limited and hence does not cause a change in relative prices. Restrictiveness of written laws and regulations is one thing and their actual enforcement and effects are another, especially in the context of India. The other possibility is, even if the price of labour becomes higher, the marginal product of labour increases so that it is equal to the shifted relative prices. Our future task is to further investigate these possibilities.

Appendix 8.1 Abbreviation of names of major states and union territories

AP Andhra Pradesh
GR Gujarat
HR Haryana
HP Himachal Pradesh
KN Karnataka
KL Kerala
MP Madhya Pradesh
MH Maharashtra
OR Orissa
PJ Punjab

RJ	Rajasthan
TN	Tamil Nadu
UP	Uttar Pradesh
WB	West Bengal
DL	Delhi

Appendix 8.2 Definition and construction of variables

real gross output (*Q*)

Gross output consists of ex-factory value of output, work done for others, non-industrial services, increase in semi-finished goods, electricity sold and value of own construction.

Gross output is deflated by the wholesale price of manufacturing of textiles not elsewhere classified.

real capital (*K*)

Capital stock is fixed assets at the closing of the year minus capital work in progress. Capital stock is deflated by the deflator of gross fixed capital formation from *National Account Statistics*.

real intermediary input (*M*)

Intermediary input consists of major material consumed and fuel and electricity consumed. Intermediary input is deflated by the wholesale prices of each item.

man-days employed (*L*)

Man-days employed represent the total number of days worked during the accounting year. This includes man-days of workers, managers and other employees.

loan dummy (loan)

loan dummy = 1 if outstanding amount of bank loan is positive.

rural location dummy

rural dummy = 1 if firm is located in rural area.

metro dummy (metro)

metro dummy = 1 if firm is located in metropolitan area.

backward location dummy (back)

backward location dummy = 1 if firm is located in scheduled backward area.

captive power dummy (elec)

captive power dummy = 1 if firm possesses captive power generation.

import input dummy (impint)

import input dummy = 1 if firm utilizes imported materials.

initial year dummy (init)

init = 1 if firm was established more than five years ago.

minimum wage dummy (min wage)

minimum wage dummy = 1 if firm is located in states and union territories where the minimum wage is fixed.

advanced states dummy (advanced states)

advanced states dummy = 1 if firm is located in advanced states. States and union territories classified as advanced states according to this criteria are: Delhi, Goa, Gujarat, Haryana, Maharashtra, Punjab and Chandigarh.

backward states dummy (backward states)

backward states dummy = 1 if firm is located in backward states. States and union territories classified as backward states according to this criteria are: Orissa, Uttar Pradesh, Assam, Bihar, Himachal Pradesh, Jammu and Kashmir, Madhya Pradesh, Manipur, Megaland, Rajasthan, Sikkim, Tripura, West Bengal, Mizoram and Negaland.

interest rate (intrate)

intrate = (interest paid)/(total outstanding of loan).

wage rate

wage rate = (total wage paid)/(man-days employed).

wage rate * min

wage rate * min = (wage rate) * (minimum wage dummy).

Notes

1. Although formal policy reforms are lagging, it must be noted that many observe that their enforcement has been diluted or government has ignored their evasion by employers. Nagaraj (2004) claims this phenomenon is 'reform by stealth'.
2. 'Organized labour' refers to people employed in the public sector, government services, and private sector firms employing more than 10 employees if they utilize electric power and more than 20 employees if they do not utilize electric power.
3. For example, see Besley and Burgess (2004), Stern (2001) and Sachs et al. (1999).
4. Figures concerning the labour force in this paragraph are from the Ministry of Labour and Employment (2004).
5. In India, certain commodities are reserved for the SSI to engage in production. But as mentioned later, there are ways to escape from this regulation for larger firms to enter into production of reserved commodities.
6. Development of the SSI has been an important objective of the Government of India. The growth of SSI is promoted through reservation of items exclusively for SSI, e.g. the number of items was 822 in 1999 and 748 in 2004, and there were various kinds of tax concession and subsidies.

7. In case of other industries, this export obligation had been 75 per cent and was reduced to 50 per cent on 18 December 1997.
8. 'Before and after' methodology is employed by Fallon and Lucas (1993) to examine the impact of the 1976 and 1982/84 amendments of the Industrial Disputes Act of 1947 on employment in manufacturing at the national and industry level.
9. As Bhattacharjea (2006) cited, the *Economic Survey 2005–6* refers to Besley and Burgess (2004), although the name is not explicitly mentioned, in claiming 'Evidence suggests that States, which have enacted more pro-worker regulations, have lost out on industrial production in general' (Ministry of Finance 2006: 209).
10. Such as Hasan et al. (2003), Topalova (2004) and Sanyal and Menon (2005).
11. Scheduled employment is employment in the area which is included in the schedule appended to the Minimum Wages Act, 1948, and those added to the schedule subsequently.
12. Goldar and Banga (2005) is one of the few works that include the minimum wage as one of the explanatory variables for estimation concerning wages. It shows that the employment size under the minimum wage rate has a positive effect on reduction of the gap between the predicted and the actual wage.
13. As for the developing countries, Saget (2001) finds that the minimum wage level has an insignificant impact on the employment level in Latin America.
14. Efficiency is one minus inefficiency and correspondence is one-to-one. Please note that we argue in terms of both efficiency and inefficiency, which are two sides of the same coin.
15. For the details of SFA and DEA, see Coelli et al. (1998).
16. SFA estimation is conducted by using software Frontier Version 4.1 developed by Dr T. J. Coelli.
17. States and union territories classified as advanced states according to this criterion are: Delhi, Goa, Gujarat, Haryana, Maharashtra, Punjab and Chandigarh. States and union territories classified as backward states according to this criterion are: Orissa, Uttar Pradesh, Assam, Bihar, Himachal Pradesh, Jammu and Kashmir, Madhya Pradesh, Manipur, Megaland, Rajasthan, Sikkim, Tripura, West Bengal, Mizoram and Negaland. States and union territories classified as neither advanced nor backward are: Andra Pradesh, Arunachal Pradesh, Karnataka and Tamil Nadu.
18. DEA estimation is conducted by using DEAP software developed by Dr T. J. Coelli.

References

Anant, T. C. A., R. Mohapatra, R. Nagaraj and S. K. Sasikumar (2006) 'Labor Markets in India: Issues and Perspectives'. In J. Felipe and R. Hasan (eds) *Labor Market in Asia: Issues and Perspectives*. Basingstoke: Palgrave Macmillan.

Besley, T. and R. Burgess (2004) 'Can Labor Regulation Hinder Economic Performance? Evidence from India'. *Quarterly Journal of Economics* 119 (1): 91–134.

Bhattacharjea, A. (2006) 'Labour Market Regulation and Industrial Performance in India'. Working Paper no. 141, Centre for Development Economics, Department of Economics, Delhi School of Economics.

Card, D. and A. Krueger (1995) *Myth and Measurement: the New Economics of the Minimum Wage*. Princeton: Princeton University Press.

Central Statistical Organization, Ministry of Planning and Programme Implementation, Government of India (1995) *Annual Survey of Industries 1998–99*.

Coelli, T., P. Rao and G. Battese (1998) *An Introduction to Efficiency and Productivity Analysis*. Norwell: Kluwer Academic Publishers.

Fallon, P. and R.E.B. Lucas (1993) 'Job Security Regulations and the Dynamic Demand for Labor in India and Zimbabwe'. *Journal of Development Economics* 40: 241–75.

Goldar, B. and R. Banga (2005) 'Wage–Productivity Relationship in Organised Manufacturing in India: a State-Wise Analysis'. *The Indian Journal of Labour Economics* 48: 241–75.

Hasan, R., D. Mitra and K. V. Ramaswamy (2003) 'Trade Reforms, Labor Regulations and Labor–Demand Elasticities: Empirical Evidence from India'. Working Paper 9879, National Bureau of Economic Research.

Labour Bureau, Ministry of Labour, Government of India (1997) *Report on the Working of the Minimum Wages Act, 1948 for the Year 1993*. Shimla/Chandigarh: Printing Unit, Labour Bureau Shimla.

—— (1998) *Report on the Working of the Minimum Wages Act, 1948 for the Year 1994*. Shimla/Chandigarh: Printing Unit, Labour Bureau Shimla.

—— (1999) *Report on the Working of the Minimum Wages Act, 1948 for the Year 1995*. Shimla/Chandigarh: Printing Unit, Labour Bureau Shimla.

—— (2000) *Report on the Working of the Minimum Wages Act, 1948 for the Year 1996*. Shimla/Chandigarh: Printing Unit, Labour Bureau Shimla.

Ministry of Finance, Government of India (2006) *Economic Survey 2005–06*.

Ministry of Labour and Employment, Government of India (2004) *Indian Labour Year Book 2004*. Shimla/Chandigarh: Printing Unit, Labour Bureau Shimla.

Nagaraj, R. (2004) 'Fall in Manufacturing Employment: a Brief Note'. *Economic and Political Weekly* 39 (24–30 July): 3387–90.

Niimi, K. (1999) 'Financial Liberalization and Efficiency in the Banking Industry' (in Japanese). PhD dissertation presented to Yokohama National University.

Patibandla, M. (2006) *Evolution of Markets and Institutions: a Study of an Emerging Economy*. Abingdon: Routledge.

Sachs, J.D., A. Varshney and N. Bajpai (eds) (1999) *India in the Era of Reforms*. Delhi: Oxford University Press.

Saget, C. (2001) 'Poverty Reduction and Decent Work in Developing Countries: Do Minimum Wages Help?' *International Labour Review* 140(3): 237–69.

Sanyal, P. and N. Menon (2005) 'Labor Disputes and the Economics of Firm Geography: a Study of Domestic Investment in India'. *Economic Development and Cultural Change* 53: 825–54.

Sharma, A. N. (2006) 'Flexibility, Employment and Labour Market Reforms in India', *Economic and Political Weekly* 41 (27 May): 2078–86.

Shimane, Y. (2005) 'Competitiveness of SSI-Reserved Items: Evidence from Trade Data after Import Liberalization' (in Japanese). In S. Uchikawa (ed.) *Economic Relations Between China and South Asia*. Chiba: Institute of Developing Economies.

Stern, Nicholas (2001) *A Strategy for Development*. Washington, DC: World Bank.

Topalova, P. (2004) 'Trade Liberalization and Firm Productivity: the Case of India'. Working Paper WP/04/28. Washington, DC: International Monetary Fund.

Part IV

Migration, Employment and Well-Being

9

Migration and Well-Being at the Lower Echelons of the Economy: a Study of Delhi Slums

Arup Mitra and Yuko Tsujita

9.1 Introduction

Globalization seems to have ushered in economic growth in areas which are endowed with higher levels of infrastructure and have already experienced higher levels of per capita income and urbanization.[1] This implies rising inequality, which is indeed a matter of serious concern. These interregional development disparities lead to increasing migration, and hence it is important to examine whether such population movement has been beneficial or not.

Other than the migration issue, an important concern, which has been intriguing researchers in a major way, is whether the growth process is able to generate adequate employment opportunities, particularly for the poor, since they largely depend for their livelihood on labour rather than assets. At the aggregate level despite the recent robust economic growth and the accelerated shift of the economy towards services and industry in terms of value added, a large majority of the workforce is still engaged in the informal or unorganized sector with meagre earnings. Only a handful of the workforce is absorbed into globally competitive industries and services. One way of testing the hypothesis more rigorously is to examine the employment and living standards of those who moved from poor areas to one of the most relatively developed regions. Delhi, being the national capital of India, has attracted considerable investment in infrastructure, and after the initiation of economic reforms and the process of globalization, several new activities including business process outsourcing services (BPOs), and firms, both domestic and multinational, offering specialized services, have cropped up in a significant way. It is understandable that labour with poor human capital cannot get absorbed in such activities directly. However, it is still important to assess if the indirect effects of globalization have been beneficial to those who are located at the lower echelons of the socio-economic ladder. It is in this context that the present chapter examines the living standards of those who migrated to Delhi slums in the recent and remote past.

The voluminous literature on rural–urban migration and its causes encompasses a vast spectrum of social, cultural and economic factors. One class of studies that long dominated policy planning in developing economies viewed migration in terms of the increasing pressure of population on farmland. A deficiency of reproducible tangible capital, as seen in the Harris–Todaro (1970) framework, exacerbates the problem of rural unemployment, underemployment and poverty, thus pushing landless labour into cities (see Dasgupta, 1987). Another class of literature has assessed the impact of economic forces on migration in terms of domestic terms of trade squeezing agriculture, diffusion of technology from the developed world, and the flow of foreign capital into the urban infrastructure and into housing, power, transportation and large-scale manufacturing (Becker et al. 1986).

In relation to job market information flow, past studies highlighted the role of informal channels operating though caste–kinship bonds, co-villagers, and other forms of 'social capital' held by low-income households (Banerjee 1986, 1991; Kannapan 1985; Mitra 2003). Stark (1995) showed ways in which the preferences and actions of one family member can impinge upon and modify the choice set, behaviour and well-being of another. On the whole, the issue of upward mobility (Kuznets 1966) and the interplay of various factors that qualify a migrant to experience upward mobility is complex, and rich quantitative information is required to lend support to theoretical underpinnings.

Though the overall rural–urban migration rates have been much lower compared to the historical experience of present-day developed nations, migration from rural areas to million-plus cities in India has been rapid in spite of the lack of an adequate rural–urban continuum perceived in terms of both economic and cultural factors (Sundaram 1989; Mitra 1992; Williamson 1988). This may be due to a concentration of activities in large cities that gives rise to agglomeration economies (see Fujita and Thisse 2003), particularly in manufacturing industry in Asia, where industrial zones together with a combination of infrastructure and institutions play crucial roles in the development of industrial agglomerations (Kuchiki 2005). On the whole, the pull factors in large cities in the face of push factors in rural areas have propelling effects on the rural population. Further, social networks, as mentioned above, help population mobility across space by supplying information to potential rural migrants about job availability at the place of destination. Also, as Fujita and Weber (2004) point out at the international level, a higher degree of labour complementarities and a lower degree of cultural friction between natives and migrants, yield higher immigration flows. In fact, except for politically motivated violence along religious or caste lines and conflicts such as those in highly populated cities like Mumbai that have been instigated by builders in cooperation with political parties to grab land, there is little evidence of friction between natives and migrants in Indian cities, despite the limited and overused infrastructure that they must share.

For a long time, policy planners perceived migration to be a flow of rural poor and destitute in search of employment. Due to their absorption in low-productivity informal sector jobs, urban poverty was seen as merely a 'spillover' effect of rural poverty (Dandekar and Rath 1971). Even in the theoretical literature, the relationship between urban and rural poverty is perceived to be dominant. For example, Bhagwati and Srinivasan (1974) argue that a production subsidy policy should be extended to agriculture. Other studies suggest that the sluggish employment growth in the industrial sector, resulting from its limited spread and adoption of capital-intensive technology, has led to a residual absorption of labour (both native and migrant) in the informal urban sector. From this point of view, there seem to be overlaps among informal sector employment, slum dwelling and poverty (Mitra 1994). However, the elasticity of urban poverty with respect to rural poverty has been found to be negligible, and this suggests the inadequacy of rural development programmes to tackle urban poverty (Mitra 1992).

Determination of urban poverty extends far beyond labour market outcome. It cannot be captured only in terms of the headcount ratio of poverty. Multiple dimensions of deprivation have been discussed in the past (Sen 1981, 1985; Haq 1995; World Bank 2001). These dimensions include education, health, shelter, drinking water and sanitation, freedom, security, opportunity, asset, and vulnerability among others. In this context the present study examines the well-being of slum dwellers based on a micro survey carried out in Delhi (2004–5) and relates the analysis to migration of low income households from rural areas.

The organization of the chapter is as follows: Section 9.2 examines the employment characteristics of slum households and their living standards. Section 9.3 provides an explanation of inter-household variations in expenditure per capita in terms of employment characteristics and other household attributes. Based on a binomial logit framework, it examines if the probability of falling into poor households declines with a rise in duration of migration. Recognizing the limitations of the unidimensional headcount measure, Section 9.4 includes the development of a well-being index based on factor analysis of a large number of diverse characteristics of households, and relates it to the duration of migration. A summary of major findings is presented in Section 9.5.

This study is based on data collected from a slum survey carried out by the first author in 2004–5 in Delhi.[2] A three-stage stratified random sampling technique was used. In the first stage, using the *Jhuggi-Jhompdi* list prepared by the Delhi Development Authority (DDA), slum clusters with 200 and more households were considered, and they were distributed across nine administrative zones. Given the fact that the sample was to be confined to a total of 30 clusters, the proportion of the number of clusters in each zone to the total (each with 200 and more households) was used as the weight in deciding the number of clusters to be picked up from each zone. Once the number of clusters to be picked up from a particular zone was estimated, the specific clusters were randomly selected. The proportion of the number of households in each of the sample clusters to the total households in 30 clusters was then calculated to assign weights in distributing about 200 sample households across the city. Finally, households were randomly selected for interviews.

9.2 Incidence of poverty among migrants and others

Based on census data, those whose duration of migration extends up to one year are treated as seasonal migrants, those from one to three years as short-duration migrants, those from three to five years as medium-duration migrants, and those from five to ten years as long-duration migrants (Mitra 1994). Those whose

Table 9.1 Percentage of population below poverty line and mean monthly household income

	Migrants	*Others*
Percentage of individuals below poverty line	57.08	61.85
No. of total individuals	226	899
Mean household monthly income (Rs.)	4,223	4,239
Household size (persons)	4.85	5.53
	BPL Household	*APL Household*
Mean household monthly income (Rs.)	3,671.0	5,011.7
Household size (persons)	5.76	5.06

Notes:
1. BPL (APL) stands for below (above) poverty line.
2. Migrant and 'other' households are defined on the basis of the migration status and duration of migrant migration of the household head/principal earner. At the individual level to identify a person as migrant or 'other' the migration status and duration of migration of the individuals are considered.
Source: Authors' filed survey 2004–5.

duration of migration exceeds 10 years are seen to be as good as non-migrants since differentials in terms of job market accessibility and other characteristics between fresh migrants and non-migrants are expected to subside over time. Hence, dividing the total number of population into migrants (duration being up to 10 years) and 'others' (migrants of duration more than 10 years and non-migrants) we present certain descriptive characteristics below.[3] The incidence of poverty defined as the percentage of population below the poverty line in terms of minimum per capita consumption expenditure,[4] turns out to be 57.1 and 61.9 per cent among migrants and 'others' respectively (see Table 9.1). This is quite surprising, as one would expect the incidence to be lower among the non-migrants or migrants of very long duration.

Next, we analyse workers' poverty (non-poverty) status and income levels cross-classified by migration status. In other words, we estimate average income of migrant and 'other' workers in different occupation groups across poor and non-poor households. This is pursued to examine the income variations across occupations and to have a feel for the differences corresponding to migrants and others. Based on a very detailed listing of specific occupations that each slum worker was engaged in (see Appendix 9.1), eight broad occupation categories were developed: semi-professional (OCCP1), sales and trade (OCCP2), personal services (OCCP3), manufacturing and repairing (OCCP4), commercial and security (OCCP5), transport (OCCP6), tailoring and knitting (OCCP7) and construction (OCCP8).[5] The total numbers of workers and non-workers (including infants and very old persons) were 376 and 749 respectively. The incidence of poverty was calculated among workers corresponding to each of the occupation categories and non-workers as well, cross-classifying them as per their migration status (Table 9.2). Workers in the occupation categories of tailoring and knitting, transport, and construction, reported a higher incidence of poverty if they were migrants (up to 10 years of duration) compared to the category of 'other' (representing those

Table 9.2 Percentage of workers below poverty line and average income by occupation

Occupation	*Percentage of individuals below poverty line*		*Average income (Rs.)*			
	Migrant	*Other*	*Migrant*		*Other*	
			Poor	*Non-poor*	*Poor*	*Non-poor*
Semi-professional	–	36.36	–	–	2,075	3,736
Sales and trade	44.44	61.29	1,294	2,418	1,929	2,526
Personal services	40.00	60.90	1,350	1,208	1,250	3,239
Manufacturing and repairing	25.00	65.70	2,150	1,967	2,337	2,176
Commercial services and security	25.00	47.60	3,150	2,375	2,428	2,791
Transport	80.00	50.00	1,862	3,500	2,700	3,715
Tailoring and knitting	80.00	70.00	1,950	5,000	2,569	1,450
Construction	62.50	46.10	1,510	2,617	2,314	2,864
Non-workers	60.74	64.99	–	–	–	–

Note: Migrant and 'other' workers are defined on the basis of the migration status and duration of migration of the individuals.
Source: Authors' filed survey 2004–5.

whose migration is more than 10 years in duration and non-migrants). However, in the rest of the occupation classes, workers belonging to the category of 'other' seemed to have a higher incidence of poverty than those who were migrants of up to 10 years' duration. Among non-workers, both migrants and the category of 'other' reported more than 60 per cent incidence of poverty, though the former was slightly (3 percentage points) lower than the latter. Migrants seemed to be relatively better off than others and this can be explained by the fact that they have strong informal channels of information flow. It is possible that in the sample, poor migrants of very long duration (more than 10 years) belonged to the landless destitute class and hence, decided not to return to rural areas even when they did not manage to escape poverty in the place of destination. However, this is based on the assumption that the intensity of urban poverty is possibly lower than its rural counterpart. Before any final conclusion, it is important to make a more thorough assessment in order to determine whether or not migrants of very long duration actually did not fare well over time.

Comparing the average income of workers from below-poverty-line (BPL) and above-poverty-line (APL) households, workers from APL households are seen to have a higher income than those from BPL. Exceptions include the following: the average income of migrant workers from BPL households in personal services and commercial services is higher than the income of migrant workers from APL households; in manufacturing, both migrant and 'other' workers from BPL households have a higher average income than their APL counterparts; in tailoring and knitting, 'other' workers from BPL households have a higher mean income than their APL counterparts.

Based on Table 9.3, a rough comparison shows that migrant workers from non-poor households have a relatively better income profile than migrant workers from poor households. More than 9 per cent of migrant workers from non-poor households earn above Rs.3500 per month, whereas only 6 per cent of those from poor households earn more than Rs.3000 per month. Similarly, in the lowest income size class, the percentage of migrant workers in non-poor households is lower than that of their counterparts in the poor households.

Among 'other' workers (migrants of more than 10 years' duration and non-migrants), the poor and non-poor distinction is very sharp (see Table 9.3). While more than 10 per cent of workers from non-poor households are in the top size class (Rs.4500 and above), only 2 per cent of those from poor households are in this size class.

Migrant poor workers appear to be worse off than 'other' poor workers. Nearly 23 per cent of migrant poor workers earn an income of less than Rs.1000 per month, whereas the corresponding figure for 'other' is only 14 per cent. Similarly, more than 8 per cent of 'other' poor workers earn above Rs.3000 per month, and this is higher than the percentage of migrant poor. The distinction between the migrant and 'other' workers from non-poor households is also evident. About 11 per cent of 'other' workers earn an income of more than Rs.4500 per month whereas the corresponding figure for migrant workers is only 3 per cent. This seems to mean that 'other' workers are better off than those who migrated in last 10 years or so, though in terms of poverty incidence measured on the basis of consumption

Table 9.3 Percentage distribution of workers as per monthly income classes (Rs.)

Migrant workers		*Other workers*	
Monthly income	*Poor*	*Monthly income*	*Poor*
		Below 500	3.98
Below 1,000	22.58	500–1,000	10.23
1,000–1,500	22.58	1,000–1,500	18.75
1,500–2,000	32.26	1,500–2,500	41.48
2,000–2,500	9.68	2,500–3,500	17.05
2,500–3,000	6.45	3,500–4,500	6.25
3,000 and above	6.45	4,500 and above	2.27
Monthly income	*Non-poor*	*Monthly income*	*Non-poor*
		Below 500	3.76
Below 1,000	18.18	500–1,000	6.77
1,000–1,500	12.12	1,000–1,500	16.54
1,500–2,500	36.36	1,500–2,500	31.58
2,500–3,500	24.24	2,500–3,500	17.29
3,500–4,500	6.06	3,500–4,500	12.78
4,500 and above	3.03	4,500 and above	11.28

Note: See note below Table 9.2.
Source: Authors' filed survey 2004–5.

expenditure, the opposite appears to be true. We may therefore have to look into factors that may explain variations in per capita consumption expenditure at the household level, which is pursued in the next section.

9.3 Determinants of per capita consumption expenditure and poverty

In poverty estimates, expenditures largely on food (and a few non-food items like fuel, transport, etc.) have been considered. However, it may also be useful to consider the total per capita consumption expenditure inclusive of other items like clothing and non-clothing expenditures incurred during festivals as well as expenditures on footwear, medicines and other durable goods such as radios, televisions, sewing machines and bicycles. Five sets of per capita monthly consumption expenditure figures have been generated: (a) FPCE – total food expenditure per capita, (b) NFPCE – nutritious food expenditure per capita,[6] (c) PCE1 – food and non-food1[7] expenditure per capita, (d) PCE2 – food and non-food1 and non-food2[8] expenditure per capita and (e) PCE3 – food and non-food1, non-food2 and non-food3.[9] Table 9.4 includes average estimates of these five variables for migrant and 'other' households[10] as well as poor and non-poor households.

Viewing Table 9.4, it is evident that per capita expenditure figures are larger among 'other' households than migrant households of duration up to 10 years. However, poverty estimates seen in Section 9.2 (Tables 9.1 and 9.2) reflect the opposite. This can be explained in part by differences in household size as seen from Table 9.4. Thus, it would be interesting to explain household level per capita consumption expenditure variations in terms of certain important factors, including household size.

To explain variations in total monthly per capita expenditure (PCE) exclusive of medical expenses across households, the following variables have been considered: household size (HHSZ), access to political contact (PD) in terms of basic amenities (treated as a dummy variable), child–woman ratio (CWR), proportion of working

Table 9.4 Monthly per capita household consumption expenditure (Rs.)

Variables	*Migration status*		*Poverty status*	
	Migrant HH	*Other HH*	*Poor HH*	*Non-poor HH*
FPCE	362.79	427.59	290.87	599.71
NFPCE	144.13	200.69	123.99	292.60
PCE1	480.06	578.30	393.18	808.94
PCE2	597.77	737.00	461.94	1,081.23
PCE3	618.55	761.41	466.83	1,131.50
HH Size	4.85	5.53	5.76	5.06

Note: Variables are defined in the text and the corresponding footnotes. For the definition of migrant and 'other' households see note below Table 9.1.
Source: Authors' filed survey 2004–5.

members in the household (WM), occupational categories of the head of household (the same sequence as listed in Table 9.2 and captured in terms of eight occupation dummy variables (OCCPi = 1, . . . , 8) with non-workers as the comparison group, two migration dummy variables (MIGi = 1, 2) representing migration up to 10 years (MIG1) and 10 years and above (MIG2) respectively with non-migrants as the comparison group, education level of the head of household or principal earner in terms of three dummy variables (EDUi = 1, 2, 3) with illiterates as the comparison group,[11] a gender dummy variable (GD) representing the sex of the head of household or principal earner (0 for males and 1 for females), age of the head of household or principal earner taken as a proxy for job market/work experience (AG), and the monthly health expenditure per capita (HPC). Though the amount of medical expenditures does not make up a significant percentage of total expenditures, two alternative views may be taken in this context. One suggests a direct relationship between health expenditure per capita and overall expenditure per capita by envisaging the positive effect of health investment on the capability of household members to pursue productive activity, which results in higher incomes and higher levels of consumption expenditure (see Gupta and Mitra 2004). A more conventional view suggests an inverse relationship between them. Higher medical expenses mean increased illness and larger numbers of days for which the workers may be absent from work, which in turn reduces household income as well as consumption expenditure per capita.

The results given in Table 9.5 show that household size, health expenditure per capita, proportion of working members in the household, and levels of education are statistically significant determinants of per capita consumption expenditure. Household size tends to reduce PCE, while other variables show a positive effect. The dummy variables used for duration of migration are not statistically significant. Neither are the occupational dummy variables, except for OCCP5, which has a positive coefficient. Further, variations across male and female-headed households are not statistically significant. However, this result does not mean that both kinds of households have equal access to job market opportunities and hence to equal income and consequent consumption expenditure.

Occupational dummies have been replaced by household per capita income (HHPCI) in an alternative specification, and this is statistically significant with a positive coefficient. Occupation dummies are not statistically significant possibly because occupation categories encompass both low- and high-income-yielding jobs. However, inter-household variations in income are substantial and have a positive effect on per capita consumption expenditure.

Dividing the households into poor and non-poor categories on the basis of the poverty line taken in terms of the per capita food consumption expenditure plus non-food consumption expenditure1 (PCE1), we have estimated a binomial logit model (0 for poor and 1 for non-poor). Results are reported in Table 9.6 and support the hypothesis that an increase in household size reduces the probability of being non-poor. Further, health expenditure per capita and the percentage of working members in a household each raise the probability of escaping poverty. Migrants of duration more than 10 years show a higher probability of being non-poor than

Table 9.5 Regression results: dependent variable: household-specific PCE

Variable	*Coefficient (Equation 1)*	*Coefficient (Equation 2)*
HHSZ	−50.11	−40.36
	(−2.21)*	(−1.97)*
PD	85.06	119.98
	(1.00)	(1.59)
HPC	1.07	0.92
	(3.27)*	(3.11)*
CWR	−10.8	7.1
	(−0.19)	(0.13)
WM	592.69	−255.24
	(2.54)*	(−1.04)
AG	3.11	3.15
	(0.69)	(0.83)
OCCP1	111.49	–
	(0.51)	
OCCP2	−74.03	–
	(−0.49)	
OCCP3	−223.35	–
	(−1.21)	
OCCP4	−64.4	–
	(−0.42)	
OCCP5	267.29	–
	(1.66)**	
OCCP6	−32.81	–
	(−0.20)	
OCCP7	−196.65	–
	(−0.90)	
OCCP8	−44.05	–
	(−0.25)	
MIG1	−25.13	23.85
	(−0.13)	(0.13)
MIG2	87.13	179.71
	(0.52)	(1.2)
GD	91.9	9.64
	(0.51)	(0.06)
EDU1	141.64	111.61
	(1.70)**	(1.47)
EDU2	274.42	194.47
	(2.58)*	(2.02)*
EDU3	387.35	241.15
	(2.05)*	(1.66)*
HHPCI	–	0.5
		(6.25)*
Constant	385.84	129.81
	(1.18)	(0.54)

Note: Adjusted R^2 is 0.20 and 0.31 for Equations (1) and (2) respectively. The number of observations is 199. * and ** denote significance at 5 and 10% levels respectively. The equations are estimated by OLS.
Source: Authors' filed survey 2004–5.

Table 9.6 Bionomial logit model with marginal effects (dep. var.: POOR: 0 for poor households and 1 for non-poor households, maximum likelihood estimate)

Variable	*Equation (1)*		*Equation (2)*	
	Coefficients	*Marginal effects*	*Coefficients*	*Marginal effects*
HHSZ	−0.27	−0.07	−0.23	−0.06
	(−2.02)*	(−2.02)*	(−1.77)**	(−1.77)**
PD	0.04	0.009	0.08	0.02
	(0.08)	(0.08)	(0.18)	(0.18)
HPC	0.03	0.007	0.03	0.008
	(4.39)*	(4.41)*	(4.54)*	(4.48)*
CWR	−0.35	−0.09	−0.3	−0.07
	(−1.01)	(−1.01)	(−0.83)	(−0.83)
WM	4.09	1.02	1.45	0.36
	(2.77)*	(2.77)*	(0.9)	(0.9)
AG	0.008	0.002	0.007	0.002
	(0.33)	(0.33)	(0.3)	(0.3)
OCCP1	−0.32	−0.08	–	–
	(−0.27)	(−0.27)		
OCCP2	−0.3	−0.75	–	–
	(−0.34)	(−0.34)		
OCCP3	−0.53	−0.13	–	–
	(−0.48)	(−0.49)		
OCCP4	−0.42	−0.105	–	–
	(−0.47)	(−0.47)		
OCCP5	0.3	0.075	–	–
	(0.31)	(0.31)		
OCCP6	−0.11	−0.03	–	–
	(−0.11)	(−0.11)		
OCCP8	−0.04	−0.009	–	–
	(−0.03)	(−0.03)		
MIG1	1.01	0.24	1.61	0.35
	(0.90)	(1.02)	(1.27)	(1.69)**
MIG2	1.56	0.35	2.55	0.48
	(1.66)**	(1.97)*	(2.20)*	(3.63)*
GD	1.79	0.36	1.15	0.27
	(1.66)**	(2.37)*	(1.13)	(1.34)
EDU1	1.47	0.35	1.37	0.33
	(2.94)*	(3.24)*	(2.68)*	(2.88)*
EDU2	1.8	0.40	1.44	0.34
	(2.94)*	(3.70)*	(2.33)*	(2.71)*
EDU3	2.18	0.41	1.82	0.38
	(2.20)*	(3.67)*	(1.97)*	(2.84)*
HHPCI	–	–	0.002	0.0005
			(3.63)*	(3.63)*
Constant	−3.73	–	−5.71	–
	(−1.96)*		(−3.21)*	

Notes: Pseudo-R^2 for Equations (1) and (2) are 0.27 and 0.33 respectively. Number of observations is 192 and 199 for Equations (1) and (2) respectively. Chi-square values are 70.79 and 89.30 respectively. These are highly significant at the 1% level. * and ** represent significance at the 5 and 10% levels respectively. OOCP7 was dropped in Equation (1), and 7 observations were not used as the non-poor households in this category were predicted perfectly.
Source: Authors' filed survey 2004–5.

do non-migrants, though there is no statistically significant difference between migrants up to 10 years' duration and non-migrants in this respect. All education-specific dummy variables have positive coefficients, indicating a higher probability of the educated escaping poverty compared to illiterates. It is interesting to note that households headed by females have a lower probability of falling below the poverty line than do those headed by males. This may be due to the fact that alcohol consumption is much higher in households headed by males and often occurs in place of food and other essential items. When occupation dummy variables are replaced by household income per capita, there is statistical significance, but the percentage of workers in the household does not become statistically significant. It is possible that its effect becomes captured in the income variable.

Viewing marginal effect calculated from the equation with occupation dummies, very long duration migrants (more than 10 years) show an almost 0.35 point rise in the probability of not being poor compared with non-migrants (Table 9.6). The three categories of education, (a) literates but below secondary, (b) secondary and above but below graduation, and (c) graduates and above, show a rise of 0.35, 0.40 and 0.41 points respectively in the probability of escaping poverty relative to illiterates. Compared to male counterparts, households headed by females show a rise of 0.36 points in the probability of being above the poverty line. In the equations without occupation dummies but including household income, similar patterns are also indicated though with differences in magnitude of marginal effects.

In Section 9.2, the average incidence of poverty is seen to be lower among households representing migrants of duration up to 10 years than those representing migrants of more than 10 years' duration and non-migrants. However, the binomial logit model suggests that the very long duration migrants show a higher (lower) probability of being non-poor (poor) compared to non-migrants, whereas migrants up to 10 years' duration are on a par with non-migrants. These findings are consistent with the view that over time, migrants tend to improve their living conditions. Otherwise, the whole enterprise of migration would seem to be futile and irrational. Why would migrants continue to reside in urban areas if in due course they are unable to experience upward mobility? Of course this question can be answered by asserting that migrants do not return to rural areas because as mentioned in Section 9.2, the intensity of poverty in rural areas may be higher than that in urban areas. Findings in the present section, however, suggest that for very long duration migrants the probability of falling below the poverty line tends to decline. These findings may still be criticized on the grounds that assessment of living standard based only on consumption poverty is too narrow. Thus, there is still scope to improve the quantification of the well-being of households, and this is considered in the next section.

9.4 Well-being index and migration

The following variables have been considered in constructing the household-specific well-being index: household size, child–woman ratio, per capita total expenditure (PCE3NH, food and all categories of non-food excluding health expenditure), proportion of persons in the household who reported illness one year preceding the date of survey (ILL), percentage of household members who acquired at least primary level education (PRIM), percentage of members in the age group 15–59, proxy for adult potential earners (PER15–59), percentage of working individuals (WM), age of the household head/principal earner, proxy for experience particularly in the job market (AG), health expenditure per capita (HPC), and per capita household income (HHPCI). Variables such as household size, child–woman ratio, and percentage of ill members in the household, are likely to reduce the well-being of the household. Health expenditure per capita on an a priori basis may reduce or raise the well-being of the household, though regressions reported in the preceding section indicate that such expenditure has a positive effect on PCE. On the other hand, other variables would be expected to enhance well-being. Since these variables are heterogeneous, it is difficult to combine them to indicate an overall living standard of households. Hence, factor analysis was conducted, and using factor loadings as weights, variables were combined to generate a composite index of well-being (or deprivation), denoted as WELLINDEX(i). This was repeated for each of the significant factors (factors with eigenvalues greater than 1):

$$\text{WELLINDEX}(i) = \sum_{j=1}^{n} \text{FL}j\ (i)\ Xj$$

where FL is the factor loading, $j = 1 \ldots n$ corresponding to the number of variables, and i represents the ith significant factor.

In the second stage the composite indices generated on the basis of factor loadings for each of the significant factors were combined using the proportion of eigenvalues as weights:

$$\text{WELLINDEX} = \sum_{i=1}^{k} \left[\frac{\text{EV}(i)}{\sum \text{EV}(i)} \right] \text{WELLINDEX}(i) \quad k < n$$

where i ranges from 1 to k, the number of significant factors.

Using varimax rotation (in order to obtain statistically independent factors), results of the factor analysis suggest the presence of two significant factors (Table 9.7). For Factor 1 (the most dominant, explaining around 69 per cent of the total variation), household income per capita and the number of working members relative to household size had the highest loadings. Variables with moderate loadings on this factor included proportion of persons in the age group 15–59 to total household size, child–woman ratio, household size and per capita consumption expenditure. Household size and child–woman ratio take negative factor loadings while the other two correspond to positive values. Factor loadings for number of ill population relative to household size, health expenditure per capita and percentage of household members who acquired at least primary level education are highly negligible.

Table 9.7 Results of factor analysis based on household data

Variables	*Factor 1*	*Factor 2*
HHSZ	−0.29	0.56
PCE3NH	0.29	−0.10
HPC	−0.004	0.08
ILL	−0.063	−0.35
PRIM	0.008	0.04
PER15−59	0.46	0.05
CWR	−0.33	−0.16
WM	0.74	0.01
AG	0.14	0.57
HHPCI	0.63	−0.11
Eigenvalue	2.19	1.01

Note: Factor loadings were determined using varimax rotation.
Source: Authors' filed survey 2004–5.

Table 9.8 Distribution of households as per well-being index

Well-being size class	*No. of households*	*Percentage share*	*Coefficient of variation in well-being index*
≤270	30	14.56	16.95
271–420	81	39.32	12.67
421–570	50	24.27	9.36
571–720	21	10.19	7.61
721–1020	12	5.83	8.61
>1021	12	5.83	35.18
Total	206	100	13.05

Source: Authors' filed survey 2004–5.

For Factor 2 (which had an eigenvalue of a little over 1), household size and the age of the household head/principal earner have the highest loadings. Proportion of ill population per household corresponds to a moderate value with a negative sign. Child–woman ratio, household income per capita and consumption expenditure per capita have low but not negligible factor loadings.

Table 9.8 shows that almost 15 per cent of the sample households correspond to the lowest size class formed on the basis of composite well-being index. On the other hand, around 12 per cent are located in the top two size classes. The second size class from the bottom constitutes the largest percentage of households (39.3).

The composite well-being index shows that there is a nonlinear relationship between the average well-being index and duration of migration (Table 9.9). Those who have migrated in the last 1–10 years and those who have been residing in the city for the last 21–25 years have virtually the same level on the well-being index, and this is considerably higher than the well-being index for migrants of 11–15 years' duration. Conversely, migrants with duration of 16–20 years have the lowest index value, and this is again quite close to the index value of migrants

Table 9.9 Household-specific well-being index and duration of migration

Duration of migration (years)	*Percentage of households*	*Average well-being index*
1–10	9.71	508.85 (53.87)
11–15	14.56	437.38 (59.18)
16–20	21.84	407.86 (45.44)
21–25	24.76	509.66 (411.66)
26–30	9.22	411.66 (35.47)
Above 30 + non-migrants	19.90	574.84 (80.65)
Above 26 + non-migrants	29.13	523.16 (76.00)

Notes: Figures in parentheses are coefficients of variation. Duration of migration of the household is defined on the basis of the duration status of the household head or the principal earner.
Source: Authors' filed survey 2004–5.

whose duration is 26–30 years. Those whose duration of migration is more than 30 years (including natives or non-migrants) have the highest value for the well-being index though the coefficient of variation for this category is relatively higher than for others. The regression of the composite well-being index on the duration of migration (excluding the non-migrant households) reveals a statistically insignificant *t*-ratio, which supports of the absence of any stable relationship between duration of migration and the well-being index.[12] On the whole, though there is no strong evidence of gains associated with migration per se, those who have been residing for a very long time in the urban areas show some possibility of improvement in the well-being index. This may explain why migrants do not return to rural areas, even when mobility does not seem to have improved their living standard in the short or medium term. With a high intensity of poverty and lack of employment opportunities in the rural areas, the hope that they will be able to experience upward mobility in urban areas seems to motivate migrants to stay on, particularly recalling the experiences of their neighbours, relatives, friends, co-villagers, and kith and kin who have resided in urban areas for more 30 years or so.

9.5 Conclusion

This chapter in the context of economic reforms and globalization makes an attempt to assess if migration to a developed city from rural areas with inadequate sources of livelihood, results in economic gains, i.e. whether or not migrants benefit significantly at the place of their destination. Since information is not available on income levels at the place of origin prior to migration, it is difficult to obtain conclusive answers to this question. Hence, we have tried to examine if there exists a positive relation between duration of migration and living standards.

In terms of the incidence of poverty (headcount ratio), though 'others' (migrants of more than 10 years' duration and non-migrants) are not better off compared to the migrants (up to 10 years' duration), average income and consumption expenditure per capita of 'others' are higher than those for migrants. However, in the regression of per capita consumption expenditure the duration of migration does not turn out to be a significant determinant. Nevertheless the binomial logit model estimated to identify factors that explain the probability of being poor (or non-poor) shows that there is a positive association between those who migrated more than 10 years ago and the probability of being non-poor.

Since the concept of poverty goes beyond monetary terms, there is a need to construct a more comprehensive index of well-being (or deprivation) based on demographic, social, economic, health and education-specific characteristics. This has been done using factor analysis of certain household-level attributes. The composite well-being index, generated by using the factor loadings and the eigenvalues as weights, suggests that a very large percentage of the sample households are located in the lowest two size classes formed on the basis of the index values. Further, there is no clear-cut relationship between the duration of migration and the household-level well-being index. Only the average index value of those who migrated almost 30 years ago appears to be greater than that of the rest.

On the whole, as we piece together all these findings it is difficult to assert that migrants have benefited significantly at the place of their destination. An important policy implication of this finding is that while rural development programmes may reduce migration to urban areas, urban poverty reduction programmes including employment, shelter and basic amenities programmes, are still important for harnessing the enhanced opportunities for informal jobs created directly or indirectly by economic reforms and globalization and also for empowering urban low-income households, many of whom have been residing in the urban areas for a very long time and possess only limited ties with the rural sector. The fact that only in the very long run does slum dwellers' well-being improve suggests that a distinction has to be made between short- and long-term poverty reduction programmes. In the short run public work programmes are of great relevance while in the long run emphasis has to be laid on human capital formation, particularly for the second generation of migrant households.

Appendix 9.1

1. OCCP1 = Semi-professional (Category 1)
2. OCCP2 = Sales and trade (Categories 2 and 3 have been merged)
3. OCCP3 = Personal services (Category 4)
4. OCCP4 = Manufacturing and repairing (Categories 5 and 11 have been merged)
5. OCCP5 = Commercial and security (Categories 6 and 10 have been merged)
6. OCCP6 = Transport (Category 7)
7. OCCP7 = Tailoring and knitting (Category 8)
8. OCCP8 = Construction (Category 9)

- *Category 1*: clerk, computer operator, engaged in fieldwork, government service as typist, owner of a health clinic, supervisor in a company, supervisor in NGOs, teaching and giving tuition, technical assistant in Air India.
- *Category 2*: selling books, magazines and newspapers, egg seller, working in a garment-exporting agent, washing clothes in a garment exporting agent, stock checking, fish vendor, flower vendor, fruit packing in wholesale market (*mandi*), working in a general store, helper in a store, helper in an export agent, helper in a footwear shop, helper in a chemical store, helper in a shop, helper in an export company's shop, helper in a garment-export shop, helper in a fruit *mandi*, helper in a garment shop, helper in a general store, helper in a hardware shop, helper in Indian Airlines, helper in a shop selling jeep batter, helper in a juice shop, helper in a medicine shop, helper in a company selling snacks (*namkeen*), helper in a shop selling sauce, helper in a shop selling TVs, helper in a shop selling woodwork, ice cream vendor, collecting garbage and waste (*kabariwala*), peanut seller, pan seller, seller of *bidi* and cigarettes on the road, salesman (medicines, cold drinks, etc.), selling vegetables, selling wood, dealing with sale and purchase of cars, sweet vendor, working in the 'go-down' of waste and garbage collection.
- *Category 3*: trading in cloth, fisherman and trading in fish, trading in hosiery, helper in an iron/steel shop, helper in a sweet shop, helper in a workshop, working in a hotel, providing room service in hotels, working in shops, suitcase fitting, working in a tea shop, owning a tea stall, working in a hotel, working in ready-made garment shop, working in a canteen.
- *Category 4*: barber, *basti sewika* (paid social worker), cleaning utensils and washing, cook, traditional midwife, domestic maid or servant, helper in a kitchen, gardener in a farmhouse, serving drinking water in *mandi*, sweeper and working in small eating places (*dhaba*) or tea stalls as a cleaner or sweeper.
- *Category 5*: bamboo work, box making, brick-making unit, bulb factory, candle making, manufacturing decorative items made of paper, factory worker, foreman, furniture work, glass work, helper in a plastic factory, helper in a factory, helper in a mineral water factory, helper in an iron factory, helper in a plastic factory, helper with a printing press, helper in a rubber factory, helper in a leather factory, labour in an iron factory, lamination work, operator, printing job, printing press, working in ready-made cloth manufacturing units, screen printing, steel almira work, supervisor in a steel factory, tube light and bulb factory, utensil polish work, woodwork, woollen work, working in a '*bidi* company', working in a footwear factory, working in an electric shop, manufacturing of food products and working in a radio and TV parts company.
- *Category 6*: bill collection, cable TV operator, courier service, helper in an embassy, loading goods, Municipal Corporation of Delhi (MCD) worker, packaging, peon in commercial units, class four employees/peon (at airport, private hospital and MCD worker), working in a video library and working in Delhi Electricity Supply Undertaking (DESU).

- *Category 7*: auto-rickshaw and tempo driver, conductor, driver (car, bus, truck, etc.), helper in the transport sector, helper in transporting goods, rickshaw puller and truck supervision.
- *Category 8*: embroidery, stitching and tailoring (both tailor master and worker), colouring thread and cutting thread.
- *Category 9*: construction workers (*beldar, dehari*), carpenter (daily wage carpenter), labour in construction work, mason (*mistri*), polishing, supervisor in building construction and whitewashing.
- *Category 10*: security guard and watchman.
- *Category 11*: car mechanic, cycle repairing, electrician, fitter, auto mechanic, learning electric work, machine repairing work, mechanic, mechanic of electronic items, motor fitter, and other repairing work.

Notes

1. Sachs et al. (2002).
2. This survey is in line with earlier surveys conducted by the first author (see Gupta and Mitra 2002; Mitra 2003).
3. In order to divide the individuals into migrant and 'other' categories the migration status and duration of migration at the individual level are considered. At the household level this distinction is made in reference to household head/principal earner.
4. The official poverty line of Rs.56.6 per capita per month (in 1973–74 prices) has been adjusted for price changes using the consumer price index for Delhi to update it for the year 2004–5. The per capita consumption expenditure used in estimating poverty among the slum dwellers includes largely food along with some minor non-food items like fuel, washing soap, transport, etc.
5. Some occupations like manufacturing and repairing were put together as the latter had few respondents. Similarly, commercial services and security workers were combined.
6. Only a subset of expenditures on food items is considered: pulses, milk, fish, meat and eggs, and vegetables.
7. Non-food1 includes expenditures for fuel, transport, washing soap, etc.
8. Non-food2 includes clothing, footwear, medical, religious and social expenditures.
9. Non-food3 covers expenditure on durable goods, jewellery, modern kitchenware, etc.
10. Migrant and 'other' households are defined on the basis of the migration status and the duration of migration of the household head/principal earner.
11. With illiterates as the reference category, EDU1 represents those who are literate and those who have studied up to class 9, EDU2 encompasses those who have studied above class 9 and completed secondary education but not graduation, and EDU3 represents graduates or those who have acquired a higher level of education including technical and non-technical, professional and vocational courses.
12. Well-being index $= 445.56 + 0.90$ duration of migration; $R^2 = 0.0012$.
    (9.94) * (0.48)

References

Banerjee, B. (1986) *Rural to Urban Migration and the Urban Labour Market: a Case Study of Delhi*. Bombay: Himalaya Pub. House.

—— (1991) 'The Determinants of Migrating with a Pre-Arranged Job and of the Initial Duration of Urban Unemployment: an Analysis Based on Indian Data on Rural-to-Urban Migrants'. *Journal of Development Economics* 36: 337–51.

Becker, Charles, E.S. Mills and J. Williamson (1986) 'Modeling Indian Migration and City Growth, 1960–2000'. *Economic Development and Cultural Change* 35(1): 1–33.

Bhagwati, Jagadish N. and T.N. Srinivasan (1974) 'On Reanalyzing the Harris–Todaro Model: Policy Rankings in the Case of Sector Specific Sticky Wages'. *The American Economic Review* 64(3): 502–8.

Dandekar, V.M. and N. Rath (1971) *Poverty in India*. Pune: Indian School of Political Economy.

Dasgupta, Monica (1987) 'Informal Security Mechanisms and Population Retention in Rural India'. *Economic Development and Cultural Change* 36(1): 101–20.

Fujita, M. and J.F. Thisse (2003) 'Does Economic Agglomeration Foster Economic Growth? And Who Gains and Loses from It?' *Japanese Economic Review* 54(2) (June): 121–45.

Fujita, M. and S. Weber (2004) 'On Labour Complementarity, Cultural Frictions and Strategic Immigration Policies'. Discussion Paper no. 8. Chiba: Institute of Developing Economies.

Gupta, Indrani and Arup Mitra (2002) 'Rural Migrants and Labour Segmentation: Micro-Level Evidence from Delhi Slums'. *Economic and Political Weekly* 37(2): 163–8.

—— (2004) 'Economic Growth, Health and Poverty: an Exploratory Study for India'. *Development Policy Review* 22(2): 193–206.

Haq, Mahbub (1995) *Reflections on Human Development*, expanded edn. Oxford: Oxford University Press.

Harris, John and M.P. Todaro (1970) 'Migration, Unemployment and Development: a Two Sector Analysis'. *The American Economic Review* LX(1): 126–42.

Kannapan, S. (1985) 'Employment Problem and the Urban Labour Market in Developing Nations'. *Economic Development and Cultural Change* 33(4): 699–733.

Kuchiki, Akifumi (2005) 'Theory of a Flowchart Approach to Industrial Cluster Policy'. Discussion Paper no. 36, Discussion Paper Series. Chiba: Institute of Developing Economies.

Kuznets, S. (1966) *Modern Economic Growth: Rate, Structure and Spread*. New Haven: Yale University Press.

Mitra, Arup (1992) 'Urban Poverty: a Rural Spill-Over?' In V. Pandit and Suresh D. Tendulkar (eds) *Indian Economic Review* 27: 403–19 (special no. in memory of S. Chakravarty).

—— (1994), *Urbanisation, Slums, Informal Sector Employment and Poverty: an Exploratory Analysis*. Delhi: D.K. Publishers.

—— (2003) *Occupational Choices, Networks and Transfers: an Exegesis Based on Micro Data from Delhi Slums*. New Delhi: Manohar.

Sachs, J. D., Bajpai N. and A. Ramiah (2002) 'Understanding Regional Economic Growth in India', CID Working Paper 88, Center for International Development at Harvard University.

Sen, Amartya (1981) *Poverty and Famines: an Essay on Entitlement and Deprivation*. Oxford: Clarendon Press.

—— (1985) *Commodities and Capabilities*. Amsterdam: North-Holland.

Stark, Oded (1995) *Altruism and Beyond: an Economic Analysis of Transfers and Exchanges within Families and Groups*. Cambridge: Cambridge University Press.

Sundaram, K. (1989) 'Agriculture–Industry Inter-Relations: Issues of Migration', World Congress of the International Economic Association, 1986, in S. Chakravarty (ed.) *Proceedings: Balance between Industry and Agriculture in Economic Development, Manpower and Transfers*, vol. 3. London: Macmillan.

Williamson, J. (1988) 'Migration and Urbanisation'. In H. Chenery and T. N. Srinivasan (eds) *Handbook of Development Economics*, vol. I. Amsterdam: Elsevier Science Publishers, BV.

World Bank (2001) *World Development Report 2000/01: Attacking Poverty*. New York: Oxford University Press.

10
The Impact of Labour Migration on Household Well-Being: Evidence from Villages in the Punjab, Pakistan[1]

Hisaya Oda

10.1 Introduction

One of the most significant features of the era of globalization is the cross-border movement of people, especially the migration of those who are looking for job opportunities overseas. It seems evident that international labour migration is rapidly growing. South Asian countries are major sources of migrants due to the lack of employment opportunities and low-income generation within those countries. Thus, the movement of the labour force from rural areas is particularly noticeable in these countries. Migrating to cities or to countries overseas in order to obtain work is one of the few options available to poor villagers.

As international labour migration has grown, workers' remittances have increased steadily for the last 10 years. The amount of remittances that flow to developing countries has already surpassed that of official resource inflows. Since 1999, workers' remittances have been the second largest resource flowing into developing countries with foreign direct investment (FDI) being first. The relative importance of official assistance has been diminishing and is no longer the most reliable source of capital for developing countries (World Bank 2003, 2006a). In 2005, the volume of recorded remittances was $US188 billion. This was roughly 80 per cent of the volume of FDI and twice that of flow from official resources (World Bank 2006b).[2] Particularly in South Asian countries, the volume of workers' remittances far exceeds the volume of FDI. As a result, there has been growing interest in using workers' remittances as a tool for development and for poverty reduction.

Compared to other types of resource flows, remittance flows possess several favourable features. One oft-noted characteristic is that they are more stable than private flow that fluctuates up and down in response to business cycles. This is evident in the movement of capital flow before and after the Asian financial crisis. While private flow went through an erratic boom-and-bust-type cycle, remittances continued to rise steadily and showed greater stability. Part of this stability may have arisen from workers' concern about families back home and been driven by altruistic motivations. Workers' remittances thus provide a kind of insurance or safety net for residents in developing countries. This is especially important for those bordering on subsistence living. From a macroeconomic viewpoint, workers' remittances are not liabilities but rather cash transfers from overseas. In principle, they do not cost recipient countries anything. There has been much debate about the negative effects of external debt on growth, so this feature is a very attractive force. It should be noted, however, that remittance flows are easily affected by the economic situation and immigration policies of labour-importing countries.

During the period from independence until the 1960s, Pakistani workers migrated to several countries such as Saudi Arabia, Libya, the UK, the USA and Canada. However, these migrations were limited in number. A large-scale international labour migration from Pakistan started in the mid-1970s in connection with oil booms in Middle Eastern countries.[3] The number of Pakistani workers who left for overseas through formal channels was 3534 in 1971 but increased to 140,445 in 1977.[4] From a peak of 153,081 in 1981, the number decreased dramatically in the subsequent five years. This was mainly due to low demand for Pakistani workers in the Gulf region. In the early 1990s, the number of Pakistani workers going overseas steadily increased and reached a peak of 191,506 in 1992 after the Gulf War. In 2003, the highest figure for labour migration, 214,039, was recorded. One reason for this was due to changes in the visa policy of Saudi Arabia and the UAE. These two countries alone received 187,726 workers.[5] Globalization appears to have facilitated the flow of cross-border migrants; however, it should also be noted that the volume of international migration is easily affected by a number of factors and can rise or fall by a significant margin.

As the number of migrants to Middle Eastern countries increased in the 1970s, the amount of remittances sent back to Pakistan also increased. At its peak, the amount rose to $US2.3 billion.[6] This was larger than export earnings of the same year. However, due to the falling price of oil in the 1980s, the subsequent economic downturn in the Middle East, and the shift in demand from unskilled manual labour to skilled labour, the number of Pakistani migrants as well as the volume of remittances fell. In addition, competition of new migrants from Thailand, Korea and the Philippines accelerated the decline in the number of Pakistani workers going abroad.

The declining trend in official remittance flows to Pakistan was reversed after 11 September 2001, due to an international crackdown on informal routes of money transfer. It was suspected that international terrorist groups had used informal routes such as *hundi* and *hawala*. Tough control on the use of these informal channels led overseas migrants (including Pakistani workers) to channel money through formal routes such as banks and post offices, and this resulted in a significant boost to official remittance statistics.[7] The remittance flows through official channels were $US920 million in 2000–1, but a sharp increase to $US2.3 billion was recorded in 2001–2 followed by $US4.1 billion recorded in 2002–3. These surges in remittances contributed to easing Pakistan's balance of payments.

Examining the impact of remittances at the macro and micro levels is an important research agenda in development studies.[8] This is particularly so in the context of Pakistan. With increases in the number of migrants from Pakistan and the amount of remittances sent home, interest has grown in examining the issues related to remittances. Since one-third of the population live below the poverty line in Pakistan,[9] the study of how remittances impact on household well-being and poverty reduction has gained importance. Large-scale migration surveys were conducted in the 1970s and 1980s, and a number of studies were initiated (e.g. Gilani et al. 1981; Abbasi and Irfan 1986; Kazi 1989; Ahmed and Sirageldin 1994; Arif 1999).[10] Despite growing importance, studies on this issue in recent years have been limited except for a few that examined the impact of migration and remittance at the micro level based on household surveys (Arif 2004, 2005; Mansuri 2006). This is probably due to the lack of new data pertinent to analysis, as there has been no large-scale survey appropriately designed for the study of migration since the late 1980s.

In an attempt to fill the aforementioned gap in the existing literature, this chapter endeavours to analyse labour 'out-migration' from a household perspective based on data from a survey of migrant-sending areas. The impact of remittances on household well-being is analysed using comparative studies of migrant and non-migrant households. Specifically, impacts of remittances on income level and school enrolment are analysed. This chapter considers not only international migration (external migration) but also domestic migration (internal migration). These two types of migration are not independent but rather interrelated; not all households are able to send family members overseas, and those who cannot afford to engage in overseas labour migration may resort to internal migration instead. By using internal remittances (remittances sent by internal labour migrants) as a yardstick, the impact of external remittances (remittances sent by international labour migrants) may be more precisely investigated.

The Chakwal district, one of the four rain-fed (*barani*) districts in the Punjab Province of Pakistan, was selected for this study. There has been active labour migration from the *barani* areas, where agricultural activities are weather-dependent and non-farm job opportunities are limited. Migration has been used as one of the important instruments to supplement household income and has become a part of life for villagers.

Section 10.2 describes the villages where field surveys were carried out. The methodology of data collection is also explained. Section 10.3 presents the profile of migrants and migrant households in comparison with non-migrant households and includes a discussion of factors that may affect migration decisions at household levels. Section 10.4 includes a brief discussion of remittance issues as well as aspects of non-migrant households and their livelihoods. Conclusions are presented in Section 10.5.

This study reveals the poor economic condition and resultant widespread poverty of non-migrant households. In surveyed villages, external migration plays a very important role and remittances from external migrants serve to upgrade the living standard of the households. However, this option is available only to a small number because of high initial costs associated with migration. Further, non-migrant households with returned migrants appear to be no better off than those with no returned migrants. Results of the study indicate that the use of remittances for more productive purposes is necessary to maintain higher income levels of households even after migrants have returned.

10.2 Data collection and profile of study villages

10.2.1 Data collection

The field survey was conducted in three villages of the Chakwal district in northern Punjab. This is one of four rain-fed (*barani*) districts in the Punjab Province of Pakistan.[11] The district is situated on the Potohar plateau and lies north of the Salt Range. Because of its *barani* nature, the production of farm crops is dictated by changes in the weather. As a result of unpredictability in production, migration has been used to supplement low and fluctuating household income and has become a part of life for villagers. The area has been known as one of the main recruiting grounds for the military in Pakistan. Expected high rates of labour migration formed one reason for using the Chakwal district in this research.

One criterion used to select study villages was their distance from Rawalpindi. Rawalpindi, with a population of 1.4 million, is the largest city in the region and also the nearest commercial centre to the Chakwal district.[12] Improved roads and availability of transportation have made commuting between rural areas and nearby big cities more common. Many villagers leave home early in the morning and travel by coach or motorbike to the nearby urban centre; they then return in the evening. In the past, these commuters would probably have migrated, but they now live in their home village and work elsewhere. Since this type of labour movement is beyond the scope of this study, villages within a 40 mile (64 km) radius of Rawalpindi were excluded in order to avoid surveying such commuters.

The urban sector in Chakwal is very small, and the industrial sector is undeveloped. Around 85 per cent of the total district population lives in rural areas.[13] For villagers, the chances of being a commuter within the Chakwal district are minimal. They must migrate outside the district for employment opportunities. This further made the Chakwal district an attractive base for this study.

A basic village census was conducted for selection of households for interviews. At this stage, information on access to farmland, size of land owned, size of cultivated land, number of migrants (both internal and external), and occupation in the case of non-farm households was collected from all the households in each village. From these results, households in the village were stratified into several categories. Sample households for the interview were selected randomly from each category according to their actual prevalence so that the sample would represent the population of each village. The number of sample households per village was weighted according to the actual number of households per village.

In total, 171 households were selected for interview.[14] For protection of privacy, villages will be referred to as Villages A, B and C; 67, 46 and 58 households were chosen from these villages respectively. Complete household migration is not included in the survey.[15]

10.2.2 Definitions

Though not exactly the same, most definitions used in this chapter closely follow those used in the *Pakistan Integrated Household Survey* (PIHS), the *Labour Force Survey of Pakistan* (LFS), and *Pakistan Agricultural Census*.

A household is defined as a collective of individuals who usually sleep in the same house, eat meals together, and share the same kitchen and food expenses. Persons who live in the same house but do not eat meals together and do not share food expenses are not included in the same household.

Household members are defined as persons who normally live and eat in the household. Those who are temporarily absent for reasons such as travelling, attending school, being hospitalized, etc., are treated as household members. Absent household members such as migrant workers are also considered to be part of the household.

In this chapter, a household with at least one migrant member is called a migrant household, and a household with no migrant members is called a non-migrant household. Migrant households are further categorized as follows: (1) internal migrant household: a household with only internal migrants, (2) external migrant household: a household with only external migrants, and (3) mixed migrant household: a household with both internal and external migrants.

The definition of a labour (out-) migrant is a person who is currently away from the village for the purpose of working for more than one year. If villagers have left the village within the 12 months preceding the interview, only those who have no intention of returning to the village within one year of departure are considered as labour migrants. This excludes temporary migrant workers such as seasonal labourers. Since no labour in-migrants are found in the three villages, labour migrants in this study refer to labour out-migrants. Only labour migration is considered in this chapter; thus the words 'migration' and 'labour migration' are used interchangeably.

Farm households are defined as households that cultivate a farm area. These include three types of households: (1) a household cultivating its own land (owner cultivator), (2) a household that cultivates both its own land and land under contract (landowner cum tenant), and (3) a household cultivating land under contract (tenant). Non-farm households are defined as households not operating a farm area. Households that own land but do not operate on it are also considered as non-farm households.

The reference period for the survey included the 12 months preceding the interview. This basically corresponded to the period from the beginning of March 2004 to the end of February 2005. This covered two distinct agricultural seasons in the Punjab: (1) the *rabi* 2003 (dry season planted from November to December 2003 and harvested from April to early June 2004) and (2) the *kharif* 2004 (rainy season planted from May to August 2004 and harvested from October to November/December 2004).

10.2.3 Profile of study villages

The study villages are located within a 25–30 km range north of Chakwal town. The distance to Rawalpindi, the closest large commercial centre, is around 80–88 km. Village A is most conveniently located and is on a main road to Rawalpindi. Village B is 12 km off the main road to the west, and Village C, the most remote, is 10 km west of Village B.

Table 10.1 includes a summary of key statistics for the study villages. Farm households constitute about 70 per cent of total sample households. Non-farm households need some explanation. Because of the limited nature of agricultural activities in the region, the number of non-farm households providing traditional services to farm households is also limited.[16] This presents a sharp contrast to villages in irrigated areas in the Punjab where a sizeable number of non-farm households that retain a traditional complementary relationship with farm households may still be observed.[17]

Though limited in size, the number of non-farm households is clearly related to agricultural activities in the study villages. Note the following contrast in Villages B and C: Village B (Village C) is most active (inactive) in farming as the size of the cultivated area per household is largest (smallest) and gross values of crops are the highest (lowest). The proportion of non-farm households to the total sample households is the highest (lowest), accordingly. Non-farm work is of a heterogeneous nature. It is thus not really appropriate to bundle such households under the single category of non-farm households. However, they are treated here as a counterpart to farm households due to the small sample size.

The ratio of landownership among farm households is very high. The average for the three villages is 96 per cent. This figure is higher than that of the Punjab, which is around 90 per cent.[18] Except in Village A, renting and sharecropping do not seem to be usual practices in the study villages.

Because of hilly terrain and forests, it was found that some parts of owned land were not available for cultivation. This was especially true in Village B where an average of about 10 acres per household were not used during the previous year.

Acreage of cultivated land is defined as farmland net of uncultivated land. More than 50 per cent of farm household holdings of cultivated land fall in the range of 0–5.0 acres. In the study sample, only 6 out of 122 farm households, less than 5 per cent, possess cultivated areas greater than the 12.5 acres.

Wheat, which is grown during *rabi*, is the major crop grown in the region. Its production comprises 40–50 per cent of the total cultivated area in the *rabi*. The average production of wheat per acre in the *rabi* 2003 season was 15.1 *maunds* or roughly 600 kg (Table 10.1). This value is around 40 per cent less than the Pakistan average (24.5 *maunds*).[19] For the most part, wheat is grown for home consumption and little is grown for commercial purposes. Only a few households keep surplus wheat for sale.

Around 30 per cent of the cultivated area is devoted to fodder crops during both *rabi* and *kharif* seasons. This reflects the importance of livestock in these village economies. Around 90 per cent of farm households keep milk animals such as she-buffaloes and cows. Milk is an important source of protein as well as an alternative source of cash income. The contribution of milk production to household income is large in the study villages. Fodder crops grown in these villages include *sarson* (mustard) which is intercropped with wheat during *rabi*, and *jowar* (sorghum) and *bajra* (millet) which are grown during *kharif*.[20] Pulses (legumes) are also grown during both *rabi* and *kharif* seasons. Most of the farm households in Village B grow *moongphali* (groundnuts) in the *kharif* season as a cash crop.

Table 10.1 Key statistics of sample households and study villages

	Village A	*Village B*	*Village C*	*Total sample*
Household				
No. of sample households	67	46	58	171
No. of sample farm households	45	29	48	122
Sample non-farm households/ total sample households (%)	32.8	36.9	17.2	28.6
Farm households with off-farm income/total farm households (%)	26.7	37.9	14.6	24.6
Farm households holding milk animals/total farm households (%)	84.4	93.0	91.7	89.3
Household size (numbers)	6.91	7.48	7.74	7.36
	(2.78)	(3.09)	(3.09)	(2.97)
Household size (MAE*)	3.64	3.97	4.05	3.87
	(1.51)	(1.85)	(1.60)	(1.63)
Land access				
Landownership among farm HHs**	44/45	27/29	46/48	95.9%
Land owned per HH (acres)	4.54	17.41	8.53	8.99
	(5.88)	(15.68)	(6.38)	(10.37)
Cultivated area per HH (acres)	5.93	7.50	4.71	5.82
	(6.17)	(5.13)	(2.88)	(4.93)
% of farm households with farm size less than 5 acres	55.6	34.5	68.8	55.7
Crops				
Wheat area (acres)	3.02	3.13	2.11	2.70
	(2.68)	(1.59)	(1.18)	(2.00)
Wheat yield (*maund****)	18.89	13.60	12.36	15.13
	(6.63)	(7.47)	(6.83)	(7.48)
Gross value of farm output/HH (Rs.)	44,096	51,675	26,527	38,985
	(68,820)	(54,371)	(20,339)	(51,739)
Gross value of farm output per acre per HH (Rs.)	6,877	6,251	5,849	6,341
	(2,907)	(3,280)	(3,383)	(3,188)
Livestock				
Milk animals per farm HH (AU****)	2.72	3.71	2.34	2.74
	(2.20)	(2.92)	(1.84)	(2.25)
Draught animals per farm HH (AU****)	0.48	0.28	0.47	0.43
	(0.62)	(0.44)	(0.46)	(0.52)

*MAE stands for male adult equivalent units. It is a unit of labour and a weighted sum of male and female workers. The weights are: for males, 16–60 years = 1.0 MAE, above 60 years and 12–15 years = 0.5 MAE, 10–12 years = 0.25 MAE, and below 10 years = 0; for females, 16–60 years = 0.5 MAE, above 60 years and 12–15 years = 0.25 MAE, 10–12 years = 0.12 MAE, and below 10 years = 0.
**HH stands for 'household'.
****Maund* is a local unit of weight. 1 *maund* is about 40 kg.
****AU stands for adult equivalent units. It is a weighted sum of adult and young livestock animals. The weights used are: for draught animals, 1.0 for adult bullocks/he-buffaloes/horses, 0.57 for young bullocks/he-buffaloes and adult donkeys, 0.28 for young donkeys; for milk animals, 1.28 for adult she-buffaloes, 0.96 for young she-buffaloes, 0.72 for adult cows, 0.54 for young cows, and 0.20 for adults goats/sheep. Adult animals are defined as those 3 years and older. Young are those aged under 3 years. However, for sheep and goats, the threshold between adult and young is one year old.
Source: Author's calculation. Standard deviations appear in parentheses.

Table 10.2 Incidence of migration at the household level

Migration status	*Farm households*	*Non-farm households*	*Total*
Non-migrant	55 (45.1)	27 (55.1)	82 (48.0)
w/No return migrant	28	9	37
w/Return internal migrant	19	17	36
w/Return external migrant	4	1	5
w/Return mixed migrant	4	0	4
Internal migrant	30 (24.6)	14 (28.6)	44 (25.7)
w/No return migrant	13	6	19
w/Return internal migrant	16	8	24
w/Return external migrant	0	0	0
w/Return mixed migrant	1	0	1
External migrant	26 (21.3)	6 (12.2)	32 (18.7)
w/No return migrant	15	6	21
w/Return internal migrant	10	0	10
w/Return external migrant	1	0	1
w/Return mixed migrant	0	0	0
Mixed migrant	11 (9.0)	2 (4.1)	13 (7.6)
w/No return migrant	3	2	5
w/Return internal migrant	5	0	5
w/Return external migrant	2	0	2
w/Return mixed migrant	1	0	1
Total	122 (100)	49 (100)	171 (100)

Note: Percentage figures in parentheses.
Source: Author's calculation.

10.3 Profile of labour migrants

10.3.1 Overview

Migration status of sample households is summarized in Table 10.2. Out of the 171 households, 89 have at least one migrant member; 67 of these are farm households, and 22 are non-farm households. Thirty-five migrant households have multiple migrants, and 13 of them have both internal and external migrants. The table shows that the incidence in migration is higher among farm households than non-farm households. It is also evident from the table that the proportion of internal migrant households among non-farm households is higher than that of farm households. It should be noted that there are variations in the pattern of migration at household levels from village to village (Appendix Tables 10A.1 and 10A.2).

In the case of non-migrant households, 45 have returned migrants; 36 of these have returned internal migrants, 5 have returned external migrants, and the remaining 4 have both. Combining this with the information on the current status of migration, 37 households (corresponding to 21.6 per cent of the total sample households) have neither returned nor current migrants. In the farm/non-farm classification, 28 farm households and 9 non-farm households have no returned or current migrants. This corresponds to 23.0 and 18.4 per cent of each category

Table 10.3 Incidence of labour migration at the individual level

	Total sample individuals	*Farm household members*	*Non-farm household members*
No. of individuals (1)	1,243	900	343
Labour migrants (2)	137	105	32
Internal migrants	78	56	22
External migrants	59	49	10
(2)/(1) (%)	11.0	11.7	9.3
% of Labour migrants	100.0	76.6	23.4
Male 16–60 yrs (3)	375	280	95
(2)/(3) (%)	36.5	37.5	33.7

Source: Author's calculation.

respectively. Looking at the current status of migration, the incidence of migration appears to be higher among farm households than among non-farm households. However, when information on returned migrants is included, a different picture emerges. Further, if the information for complete household migration is considered, the incidence of migration among non-farm households is even higher. In the past, 29 non-farm and landless households left the three villages.[21] The high incidence of migration from these villages confirms active labour migration from the *barani* areas.

Table 10.3 shows the current migration status of individuals from the sample. At the time of the interviews, 137 villagers of three villages were either internal or external migrants. The rate of labour migration from these villages was 11.0 per cent. Out of 137 migrants, 78 villagers were internal migrants and 59 were external migrants. The proportion of internal migrants to total migrants (56.9 per cent) was higher than that of external migrants (43.1 per cent). It might be expected that labour migrants from rural areas would be mostly males. This proved to be the case and all the migrants were males in our study.[22]

Table 10.3 shows that migrants who belong to farm households constitute 76.6 per cent of the total labour migrants, and the propensity for labour migration among farm household members (11.7 per cent) is slightly higher than that among non-farm household members (9.3 per cent). These figures are consistent with Eckert and Khan (1977) and Nabi et al. (1986). However, caution is necessary in saying this as the information on the current status of migration does not include returned and complete migration. Migrants from non-farm households tend to migrate more internally than do migrants from farm households. The ratio of internal migrants to total migrants among sample non-farm individuals is 68.8 per cent, whereas it is 53.3 per cent among farm samples.

Each village displays distinct patterns of migration. For example, in Village A, external migration is more likely to occur, especially among farm household members. On the other hand, the incidence of internal migration is high in Village C. No external migrants among non-farm household members are found in Village B

Table 10.4 Destinations of internal migrants

Destination	*Farm household members*	*Non-farm household members*	*Total*	
			No.	*Share (%)*
Army/PAF*/Police	25	7	32	41.0
Rawalpindi	14	6	20	25.6
Lahore	5	7	12	15.4
Karachi	8	0	8	10.3
Others	4	2	6	7.7
Total	56	22	78	100.0

*PAF stands for Pakistan Air Force.
Source: Author's calculation.

(Appendix Table 10A.1). There are variations from village to village, but on average, approximately one-third of male village members of age 16–60 are internal or external migrants.

10.3.2 Destination of migrants

Table 10.4 shows the destinations of internal migrants. Traditionally the *barani* areas have been a major source for military recruitment in Pakistan. The tradition still remains. Around 40 per cent of total internal migrants left villages to join the military or the police. This tradition seems especially strong in Village C; 22 out of 32 migrants who joined the military are from Village C. Joining the military or any other type of public service is an attractive option for villagers. In addition to a stable salary, a lump sum retirement payment and pension may also be expected.

The next favourite destination is Rawalpindi. This is easily understandable because of its geographical proximity to the Chakwal district. The direct distance between Rawalpindi and the villages is less than 100 km. Two big cities, Lahore and Karachi, are also major destinations. Apart from joining the military, the nearby commercial centre and the big cities tend to attract migrants.

Table 10.5 shows destinations of external migrants. The UAE is the number one destination, followed by the Kingdom of Saudi Arabia. Migrants to oil-rich countries in the Middle East comprise 70 per cent of total migrants from the three villages. Hong Kong is also a popular destination. In fact, this is the most favoured destination of migrants from Village A. Nine out of 10 Hong Kong migrants in the sample are from this village. More than 30 years ago, one person from this village left for Hong Kong to seek employment. He settled in Hong Kong and developed a network. This kind of network within a village or within a broader kinship is very influential when it comes to choosing a migration destination. There are ample anecdotal examples in this regard. Such examples include migratory flows from Mirpur in Azad Jammu Kashmir to the United Kingdom and from Gujrat, Punjab, to Norway.

Table 10.5 Destinations of external migrants

Destination	*Farm household members*	*Non-farm household members*	*Total*	
			No.	*Share (%)*
UAE	19	5	24	40.7
Abu Dhabi	(16)	(3)	(19)	(32.2)
Dubai	(3)	(2)	(5)	(8.5)
Saudi Arabia	11	1	12	20.3
Oman	5	0	5	8.5
Kuwait	1	0	1	1.7
Hong Kong	8	2	10	16.9
Korea	2	0	2	3.4
UK	3	2	5	8.5
Total	49	10	59	100.0

Source: Author's calculation.

10.3.3 Determinants and characteristics of labour migrants and their households

Since migration is a result of a selective process, not all people and households are able to migrate. Migrants and their households have common characteristics.[23] In this section, individual (age, education) and household (size, landholding) characteristics that determine labour migration are described and discussed.

10.3.3.1 Age

Existing studies indicate that the probability of migration is higher among the young than the old because the young are more mobile and can expect higher returns over a long period of time (see e.g. Sjaastad 1962). Khan and Shehnaz (2000) and Akram et al. (2002) support this view for cases in Pakistan. The average age of internal and external migrants in the study sample was 31.7 and 34.3 years respectively (Table 10.6). The minimum age was 17, and 60 was the maximum. Part of the difference in the current age of internal and external migrants may be explained by the duration of migration. The average duration of migration for internal migrants is 7.5 years, while it is 8.2 years for external migrants (Table 10.7). The age distribution of migrants shows that migrants aged 21–30 years account for more than 40 per cent of total migrants. Thereafter, the number of migrants decreases as age increases. However, external migrants 41 years of age or older still constitute more than 25 per cent of total external migrants, in contrast to 12 per cent for internal migrants. More useful information is the age of migrants at the time of migration. Table 10.8 presents the distribution of age at the time of migration. It shows that more than 60 per cent of migrants left their village when they were 25 or younger. Internal migrants tend to leave at younger ages than external migrants.

Table 10.6 Age distributions of migrants and non-migrants

Age	*Internal migrants*		*External migrants*		*Non-migrant males age 16–60*	
	No.	*Share (%)*	*No.*	*Share (%)*	*No.*	*Share (%)*
16–20	7	9.0	4	6.8	59	24.8
21–30	36	46.2	25	42.4	56	23.5
31–40	25	32.1	14	23.7	41	17.2
41–50	7	9.0	11	18.6	34	14.3
51 and above	3	3.8	5	8.5	48	20.2
Total	78	100.0	59	100.0	238	100.0
Mean	31.7		34.3		34.5	
Std.	9.0		11.3		14.5	
Min.	17		18		16	
Max.	55		60		60	

Source: Author's calculation.

Table 10.7 Duration of migration

Years of migration	*Internal migrants*		*External migrants*	
	No.	*Share (%)*	*No.*	*Share (%)*
Less than 1	8	10.3	9	15.3
1–4	27	34.6	20	33.9
5–9	16	20.5	8	13.6
10–14	9	11.5	8	13.6
15–19	14	17.9	6	10.2
20 and above	4	5.1	8	13.6
Total	78		59	
Average	7.5		8.2	
Std.	6.9		9.0	
Max.	25		36	

Source: Author's calculation.

10.3.3.2 Education

Along with age, it has been argued that characteristics of human capital for individuals are important in making decisions about migration. Though there are several studies that provide counter-evidence (e.g. Beals et al. 1967), studies in the past have generally shown that migrants tend to be better educated or skilled than non-migrants because they can expect higher wages and also higher chances of getting employment (Levy and Wadycki 1974). In the context of Pakistan, this hypothesis has been validated by several empirical studies (Ahmed and Sirageldin 1993; Khan and Shehnaz 2000; Akram et al. 2002).

Proxy indicators of human capital derived for our survey included literacy rates, average years of completed schooling and completed level of education. They are

Table 10.8 Age distribution of internal and external migrants at the time of migration

Age	*Internal migrants*		*External migrants*		*Total*	
	No.	*Share (%)*	*No.*	*Share (%)*	*No.*	*Share (%)*
Up to 20	34	43.6	12	20.3	46	33.6
21–25	19	24.4	24	40.7	43	31.4
26–30	13	16.7	9	15.3	22	16.1
31–35	5	6.4	8	13.6	13	9.5
36–40	4	5.1	5	8.5	9	6.6
41–50	3	3.8	0	0.0	3	2.2
51 and above	0	0.0	1	1.7	1	0.7
Total	78	100.0	59	100.0	137	100.0

Source: Author's calculation.

Table 10.9 Literacy rates and schooling of migrants

	*Non-migrant males 16 to 60 yrs**		*Internal migrants*		*External migrants*	
Literacy rate (%)		83.8		100.0		96.3
Average schooling years		6.90		8.72		8.52
Completed education	No.	Share (%)	No.	Share (%)	No.	Share (%)
No education	33	16.2	1	1.3	2	3.4
Below primary	8	3.9	2	2.6	0	0.0
Below middle	45	22.1	14	17.9	12	20.3
Below matric	54	26.5	26	33.3	22	37.3
Below higher secondary	49	24.5	25	32.1	13	22.0
Above higher secondary	15	7.4	10	12.8	10	16.9
Total	204	100.0	78	100.0	59	100.0

Notes: *Males aged 16–60 who are not enrolled in school.
Source: Author's calculation.

reported in Table 10.9. The figures on non-migrants are those of males aged 16–60 years who were not enrolled in school at the time of interview; this makes them comparable with values for migrants. On average, migrants attain higher rates of literacy and have more years of schooling. A conspicuous difference is seen in the category of 'No education'. Thirty-three out of 204 non-migrants, or 16.2 per cent, never received formal education. The ratio is just 1.3 per cent for internal migrants and 3.4 per cent for external migrants. Overall, migrants are richer in human capital than non-migrants.

10.3.3.3 Household size

The size of migrant households tends to be larger than that of non-migrant households, and this is supported by figures reported in Table 10.10. One possible explanation for this tendency may be found in evidence that the migration of

Table 10.10 Household size and migrants

Migration status	*Total household members*	*Active males aged 16 and above**	*Male adult equivalent***	*Average no. of migrants per household*
Non-migrant households	6.3	1.7	3.0	n/a
Internal migrant households	8.1	3.1	4.4	1.45
External migrant households	7.7	2.6	4.0	1.28
Mixed migrants households	9.5	4.1	5.5	2.46

Notes: *This excludes those who are not able to work due to old age, sickness or disability.
**For the definition of male adult equivalent, please see the footnote of Table 10.1.
Source: Author's calculation.

household members does not necessarily cause the reduction of domestic production (Connell et al. 1976; Hampshire 2002). Work that would normally be done by absent migrants can be maintained and easily shared by remaining members. This is particularly true for farm households that have many adult males. Basically, the number of adult males per household relates to the opportunity cost for farm households. Given the agricultural output, as the number of males increases, the opportunity cost per male member decreases, and this makes it easier for households to send adults to work outside the village.

Table 10.11 shows the number of households with no active male members aged 16 and above in farm and non-farm households. An interesting observation from this table is that among farm households, only 3 out of 67 migrant households have no active male adults. This presents a sharp contrast to non-farm migrant households where 11 out of 22 are without adult male members. This clearly indicates that the number of active adult male members is a crucial factor in migration decisions of farm households. Although female farm household members are often responsible for tending livestock not only in the *barani* areas, but also in other rural areas in Pakistan, males appear to contribute to farming activities that require large amounts of physical strength.

10.3.3.4 Landownership

Possession of land has considerable influence on household decisions, including those on migration. Land is the most important source of income in the rural economy, where with the exception of agricultural activities, job opportunities are limited. Since the income level of farm households is constrained by the size of cultivated land, income from farming may not be sufficient for marginal and small landowners to support their families. This low level of income motivates them to engage in migration activities. However, not everyone can afford to migrate

Table 10.11 Households without active adult male

Migration status	*No. of HH without active males aged 16 and above*	
	Farm households	*Non-farm households*
Internal migrant HH	0/30	4/14
External migrant HH	3/26	5/6
Mixed migrant HH	0/11	2/2

Source: Author's calculation.

because it is an expensive process, including expenses such as travelling and initial living costs at the destination. Costs of internal migration do not seem so high, and even poor villagers can afford them. External migration is prohibitively expensive as it includes airfares, commission charges to brokers, and so on.[24] As landholding size increases, farmers become more capable of financing even costly external migration. At the same time, migration becomes less attractive to large landholders because income from farming is sufficient, and the monetary benefit of sending a member of the household elsewhere may not cover the reduction of agricultural output due to the loss of labour.

In addition to the above economic motivations, the social value of land may have a significant impact on migration decisions. Traditionally the landowning classes (or *zamindar* in the local language) are considered to be superior, not only in economic status, but also in social status. There is a clear social and economic division between landholder and landless. Even when a household owns no land but operates land under a tenancy contract, it is considered superior to one that is landless. From a social point of view, large landowners are likely to enjoy higher social status, so they are not interested in leaving the village for work while the landless and marginal/small farmers are different in this regard. Thus, the social value of land also influences migration decisions.

The relationship between land and migration has been analysed in a number of studies.[25] These have produced somewhat ambiguous results since the impact of each factor discussed above on migration decisions differs from household to household and from place to place. Studies of internal migration in Pakistan tend to show a negative relationship between landholding and migration (Nabi 1981, 1984; Ahmed and Sirageldin 1993). On the other hand, Oda (2007) found no significant relationship between landholding and migration in the case of internal migration but a positive and nonlinear relationship in the case of external migration.

Table 10.12 presents the migration status of households according to landownership. The proportion of migrant households among landless households is 40.0 per cent when internal, external and mixed migrant households are considered. It is 56.3 per cent among landowning households. Note that only 5 landless households out of 18 landless migrant households have external migrants. The corresponding figure among landowning migrant households is 40 out of 71 households. Caution is necessary in interpreting these data since 29 non-farm and landless households completely left these villages in the past. However, the difference between landless and landowners is quite significant, particularly regarding the proportion of external migrants, and this probably suggests that landownership signifies owners' ability to finance costly external migration.

Table 10.13 shows the incidence of migration according to the size of farmland under ownership. Only those households owning farmland are considered here. The figures presented do not show a clear association between land size and incidence of migration for both internal and external migrations. Due to the limited size of the sample and possible changes in the size of farmland due to purchasing or

Table 10.12 Landownership and labour migration

Landownership	*Non-migrant HH w/no returned migrants*	*Non-migrant HH w/returned migrants*	*Internal migrant HH*	*External migrant HH*	*Mixed migrant HH*	*No. of HH per category*	*% Migrant HH(1)*	*% Migrant HH(2)*
Landless	12	15	13	2	3	45	40.0	73.3
Landowner	25	30	31	30	10	126	56.3	80.2
Total	37	45	44	32	13	171	52.0	78.4

Notes: %Migrant HH(1) is the percentage ratio of the sum of internal, external and mixed migrant households to the total number of households per category. %Migrant HH(2) is the percentage ratio of the sum of internal, external, mixed migrants households plus non-migrant households with returned migrants to the total number of households per category.
Source: Author's calculation.

Table 10.13 Landholding size and labour migration

Landholding size (acres)	*Non-migrant HH w/no returned migrants*	*Non-migrant HH w/returned migrants*	*Internal migrant HH*	*External migrant HH*	*Mixed migrant HH*	*No. of HH per category*	*% Migrant HH(1)*	*% Migrant HH(2)*
$0 < L \leq 2.5$	8	10	6	9	2	35	48.6	77.1
$2.5 < L \leq 5.0$	2	6	9	5	3	25	68.0	92.0
$5.0 < L \leq 7.5$	4	4	6	2	2	18	55.6	77.8
$7.5 < L \leq 10.0$	3	6	2	6	0	17	47.0	82.3
$10.0 < L \leq 12.5$	2	0	4	0	0	6	66.7	66.7
$12.5 < L \leq 25.0$	2	4	3	6	0	15	60.0	86.7
$25.0 < L$	4	0	1	2	3	10	60.0	60.0
Total	25	30	31	30	10	126	56.3	80.2

Notes: %Migrant HH(1) is the percentage ratio of the sum of internal, external and mixed migrant households to the total number of households per category. %Migrant HH(2) is the percentage ratio of the sum of internal, external, mixed migrants households plus non-migrant households with returned migrants to the total number of households per category.
Source: Author's calculation.

selling with the passage of time, it is difficult to investigate the genuine relationship between the size of landholding and incidence of migration.

10.4 Remittances

10.4.1 Overview

Table 10.14 shows the percentage of migrants who sent money back home and the average amount per migrant during the 12 months preceding the interview. Those who left the village within one year prior to the interview were not included.[26] More than 90 per cent of migrants sent a portion of their earnings back home. As observed, there is a strong linkage between migrants and their families of origin. This supports the argument of New Economics of Labour Migration (NELM) that migration is a family (or household) strategy and that there exists an implicit contract in the form of remittance between migrants and their households (note 23).

Remittance by external migrants (Rs.86,120) is about three times as much as that of internal migrants (Rs.29,803). Higher pay abroad is undoubtedly attractive to most Pakistani workers. Eighty-five out of 89 migrant households received remittances during the 12 months preceding the survey, and the average was Rs.75,116 per household.[27] From these figures, it seems obvious that remittances significantly boost recipient household income levels.

The size of remittances varies according to the duration of migration. Table 10.15 shows that remittances during the 12 months prior to the survey from both internal and external migrants increased as the duration of their stay increased. This is consistent with the findings of Ahmed and Sirageldin (1994). This is one reason why migration at a younger age is desirable; the young can work for a longer period of time and reap greater benefits.

Factors affecting the size of worker remittances were formally analysed using an OLS technique. The dependent variable was the logarithm of worker remittances, and the explanatory variables were: (1) a dummy that indicates if the destination is either domestic ($d=0$) or overseas ($d=1$), (2) duration of migration, (3) the number of active adult male members per household, and (4) educational level of migrants. To examine the effect of education level, completed years of education and the attained level of education were used.

Table 10.14 Summary of remittance data

	Internal migrant	*External migrant*
% of migrants who remitted home	94.3 (66/70)	92.0 (46/50)
Average amount per migrant (Rs.)	29,803	86,120

Source: Author's calculation.

Table 10.15 Amount of remittances during the past 12 months and duration of migration

Years of labour migration	*Remittances from internal migrants (Rs.)*		*Remittances from external migrants (Rs.)*	
	No.	*Remittance per migrant*	*No.*	*Remittance per migrant*
1–4	27	22,815	20	57,550
5–9	16	25,375	8	78,500
10–14	9	35,556	8	114,375
15 and above	18	42,000	14	114,643
Average	70	29,803	50	86,120

Source: Author's calculation.

Table 10.16 OLS estimates of workers' remittances

Variables	*Model 1*	*Model 2*
Constant	9.852***	9.841***
	(0.238)	(0.276)
Destination (External = 1)	0.909***	0.915***
	(0.121)	(0.121)
No. of adult males per household	−0.487***	−0.467**
	(0.235)	(0.234)
Duration of migration	0.040***	0.038***
	(0.007)	(0.007)
Completed schooling years	0.021	
	(0.023)	
Education level		
Primary		−0.063
		(0.286)
Middle		0.317
		(0.266)
Matric		0.255
		(0.272)
Above matric		0.151
		(0.299)
No. of observations	120	120
Adjusted R-square	0.431	0.440

Notes: Standard errors are in parentheses. ***significant at 1%, **significant at 5%.
Source: Author's calculation.

Results are presented in Table 10.16. As expected, the destination and duration of migration have a positive effect on the size of remittance. Results also show that the amount of remittance decreases as the number of active adult male members increases. This means that migrants have less pressure to send money back home when other active male adults of their household can also earn money. Educational level of migrants did not turn out to be statistically significant, though signs are

Table 10.17 Use of remittances by recipient households

Use of remittances	*Farm households*		*Non-farm households*	
	Multiple	*Primary*	*Multiple*	*Primary*
1. Purchase land	5	2	n/a	n/a
2. Rent more land	2	0	n/a	n/a
3. Purchase farm inputs (pesticides, seeds, etc.)	18	1	n/a	n/a
4. Improve land	5	0	n/a	n/a
5. Buy farm equipment (tractor, thresher, etc.)	6	1	n/a	n/a
6. Pay for schooling/training of the household members	23	1	13	2
7. Buy non-farm productive equipment	0	0	2	0
8. Purchase/pay for house/dwelling	22	8	6	1
9. Contribute to consumption (food, clothes, etc.)	59	36	21	17
10. Purchase consumer durables (TV, fridge, car, etc.)	14	1	5	0
11. Finance marriage/ceremony	9	6	1	0
12. Pay off debt	5	3	1	1
13. Other	6	3	0	0
Total	174	62	49	21

Source: Author's calculation.

generally positive as expected. This may be because many migrant workers at the destination may take jobs such as that of labourer, a position that does not need higher education and/or skills. In addition, since migrants are as a whole better educated than non-migrants, regardless of the type of migration, there may be no significant differences in the level of education among them, thus making the effect of education less significant.

An interesting question regarding remittances is how they are spent by recipients. This question has been a focus of attention in many studies because of interest in the impact of remittances on economic development. Unfortunately, many survey respondents report that remittances are often used on unproductive items such as those related to daily consumption or on housing/real estate investment. For example, Gilani et al. (1981), in their analysis of external remittances in Pakistan, report that 62 per cent of remittances were spent on current consumption, 22 per cent on real estate, 13 per cent on direct investment, and 3 per cent on financial investment.[28]

Table 10.17 shows how recipient households in the current study spent remittances. In the column titled 'multiple', results are given for how households responded when asked if remittances were or were not spent on each item in the list. The number in the column indicates the number of 'yes' answers. Similarly, in the column titled 'primary', results are given for how households responded when asked on which item remittances were spent most. The survey shows that most remittances were spent on daily consumption, the purchase of consumer durables, and housing construction. Table 10.17 also indicates that remittances were used to finance the schooling of household members, and this is considered a productive investment in the long run. Caution should be exercised in making too great a generalization based on evidence of three villages, but the relatively high literacy rates and high levels of educational attainment in the Chakwal district may be explained by remittance-financed spending on education.[29] This point as well as further analysis of the relationship between school enrolment and remittance is discussed in the next section.

There were five 'yes' answers in the category titled 'purchase land'. Four of these respondents had been landowners and had purchased additional plots.[30] Only one household had newly acquired land and had only recently become a landowner. The head of this household worked as a barber (*nai*) and cultivated the acquired land for home consumption. This may be the only way that landless non-farm households can raise their economic and potential social status in the villages of Pakistan.[31]

Another interesting feature found in Table 10.17 is the role of ceremonial events in villages of Pakistan. Six farm migrant households reported that remittances were spent primarily for ceremonial purposes. Interestingly, five of them received remittances from overseas. As honour and shame dictate social life in the villages, events (especially marriage ceremonies) need to be as lavish as possible.[32] There is little difference between farm and non-farm households in the use of remittances, except in the case of ceremonial events. No non-farm migrant households spent funds primarily on ceremonial events. This reflects the fact that the social status of farm households (generally landowners) is high in rural areas and probably related to holding extravagant functions.

10.4.2 The impact of remittances on household income and school enrolment

To quantitatively examine the impact of remittance on households, a concept of poverty set by the Centre for Research on Poverty Reduction and Income Distribution (CRPRID) was introduced. Based on the official poverty line of Rs.749 per adult equivalent per month at the prices of 2000–1, the poverty line at 2004 prices was set at Rs.875 per adult equivalent, which roughly corresponds to Rs.10,500 per annum. The per adult equivalent is a scale that counts all household members younger than 18 as 0.8 and all the other household members as 1. Those who are living on a budget below Rs.10,500 per annum were considered to be in poverty.

Following the centre's classifications and taking inflationary changes into account, the non-poor (above Rs.20,500), transitory non-poor (above Rs.12,750 and below Rs.20,500), and the transitory vulnerable (above Rs.10,500 and below Rs.12,750) were defined (all figures are per adult equivalent per annum).[33] A household with an income of Rs.10,500 per adult equivalent per annum or below was defined as poor. For analysis, these figures were compared with household income per capita obtained from the field survey. Income here was defined as gross revenue and income from all sources minus gross cost. Gross revenue and income included agricultural income, off-farm income, revenue from business, and remittance and transfer income. A money value was imputed to receipts in kind. Gross cost included input costs and expenditures but excluded imputed land rent, family labour wages, rent to owned agricultural machinery, and rent to owned off-farm machinery and equipment.

The figures of average income per adult equivalent by household migration status, stratified by the poverty definitions, are presented in Table 10.18 for farm households and in Table 10.19 for non-farm households.

Both tables show that regardless of migration status, average income per adult equivalent exceeds the poverty line of Rs.10,500. Even non-migrant household income per adult equivalent crosses the line of the transitory vulnerable and is in the category of transitory non-poor. The average income per adult equivalent

Table 10.18 Income per adult equivalent by migration status, stratified by poverty categories (farm households)

Income (Rs.)	*Non-migrant households*		*Internal migrant HH*		*External migrant HH*		*Mixed migrants HH*		*Total households*	
	No.	*%*	*No.*	*%*	*No.*	*%*	*No.*	*%*	*No.*	*%*
0–10,500	25	45.5	6	20.0	1	3.8	1	9.1	33	27.0
10,501–12,750	2	4.4	3	10.0	3	11.5	1	9.1	9	7.4
12,751–20,500	14	25.5	9	30.0	1	3.8	3	27.3	27	22.1
20,501–40,000	9	16.3	12	40.0	8	30.8	3	27.3	32	26.2
40,001+	5	9.1	0	0.0	13	50.0	3	27.3	21	17.2
Total	55	100.0	30	100.0	26	100.0	11	100.0	122	100.0
Average income	17,605		18,198		43,218		32,557		24,557	

Source: Author's calculation.

Table 10.19 Income per adult equivalent by migration status, stratified by poverty categories (non-farm households)

Income (Rs.)	*Non-migrant households*		*Internal migrant HH*		*External migrant HH*		*Mixed migrants HH*		*Total households*	
	No.	*%*	*No.*	*%*	*No.*	*%*	*No.*	*%*	*No.*	*%*
0–10,500	11	40.7	1	7.1	0	0.0	0	0.0	12	24.5
10,501–12,750	4	14.8	1	7.1	0	0.0	0	0.0	5	10.2
12,751–20,500	6	22.2	5	35.7	1	16.7	0	0.0	12	24.5
20,501–40,000	5	18.5	6	42.9	4	66.7	1	50.0	16	32.7
40,001+	1	3.7	1	7.1	1	16.7	1	50.0	4	8.2
Total	27	100.0	14	100.0	6	100.0	2	100.0	49	100.0
Average income	14,125		23,112		49,793		35,686		21,718	

Source: Author's calculation.

of migrant households also appears larger than that of non-migrant households. The difference between income figures of non-migrant households and those of internal migrant households, however, is relatively small. The income figures of external migrant households far surpass those of non-migrants and internal migrant households. The income figures of mixed households lies between those of internal and external migrant households.

Though the average income per adult equivalent is in the range of the transitory non-poor and higher categories, Tables 10.18 and 10.19 show that the highest concentration of poverty is found among non-migrant households, irrespective of farm/non-farm classification. Among farm non-migrant households, 45.5 per cent are below the poverty line. This poverty class constitutes about 75 per cent of farm households in poverty. For more than 70 per cent of this class, landholding sizes are less than 5 acres. Among non-farm non-migrant households, about 41 per cent of them live in poverty, and this accounts for 92 per cent of non-farm households in poverty.[34]

These tables also show a noticeable number of internal migrant farm households below the poverty line. They constitute close to 20 per cent of farm households in poverty. This suggests that internal migration is not necessarily a panacea for villagers wishing to escape poor living conditions. In general, external migrant households are most well off in the villages. Thanks to greater remittances, the majority of these households belong to the non-poor class. Only one external household was found to be in the range of the poor. A closer examination indicated that this household did not receive any remittances because it had been less than one year since the migrant left for work overseas, and he did not have enough to send funds back home.

There are a considerable number of returned migrants in the villages considered in this study. For example, among 82 non-migrant households, 36 have returned internal migrants, 5 have returned external migrants, and 4 have returned mixed migrants. It might be expected that there are differences in income distribution between households with no returned migrants and those with returned migrants. Results of an examination of the case of non-migrant households are presented in Tables 10.20 and 10.21. Surprisingly, these results show that non-migrant households with returned migrants are no better off than those with no returned migrants. Particularly, income levels of those of non-farm households seem worse; 10 out of 18 non-migrant, non-farm households with returned migrants are in the poor category, while only 1 out of 9 without returned migrants fall into the same range. In the case of farm households, 12 out of 27 non-migrant households with returned migrants are in poverty. These imply that, after the return of migrants, migrant households are not able to sustain the higher living standard that they may have enjoyed, and that stoppage of remittance flows pushed them back to their pre-migration income level. Thus, the impact of migration on income levels seems temporary. While this result contradicts Burki (1991), who found a significant permanent change of economic status of migrant households, it supports the findings of higher unemployment levels among returned migrants reported by Kazi (1989) and Arif (1998).

Table 10.20 Income per adult equivalent of non-migrant households with/without returned migrants, stratified by poverty categories (farm households)

Income (Rs.)	*Non-migrant households without returned migrants*		*Non-migrant households with returned migrants*		*Total non-migrant households*	
	No.	*%*	*No.*	*%*	*No.*	*%*
0–10,500	13	46.4	12	44.4	25	45.5
10,501–12,750	0	0.0	2	7.4	2	4.4
12,751–20,500	5	17.9	9	33.3	14	25.5
20,501–40,000	6	21.4	3	11.1	9	16.3
40,001+	4	14.2	1	3.7	5	9.1
Total	28	100.0	27	100.0	55	100.0
Average income	21,348		13,724		17,605	

Source: Author's calculation.

Table 10.21 Income per adult equivalent of non-migrant households with/without returned migrants, stratified by poverty categories (non-farm households)

Income (Rs.)	*Non-migrant households without returned migrants*		*Non-migrant households with returned migrants*		*Total non-migrant households*	
	No.	*%*	*No.*	*%*	*No.*	*%*
0–10,500	1	11.1	10	55.6	11	40.7
10,501–12,750	2	22.2	2	11.1	4	14.8
12,751–20,500	2	22.2	4	22.2	6	22.2
20,501–40,000	3	33.3	2	11.1	5	18.5
40,001+	1	11.1	0	0	1	3.7
Total	9	100.0	18	100.0	27	100.0
Average income	19,860		11,257		14,125	

Source: Author's calculation.

More interesting findings can be discerned in Table 10.20. Note that there are four non-poor households among non-migrant farm households with no return migrants. Two of them possess cultivated areas greater than 25.0 acres. One owns 56.0 acres, the largest farmland acreage among the sample households. The other owns 36.6 acres, which is the fifth largest. These non-migrant households are land-rich households that obtain sufficient income from farming. For them, labour migration is not an attractive household strategy. Also from a social point of view, labour migration is not appealing to large landowners as already discussed in the previous section. Since they are usually influential figures in the village, it is easy to imagine that they do not want to leave the village because they would lose the social status that they enjoy.

Table 10.22 School enrolment by migration status

	Households receiving no remittances		*Households receiving internal remittances*		*Households receiving external remittances*	
	Male	*Female*	*Male*	*Female*	*Male*	*Female*
Age 10–13						
Not enrolled	0	2	0	0	0	0
Enrolled	20	24	6	5	12	11
Enrolment ratio (%)	100.0	92.3	100.0	100.0	100.0	100.0
Age 14–16						
Not enrolled	8	10	0	3	0	3
Enrolled	18	12	5	6	8	6
Enrolment ratio (%)	69.2	54.5	100.0	66.7	100.0	66.7
Age 10–16						
Not enrolled	8	12	0	3	0	3
Enrolled	38	36	11	11	20	17
Enrolment ratio (%)	82.6	75.0	100.0	78.6	100.0	85.0

Source: Author's calculation.

In addition to analysing the impact of remittance on income levels, its impact on gross school enrolment was also examined.[35] Due to data limitations, only the enrolment of children age 10–16 was examined. This age group corresponds to middle (10–13 years old) and matriculation (14–16 years old) levels in Pakistan. For this analysis, households receiving both internal and external remittances were excluded. Table 10.22 shows a high rate of school enrolment in these villages. Overall, the enrolment rate at the time of the survey was 83.6 per cent, with 89.6 per cent males and 78.0 per cent females. These figures are considerably higher than the average figures for Punjab Province. SPDC (2003) reports indicate that the overall average gross secondary enrolment rate of Punjab Province was 44 per cent. The figure was 48 per cent for males and 39 per cent for females. High rates of school enrolment may be explained by migration-enabled remittances, as a number of migrant households that receive remittances report that these funds were used to finance schooling of household members. In addition, the minimum educational requirement for joining the military has been raised to the matriculation level, and this may motivate villagers to invest in schooling at least until their children complete matriculation. The same motivation applies to overseas employment, as countries in the Middle East now set matriculation as a minimum level of education.

Generally, as expected, male gross enrolment rates are higher than those for females. The average enrolment rates of middle schools are higher than those of matriculation. It would appear that school enrolment rates are higher among remittance-receiving households than those of non-remittance-receiving households, and that they are higher in households which received remittances from overseas than in households which received remittances from domestic sources.

Table 10.23 Logistic regression of the effects of remittances on school enrolment

Variables	*Model 1*	*Model 2*
Constant	0.942	0.985
	(0.684)	(0.695)
Sex	1.042**	1.021**
	(0.488)	(0.490)
HH head's education	0.099*	0.110*
(completed years of schooling)	(0.058)	(0.060)
Remittances	0.807	
	(0.523)	
Internal remittances		1.225*
		(0.089)
External remittances		0.173
		(0.729)
Village dummies (Village A = 0)		
Village B	−1.148*	−1.222*
	(0.610)	(0.620)
Village C	−0.285	−0.469
	(0.605)	(0.693)
No. of observations	159	159
LR χ-square	18.57	19.79
Pseudo-R-square	0.131	0.140

Notes: Standard errors are in parentheses. **significant at 5%, *significant at 10%.
Source: Author's calculation.

To investigate the independent effect of remittance on school enrolment, a logit analysis was carried out. As the dependent variable, an enrolment dummy having a value of one for those enrolled and zero otherwise was used. Explanatory variables included a gender dummy (one for male and zero for female), completed years of education for the head of household, a remittance dummy, and village dummies. In model 1, the remittance dummy had values of one for remittance-receiving households and zero otherwise. In model 2, two remittance dummies were used: one for remittances from within Pakistan (internal remittance dummy) and one for remittances from overseas (external remittance dummy).

The results of the estimation are reported in Table 10.23. The gender dummy and completed years of education for the head of household are positive and significant. This means that girls are less likely than boys to go to school, and that the household head's education has a positive effect on school enrolment. The dummy for Village B is negative and significant. This is probably due to its location. Village A sits near the main road, facilitating easier access for children to go to school.

The remittance dummy in model 1 is positive but not statistically significant. In model 2, the internal remittance dummy is positive and significant while the external remittance dummy turns out to be positive but not significant. These findings indicate that internal remittances help households finance schooling for their children and increase the probability of school enrolment. However, the impact of external remittances on school enrolment may not be evident. This is somewhat consistent with results of Arif (2004) who found no significant impact of overseas remittance on school enrolment of boys.

10.5 Concluding remarks

Globalization has made the movement of people and the transfer of money easier. In fact, cross-border labour migration from, and associated remittance of funds to, developing countries are not new. However, they are increasing rapidly and have considerable social and economic impact on both developed and developing countries. Impacts on households in developing countries seem to have been particularly strong.

This chapter included an analysis of the impact of worker remittances viewed from a household perspective and based on a field survey carried out in the Chakwal district of the Punjab Province in Pakistan. The study reveals the poor economic condition of non-migrant households and associated widespread poverty in the *barani* areas. In these areas, agricultural activities are weather-dependent, and non-farm job opportunities are limited. Migration has been an important means of supplementing household income. Migrant households expect to get remittances from their migrant members. They hope that these funds will pay daily consumption needs as well as expenses related to unexpected events and thus keep them above the poverty line. In fact, respondent households indicated that remittances were mainly used for daily consumption.

Although remittances from migrant members increase migrant household income, the contribution made by internal remittances seems insufficient. This is supported by survey results presented in this chapter. Our analysis also shows a non-negligible incidence of poverty among internal migrant households. This suggests that internal migration is not necessarily a panacea for villagers wishing to escape poor living conditions. While internal migration and associated remittances fail to lift the income levels of a number of households, external migration appears to raise the living standard of households in villages like those surveyed in this study. Since remittances from external migrants are far larger than those from internal migrants, external remittances supplement household income to a large extent. In fact, only one household receiving remittance funds from overseas was found to be in poverty. Although globalization has made the movement of human beings easier, the option of migrating overseas in order to work and sending remittances back home is available only to a few. It involves high initial costs such as travel expenses, commissions to brokers, and costs associated with obtaining job information. The poor simply cannot afford such costs.

There are exceptions to this, however. Even poor families can have overseas migrant members if they can cover the cost of migration by borrowing from their extended family and close relatives. In NELM literature, it is argued that there exists an informal credit arrangement between the migrant and those who help in the financing of migration. Based on data from Pakistan, Ilahi and Jafarey

(1999) point out the important role of the extended family in financing costly international migration. In some cases, overseas employers may pay the cost of migration with the migrant later using salary to repay. This arrangement does not cost much upfront, so poor households can send their members abroad. However, it may still cost a lot to find such arrangements as such must usually be made through private recruiters.

Economic conditions of non-migrant households with returned migrants were also examined in comparison to those without returned migrants. It was found that non-migrant households with returned migrants were no better off than those without returned migrants. In particular, the income levels of non-migrant households with returned migrants among non-farm households were even lower. This implies that income levels financed by remittances are not sustainable following the return of migrants, and that the impact of remittances on income level is temporary. Continued migration and remittances are thus necessary for poor households to keep their daily lives above the subsistence level. This practice seems unsustainable.

This study shows that the primary use of remittances is for daily consumption, followed by housing construction and wedding ceremonies. While these are not considered productive, it is found that remittances were also spent on schooling, which is productive in the long term. Our econometric results show a positive impact of remittances, internal remittances in particular, on school enrolment. This use of remittances on schooling or human capital development in general is a good sign and should be welcome, but our survey suggests that a policy that directs remittance flows to more productive purposes is necessary to maintain the higher income level of households even after the return of migrants and the subsequent halt of remittances.

Appendix 10.1

Table 10A.1 Current migration status of sample individuals

	Total sample	*Village A*	*Village B*	*Village C*
Total sample individuals (1)	1,243	449	353	441
Labour migrants (2) ((2)/(1)%)	137 (11.0)	51 (11.4)	33 (9.3)	53 (12.0)
Internal migrants (3) ((3)/(2)%)	78 (56.9)	19 (37.3)	19 (57.6)	40 (75.5)
External migrants (4) ((4)/(2)%)	59 (43.1)	32 (62.7)	14 (42.4)	13 (24.5)
Farm sample (5)	900	313	217	370
Labour migrants (6) ((6)/(5)%)	105 (11.7)	34 (10.9)	22 (10.1)	49 (13.2)
Internal migrants (7) ((7)/(6)%)	56 (53.3)	10 (29.4)	8 (36.4)	38 (77.6)
External migrants (8) ((8)/(6)%)	49 (46.7)	24 (70.6)	14 (63.6)	11 (22.4)
Non-farm sample (9)	343	136	136	71
Labour migrants (10) ((10)/(9)%)	32 (9.3)	17 (12.5)	11 (8.1)	4 (5.6)
Internal migrants (11) ((11)/(10)%)	22 (68.8)	9 (52.9)	11 (100.0)	2 (50.0)
External migrants (12) ((12)/(10)%)	10 (31.3)	8 (47.1)	0 (0.0)	2 (50.0)

Source: Author's calculation.

Table 10A.2 Current migration status of sample households

Farm/non-farm	*Household by migration status*	*Village A*		*Village B*		*Village C*		*Total*	
		No.	*%*	*No.*	*%*	*No.*	*%*	*No.*	*%*
Farm households	Non-migrant HH	19	42.2	17	58.6	19	39.6	55	45.1
	Internal migrant HH	8	17.8	2	6.9	20	41.7	30	24.6
	External migrant HH	16	35.6	5	17.2	5	8.3	26	21.3
	Mixed migrants HH	2	4.4	5	17.2	4	8.3	11	9.0
	Farm HH per village	45	100.0	29	100.0	48	100.0	122	100.0
Non-farm households	Non-migrant HH	10	45.5	11	64.7	6	60.0	27	55.1
	Internal migrant HH	6	27.3	6	35.3	2	20.0	14	28.6
	External migrant HH	4	18.2	0	0.0	2	20.0	6	12.2
	Mixed migrants HH	2	9.1	0	0.0	0	0.0	2	4.1
	Non-farm HH per village	22	100.0	17	100.0	10	100.0	49	100.0
Total households	Non-migrant HH	29	43.3	28	60.9	25	43.1	82	48.0
	Internal migrant HH	14	20.9	8	17.4	22	37.9	44	25.7
	External migrant HH	20	29.9	5	10.9	7	12.1	32	18.7
	Mixed migrants HH	4	6.0	5	10.9	4	6.9	13	7.6
	Household per village	67	100.0	46	100.0	58	100.0	171	100.0

Source: Author's calculation.

Notes

1. I would like to express my deepest gratitude to M. Jameel Khan, Director of Punjab Economic Research Institute (PERI), for providing me with enumerators for field surveys and for his advice at every step of the research. Without his help, this chapter would have not been completed. I am deeply indebted to PERI field staff members Ghulam Hussain, Ghulam Abbas Khan, Muhammad Imran and Zafar Abbas Zafar. I am also thankful to Khawar Ata of PERI for keeping things in order. I was aided by Muhammad Avais Tahir, Muhammad Faisal, Muhammad Shafique, Nayab Sarwal, Ahmad Yar Siddiquee and Noor Ahmad of PERI on various counts. Discussions with Abid A. Burki, Mushtaq A. Khan and S.M. Turab Hussain of Lahore University of Management Sciences, and Raishad of the Federal Bureau of Statistics were helpful in identifying problems in labour migration in Pakistan. The materials provided by S. Hirashima helped me understand non-farm households in Pakistani villages. I am also grateful to Saad Paracha for valuable comments. Last but not least, I am deeply indebted to all the villagers who kindly spared their time for this study. I am, of course, responsible for any remaining errors.
2. A serious issue in the calculation of remittance flow arises from workers' use of informal channels such as *hundi* and *hawala*, traditional methods of remitting money. IMF statistics only capture remittance flow made through formal channels such as banks and post offices. However, it is quite evident that many workers use informal channels for sending money back to their home country. Migrants also bring in cash transfers when they return home. It is believed that the amount of money that makes its way into countries through informal channels and carried in by hand is quite substantial. It may add 50 per cent or more to recorded flow (World Bank 2006b). If this unrecorded flow is included, the true size of remittances far exceeds the amount of FDI. Though a recent study by El-Qorchi et al. (2003) attempts to estimate the size of remittances through

unofficial channels, blind spots in remittance data have caused actual financial inflow to be underestimated. This is indeed a sensitive issue for research.

3. Labour migration from Pakistan to the Middle East dates back to the 1930s when oil reserves were found in the Gulf region. See Arif and Irfan (1997) for a brief history of international labour migration from Pakistan.
4. Data on the number of workers headed overseas come from the website of the Bureau of Emigration and Overseas Employment (BEOE), Government of Pakistan (http://www.beoe.gov.pk/).
5. Middle Eastern oil-exporting countries have been major recipients of Pakistani labourers since the 1970s. In particular, Saudi Arabia and the UAE are two of the most popular destinations. However, the progress of globalization, changes in the political landscape, and diversion of the demand of host countries have gradually affected the selection of destination countries. Despite their 'nativization' policies, countries in the Middle East are still attracting many workers from Pakistan. However, new destinations such as Korea and Malaysia are among the top 10 for the period from 2001 to 2005. Other countries that should be noted as host countries in recent years are the United Kingdom, Italy, the US and Spain. Data are taken from the website of the Bureau of Emigration and Overseas Employment (BEOE), Government of Pakistan (http://www.beoe.gov.pk/).
6. Data on remittances are from various *Economic Surveys* by the government of Pakistan.
7. See World Bank (2005) for a summary of unofficial channels of remittances and for a comparison of official and unofficial remittances for Pakistan.
8. See Taylor (1999) for a review of literature on this topic.
9. See *Economic Survey, 2004–5* of the government of Pakistan.
10. See Arif (2005) for a review of literature on Pakistan on this issue.
11. Others are Jhelum, Rawalpindi and Attock. The Chakwal district was created by combining parts of Attock and Jhelum and was given the status of 'district' in 1985.
12. The combined population of Rawalpindi city and adjacent Islamabad exceeds 2 million. This constitutes one of the largest urban centres in Pakistan. See Government of Pakistan (2001).
13. The population of the Chakwal district is around 1,060,000 (as of 1998). Only 12.3 per cent of the population lives in urban areas. See Government of Pakistan (2001).
14. The basic census was conducted in December 2004. The field survey was carried out in March 2005. Prior to the field survey, questionnaires were tested in the Sheikhupura district of the Punjab Province, in January 2005.
15. This may be a source of selectivity bias because no information is available on entire household migration. See Bilsborrow et al. (1984) for a discussion of selectivity bias arising from sampling.
16. Landowning castes are called *zamindars*, and the classes that provide various services to *zamindars* are called *kammees*. The latter are considered inferior to *zamindars*. The traditional complementary relationship between *zamindars* and *kammees* is called *seypidar* in the local language.
17. For studies on non-farm households in Pakistan, see Hirashima (1978) and Irfan (1989). A parallel study conducted by the author in irrigated villages of the Sargodha district included observation of quite a large proportion of non-farm households that provide traditional services to *zamindars*.
18. The figure is taken from *Pakistan Agricultural Census, 2000*. It is the ratio of the combined number of owner and owner-cum-tenant farms to total farms.
19. In the Punjab province in 1999–2000, the average yield per acre of wheat in *barani* areas was 9.6 *maunds* while it was 32.7 *maunds* in irrigated areas (see Saleem and Jami, 2001).
20. *Jowar* and *bajra* can also serve as a food crop. However, in the study villages, they are mainly used as fodder. Please refer to Byerlee et al. (1992) for details of farming in the *barani* areas of Pakistan.

21. This is based on information obtained from village elders. According to these elders, five non-farm (and landless) households from Village A, 14 from Village B and 10 from Village C completely moved away in the past.
22. There was one female who had migrated to Hong Kong. Her father had migrated to Hong Kong and started a business. Later, she was called in to help with her father's business. This is a very special case and therefore excluded from the study.
23. The New Economics of Labour Migration (NELM) sheds light on the role of household characteristics on migration decisions. Stark and Bloom (1985) and Stark (1991) argue that migration decisions are not taken by individuals but are collectively taken within a group of related people such as a family or household. The proposition that households use migration in order to overcome constraints and risks caused by market failures is the central tenet of the NELM.
24. These are direct costs that are incurred upon migrating. There are also indirect costs associated with migration such as investment in education for potential migrants.
25. See Bilsborrow et al. (1984) and Van Wey (2005) for a literature review of the relationship between landholding and migration.
26. Seventeen males left the villages during the 12 months prior to the interview. Two of them (both external migrants) received financial assistance from their households to finance their stay at the beginning. Their households remitted out to them when they first went overseas in the expectation of financial returns in the future. This is another indication as argued in NELM analysis that migration is a family strategy and that there exists an implicit contract between migrants and households.
27. Two households received remittances from persons who were not household members. Figures relating to such cases are not included here when calculating the average amount of remittances at the household level.
28. Based on different data sets, Arif (1999) claims that a substantial portion of remittances were spent on investment and further shows that 37 per cent of external remittances were directed to investment by recipient households. A detailed breakdown of the use of remittances, however, reveals that 62 per cent of total investment went to real estate (land and housing).
29. The share of population with no education in the Punjab Province is 11 per cent, while it is only 4 per cent in the Chakwal district. The share of population that has matriculated is 29 per cent in the Punjab Province; it is 43 per cent in the Chakwal district. Figures are from Government of Pakistan (2000).
30. Adams (1998) examined the use of remittances based on household data from Pakistan and found that external remittances have a positive impact on the accumulation of farmland. However, internal remittances do not have such an effect and are more likely to be used for consumption.
31. In fact, there is hardly any social mobility in the villages of Pakistan. Lefevbre (1999) reports that even if a *kammee* acquires land, there is no change in social status, and such a person is still considered *kammee*.
32. The government of Pakistan has been trying to ban exorbitant expenditures for marriage ceremonies. The Marriage Ordinance of October 2006 allows the serving of only a one-dish meal during wedding ceremonies. Still, the custom of giving a dowry remains.
33. See *Economic Survey, 2003–4*, Government of Pakistan for details.
34. In general, the incidence of poverty is said to be more acute among non-farm households. However, there is a shortage of studies examining poverty among non-farm households in Pakistan. Hirashima (2001) describes these rural non-farm households as 'the neglected poor'.
35. The gross school enrolment ratio is defined as the share of total school enrolment at a certain level of education, regardless of age, divided by the population of the age group that corresponds to that level of education.

References

Abbasi, N. and M. Irfan (1986) 'Socio-Economic Effects of International Migration on the Families Left Behind'. In Fred Arnold and Nasra M. Shah (eds) *Asian Labour Migration: Pipeline to the Middle East*. Boulder, USA: Westview.

Adams, Richard H., Jr (1998) 'Remittances, Investment, and Rural Asset Accumulation in Pakistan'. *Economic Development and Cultural Change* October: 155–73.

Ahmed, A. Maqsood and Ismail Sirageldin (1993) 'Socio-Economic Determinants of Labour Mobility in Pakistan'. *The Pakistan Development Review* 32(2) (Summer): 139–57.

—— (1994) 'Internal Migration, Earnings, and the Importance of Self-Selection'. *The Pakistan Development Review* 33(3) (Autumn): 211–27.

Akram, M., Surayya and Lubna Shahnaz (2002) 'Factors Affecting Male Internal Migration in Punjab-Pakistan'. *The Lahore Journal of Economics* 7(2): 93–107.

Arif, G. M. (1998) 'Reintegration of Pakistani Return Migrants from the Middle East in the Domestic Labour Market'. *The Pakistan Development Review* 37(2): 99–124.

—— (1999) *Remittances and Investments at the Household Level in Pakistan*. PIDE Research Report no. 166. Islamabad: Pakistan Institute of Development Economics.

—— (2004) 'Effects of Overseas Migration on Household Consumption, Education, Health and Labour Supply in Pakistan'. In Hisaya Oda (ed.) *International Labour Migration from South Asia*. ASEDP no. 70. Chiba: Institute of Developing Economies.

—— (2005) 'Internal Migration and Households Well-Being: Myth or Reality'. In Hisaya Oda (ed.) *Internal Labour Migration in Pakistan*. ASEDP No. 72. Chiba: Institute of Developing Economies.

Arif, M. and M Irfan (1997) 'Population Mobility across the Pakistani Border: Fifty Years Experience'. *The Pakistan Development Review* 36(4): 989–1009.

Beals, R. E., M. B. Levy and L. N. Moses (1967) 'Rationality and Migration in Ghana'. *Review of Economics and Statistics* 49(4): 480–6.

Bilsborrow, R.E., A.S. Oberai and Guy Standy (1984) *Migration Surveys in Low Income Countries: Guidelines for Survey and Questionnaire Design*. London: Croom Helm.

Burki, S. J. (1991) 'Migration from Pakistan to the Middle East'. In G. D. Papademetriou and P. L. Martin (eds) *The Unsettled Relationships: Labour Migration and Economic Development*. London: Greenwood Press.

Byerlee, D., A.D. Sheikh and Muhammed Azeem (1992) 'Food, Fodder, and Follow: Analytics of the Barani Farming Systems of Northern Punjab'. In D. Byerlee and T. Hussain (eds) *Farming Systems of Pakistan*. Lahore: Vanguard Books.

Connell, J., B. Dasugupta, R. Laishley and M. Lipton (1976) *Migration from Rural Areas: the Evidence from Village Studies*. Delhi: Oxford University Press.

Eckert, J. B. and D. A. Khan (1977) 'Rural–Urban Labour Migration: Evidence from Pakistan'. Occasional Paper. Punjab Economic Research Institute, Lahore, Pakistan.

El-Qorchi, M., S.M. Maimbo and J.F. Wilson (2003) 'Informal Funds Transfer Systems: an Analysis of the Informal Hawala System'. IMF Occasional Paper 222. International Monetary Fund, Washington, DC.

Gilani, I., F.M. Khan and M. Iqbal (1981) 'Labour Migration from Pakistan to the Middle East and Its Impact on the Domestic Economy'. Research Report Series no. 126. Pakistan Institute of Development Economics, Islamabad.

Government of Pakistan (2000) *Pakistan Agricultural Census 1999–2000, Punjab Province Report*. Islamabad: Agriculture Census Organization, Government of Pakistan.

—— (2001) *1998 Census Report of Pakistan*. Islamabad: Population Census Organization, Statistics Division, Government of Pakistan.

—— *Economic Survey* various issues. Islamabad: Economic Advisor's Wing, Finance Division, Government of Pakistan.

Hampshire, Kate (2002) 'Fulani on the Move: Seasonal Economic Migration in the Sahel as a Social Process'. In Arjan De Hann and Ben Rogaly (eds) *Labour Mobility and Rural Society*. London, UK: Frank Cass.

Hirashima, S. (1978) *The Structure of Disparity in Developing Agriculture: a Case Study of the Pakistan Punjab*. Tokyo: Institute of Developing Economies.

—— (2001) 'Rural Poverty and the Landed Elite: South Asian Experience Revisited'. Working Paper. Department of Applied Economics and Management, Cornell University.

Ilahi, Nadeem and Saqib Jafarey (1999) 'Guestworker Migration, Remittances and the Extended Family: Evidence from Pakistan'. *Journal of Development Economics* 58(2): 485–512.

Irfan, M. (1989) 'Poverty, Class Structure and Household Demographic Behavior in Rural Pakistan'. In Gerry Rodgers (ed.) *Population Growth and Poverty in Rural South Asia*. New Delhi: Sage.

Kazi, Shahnaz (1989) 'Domestic Impact of Overseas Migration: Pakistan'. In Rashid Amjad (ed.) *To the Gulf and Back: Studies on the Economic Impact of the Asian Labour Migration*. New Delhi: UNDP/ILO/ARTEP.

Khan, Aliya H. and Lubna Shehnaz (2000) 'Determinants of Internal Migration in Pakistan: Evidence from the Labour Force Survey, 1996–97'. *The Pakistan Development Review* 39(4) (Part II) (Winter): 695–712.

Lefebvre, A. (1999) *Kinship, Honour and Money in Rural Pakistan: Subsistence Economy and the Effects of Internal Migration*. Richmond: Curzon Press.

Levy, M.B. and W. J. Wadycki (1974) 'Education and the Decision to Migrate: an Econometric Analysis of Migration in Venezuela'. *Econometrica* 42(2): 377–88.

Mansuri, Ghazala (2006) 'Migration, School Attainment and Child Labour: Evidence from Rural Pakistan'. World Bank Policy Research Working Paper 3945. World Bank, Washington, DC.

Nabi, Ijaz (1981) 'An Empirical Analysis of Rural–Urban Migration in Less Developed Economies'. *Economic Letters* 8: 193–9.

—— (1984) 'Village-End Considerations in Rural–Urban Migration'. *Journal of Development Economics* 14: 129–45.

Nabi, Ijaz, N. Hamid and Z. Shahid (1986) *The Agrarian Economy of Pakistan: Issues and Policies*. Karachi: Oxford University Press.

Oda, H. (2007) 'Dynamics of Internal and International Migration in Rural Pakistan: Evidence of Development and Underdevelopment'. *Asian Population Studies* 3(2): 169–79.

Saleem, M.A. and A. R. Jami (2001). *Farm Accounts, Family Budgets of Rural Families and Cost of Production of Major Crops in Punjab: 1999–2000*. Lahore, Pakistan: Punjab Economic Research Institute.

Sjaastad, L.A. (1962) 'The Costs and Returns of Human Migration'. *Journal of Political Economy* 70(5) (Part 2): 80–93.

Stark, Oded (1991) *The Migration of Labour.* Oxford and Cambridge, Mass.: Basil Blackwell.

Stark, Oded and David E. Bloom (1985) 'The New Economics of Labour Migration'. *The American Economic Review* 75(2): 173–8.

SPDC (2003) *Annual Review of Social Development in Pakistan: the State of Education*. Karachi: Social Policy and Development Centre.

Taylor, J. Edward (1999) 'The New Economics of Labour Migration and the Role of Remittances in the Migration Process'. *International Migration* 37: 63–88.

Van Wey, Leah K. (2005) 'Land Ownership as a Determinant of International and Internal Migration in Mexico and Internal Migration in Thailand'. *International Migration Review* 39(1): 141–72.

World Bank (2003) *Global Development Finance 2003*. Washington, DC: World Bank.

—— (2005) *Migrant Labour Remittances in the South Asia Region*. Report no. 31577. Washington, DC: World Bank.

—— (2006a) *Global Economic Prospects 2006*. Washington, DC: World Bank.

—— (2006b) *Migration and Development Brief 2*. Development Research Group. Washington, DC: World Bank.

Index